Leadership in
Abuse Preve[...]

Leadership in Drug and Alcohol Abuse Prevention blends the wisdom of numerous long-term professionals addressing drug and alcohol issues with helpful strategies and current science.

Organized around the Pyramid of Success that emphasizes Competence, Confidence, and Commitment, this book offers practical and grounded approaches for better addressing substance abuse issues. Included are insights from 50 contributors, featuring professional perspectives from practitioners with decades of experience. While issues of substance abuse are not readily solved or cured, they can be better addressed – more effectively, more efficiently, and more appropriately. This timely resource offers a unique blend of science-based strategies and resourceful foundations for implementation.

Designed for those working either directly or indirectly with problems associated with substance use disorders, this book will aid those in a wide variety of settings, whether in schools, communities, business, or government.

David S. Anderson, Ph.D., is Professor Emeritus of Education and Human Development at George Mason University. His research focuses primarily on drug and alcohol abuse prevention, wellness, and health promotion, with attention to youth, young adults, and professional development; specialty areas include substance abuse prevention and wellness promotion, strategic planning, program development, health communication, and needs assessment and evaluation. Noteworthy publications include *Health and Safety Communication: A Practical Guide Forward*, *Wellness Issues for Higher Education*, *Further Wellness Issues for Higher Education*, *Promising Practices Sourcebook*, and *Charting Your Course: A Lifelong Guide to Health and Compassion*.

Leadership in Drug and Alcohol Abuse Prevention
Insights from Long-Term Advocates

David S. Anderson

Routledge
Taylor & Francis Group
NEW YORK AND LONDON

First published 2020
by Routledge
52 Vanderbilt Avenue, New York, NY 10017

and by Routledge
2 Park Square, Milton Park, Abingdon, Oxon, OX14 4RN

Routledge is an imprint of the Taylor & Francis Group, an informa business

© 2020 Taylor & Francis

The right of David S. Anderson to be identified as author of this work has been asserted by him in accordance with sections 77 and 78 of the Copyright, Designs and Patents Act 1988.

All rights reserved. No part of this book may be reprinted or reproduced or utilised in any form or by any electronic, mechanical, or other means, now known or hereafter invented, including photocopying and recording, or in any information storage or retrieval system, without permission in writing from the publishers.

Trademark notice: Product or corporate names may be trademarks or registered trademarks, and are used only for identification and explanation without intent to infringe.

Library of Congress Cataloging-in-Publication Data
A catalog record for this title has been requested

ISBN: 978-1-138-58841-7 (hbk)
ISBN: 978-1-138-58842-4 (pbk)
ISBN: 978-0-429-49199-3 (ebk)

Typeset in Goudy
by Newgen Publishing UK

This book is dedicated to all those who share their heart-felt commitment and service, seeking to make the world a healthier and safer place for all. This book is for the legacy of Rich and Mary and the countless individuals and families whose lives and dreams were shattered by the preventable behavior of others.

Contents

List of Figures x
List of Professional Perspective Articles xi
About the Author xiv
Interviewees: Long-Term Advocates xvi
Preface xxiii

Introduction 1

PART I
Competence 9

1 Understanding the Nature of the Concern: Individual
　Perspectives 11
　　Overall Context and Definitions 12
　　Usage Patterns among Adults 13
　　Usage Patterns among Youth 15
　　Other Higher Risk Groups 20
　　Reasons for Use 24
　　Consequences 25
　　Dependence Considerations 30
　　Limitations with Data and Information 31
　　Future Implications 32
　　Summary 33

2 Understanding the Nature of the Concern: Environmental
　Perspectives 34
　　Defining the Environment 35
　　Consequences of Drug and Alcohol Abuse 37
　　The Environment as a Cause or Contributor 42
　　The Environment as a Blockage or Disinhibitor of Progress or Change 47
　　The Environment as a Facilitator of Change 51
　　Summary 58

3 Why Be Concerned?   60
Clarifying the Concern 60
Consistency and Followthrough 63
The Evolution of Science and Knowledge 65
The Context of Blockages and Roadblocks 74
Root Causes of Use and Abuse 80
The Importance of Values 83
The Integration of Values 86
Summary 87

4 Foundational Factors   89
Paradigms 90
Brain Health 95
Principles Defining the Effects of a Drug 99
Continuum of Use 101
Continuum of Care 107
Nature of Strategies 114
Summary 115

5 Skills for Intervention, Treatment, and Recovery   116
Intervention: The Response Process 116
Treatment 127
Recovery 145
Summary 151

6 Skills for Prevention and Education   153
Defining Prevention 153
Prevention Outcomes 156
The Role of Health Promotion 159
Risk and Protective Factors 164
Prevention Framework 165
Prevention Methodologies 168
Prevention Messages 173
Education and Training 179
Summary 184

PART II
Confidence   185

7 Helpful Processes   187
Planned Change 187
Force Field Analysis 189
Planning Framework 191
Engaging Others 208
Summary 211

Contents ix

8 Resourceful Approaches 212
Evidence-Based Foundations 212
Guiding Principles from an Organizational Perspective 215
A Menu of Strategies 219
Pulling It Together: A Planning Grid 226
Summary 232

9 Personal and Professional Strategies 233
Communication Foundations 233
Tools and Resources 239
Persuasive Components 245
Advocacy 251
Summary 252

PART III
Commitment 255

10 Leadership and Advocacy within an Evolving Societal Context 257
Leadership 258
Ethics 267
Continually Changing Society 273
Movements and Campaigns 279
Synthesis of Leadership and Advocacy 285
Summary 287

11 Believing in and Taking Care of Yourself 289
Mission 290
Growth 291
Support 296
Balance 297
Management 300
Perseverance 302
Refreshment 307
Legacy 309
Summary 312

12 Vision for the Future 313
What Having a Vision Means 313
Why Have a Vision 317
Contents of a Vision 318
How to Prepare a Vision 326
Summary 331

Index 332

Figures

0.1	Pyramid of Success	4
1.1	Reasons for Use	25
1.2	Consequences of Use	26
3.1	COMPASS Topics	82
6.1	The Role of the School in Responding to Chemical Health Issues and Problems	162
7.1	Planning Framework	194
8.1	Comprehensive Approaches	229

Professional Perspective Articles

1.1	Underage Drinking *Michael E. Dunn and Jessica N. Flori*	16
1.2	Substance Use Disorder Prevention with LGBTQ/Sexual Minorities *Philip T. McCabe*	21
1.3	Impacts of Drug-Impaired Driving Means Increased Risk for Roadways *Ryan Snow*	26
2.1	Family Considerations *Jenny Wagstaff*	39
2.2	Sober Privilege – I'm Not Bad. I'm Drawn That Way: The Public Persona of Substance Use Disorders *Thomas Hall*	44
2.3	Coalitions for Impact: Collaboration, Teamwork, and More *Maureen Earley*	53
2.4	The Practice of Prevention: An Ecological Approach *Jim Lange*	56
3.1	The Biology of Addiction: Knowing Fact from Fiction *Michael L. Wenzinger and Mark S. Gold*	66
3.2	The Opioid Epidemic: How Did We Get Here? *Dana Ripley and Jenny Wagstaff*	69
3.3	Reflections on Substance Abuse Prevention Strategies: Overcoming Obstacles *Gail Gleason Milgram*	76
4.1	On the Prevalence of Old Paradigms or Knowledge *Allan Cohen*	90
4.2	The Brain Disease Model of Addiction Should Be Reevaluated *Christopher Medina-Kirchner, Kate Y. O'Malley, and Carl L. Hart*	96
4.3	Understanding the DSM-5 *Diane Rullo*	101
4.4	Continuum of Use *Randy Haveson*	105
4.5	Comprehensive Approaches to Prevention *William DeJong*	109

xii Professional Perspective Articles

5.1	Redefining Intervention: Altering Trajectories to Reduce Harms *Jason R. Kilmer and Shannon K. Bailie*	124
5.2	Assessment and Diagnosis of Substance Use Disorders *Michael E. Dunn and Jessica N. Flori*	129
5.3	The Role of the Family *Randy Haveson*	134
5.4	Self-Help/Mutual Aid Groups for Sustained Recovery from Substance Use Disorders *Thomasina Borkman*	139
5.5	Medication-Assisted Treatment … A Drug to Treat a Drug? *Dana Ripley and Jenny Wagstaff*	143
5.6	Steps Toward Effectively Supporting Recovery *Jenna Parisi*	146
5.7	Mutual Aid Groups' Contribution to Recovery-Oriented Systems of Care *Thomasina Borkman*	149
6.1	Promoting Health/Preventing Problems *Thomas M. Griffin and Jennifer Griffin-Wiesner*	161
6.2	Choices and Guidelines about Alcohol and Other Drugs *Thomas M. Griffin and Jennifer Griffin-Wiesner*	169
6.3	Words Matter *Barbara E. Ryan*	174
6.4	Building Capacity for Community Change *Joseph Espinoza and Kelly Schlabach*	181
7.1	Strategic Planning: The Power Is in the Process *Dave Closson*	192
7.2	Blending Research and Practice: Recognizing the *Question* in Program Design *Jim Lange*	195
7.3	Rising above Politics in Alcohol and Drug Abuse Prevention *Richard Lucey*	198
7.4	When an Adult Organization Needs to Engage Young People to Drive Change *Robert Heard*	204
8.1	The Dichotomy of Data: Slow Is Smooth and Smooth Is Fast *Dave Closson*	213
8.2	Let's Dream! Employing Creativity and Innovation in Working with Alcohol, Other Drugs and Related Issues *John Watson*	216
8.3	Successful Leadership Requires Collaboration in Law Enforcement *Ryan Snow*	230
9.1	Translating Research into Practice on a Global Scale: The Health Information National Trends Survey Global Research Program *Gary L. Kreps*	235

9.2	Coming to Grips with a Common Language *Barbara E. Ryan*	242
9.3	Don't Fear Change – Initiate It *Thomas Hall*	247
10.1	Strategies to Minimize College Drinking and Related Problems *Gail Gleason Milgram*	264
10.2	The Changing Legal Landscape for Prevention in Higher Education *Peter Lake*	270
10.3	Knowing What's New: How to Stay Current and Effective in an Ever-Evolving Landscape of Prevention, Intervention, and Initiatives *Shannon K. Bailie and Jason R. Kilmer*	276
10.4	Movements: Key to Making Change! *John Watson and Brad Luna*	281
11.1	Keepin' It Green: Staying Professionally Challenged *Robert J. Chapman*	292
11.2	Staying Refreshed *Darlind Davis*	299
11.3	Accepting the Role of Role Model: A Work in Progress *Ann Quinn-Zobeck*	303
12.1	Substance Abuse Prevention: A Retrospective *Darlind Davis*	315
12.2	The Power of an Idea *Gerardo M. González*	324
12.3	Helping Others Create Shared Visions: Generating More Light Than Heat *Robert J. Chapman*	329

About the Author

David S. Anderson, Ph.D., is Professor Emeritus of Education and Human Development at George Mason University. With his professional work spanning over four and a half decades, his specialty areas include drug and alcohol abuse prevention, strategic planning and mobilization, communication and education, health promotion, and needs assessment and evaluation. He conducts needs assessments; prepares evaluation and analysis; and assists with strategic planning. His work emphasizes program planners, policymakers, school and community leaders, college students, and youth.

At George Mason University, he served on the faculty for 28 years, finishing his career there as Professor and Director, Center for the Advancement of Public Health. In addition to teaching taught graduate and undergraduate courses on drug and alcohol issues, community health, and health communications, he served as project director and researcher on over 180 grants and contracts. These projects encompassed research, evaluation, program implementation, curriculum, and community service at the national, state and local levels. He has also produced, moderated, or been a guest on several television programs and has produced several multi-media resources.

His research and evaluation experience is extensive. He co-authors the *College Alcohol Survey* (1979–2018), the nation's longitudinal assessment of alcohol, drug, tobacco, violence, and related issues on four-year campuses. He co-directed the *Understanding Teen Drinking Cultures in America* research project, with attention to high school youth decisions to use or not use alcohol. He co-authored the *Wellness Assessment for Higher Education Preparation Programs* and the *Student Affairs Professionals Wellness Assessment*.

His numerous publications are applied in focus. He co-authored *Health and Safety Communication: A Practical Guide Forward* (2017). He edited *Wellness Issues for Higher Education* (2015) and *Further Wellness Issues for Higher Education* (2016). He co-directed *Promising Practices: Campus Alcohol Strategies* from 1994 to 2001, with its three primary products distributed nationwide (*Sourcebook 2001*, *Action Planner*, and *Task Force Planner*). He produced COMPASS: *A Roadmap to Healthy Living*, and *COMPASS Roadmap: Destination Health*, both focusing on a positive approach to wellness choices among young adults; these were based on his co-edited *Charting Your Course: A Lifelong Guide to Health and Compassion* (1998). For the National Collegiate Athletic Association, he has served as evaluation consultant for nearly two decades, and has authored the *IMPACT Evaluation Resource* and produced *Best of CHOICES: Alcohol Education 1998–2008*. With Boat People SOS, he developed *STEP (Seniors and Trauma survivors Empowerment Program) Peer Companion Curriculum* (2009). Early in his career, he served as senior editor for *A Winning Combination: An Alcohol, Other Drug and Traffic Safety Program for College Campuses* (1988) and *That Happy Feeling: An Innovative Model for a Campus Alcohol Education Program* (1979).

In a service role in Celebration, Florida, he serves as President of the Board of Directors of the Celebration Residential Owners Association. Early in his career, he served as a student affairs administrator, with positions as Director of Residence Life at Ohio University, Director of Residential Life at Radford University, and Residence Hall Director at The Ohio State University. He received his bachelor's degree from Duke University, with a major in Psychology and a minor in Business Administration. His master's degree, from The Ohio State University, is in Student Personnel Administration. His Ph.D. in Public Policy/Public Affairs is from Virginia Polytechnic Institute and State University.

Interviewees: Long-Term Advocates

As highlighted in the introduction of this book, numerous interviews were conducted with a range of long-term advocates in the field of drug and alcohol abuse prevention. Included here are short biographies illustrating their long and productive careers of service, scholarship, and societal impact.

Claudia A. Blackburn, Psy.D., is responsible for content direction and development of Treatment Improvement Protocols (TIPs) for the Substance Abuse and Mental Health Services Administration (SAMHSA) Knowledge Application Program. A licensed psychologist, consultant, and administrator, she has held executive management, clinical, research, technical assistance, and training positions within the U.S., Europe, and Middle East in integrated treatment settings for substance use and co-occurring disorders. She received the highest honor, The Officer's Cross of Merit, Presidential medal from Poland, for her humanitarian work in the field of addiction, and in the development of family-oriented treatment programs post-Communism. Currently, she holds a faculty appointment at the University of Maryland, University College.

Ralph S. Blackman, M.A., is President and CEO of the Foundation for Advancing Alcohol Responsibility, which is funded by the nation's leading distillers and works to eliminate underage drinking and drunk driving. He staffed the White House Conference on Small Business in 1986 and served as Assistant Administrator for Private Enterprise at the U.S. Agency for International Development. He also held positions with the state of Illinois and the Republican National Committee. He obtained a B.A. degree from Western Illinois University and an M.A. degree from the University of Illinois-Springfield.

Thomasina Borkman, Ph.D., Professor of Sociology Emerita, George Mason University, Fairfax, Virginia and Affiliate Scientist, Alcohol Research Group of the Public Health Institute, Emeryville, California. Peer-run and other citizen-based solutions to health and social issues, such as self-help/mutual aid groups (e.g., Alcoholics Anonymous or Recovery, Inc.) or consumer-run mental health programs have been her primary research interest. She publishes in social science journals and her book *Understanding Self-Help/Mutual Aid: Experiential Learning* *in the Commons* (1999), summarizes her early research. She is known internationally for her concept of experiential knowledge, i.e., the authoritative voice of lived experience honored in peer-run solutions.

Darlind J. Davis, M.Ed., was coordinator of prevention for Pennsylvania, then Maryland; first chair of the National Prevention Network, then developed the drug prevention program in higher education at the U.S. Department of Education. At the Center for Substance Abuse Prevention, she was a manager in community prevention and training. Her career continued as prevention branch chief at the White House Office of National Drug Control Policy. She is the recipient of many awards and served as a coalition director in North Carolina. She holds a B.A. in Psychology from the State University of New York at Potsdam and an M.Ed. from Springfield College.

Kim Dude, M.A., worked at the University of Missouri for 38 years and has a degree in secondary speech education, a master's in counseling, and a Missouri Prevention Specialists Certification. She created the Wellness Resource Center (WRC) in 1990 that dealt with alcohol, tobacco, and other drug prevention, stress, depression, sleep, and self-esteem. She was recognized by the U.S. Department of Education's Network: Addressing Collegiate Alcohol and Other Drug Issues as the recipient of the Outstanding Contribution to the Field award in 2003. Under her leadership the WRC was recognized as a model program by the U.S. Department of Education four times.

Kurt Erickson serves as President and CEO of the award-winning nonprofit organization, the Washington Regional Alcohol Program. In addition to serving as CEO and lead public affairs strategist for the 36-year-old public–private partnership, working to prevent drunk driving and underage drinking in the District of Columbia, Maryland, and Virginia, he is a registered multi-state lobbyist for the nationally heralded coalition. He is a recipient of numerous honors including the National Highway Traffic Safety Administration's Public Service Award, the Maryland Highway Safety Office's Kevin E. Quinlan Advocacy Award, D.C.'s Metropolitan Police Department's Chief of Police Special Award, and, as part of the WRAP coalition, Virginia's Governor's Transportation Safety Award, among others.

Mark S. Gold, M.D., is a translational researcher, author, mentor, and inventor best known for his work on the brain systems underlying the effects of opiate drugs, cocaine, and food. He has worked as an advisor to many White House Drug Czars, White Houses, and NIDA and NIMH directors over his 40+ year career. He has published over 1000 peer reviewed scientific articles, texts, and practice guidelines. He was Professor, Eminent Scholar, Distinguished Professor, Distinguished Alumni Professor, Chairman, and Emeritus Eminent Scholar during his 25 years at the University of Florida. He regularly lectures at national and international meetings, medical societies, and grand rounds. He is Adjunct Professor in the Department of Psychiatry at the School of Medicine at Washington University.

xviii Interviewees: Long-Term Advocates

Thomas M. Griffin, Ph.D., M.S.W., retired as Associate Executive Director of the Minnesota Institute of Public Health in 2010. He has 50 years of experience in a variety of leadership roles in education and public health, including supervisor of drug education for the Minnesota Department of Education and manager of community and professional education for the Hazelden Foundation. He has taught courses for the Rutgers University Center of Alcohol Studies since 1984. He has directed program evaluations at the national, state, and community levels and has contributed over 75 publications. His evaluation work focused on multi-method participatory approaches that emphasized use of findings to improve programs, policies, and practices.

Mary Hill, Ph.D., served as Senior Administrator, Dean of Students, Professor, and Coach at West Texas A&M University. For decades, she served as a consultant for higher education; she was a national trainer for the Office of Juvenile Justice and Delinquency Prevention/Underage Drinking and other Drug Enforcement Training, a grant reviewer and site visitor for model programs for the U.S. Department of Education, and a consultant for the Texas Alcoholic Beverage Commission, Texas Department of Health, Governor's Drug Demand Reduction Advisory Committee, Texans Standing Tall, and over 75 colleges and universities. She continues to provide training and prevention programs.

Teresa Johnston, M.A., L.P.C., M.A.C. serves as Assistant Dean – Student Affairs at Kennesaw State University, providing leadership and direction to the Center for Young Adult Addiction and Recovery (CYAAR) and the Health Promotion and Wellness department. As executive director of CYAAR, the Center has grown to provide recovery support services for students seeking help with addictive disorders, a thriving collegiate recovery program, alcohol and other drug prevention education, and research in recovery science. She teaches two courses in the KSU Master's of Social Work Program: Substance Abuse Seminar and Addiction Theory and Policy. She also sits on the Georgia Statewide Opioid Task Force and the Georgia Substance Abuse Research Alliance.

William J. Kane, J.D., is the founder and director of the New Jersey Lawyers Assistance Program (LAP), created in 1993. He was one of the first Certified Employee Assistance Professionals in the nation, and was selected for the 2017–2018 EAP of the Year Award. Bill has served for more than 38 years as Adjunct Faculty of the Rutgers University Center for Alcohol Studies and Summer Schools and taught throughout the U.S. and Canada on alcoholism and the law, lawyers assistance programs, confidentiality, and legal issues for EAPs and addiction professionals. Bill is a graduate of both Seton Hall University School of Law and Seton Hall undergraduate program. He served as a volunteer in the U.S. Peace Corps and was a founding faculty member at Cameroun College of Arts and Science.

Karol L. Kumpfer, Ph.D. (Pawnee), is a psychologist and University of Utah Professor Emeritus. She developed the evidence-based Strengthening Families

Program (SFP), which is considered one of the most effective drug prevention programs by states, federal government, and international websites and raters, including the Oxford University Cochrane Reviews. Until 2000, she was the SAMHSA/CSAP Center Director in Washington, D.C. In June 2008, she was awarded the prestigious Community and Cultural Research award by the Society for Prevention Research. She was also their first woman president in 1998. She has published and presented widely and internationally, including a 2017 Academic Press book on *Evidence-based Family Interventions*. Currently she is principal investgator on a NIDA SBIR grant to put SFP online.

Carla Lapelle, M.A., served as Associate Dean of Student Affairs at Marshall University for 16 years. Prior to that, she was coordinator of Marshall Student Health Education Programs. She is the co-founder and a past chair West Virginia Collegiate Initiative to Address Alcohol Abuse, served as a Department of Education Higher Education Center Associate and Higher Education Fellow; co-chaired the Network Addressing Collegiate Alcohol and Other Drug Issues; and sat on the Department of Education's Prevention Review Board. She was awarded the "Excellence in Service to Students Award" by the National Society of Leadership and Success, and the Marshall University "Stephen W. Hensley Dedication to Student Life Award." She holds a master's degree in clinical psychology.

Jeffrey Levy is President of Virginia College Parents, Inc., an outgrowth of the 1997/98 Virginia Task Force on Drinking by College Students formed after the death of several college students including his son in alcohol-related incidents. He has also been an active leader in several other organizations addressing drug and alcohol abuse by college students. He is a retired business executive and also a retired Air Force colonel fighter pilot. He graduated from the U.S. Air Force Academy, and has graduate degrees from the University of Stockholm and Marymount University.

Jeff Linkenbach, Ed.D., is Founding Director and Research Scientist at The Montana Institute, who has developed national award-winning research-based programs to change norms. He is also an affiliate faculty member with the University of Montana – Mansfield Center, and a fellow with UM-Mansfield Academy for Global Leadership. He is recognized for his pioneering development of the Science of the Positive process and the Positive Community Norms framework, which are being utilized by tribal, federal, state, and local organizations to achieve positive change and transformation around issues such as child maltreatment, substance abuse, suicide, and traffic safety.

Bob Lynn, Ed.D., is an internationally recognized lecturer, researcher, and clinician in the field of counseling psychology and drug dependency. During the past 40 years he has held leading positions in many clinical settings, levels of addiction treatment, employee assistance programs, state government, and as a professor in several universities. He is a licensed professional counselor and senior fellow in biofeedback practice. He is also a recognized expert in family therapy and behavioral therapy. He completed his doctoral studies at Rutgers University School of Graduate Education. His major research focuses on issues related to treatment outcomes.

Elizabeth S. "BJ" McConnell, M.S., is an experienced education program developer who manages national trainings and implementations. During her 30 year career, she served as executive director of the Mendez Foundation, worked at the White House Conference, served in the U.S. Department of Justice and was Deputy Director for Education for DARE America. Consulting clients include the National Institutes of Health, National Families in Action, U.S. Department of Education, The Century Council and the NFL. She has worked with hundreds of schools and communities assisting implementation of prevention efforts for children and families. Her undergraduate and graduate degrees are from the University of Florida.

Gail Gleason Milgram, Ed.D., earned her B.S. from Georgian Court University and her M.Ed. and Ed.D. from Rutgers – the State University of New Jersey. Her dissertation studied what young people knew about alcohol and what their teachers and parents wanted them to know. Her work at Rutgers' Center of Alcohol Studies spanned four decades and included annotating the literature available on alcohol; she wrote books, articles, and pamphlets. Starting in 1980, she directed the Education and Training Division, and led the School of Alcohol and Drug Studies, the Advanced School of Alcohol and Drug Studies, and the New Jersey School of Alcohol and Drug Studies.

William Modzeleski, M.P.A., is a nationally recognized leader in the area of school safety and emergency management. Currently a senior consultant with SIGMA Threat Management Associates, he served as Associate Assistant Deputy Secretary of the U.S. Department of Education's Office of Safe and Drug Free Schools. During his tenure at the Department of Education, he was instrumental in the development and implementation of several programs related to emergency management and violence prevention, including the Safe Schools/Healthy Students Program; School Emergency Response to Violence; and the REMS program. Previously, he served as Executive Director of the National Commission on Drug-Free Schools. He has a Bachelor of Arts in Political Science from the University of Bridgeport, and a Master's of Public Administration from C.W. Post College. After graduation he served in the U.S. Army for three years.

Steve Schmidt, M.S., is Senior Vice President of Public Policy and Communications for the National Alcohol Beverage Control Association (NABCA). He directs research, public policy, and communication strategies to assist states in managing alcohol control and regulatory systems. Steve has consulted with state and national organizations; authored several articles; and presented at numerous international, national, and state conferences on a variety of alcohol-related issues. He has been professionally employed for over 39 years in positions leading efforts to address alcohol-related issues at the local, state, and national levels. Steve has been an adjunct faculty member at York College of PA, Villanova University, and Pennsylvania State University.

Deb Thorstenson, M.A., has worked in the human services and prevention field for over 40 years, with almost 30 years at Northern State University (NSU) in Aberdeen, South Dakota. As the director of the counseling center, she spearheaded campus-wide prevention efforts to address alcohol and other drug, and violence prevention utilizing environmental strategies which resulted in a decrease in high-risk drinking. Spanning 25 years, she also served as Regional Coordinator/Director for the U.S. Department of Education's Network Addressing Collegiate Alcohol and Other Drug Issues with ten years on the Executive Committee and was a part of the Network's major reorganization initiative.

Helene R. White, Ph.D., is Distinguished Professor Emeritus of Sociology at Rutgers University. For over 40 years, she has been conducting longitudinal research on alcohol and drug use from adolescence through middle adulthood. Her expertise and past research has addressed theoretical, methodological, analytical, and substantive issues that are central to understanding the development of substance use and comorbidity of substance use with criminal offending and family violence. She has written one book, edited three others, and published more than 200 articles and book chapters. She has received awards from the American Sociological Association, Society for Prevention Research, and American Society of Criminology.

Mary E. Wilfert, M.Ed., Community Health Education, is a lifelong health educator. She served as the associate director of prevention and health promotion for the NCAA from 1999 to 2018. Prior to that, she was the coordinator for health education at both Western Kentucky University and Northern Kentucky University health services. As a young professional, she served the Northern Kentucky community through her work at the District Health Department and Catholic Social Services. Over her 40 year career, she focused her work on collaborations with community health specialists and higher education public health professionals, and relied on both professional and personal experience to support individuals and organizations in advancing healthy choices for lifelong well-being.

Preface

This book is part of a lifelong journey. That journey is a quest of trying to identify and share ways of making the world – at least small parts of it – a healthier and safer place. Beginning in the early 1970s, as a young college administrator, I found that virtually all of the incidents and other problems I dealt with were caused, or at least exacerbated, by others' use of drugs or alcohol. In 1975, I initiated a program "All about catchin' a good buzz, and other ways of getting high" which generated a packed room with lively discussions.

Tragedy struck a year later, with an apparent drug overdose death of a student. Following that, in a different setting in a different state, another tragedy hit, with a drunk driver killing two of my professional staff members; and this was on a sunny Saturday afternoon in autumn. My research and writing, my training and consultation, and my motivation and inspiration were propelled and continue to be so based on these tragedies, each of which could have been prevented. I am further inspired by the belief that we *can* do better – and that we *must* do better.

I realize that so many people – virtually everyone – has a story similar to mine. Some are personalized with their own life experiences, some are with family members, and some are with acquaintances. Yet, I believe everyone has been touched. What would their lives have been like had drug or alcohol issues *not* affected them, and in such a dramatic way? What if these stories were fewer in number and reach? Can something be done, in a hopeful and helpful way, to change the nature and scope of others' journeys?

The answer to the question about something being done is, and will continue to be, I believe, a resounding "yes." Progress has been made, scientific discoveries have evolved, quality efforts have been implemented, and many people have dedicated their lives to various aspects of preventing and treating so many of the issues surrounding drug and alcohol problems and concerns. However, so much more remains to be done.

As part of my own journey, I have continually sought out good works and pockets of excellence so others can learn from these. Whether through doing original research or compiling and codifying the works of others, I have sought to learn and share others' insights and strategies. My journey continues with this book, as it draws upon the experience and expertise of so many people.

The specific impetus for this book was based upon two "aha" moments. One was a talk by an esteemed professor who told stories about Bill W., a co-founder of Alcoholics Anonymous, and Dr. William Jellinek, a professor who wrote *The Disease Concept of Alcoholism*. These riveting stories gave insight into the lives and important perspectives of these two forerunners of the modern era of addiction studies. In a poignant manner, this professor concluded his remarks by saying "I can tell these stories because I knew Bill W. and Dr. Jellinek; however, who is going to tell these stories when I am gone?"

When I heard those words, I knew these were the seeds of something new. I knew that part of my life's journey was to do something to share the wisdom of others. Thus, I set out to learn from those who have dedicated a significant portion of their lives to addressing drug and alcohol issues. At the time I did this, starting five years ago, I didn't know how these insights and perspectives would be used. I didn't know if this process would result in a research study or a book; and if it were to become a book, I was not sure what shape it would take.

The other "aha" moment occurred shortly after that talk, when I had some reflections about leadership with thoughts about the nation's efforts to address drug and alcohol issues. Over many decades of working with substance abuse issues, I had clearly heard some leaders' voices. Consider former Surgeon General C. Everett Koop, particularly with tobacco issues; also consider the voice of the nation's first "drug czar" William Bennett. Think about Dr. Joseph Califano, first secretary of Health, Education and Welfare, and the founder of the National Institute on Alcohol Abuse and Alcoholism. Remember the 1-800-COCAINE hotline, established by Dr. Mark Gold? And we remember hearing about the sacrifices of Candy Lightner, the founder of Mothers Against Drunk Driving. Yet many of these names and their vocal leadership and inspiration were years ago. Where are the voices of today's leaders? Where are the role models, and who serves as a positive inspiration for others, whether adults or youth? Where are the leaders (whose names may never be known widely) at the state and local levels? Where is the knowledge of so many dedicated people, and how can this help promote and sustain the work so necessary for our society?

Those pivotal experiences and perspectives serve as the foundation for this book. Leadership seems to be lacking from a publicly vocal perspective. Yet leadership does exist, and wisdom is present. I believe it is important to gather and share the insights and wisdom of many of those who have been involved with drug and alcohol issues for a long period of time, learning about their challenges and opportunities, their lessons learned and regrets, and their recommendations for those working on these issues today and tomorrow.

I remain hopeful and positive. I draw inspiration from so many people because of their dedication, wisdom, selfless service, and commitment to a healthier and safer future. It is now incumbent upon each of us to find our paths, create our own journeys, and determine the ways in which we choose to dedicate ourselves.

The opportunity is before each of us to create our own legacy. The insights of long-term advocates can help us as we move forward.

Introduction

Drugs and alcohol are pervasive throughout the world, and they have been for centuries. They are found in all walks of life, and they are used by so many people for so many reasons. The range of substances included under the label of "drugs and alcohol" includes formulations old and new; these substances are used for therapeutic purposes as well as purposes strictly recreational. Cultural and hereditary considerations are part of their history; legal factors and evolving norms are also part of the context of drugs in the world.

Beyond the mere existence of drugs and alcohol throughout the world, many problems are associated with drugs and alcohol. This is not to imply that all usage of drugs or alcohol is bad – far from it. It does mean that problems do emerge, sometimes due to the substance, sometimes due to the individual, sometimes due to the context, and sometimes due to the confluence of multiple influences or idiosyncratic factors.

Further compounding this context is the fact that each of us knows of individuals and situations where problems have occurred, or are occurring. Consider knowing of someone who had too much to drink and drove a car, or someone who used a pain medication and then needed more. Consider the adolescent experimenting with marijuana, or an elderly person having a mixed drink after taking prescribed medications. Consider someone sharing a prescription with a friend with similar symptoms, or a person buying an unregulated substance from a dealer. The list goes on and on and on. The point is that so many problems can and do exist. Further, the point is also that most or all of us know of these situations, whether with ourselves, our family or loved ones, our neighbors and friends, our co-workers or acquaintances, or others who surround us.

Beyond this fact that "everyone knows something" is the fact that many controversies in the field of substance abuse exist. Even with scientific understanding progressing on numerous issues, many different perspectives remain among the professionals. Add to this the areas of specialization among professionals. And then compound this further with the gap between professionals' views and those of the rest of the public. Consider views about addiction, dependence, and substance use disorder; and the issue of disease versus disorder. Consider the respective roles of genetic backgrounds, family and environmental factors, and constitutional factors. Consider the extent to which education, punishment, values, and resiliency each make a difference with behavior. Consider the roles of family, peers, schools, community, and overall society with helping influence and shape individual and group norms. Consider how the issue is defined, and whether problem avoidance or human growth and potential are appropriate or complementary roles. The presence of these controversies, interpretations, and understandings that are or are not shared suggests a further need to address, more fully and more effectively, the areas of concern surrounding substance abuse issues.

When thinking about the range of concerns and problems related to drugs and alcohol, how many were preventable? How many of these problems could have been avoided or reduced in intensity or duration? What would the outcome have been if the individual or individuals affected had done something different, had a different attitude, or were a little more knowledgeable? Indeed, some problems may not be fully avoidable or predictable; but many – and perhaps most – could have been avoided or had reduced negative consequences.

Have problems always been present? Probably so. Data about the nature and extent of problems may not have been gathered on many of these issues, and undoubtedly many issues still exist about which data is outdated, incomplete, or nonexistent. Further, as we look across many different cultures of the world, different countries often have varied standards of measurement, or no standards at all, which makes cross-cultural comparisons difficult. Some problems may have decreased over time, in some cultures. And other problems may have decreased, although not in a particularly timely way. Other areas of concern may have remained stable, in spite of dedicated efforts to address them. The point is that we can, and should, take a hard look at what we are doing with the range of concerns and problems associated with drugs and alcohol. The reason for this is so we can do better, as we must do better.

Leadership

This book on *Leadership in Drug and Alcohol Abuse Prevention* is designed for just that purpose: leadership. The book is based on the need for grounded, needs-based, and appropriate strategies to prevent and address drug and alcohol issues. The premise is that these issues can be better addressed and managed if we, in whatever roles we occupy, take some lessons and advice from those who have worked in this arena on a long-term basis. The foundation is that each of us can have a leadership role, whether our work with drug and alcohol issues is full-time or part-time.

This book is designed for those who work with drug and alcohol issues, or who are preparing to do this kind of work. Most important, the audience for this book includes current and future counselors and therapists, social workers and community health personnel, health promotion specialists, and life coaches. Would others benefit? Absolutely. The business leader, the community volunteer, the faith community professionals, the parent, the elected official, the administrators in government, and the friend – all individuals will benefit from a greater understanding of the range of issues associated with preventing and addressing drug and alcohol issues. They will also benefit from an understanding about how they might "fit" within overall initiatives to plan and, ultimately, lead efforts on some aspect of this topic area.

Since virtually everyone (if not every person) has drug/alcohol issues in their personal, family, social, community, and/or work lives, all can benefit from perspectives and strategies encompassed in this book. Included are helpful insights, broad and narrow perspectives, knowledge overviews, and motivation embedded throughout this book. For example, a high school teacher serves an important role, whether as a role model, gatekeeper, early responder, or purveyor of positive messages and guidelines for the youth with whom she/he comes in contact. Similarly, a factory worker or fellow employee may gain insights and encouragement to become engaged in a different way regarding these pervasive issues. Further, those in policy or decision-making roles, whether in their paid work or community volunteer settings, can incorporate the wisdom from the personnel involved with the research undergirding this book. Each of these individuals, and more, can serve as a leader in their respective settings.

And why leadership, particularly with a topic as complex, controversial, and interwoven throughout society as substance abuse? In a broad sense, individuals are guided by a quest for a healthier and safer society. They want to address problems so their impact is minimal, and so they are less likely to recur. They are propelled to help individuals and groups, including their own, reach a higher potential. Ultimately, they feel a moral purpose and a calling to improve the quality of life for all. And, succinctly, because it is the right thing to do.

Within this contextual framework is found the call for leadership from multiple perspectives. With the apparent lack of publicly vocal leadership, stronger and grounded voices are required. With the wisdom that exists from so many years of experience, the foundation of this book was one of gathering the insights of many people involved with drug and alcohol issues for a long period of time.

Two sources of wisdom are included in this book. One source is individuals who have spent a substantial amount of time addressing substance abuse issues; these individuals served as the source of interviews conducted over a period of several years. The other source is professionals who have particular expertise or insight deemed especially relevant for a short essay or segment that provides additional insight on a topic or theme.

The people interviewed are those who worked in the public and private sector, who worked in prevention or treatment, who served at the local, state, or national level, or who did research or guided federal agencies. The common denominator was long-term experience working on some aspect of drug and/or alcohol issues, and doing so from a professional perspective. The same questions were asked of each individual, and these interviews were recorded and transcribed. Quotes from these interviews are found throughout each of the book's 12 chapters, providing additional perspectives and observations. Often, these individuals do not agree, and often they do agree; these varied perspectives provide much of the richness and practicality incorporated in this book.

The short segments – each named a *Professional Perspective* – are provided by professionals with a particular expertise or viewpoint. Just as with the interviewees, most of the contributors have long-term involvement with drug and alcohol issues. While some are clinicians, others are prevention specialists. Most work actively with their areas of expertise, and offer specific insights on their topical area.

4 Introduction

This book focuses on the perspectives and insights from both sets of these professionals. Their wisdom – broad and narrow – is folded into a framework designed to be helpful for those seeking a greater understanding of the important context of this work, and who are seeking skills that help them succeed. Much of the content is provided to offer attention to much of the current knowledge about drugs and alcohol, and the entire range of services and strategies.

The Book's General Framework

The general framework for this book is the *Pyramid of Success* (Figure 0.1). This comprises three elements: Competence, Confidence, and Commitment. *Competence* is having the knowledge and the skills to address the issue. It is being current and appropriate, based on the latest knowledge and scientific understandings. It means using the most appropriate protocols and approaches. It means having the grounding. While there are controversies and disagreements in the substance abuse field, as there are in so many fields of study, what is important is that an individual seeking to be involved in this area be trained and skilled, to the greatest extent possible, in the field of study. *Confidence* is having belief in oneself; it is rooted in self-esteem, that the individual believes that his or her expertise has value and worth. It is the understanding that s/he knows more and has a larger perspective about addressing the relevant issues (whether in prevention, intervention, treatment, recovery, or related areas) than most of those with whom contact is made. This confidence is important, since the field of drugs and alcohol is a persistent and challenging one, and where rewards and successes are often difficult to achieve and sustain. *Commitment* is similar to confidence, as it represents the need to persevere and be persistent with efforts to address drug and alcohol issues. Commitment means keeping on with the dedication and work for the long haul, as issues with drugs and alcohol do not lend themselves to a quick fix; they require long-term strategies, quality efforts, "booster shots," and continued effort to attain an outcome that will last.

Pyramid of Success

Commitment

Competence   Confidence

Figure 0.1 Pyramid of Success

The rationale for using this *Pyramid of Success* is that all three elements are essential for making a difference. It is not sufficient to have just one or two of these. Consider if someone working with drugs or alcohol had the competence, but didn't have the confidence to speak up about the issues; it's great that this person is knowledgeable, but if that isn't shared with others, then its value is quite limited. Similarly, if that competent person only worked on substance abuse issues for a little while, whether with a community, an organization, an individual, or other setting, that's great; however, there will be more impact and results if the work is sustained, renewed, and continued – that's the commitment. On another hand, what if an individual had great confidence and commitment, but lacked competence? What if that person really wasn't grounded in factual knowledge, or was not up to date with the latest science or expertise? That situation should cause major concern with what is being proposed or encouraged.

Thus, it is within these three broad constructs – competence, confidence, and commitment – that this book is organized. The first six chapters are subsumed under the construct of competence, three chapters constitute the confidence construct, and the final three chapters are incorporated within the construct of commitment. The details of these chapters help to capture essential elements for those seeking to make a difference with drug and alcohol problem prevention.

Some Perspectives and Some Limitations

This book is designed to accomplish multiple aims. It is designed as a high-level view of how our society can better address problems and issues associated with drugs and alcohol. It is designed to serve as a primer on multiple elements traditionally associated with substance abuse issues, whether that be prevention or treatment, recovery or dependence. It is designed to introduce practical tools from other fields of study, such as communication, management, evaluation, and strategic planning. It is designed to complement existing and emerging detailed knowledge and compendiums and repositories of knowledge. It is designed to help cut across the various fields of specialization, and often the silos, that exist within this overarching field of study.

What this book does not provide are detailed descriptions of many of the content areas. The aim of providing an overview and sharing the wisdom of long-term advocates and other professionals in the substance abuse field necessitated limitations with depth. Details about so many of the topics with drugs and alcohol are found elsewhere. For example, many textbooks and reference materials offer in-depth detail on various drug groupings, individual effects and intended uses of the wide range of substances. Volumes exist on individual characteristics associated with consequences and harms associated with various substances. Much is written about dependence and addiction, about prevention and intervention, and about treatment and recovery. While this volume includes some overview of these areas, the greatest depth will be found in other volumes. This book has limited attention to tobacco. While this book has some highlights with data, so much more is available in various formats. This book does not have the answers, but does point to successes and helpful strategies.

6 Introduction

As such, this book is intended as a complementary volume to the many resources and research that exists. Based on the framework of this volume – with the *Pyramid of Success* – individuals will round out much of their learning and inspiration with the content of this book. Readers will find direction and opportunities for new and renewed direction with their work on these issues.

This book provides individuals, whether full-time or part-time in drug and alcohol issues, whether professional or volunteer, whether highly experienced or relatively new, with some broad grounding about the range of topics and issues. With the various success stories, challenges, and strategies included, the book is designed as a motivation builder. The experience from those who have addressed these issues for years – decades – provides helpful information and motivation for continued work in this area.

Organization of This Volume

This book blends leadership and substance abuse prevention. As such, it provides a unique and compelling view of ways of understanding many of the issues surrounding drugs and alcohol; it provides structure, examples, resources, and inspiration. Each chapter includes several *Professional Perspectives*, the short articles prepared to provide in-depth insights on a focused topic. Also incorporated throughout each chapter are a variety of quotes from the individuals interviewed.

The first section focuses on *Competence*, with the premise that sound foundations of knowledge and skill are essential for effective work in this area. This section includes six chapters, all focused on the basic knowledge and skills surrounding the entire continuum of care. Chapters 1 and 2 focus on the nature of the concern; the first chapter highlights problems and issues from an individual perspective, whether adults or youth, consequences, reasons for use, and some considerations with dependence. The second chapter looks at these issues from an environmental or societal perspective; it includes consequences of substance abuse, and examines the environment as a cause of problems as well as a contributor to addressing these.

Chapter 3 highlights in detail the rationale for being concerned. Whether the evolution of science and knowledge or the context of roadblocks and obstacles, the focus is on having a firm grounding about why leadership is important. Attention to root causes of use and abuse, as well as values and consistency, are also addressed. Chapter 4 builds on this, with attention to various foundational factors. Whether it is the paradigms helpful for consideration, brain health, or principles defining drugs' effects, some basic knowledge is important for enhancing competence. This also introduces the continuum of use and the continuum of care, both essential for a comprehensive strategy.

Chapters 5 and 6 highlight the specific elements of the continuum of care. Specific attention is provided to a basic understanding of intervention, of treatment, and of recovery. The role of self-help groups, families, and treatment protocols are all included in the first of these chapters. With the latter chapter, attention to prevention, health promotion, methodologies, and messages are emphasized.

The second section of the book addresses *Confidence*, which is based on strategies and skills that will help individuals have heightened belief in themselves.

Chapter 7 includes overall organizing skills for helping orchestrate change efforts; this includes a planning framework and attention to the importance of getting others involved with these efforts. Chapter 8 highlights perspectives about what comprises a comprehensive effort for a setting, such as a community; a menu of strategies, including a planning grid, is helpful for these perspectives. In Chapter 9 the emphasis is on effective communication, whether in a large-scale organized sense or with personalized efforts; attention here is upon both persuasion and advocacy.

Commitment represents the book's third section, as this is the focus of leadership for helping create a future setting that is healthier and more productive. Chapter 10 addresses leadership within a society that is continuing to change and evolve. Attention is provided to ethical foundations and various leadership styles; the role of movements and campaigns is addressed also. With Chapter 11, the importance of taking care of oneself and providing assurance about continuing to persevere are addressed. The final chapter – Chapter 12 – includes the vision for the future. Many of those interviewed provided their wisdom and constructs for this; insight is provided about why this is an important element, and how to address it.

In total, these 12 chapters, within the overall rubric of the *Pyramid of Success*, are prepared with strategies, constructs, tools, insights, details, and perspectives. No "master roadmap" is provided, as no single approach is appropriate or relevant to address the diverse issues in widely different communities, settings, and circumstances. However, the tools and sustenance are included, and provide continuous motivation and inspiration for moving forward.

Final Considerations

For those considering being a leader, various considerations are central with this book. First, it is important to *have a general vision or dream*. It is essential to not accept what is, but to strive for improvement. It is vital that each of us dare to dream bigger than we already do. Second, it is vital to *have a broad perspective*. Showing the entire picture of drug and alcohol issues, and the large and small problems associated with them, can be helpful. This is contrasted with being limited to a narrow, focused perspective. This includes overall frameworks and paradigms. Third, *be grounded in good knowledge*. This should be accurate and current; thus, the various expert segments provide some focused information and resources for further examination. It should also be locally appropriate, based on factors and facts relevant for the specified group, community, or setting.

Fourth, *learn from others' experience and insight*. Learn from their experiences, challenges, and opportunities; adapt successful approaches, build on their accomplishments and challenges, and experiment. Fifth, *identify various resources*, whether from science, experience, collaborative planning, or other settings, that can be helpful in bringing dreams into reality. Much of this is provided in this book and much more is available in referenced resources as well as with other respectable sources. Sixth, *be both realistic and practical*. Think in terms of the short-range as well as the longer-range. Success is achievable, but only if the aim is realistic.

Finally, *be clear with what role you want to play*. Leadership can take all sorts of shapes and styles. Ultimately, the context and role go hand in hand, and a viable role is one as a transformer. The aim is transformation (to reduce existing problems). This is about looking different tomorrow. The role of each of us can be one of helping make the world around each of us a better, happier, healthier, and more joyful place.

The leader's role, with this transformation, is one of weaving the tapestry. It is like preparing a quilt, where many different pieces are stitched together. For drug and alcohol problem prevention, the master weaver is one who has the vision of the overall quilt, has the patience and perseverance to see things through, and does so in a quality way. It is also like growing a plant from a seed, starting with quality soil, adding nutrients and water, and tending to its health as it matures. This will not be a simple process, but it does require the competence, confidence, and commitment to address these issues.

Part I
Competence

Competence is a central component of the *Pyramid of Success*. This represents the knowledge base of the individual, and also includes the requisite skills for addressing the topic or issue. Competence requires that the knowledge be current and relevant, representing a sound understanding of the latest issues and strategies. Being competent means being skillful, whether through years of work and/or substantive grounding and practice. Being competent is not a particular endpoint, as skills will increase over time and new knowledge and practices will emerge.

Competence is all about having the skill and the background. Without competence, individuals will proceed in an unsubstantiated manner. Imagine any professional, service provider, laborer, or other person offering services or direction without the grounding. If a person has other elements of the *Pyramid of Success*, without the competence, this would result in a hollow effort not grounded in current science or quality practice. Thus, detailed study, renewal training, mentoring, and quality implementation are all integral to competence.

1 Understanding the Nature of the Concern
Individual Perspectives

When thinking about leadership in any field of study, the appropriate starting point is understanding the overall context of the issue. It is important to know about the current status of affairs for the issue, and also to understand what is needed or wanted. If the status quo is satisfactory, then there may be no need for change, unless the leadership wants improvement or modifications. The obvious context of this is that some type of review or assessment is needed to ascertain whether or not change is warranted, and if so, what different circumstances or outcomes are needed.

Why state the obvious at the beginning of this first chapter of this book? Simply put, it is to make very clear that, with drug and alcohol issues, the status quo is not acceptable. The current state of affairs with the misuse and abuse of substances is not where we as a society, whether in the United States or elsewhere, want to be. As leaders and as concerned individuals, we know that we do not want to leave situations surrounding drugs and alcohol as they are; we know that we are not satisfied with the presence of drug- and alcohol-related problems in families, work settings, schools, or communities, and more generally throughout states, the nation, and other nations throughout the world.

Consider for a moment the fact that every one of us is aware of at least one individual about whom we have had, or currently have, concerns about their personal use of drugs and/or alcohol. How about the eight-year-old who drank a beer, mimicking a parent's behavior. Consider a high school student who tried marijuana to escape some of life's challenges, or a college student who wanted to impress friends with how much he or she could drink. Or how about a middle-aged adult who had a couple of glasses of wine during a dinner interview with a prospective employer. Are there concerns with a factory worker who was hung over when showing up at the plant? Would this be different if it was a teacher? A bus driver? A surgeon or a lawyer, an accountant or a store clerk? An airline pilot? Is it different if this individual had smoked a joint, and that most yet not all of the immediate effects were gone when adopting these professional responsibilities?

In each of these situations, and countless more, we can identify areas of concern. Beyond that, each of us has different points of view about what behaviors are of concern, and which of these warrant some attention. Our perspectives may be based on the age of the person, the specific substance or its quantity, the effects, the circumstances, or other factors. Further attention to these areas of concern are found in Chapter 3 (Why Be Concerned?).

The main point is that substance abuse issues abound in our society. We can document areas where progress has been made, and we can also document areas where changes are needed. Significant amounts of research have been done to document areas of need; further, many areas remain where research has not been sufficient or is not conclusive.

This chapter highlights some areas of individual concern regarding drugs and alcohol. Included are some data points and contextual issues helpful as foundations for efforts addressing drug and alcohol issues, whether in prevention, treatment, or recovery. Some key factors – certainly not all! – are incorporated regarding the individual perspectives on this topic. The next chapter examines parallel issues from an environmental or overall societal perspective.

Overall Context and Definitions

The essential starting point is to provide a contextual framework and brief definitions. This is helpful for this book's readership, and also to serve as a model for dialog with others in family settings, schools, communities, workplaces, and elsewhere. While much more detail on these topics and issues is found in textbooks, monographs, scientific papers, and resources, this overview is essential for the necessary limitations of this volume. Further, this brief overview will help provide a foundation for the contents of this book; much more detail is provided in the specific chapters, as well as with many of the Professional Perspective segments found in each chapter.

First, why are both terms used when talking about "drugs and alcohol"? Generally speaking, the word "drug" encompasses any substance that, because of its chemical nature, affects a living organism. "Drug" includes alcohol; however, alcohol is separated here to specify clearly that it is to be included. Tobacco fits within the construct of "drug"; however, while most of the content of this volume is relevant, it is not the primary emphasis. *With this volume, the focus is on substances that, by their nature and use patterns, can result in immediate harm to self or others.* While "drug" includes legal and illegal substances (defined by the law), it also includes licit and illicit (what is generally accepted or not accepted by society). "Drugs" do include prescription and over-the-counter substances, which are generally used in appropriate and non-harmful ways. The primary focus within this book is upon identifying strategies to reduce the illicit, harmful, and/or inappropriate use of any drug, including alcohol.

A basic principle is that the body doesn't know what a person is putting into it; it just responds to what is placed in it. Thus, much of what is discussed throughout this book will be the same regardless of the specific ingredients. That is, when addressing prevention, intervention, treatment or recovery, much will be the same. When addressing individual factors, like the reasons for use, the substance itself may vary but the reasons may be the same. Certainly, different effects occur based on the substance itself and its innate effects; and other effects occur because of the individual, such as his/her expectations (see more in Chapter 4). Further, a protocol or procedure appropriate for one substance (e.g., heroin) may not be appropriate for another (e.g., alcohol); however, many factors cut across all substances in some form.

Finally, it is important to highlight that any use of a substance – alcohol or drug – is not necessarily harmful, bad, or undesirable. The aim espoused in this book, and reflected by so many professionals, is to reduce the negative consequences associated with substances. Research findings document that alcohol may, for some or for many people, be healthy (or at least not harmful) under certain circumstances. The important factor is to determine what is most appropriate – for this person, under these circumstances, at this point in time. Looking ahead to Chapter 4 (Foundational Factors) and Chapter 6 (Skills for Prevention and Education), it will be important to incorporate the principles defining the effects of a drug, as well as the factors of "guidelines" and the distinction between prevention and promotion. Having those more clearly defined will be most important in developing appropriate "next steps" for action.

Regarding definitions, these apply to both drugs and alcohol. Further, when considering drugs, the distinction is not made between those drugs used for medical purposes under a physician's direction and those used under other circumstances (whether prescribed or not).

- Abstainer – an individual who does not use substances
- Use – any consumption of drugs or alcohol
- Misuse – use of a substance in a problematic matter, yet done so unintentionally
- Abuse – use of a substance in circumstances or doses that significantly increase the potential for harm, or use outside generally acceptable behavior
- Harm – negative consequence (physical, emotional, cognitive, social, financial, legal, or other) to oneself or others as a result of substance use
- High-Risk Use – consumption of a substance that results in increased likelihood of short- or long-term negative consequences
- Dependence/Addiction – compulsive need to use a substance; inability to stop use, whether situational or immediate, in spite of negative consequences.

Usage Patterns among Adults

Drugs and alcohol have significant documentation regarding usage rates. These are found by looking at various patterns of use, most commonly lifetime, annual, month, and day. Similarly, the amount of use at one time (dosage), with alcohol in particular, is examined. With adults, over two-thirds of adults (70.1%) have consumed alcohol in the last year, with 56.0% reporting use in the last month; for the lifetime, this is 86.4% of individuals aged 18 or older. Binge drinking (generally four drinks for women and five drinks for men, on the same occasion) is found with one-quarter (26.9%) of adults aged 18 or above; heavier alcohol use (binge drinking on five or more days in the last month) is found among 7% of adults.

With drugs, it is estimated that 24.6 million Americans aged 12 or more used an illicit drug in the last month, from data in 2013.[1] This represents just under 10% of the population (9.4%). When excluding marijuana, use of other drugs appears to have stabilized in the past decade. Cocaine use has lowered over this time period;

currently this is 1.5 million people.[2] Methamphetamine use increased to 595,000 in 2013, up from 353,000 in 2010. Marijuana use has increased; current use (2013) was reported at 19.8 million users (7.5% of people aged 12 and older), increasing from 14.5 million people (5.8%) in 2007. Similarly, opioid use has increased, with about one-quarter of patients prescribed opioids for chronic pain misusing them.[3]

Much more information about adult drug usage patterns is available from various sources at the national level; the most helpful starting points are the federal agencies dealing specifically with these topics: the National Institute on Alcohol Abuse and Alcoholism, the National Institute on Drug Abuse, and the Centers for Disease Control and Prevention. This is not to negate other nonprofit or academic research initiatives, as these often have helpful and resourceful materials and findings.

Insights gathered from long-term advocates provide further background about the nature of the problems with drugs and alcohol, particularly as they affect individuals. Consider the following:

> When talking about drugs and alcohol, I think that they are tied together.
>
> Bill Modzeleski

> Alcohol is I think a lot more problematic. There is a huge difference because of the illegality of drugs.
>
> Thomasina Borkman

> So I wish that we could change the way people view things, bringing in more of the whole global impact of those two things, alcohol and other drugs.
>
> Carla Lapelle

> There is a group that try heroin and say "I'm never doing that again; that was really stupid." But heroin is a really fast addicting drug so you get somebody who reports that it was pleasurable, "I'm going to try it again" and then they try it again, and then they try it again, and who knows that may be enough for them to adjust and say "Well I have to, I can't snort, I have to inject, I need more" and they may then do this more frequently.
>
> Gail Milgram

> There is almost a civil rights issue associated with drug use; "it's your body, your brain, you can do what you want and if you develop a problem you need to have insurance to get treatment."
>
> Mark Gold

> Alcohol abuse is not the politically correct issue so it does not get the traction that other issues do.
>
> Kim Dude

> Alcohol continues to be our most abused drug. I think especially about the high-risk drinking, the heavy episodic drinking.
>
> Deb Thorstenson

Usage Patterns among Youth

Many of the issues surrounding drugs and alcohol focus on youth. While some of the adult behavior patterns are noted in the previous section, this section highlights the patterns of youth. Young people are of particular concern for a variety of reasons, including the fact that they are at the beginning of their lives, and that they are establishing decision-making and lifestyle patterns that will, to a large extent, sustain them for the rest of their lives. Young people are more impressionable and malleable, as their judgment and decision-making activities are in the process of being developed. Youth are learning life skills and are highly engaged in experimentation, new behaviors, and unfamiliar situations and settings. Typically, these various elements act together – a young person is learning about relationships and driving automobiles and drugs and alcohol, all at the same time. More narrowly, when putting a novice driver together with friends and drugs/alcohol, the result can be problematic and sometimes deadly.

Two main sources of information about youth use of drugs and alcohol are the Monitoring the Future Study[4] and the Youth Risk Behavior Survey.[5] Just as with the adults, the data can be overwhelming and challenging to understand. For example, with the Monitoring the Future Study, attention is provided to lifetime, annual, monthly, and daily use of substances. Primary attention is to 8th, 10th, and 12th grade youth; however, college students and other adults are also included. The particular validity and importance of this survey source is its longitudinal nature (from 1975).

When looking at high school data, for example, nearly four in ten (38.8%) of 12th graders have used any illicit drug in the past year; this compares with 41.4% 20 years earlier, and 36.6% ten years earlier. When excluding marijuana, this changes to 12.4% (2018), 18.3% (2008), and 20.2% (1998). Looking at illicit drug use in the past 30-day period, the rate was one-quarter (24.0%) among 12th grade students; this was 6.0% when excluding marijuana. Marijuana and hashish alone was found among 22.2% of 12th graders during the past month; this was 16.7% among 10th grade youth.

Annual alcohol use among 12th graders is 53.3% in 2018; for 8th graders it was 18.7%, and 37.8% for 10th graders. For those reported being drunk, the rates were 33.9% for 12th graders, 20.9% for 10th graders and 6.5% for 8th graders – all within the past year, at least once. From a 30-day use perspective, data for 12th graders showed three in ten (30.2%) youth consuming at least once; this was 8.2% for 8th graders and 18.6% for 10th graders. Regarding being drunk, this was 17.5% (12th grade), 8.4% (10th grade), and 2.1% (8th grade) over the past month.[6]

What this data demonstrates is that alcohol and drug use is common among youth. While substance use is not the dominant or majority behavior among youth, the presence of substances is noticeable. While only some highlights are noted here, data is available for a large range of substances, and this can be reviewed over time. For example, with marijuana, the monthly use rate among high school 12th graders was 15.5% in 1993; a quarter century later, in 2018, this is 22.2%.

Some detailed background information regarding underage drinking, as a specific common and long-term area of interest and concern, is provided with Professional Perspective 1.1.

Professional Perspective 1.1

Underage Drinking

Michael E. Dunn, Ph.D. and Jessica N. Flori, M.A.

Alcohol may not be listed as the leading cause of death among teens and young adults, but it is certainly the most common contributing factor to the majority of fatalities and many other serious harms. Underage individuals who consume alcohol are more likely to experience academic problems, legal problems, physical consequences, undesired and unprotected sexual activity, physical and sexual assault, lasting physical and neurological effects, higher risk of suicide and homicide, unintentional injury and car crashes, additional drug abuse, and death from unintentional injury, motor-vehicle accidents, and alcohol poisoning. Annually, almost 2000 college students die from alcohol-related motor-vehicle crashes and unintentional injuries, almost 700,000 are assaulted by another student who has been drinking, and almost 100,000 *report* experiencing alcohol-related sexual assault or date rape (the actual prevalence is much higher).

The nature of underage drinking has changed in recent decades. Overall prevalence is down, but risky alcohol use has increased. Of individuals aged 12 to 20 years old, 20% report alcohol use, and 13% report binge drinking in the past 30 days. Compared to those who start drinking at the age of 21, people who start drinking before the age of 15 are six times more likely to develop an alcohol use disorder later in life (Center for Behavioral Health Statistics and Quality, 2016). Drinking increases through childhood with 8% of 8th graders and 33% of 12th graders reporting alcohol use in the past month, and 4% of 8th graders and 17% of 12th graders reporting binge drinking in the past two weeks (Johnston et al., 2018).

The definition of underage drinking in the U.S. has changed over the years. At the end of Prohibition in 1933, the majority of states set the minimum drinking age at 21 to be consistent with the voting age at the time. In 1971, the voting age was lowered to 18, followed by 29 states lowering the minimum drinking age to 18, 19, or 20 (Wagenaar, 1993). The lowered drinking age was associated with an increase in traffic fatalities and alcohol-related car crashes with 60% of all traffic fatalities involving alcohol. Traffic crashes were the leading cause of alcohol-related deaths and over 65% of traffic deaths among individuals aged 16 to 20 involved alcohol (Fell et al., 2009).

In response to the rise in automobile crashes, the National Minimum Drinking Age Act of 1984 required states to set the minimum drinking age to 21 by 1986. There was a subsequent decrease in alcohol consumption and highway crashes among individuals aged 18 to 20. From 1982 to 1995 the number of fatal car crashes involving young drivers declined from 61% to

31%, although some of that decrease was likely the result of automobile safety improvements (McCartt et al., 2010). Overall, many studies have found that higher minimum drinking ages correspond with lower rates of alcohol consumption, later drinking initiation, and reduced heavy drinking and alcohol-related consequences (Grucza et al., 2016).

Underage drinking persists for a number of reasons. Teens are in a developmental stage in which they are seeking greater independence and beginning to explore adult roles, all of which is influenced by biopsychosocial factors. Adult societal norms are a powerful influence and children are inundated with media depictions of alcohol use as a social lubricant. Alcohol advertising has been found to influence the development of young children's understanding of alcohol in ways that encourage earlier use (Dunn & Yniguez, 1999). Peer pressure in social settings can be a factor along with internal pressure to be viewed positively by others who are drinking. Underage alcohol use is against the rules and risky, which presents teens with an opportunity to demonstrate independence. Teens may see drinking as another opportunity to experiment with adult roles and could feel like it is being denied to them unfairly. Drinking often plays a central role in underage social activities and many use alcohol to manage social anxiety.

Several strategies have been found to be effective in reducing underage alcohol use. Brief motivational interventions that provide personalized feedback about an individual's alcohol consumption, encouraging use of protective behavioral strategies, and challenging alcohol expectancies have all been successful at reducing underage alcohol use (Dimeff et al., 1999; Scott-Sheldon et al., 2012). Motivational interviewing strategies have been found to be effective in reducing alcohol consumption among adolescents in school-based programs (Hennessy & Tanner-Smith, 2015). Challenging alcohol expectancies represents a promising group-delivered prevention approach (Cruz & Dunn, 2003; Fried & Dunn, 2012), and cognitive behavioral programs like Life Skills Training have been found to be effective at reducing alcohol use among children (Botvin et al., 2001).

Much remains to be learned about effective means for reducing underage alcohol use. In 2007, the acting Surgeon General of the United States issued a *Call to Action to Prevent and Reduce Underage Drinking*. While helpful in drawing attention to the problem, reports like this tend to restate conclusions repeatedly noted by those of us doing research in this field. First and foremost, ineffective programs like DARE must be replaced with empirically supported strategies. Decade after decade, meta-analyses have repeatedly found that DARE is ineffective. Implementing effective strategies begins by understanding that important determinants of early and risky drinking are clearly evident by 3rd grade and develop throughout childhood (Dunn & Goldman, 1998). The most effective approach is based on empirically developed content, is developmentally appropriate, begins with younger children (3rd grade), is repeated in every grade, and addresses the natural drive toward risk taking and sensation seeking. Finally, a developmental approach to underage drinking prevention should be mindful that not all adolescents drink or want to drink. Supporting alcohol-free social activities is a crucial component of a successful prevention strategy. In conclusion, while this segment was entirely about alcohol consumption and underage drinking, most of the insights and lessons learned apply to use of other substances and should be incorporated into a comprehensive substance use prevention strategy.

References

Botvin, G.J., Griffirn, K.W., Diaz, T., & Ifill-Williams, M. (2001). Drug abuse prevention among minority adolescents: Post-test and one-year follow-up of a school-based preventive intervention. *Prevention Science, 2*, 1–13.

Center for Behavioral Health Statistics and Quality. (2016). *2015 National Survey on Drug Use and Health: Detailed Tables*. Rockville, MD: Substance Abuse and Mental Health Services Administration.

Cruz, I.Y. & Dunn, M.E. (2003). Lowering risk for early alcohol use by challenging alcohol expectancies in elementary school children. *Journal of Consulting and Clinical Psychology, 71*(3), 494–503.

Dimeff, L., Baer, J., Kivlahan, D., & Marlatt, G. (1999). *Brief Alcohol Screening and Intervention for College Students (BASICS): A Harm Reduction Approach*. New York, NY: Guilford Press.

Dunn, M.E. & Goldman, M.S. (1998). Age and drinking-related differences in the memory organization of alcohol expectancies in 3rd, 6th, 9th, and 12th grade children. *Journal of Consulting and Clinical Psychology, 66*, 579–585.

Dunn, M.E. & Yniguez, R.M. (1999). Experimental demonstration of the influence of alcohol advertising on the activation of alcohol expectancies in memory among fourth- and fifth-grade children. *Experimental Clinical Psychopharmacology, 7*(4), 473–483.

Fell, J.C., Tippetts, A.S., & Voas, R.B. (2009). Fatal traffic crashes involving drinking drivers: What have we learned? *Annuals of Advances in Automotive Medicine, 53*, 63–76.

Fried, A.B., & Dunn, M.E. (2012). The expectancy challenge alcohol literacy curriculum (ECALC): A single session group intervention to reduce alcohol use. *Psychology of Addictive Behaviors, 26*(3), 615–620.

Grucza, R.A., Agrawal, A., Krauss, M.J., Cavazos-Rehg, P.A., & Bierut, L.J. (2016). Recent trends in the prevalence of marijuana use and associated disorders in the United States. *Journal of the American Medical Association Psychiatry, 73*(3), 300–301.

Hennessy, E.A., & Tanner-Smith, E.E. (2015). Effectiveness of brief school-based interventions for adolescents: a meta-analysis of alcohol use prevention programs. *Prevention Science, 16*(3), 463–474. DOI:10.1007/s11121-014-0512-0.

Johnston, L.D., Miech, R.A., O'Malley, P.M., Bachman, J.G., Schulenberg, J.E., & Patrick, M.E. (2018). *Monitoring the Future National Survey Results on Drug Use: 1975–2017: Overview, Key Findings on Adolescent Drug Use*. Ann Arbor, MI: Institute for Social Research, The University of Michigan.

McCartt, A.T., Hellinga, L.A., & Kirley, B.B. (2010). The effects of the minimum legal drinking age 21 laws on alcohol-related driving in the United States. *Journal of Safety and Research, 41*(2), 173–181.

Scott-Sheldon, L.A., Terry, D.L., Carey, K.B., Garey, L., & Carey, M.P. (2012). Efficacy of expectancy challenge interventions to reduce college student drinking: A meta-analytic review. *Psychology of Addictive Behaviors, 26*(3), 393–405.

U.S. Department of Health and Human Services. (2007). *The Surgeon General's Call to Action to Prevent and Reduce Underage Drinking.* U.S. Department of Health and Human Services, Office of the Surgeon General.

Wagenaar, A.C. (1993). Research affects public policy: The case of the legal drinking age in the United States. *Addiction, 88*(suppl.), 75–85.

Michael E. Dunn, Ph.D., is a licensed psychologist (FL PY5502) and a founding faculty member of the Clinical Psychology Ph.D. program at the University of Central Florida. He has worked in the field of substance use research and treatment of Substance Use Disorders for over 30 years.

Jessica Flori is a clinical psychology doctoral student at the University of Central Florida. Her background includes work on research projects focused on treatment for Opioid Use Disorder and development of alcohol expectancy-based interventions for high-risk drinkers.

The long-term advocates interviewed had various comments regarding underage drinking, defined as being under the legal age of purchase (21 years of age). Specific comments include the following:

> *If we had an alcohol poisoning death here, then, suddenly everyone would go "we have to do something about this now"; the reality is we have close calls every single weekend.*
>
> Kim Dude

> *A real call to action on underage drinking is based upon the science and the evolution of the knowledge of just how impactful alcohol is on the developing human brain. I am convinced that if parents really knew, they would want to address it.*
>
> Jeffrey Levy

> *I am just amazed when the results could be death or dropouts or sexual assaults.*
>
> Kim Dude

> *What I believed earlier, that I no longer believe ... I thought binge drinking was the problem. That all the kids are going to drink, if we could just get them to moderate their behavior; if we could just get them to instead of drinking eight just drink five. I switched from being one of these guys who was an anti-binge drinking guy to someone who is an anti-underage drinking guy.*
>
> Jeffrey Levy

Not all the data is "bad news," however. Note, for example, that use of inhalants among 8th grade youth is down from 4.4% to 2.1% over a 30-day period, from 1991 to 2017. And 30-day alcohol use among 12th grade students has dropped from 54.0%

in 1991 to 33.2% in 2017; for 8th grade students this dropped from 25.1% to 8.0%. What this massive data set, as well as other data sources, provides is the opportunity to examine the information based on specific substances, different age groups, and demographic and other factors. Depending on the need and local context, and how the information will be used, greater and lesser examinations of the data are warranted.

Moving a bit beyond the data per se, it is helpful to review the population of "youth" from a broader perspective. As noted, youth are malleable and learning. Just as their bodies are not fully developed, their brains are not yet fully formed. While changes in the body and brain will occur throughout one's lifetime, the science now is informative that an individual's brain typically reaches full development at the age of around 25. Prior to that time, the plasticity or malleability of the brain is much more present, and an individual is found to be more susceptible to external influences at certain ages.

Other Higher Risk Groups

In addition to youth, other higher risk populations exist. These are distinguished because of some of the unique factors associated with their lives that make them at a higher risk for problems associated with the use of drugs or alcohol. Being at a higher risk does not mean that an individual with one or more of these "classifications" will become harmfully involved with substances; it simply means that they are at a higher risk of being involved, because of their affiliation with this category. For example, a person is at a higher risk of having a car crash if s/he has been using substances, because of factors such as reaction time, judgment, sight, and coordination; that does not mean that a person under the influence will definitely have a crash, but that s/he is at greater risk. Similarly, a person in a higher risk group is more likely to have problems as a result of drug/alcohol use because of the factors associated with that grouping; those may be genetic or constitutional, or they may be environmental or sociocultural.

Individuals may be at higher risk because of age, setting, affiliation group, or race/ethnicity. The Substance Abuse and Mental Health Services Administration (SAMHSA)[7] addresses many of these factors with their data collection and services. With age for example, older individuals are at risk because of compromised immune systems as well as other health situations (such as low or high blood pressure); there is also a heightened use of varied medications. For race and ethnic populations, African Americans have illegal monthly drug use at a rate of 12.4%, compared with 10.2% nationally; youth monthly alcohol use for ages 12–20 was lower – 17.3% versus 22.8% nationally. Native Americans had the highest rate of drug-induced death (17.1%). Hispanic illicit drug use was lower than the national rate of 10.2%, as it was 8.9% in the last month. With Asian Americans, illegal drug use was 4.1%, while it was 15.6% among Native Hawaiians or other Pacific Islanders. Binge alcohol use was 18.3% among this latter group, compared with 14.5% among Asian Americans.

A related category of youth focuses on college students. This is a significant transition period for many young people. Due to various factors with the traditional-age audience, individuals are at higher risk for drug/alcohol-related problems Some factors include learning to live on their own, higher risk affiliation groups, new social situations, academic pressures, and relationship development. With alcohol, most traditional age undergraduates are under the legal drinking age of 21, yet are situated in an environment that honors adulthood at age 18. Alcohol use, and heavier alcohol use, is higher among full-time college students aged 18–22, when compared with others of the same age.[8] For example, monthly use of alcohol was 58.0% (compared with 48.2%); binge drinking was 37.9% (versus 32.6%); and heavy drinking was 12.5% (versus 8.5%).

Other factors contribute to a higher risk situation. For setting, past-month alcohol use was higher in both large and small metropolitan areas (23.5% and 22.8%, respectively) than in non-metropolitan areas (46%). Other groups with unique needs and thus potentially higher risk for drug and alcohol problems are veterans, people involved with the criminal justice system, and the homeless. The important consideration is to discern what factors may be common among individuals with similar backgrounds or situations, as these may be causal for their substance use decisions and consequences. This understanding can then help guide decisions about ways of preventing problems, whether through individualized work, environmental strategies, or other approaches.

When considering high-risk groups, numerous different groups are at risk for a variety of reasons. These may include different stressors as well as genetic or environmental factors. Providing some insights about one high-risk population, as found with Professional Perspective 1.2, helps illustrate the complexities associated with addressing drug and alcohol issues in an appropriate way. Further insights are provided based on comments provided during the interviews with long-term advocates.

Professional Perspective 1.2

Substance Use Disorder Prevention with LGBTQ/Sexual Minorities

Philip T. McCabe, C.S.W.

The Centers for Disease Control and Disease Prevention acknowledges lesbian, gay, bisexual, transgender, and queer (LGBTQ) people are more likely to use alcohol, tobacco, and other drugs than the general population. They are also less likely to abstain from alcohol, tobacco, and other drugs; they report higher rates of substance abuse problems; and they are more likely to continue heavy drinking into later life. While some insights into the reasons for these differences are understood, many remain unclear. The important points, and the focus of this brief segment, are that the differential needs are significant, and appropriate attention to the needs of these individuals is warranted. Similar needs with other "minority" populations exist, and thus command understanding specific to those audiences and strategies appropriate for those needs.

In any attempt to develop materials that are culturally relevant, it is important to understand the language and terminology that is used. It is first important to consider that when discussing sexual orientation and gender identity or expression, there is not universal agreement and understanding of terminology. It is important to take into consideration that various sub-groups (social, generational, racial, cultural, and or regional) maybe comfortable with certain terms that are not used by others. Use of the term "queer" is a prime example; some individuals consider it to be a very inclusive term, while others consider it to be oppressive and derogatory. Sexual variations are not limited or unique to lesbian, gay, bisexual, or transgender individuals. Human sexuality can include a spectrum of activity, desire, and emotions. People who do not identify as fully heterosexual, or whose sexual behavior is not limited to a monogamous relationship with a person of the opposite sex, as well as individuals who express their gender in ways other than their perceived birth gender, can all be referred to as a sexual minority. Sexual minority individuals are often underserved or subject to inequitable or discriminatory practices in health care. They can also be reluctant to disclose their sexual orientation with providers based on previous experiences with heterosexism, judgment, discrimination, alienation, or mistrust.

Sexism, racism, ageism, heterosexism, transphobia, and other oppressions can have a similar impact on individuals who struggle with receiving culturally competent health care. This form of oppression is referred to as minority stress. Minority stress refers to the anxiety that comes from being a member of a marginalized group. Minority stress describes chronically high levels of stress faced by members of stigmatized minority groups. It may be caused by a number of factors, including poor social support and low socioeconomic status, but the most well understood causes of minority stress are interpersonal prejudice and discrimination. The experience of minority stress is compounded by the fact that for many LGBTQ individuals, their minority status is often kept hidden for many years. Many LGBTQ individuals have turned to substance abuse to ease the discomfort of minority stress. Minority stress, especially related to past trauma, can increase disparity in health and wellness for individuals.

Sexual minorities are not always included in national surveys. According to the 2015–2016 National Survey on Drug Use and Health (NSDUH), 64.2% (6.8 million) of sexual minorities in this survey, meaning lesbian, gay, or bisexual (LGB) only, aged 18 and older reported using alcohol in the past month; this was higher than the national average (55.5%) (Medley et al., 2015). Bisexuals aged 18 and older reported 37.4% (2.3 million) binge drinking in the past month; this was higher than the national average (26.5%). Binge drinking for bisexual women was reported at 39.9%, which is higher compared to all women (21.6%).

According to the 2016 NSDUH, 32.1% (3.4 million) of sexual minorities aged 18 and older reported using marijuana in the past year. This was higher than the national average (13.8%). Among sexual minorities aged 18 and older, 10.5% (1.1 million) reported misusing a prescription pain reliever in the past year; this was higher than the national average (4.5%).

Data from the 2017 Youth Risk Behavior Surveillance Survey reported that 60.9% of heterosexual students had at least one drink of alcohol in their lifetime (72.2% for LGB), and 29.7% of heterosexual students reported at least one drink of alcohol in the past 30 days (this was 37.4% among LGB students). In addition, 35.6% of students reported using marijuana one or more times in their lifetime (35.2% for heterosexual students, 50.4% for LGB students).

Some studies have found significantly higher rates of alcohol, cigarette, and marijuana use among transgender youth, when compared with cisgender peers. A 2017 study from Chapman University (De Pedro et al., 2017) has found that transgender teenagers are twice as likely as their cisgender peers to have substance abuse problems. Transgender students were about 2.5 times more likely as cisgender students to use cocaine/methamphetamine in their lifetime. They also were more than twice as likely to report past 30-day prescription pain medication use and more than three times as likely to use cigarettes in school.

According to a 2015 study from Harvard University (Reisner et al., 2015), transgender youth are also at disproportionate risk for depression and suicide, which can certainly factor into the social stress and health disparities.

It is important that those addressing drug and alcohol issues, understand the complexity of sexual identity and gender expression in working with LGBTQ and sexual minority individuals. Social and cultural variables, mental health, trauma, and substance abuse, in addition to specific risk behaviors, can create barriers to the effectiveness of typical and common prevention messages or treatment interventions in helping individuals enact behavior changes.

Prevention, treatment or recovery support services need to be LGBTQ inclusive and affirmative. Understanding about the variations of how LGBTQ individuals socialize, develop, and maintain relationships and families of choice along with issues with their family of origin needs to be included. The ability to have open discussion about sexual health, when appropriate, needs to be developed. Confidentiality needs always to be maintained. Never disclose a person's sexual orientation or gender identity without informed consent from the individual. For LGBTQ individuals, treatment and prevention must include a focus on the effects of stigma, homophobia, transphobia, and heterosexism in order to be beneficial to the recipient, whether a client, participant, or ally.

References

De Pedro, K., Gilreath, T., Jackson, C., & Christina Esqueda, M. (2017). Substance use among transgender students in California public middle and high schools. *Journal of School Health, 87*, 303–309. DOI:10.1111/josh.12499.

Medley, G., Lipari, R., Bose, J., Cribb, D., Kroutil, L., & McHenry, G. (2015). Sexual orientation and estimates of adult substance use and mental health: Results from the 2015 National Survey on Drug Use and Health. *NSDUH Data Review*, October.

Reisner, S.L., Vetters, R., Leclerc, M., Zaslow, S.,Wolfrum, S., Shumer, D., Mimiaga, M.J. (2015). Mental health of transgender youth in care at an adolescent urban community health center: A matched retrospective cohort study. *The Journal of Adolescent Health: Official Publication of the Society for Adolescent Medicine*, 56(3), 274–279.

U.S. Center for Behavioral Health Statistics and Quality. (2016). *2015 National Survey on Drug Use and Health: Methodological Summary and Definitions*. Retrieved from www.samhsa.gov/data/.

U.S. Centers for Disease Control and Prevention (CDC). (1991–2017). High School Youth Risk Behavior Survey Data. Available at http://nccd.cdc.gov/youth online/.

U.S. Centers for Disease Control and Prevention (CDC). (2013). Youth risk behavior surveillance: United States, 2013. MMWR *Surveillance Summary*, 63(4), 1–168.

Philip T. McCabe, C.S.W., CAS, CDVC, DRCC, is a health educator for Rutgers School of Public Health, Center for Public Health Workforce Development, an adjunct instructor for Rutgers School of Nursing and School of Social Work. Additionally he serves as the president of NALGAP – The Association of Lesbian, Gay, Bisexual, Transgender Addiction Professionals and Their Allies.

People at all economic levels get into trouble with alcohol and drugs.
Thomasina Borkman

I think that there is a global misinterpretation of who is doing what.
Gail Milgram

Reasons for Use

Integral with the extent and patterns of use of drugs and alcohol are the various reasons for use. These will vary based on numerous factors, such as the cultural and environmental factors cited in the following chapter. They will also be different based on the choice of the substance, as well as prior experiences. They may vary based on age or setting, and there may be a progression over time, such as illustrated with the gateway theory.

Overall, what is helpful is having a framework or construct that helps identify the reasons that individuals use drugs or alcohol (Figure 1.1); similarly, it is helpful to understand why individuals abuse or misuse drugs or alcohol. This organizing framework, with four overall categories, is a starting point for understanding decisions made by individuals regarding their substance use and abuse. While not all inclusive, it does help identify individuals' motivations and attitudes. If these reasons are better understood, proactive strategies and environmental approaches can be developed to address these reasons both directly and indirectly, and in the short term as well as the longer term.

PHYSICAL
→ To relax   → To calm jitters   → To frontload before a party
→ To forget   → To reduce hangovers   → To help sleep
→ To relieve stress   → It tastes/feels good   → To get drunk/high
→ To unwind   → To get a buzz   → Because of a family history

EMOTIONAL
→ To feel good about self   → To gain confidence   → To feel good
→ To believe in self   → To drown sorrows   → To numb emotions
→ To boost self-esteem   → To enjoy life   → To escape

COGNITIVE
→ To focus attention   → To appreciate setting   → Easy to get
→ To be more creative   → To avoid guilt   → Not seen as a problem
→ To organize thoughts   → Rite of passage   → Tradition

SOCIAL
→ To loosen up   → To be friendly   → To celebrate
→ To keep up with friends   → To meet expectations   → Nothing else to do
→ To become talkative   → To be liked   → To meet people
→ To be friendly   → To enjoy self   → Because others are

Figure 1.1 Reasons for Use

Consequences

It is not just the usage patterns per se that are important, but the associated consequences (Figure 1.2). If, in fact, no negative consequences existed, then there would be no need to be concerned. That is, the use of drugs/alcohol in and of itself is not the area of concern; rather, it is the consequences that are often associated with the use that are of concern.

When thinking about negative consequences, the two that typically arise are dependence and death. Regarding dependence, more about that will be provided in the next section, as well as in Chapter 4 on Foundational Factors. However, the one that probably causes the greatest concern is death. It is estimated that 88,000 people die each year, due to alcohol-related causes (National Institute on Alcohol Abuse and Alcoholism); for drugs, over 64,000 people died from drug overdoses in 2016;[9] this compares with less than one-third that number (about 18,000) in 1999 and a number that more than doubled in a decade (28,000 in 2006). With opioids alone, deaths were estimated at over 42,000 in 2016, with over 17,000 involving prescription opioids, over 19,000 included synthetic opioids (especially fentanyl), and over 15,000 involving heroin.

Concerning fatalities associated with driving, alcohol was involved with about 31% of all driving fatalities, with 9967 deaths in 2014. NSDUH shows that in 2017 21.4 million people drove under the influence of alcohol in the past year; this was 12.8 million under the influence of illicit drugs.[10] The extent to which drugs are associated with car crashes is difficult to ascertain; the National Highway Traffic Safety Administration cites one study that showed that 18% of drivers killed in a crash had a positive drug test for at least one substance.[11] Further detail about drunk and impaired driving is provided with Professional Perspective 1.3.

PHYSICAL
→ Impaired vision
→ Loss of coordination
→ Loss of balance
→ Poor decision-making
→ Limited judgment
→ Personal injury
→ Anger

→ Passing out
→ Upset stomach
→ Nausea
→ Overreaction
→ Slow reaction time
→ Sleep disturbances
→ Blackouts

→ Hangover
→ Sexual assault
→ Rape
→ STDs
→ Overdose/poisoning
→ Fights
→ Falls

EMOTIONAL
→ Loss of confidence
→ Share emotional thoughts
→ Easily moved emotionally
→ Loud comments

→ Moody
→ Irritable

→ Anxiety

→ Guilt about use

→ Argumentative
→ Depression

→ Dramatic mood swings

→ Withdrawal

COGNITIVE
→ Memory loss
→ Lack coherent thoughts
→ Slurred speech
→ Irrational judgment

→ Irrational comments
→ Slower activity level

→ Decreased attention
→ Poor judgment

→ Forgetfulness
→ Grasping for words

→ Difficulty concentrating
→ Poor work performance

SOCIAL
→ Undeveloped social skills
→ Embarrassing statements
→ Social faux pas
→ Lack personal recognition
→ Disheveled appearance

→ Isolation

→ Withdrawal

→ Family difficulties
→ Poor relationships

→ Damaged friendships

→ Damage of property

→ Later regrets for behavior

→ Legal consequences
→ Driving under influence

→ Financial constraints

Figure 1.2 Consequences of Use

Professional Perspective 1.3

Impacts of Drug-Impaired Driving Means Increased Risk for Roadways

Ryan Snow, M.Ed.

Starting in the 1970s, three tests were developed to determine whether or not a driver was impaired. The Horizontal Gaze Nystagmus, walk and turn, and one-leg stand tests have been used to correctly identify over 90% of alcohol-impaired drivers if properly administered. Training and education for police officers has increased since the development of the tests and officers from all over the nation are performing these tests on the side of the road if they suspect a driver to be impaired due to alcohol. Organizations like Mothers Against Drunk Driving (MADD), Students Against Destructive Decisions (SADD), and the National Highway Traffic Safety Administration (NHTSA) have helped develop educational campaigns that provide facts and consequences when it comes to the dangers of drinking and driving. The impact these organizations have had on society is immense. Hundreds of laws have been passed to help deter alcohol-impaired driving. The nation decided to adopt the .08 BAC (blood alcohol concentration) limit for drivers over 21 and some states are currently looking at dropping it to a .05 BAC limit. Due to the efforts of these organizations and police enforcement, the number of deaths in the United States caused by drunk drivers has dropped significantly. Since 1982, drunk driving fatalities on our nation's roadways have decreased 48% (Foundation for Advancing Alcohol Responsibility, 2018) However, the nation is beginning to see an alarming trend about which many leaders in drug prevention and law enforcement are realizing they are not prepared. Drug-impaired driving has thrust itself into the spotlight and the need for change is more apparent than ever.

Drug-impaired driving has many faces. The driver's body does not discriminate when it comes to impairment from drugs while driving. Impairment can be seen from prescription drugs, illicit drugs, marijuana, or a combination of drugs and alcohol. The steady increase in prescription drugs being issued by doctors has been well documented in the last ten years. Surveys show an 85% increase in the number of prescriptions filled between 1997 and 2016 (Preidt, 2017). When those drugs are taken into the body, especially outside of the instructions of doctors, they also greatly impact the ability for that person to drive. Most prescription bottles come with labels that attempt to deter patients from driving while using the drugs, but many people drive anyway. Their use can have effects on the body that directly impact the ability to drive safely.

Illicit drugs, especially opioids, have become a major concern for many around the country. Deaths have skyrocketed with the increase of drugs like fentanyl and other synthetics. But these are not the only drugs that concern police when it comes to impaired driving. Everything including cocaine, heroin, methamphetamine, and many other synthetic drugs can impair a driver, causing them to be involved in a fatal crash. An increasingly large sector of society believes that marijuana poses no risks to our society. Many people view it as a harmless substance taken to relax or possibly fall asleep. Although this can be perpetuated by members of media on TV and movies, there is another side to this argument. Police are struggling with drugged driving issues every day on American roadways. The true impact the legalization of marijuana will have on traffic crashes is still yet to be determined but some research has been able to connect the legalization to a higher percentage of traffic crashes in specific states (IIHS, 2018). These findings show that crashes are up by as much as 6% in Colorado, Nevada, Oregon, and Washington, compared to neighboring states that have not legalized marijuana for recreational use.

So, what can be done? There are many issues concerning drug-impaired driving. The general public does not recognize drug-impaired driving like they do alcohol-impaired driving. Many times, a typical person can pick out an over-inebriated person standing on the side of the road performing field sobriety tests. The common signs include stumbling or falling, slurred speech, and often repulsive odor. Drugs take on many forms and their impairment is also sometimes difficult to detect. Most police officers have not been provided the training needed to combat these issues. There are only a select number that have been trained as Drug Recognition Experts across the nation. These officers attend over two weeks of training specifically designed to help them identify drug-impaired drivers. Often, that is too much time for departments to allocate their precious resources to a training class. This also takes money from the budgets of departments that are already struggling to support programs currently in place. These issues prevent many officers from receiving the training to recognize and enforce drug-impaired driving laws.

If the issue of drug-impaired driving is looked at as an increasing issue today, governments on local, state, and national levels need to develop a plan to increase the awareness of the people they serve. A push for more education needs to be a focus in the coming years not only for adults but for children as well. Development of better training for law enforcement, judges, and attorneys needs to happen in order to create a more cohesive and collaborative way to tackle this problem.

References

Foundation for Advancing Alcohol Responsibility. (2018). Retrieved November 6, 2018 from www.responsibility.org/get-the-facts/research/statistics/drunk-driving-fatalities/.

Insurance Institute for Highway Safety (IIHS). (2018). Crashes rise in first states to begin legalized retail sales of recreational marijuana. Retrieved October 18, 2018 from www.iihs.org/iihs/news/desktopnews/crashes-rise-in-first-states-to-begin-legalized-retail-sales-of-recreational-marijuana.

Preidt, R. (2017). Americans taking more prescription drugs than ever: Survey. Retrieved August 3, 2018 from https://consumer.healthday.com/general-health-information-16/prescription-drug-news-551/americans-taking-more-prescription-drugs-than-ever-survey-725208.html.

Ryan Snow, M.Ed., has served as a police officer for eight years, with specialties in impaired driving and drug investigations. He also serves as a trainer on emerging drug trends and a conference speaker emphasizing the impact of drugs and alcohol on communities.

The costs of drug use, including alcohol, tobacco, and illicit drugs, is reported at a level of $740 billion annually.[12] This figure includes health care, crime, and lost work productivity. With these alcohol is estimated at $249 billion, illicit drugs at $193 billion, and prescription opioids at over $78 billion.

Emergency room visits reported in 2009 are estimated with 4.6 million drug-related visits; while 45% of these involved drug abuse, nearly one-half were linked to adverse reactions to drugs that were taken as prescribed.[13] Chapter 4 (Foundational Factors) highlights principles defining the effects of a drug; this acknowledges the interaction between an individual and the substance, without attention to the legality or illegality of consuming a substance.

A range of consequences are specified by the long-term advocates. Whether these consequences persist, have gotten better, or otherwise are illustrated with the following:

The one area that I think we've really made a lot of progress in is in regard to drunk driving because among this generation of young people almost all use designated drivers. I think that is amazing that the culture was able to make such a switch. Other protective strategies might also work; if we can get them to stop playing drinking games and pre-gaming, we might be able to reduce a lot of the problems.

Helene White

A lot of the problem is economic. People with entry level jobs don't have a living wage. Our society is so out of whack economically; I think it starts there.

Thomasina Borkman

In some respects the numbers are better, the drunk driving numbers are specifically a whole lot better.

Jeffrey Levy

When thinking about consequences from an individual perspective, it is helpful to group these into four distinct categories: physical, emotional, cognitive, and social. Many of these overlap among the categories; for example, a single consequence may be both physical and cognitive in nature (e.g., limited judgment). Some consequences may exist or be more extreme with an individual, while similar consumption patterns and circumstances may have no such consequences with other people.

Linking to the previous discussion on higher risk groups, consideration of consequences for individual groups is worthy of review. For example, among college students the consequences are significant, with 1825 college student deaths for ages 18 to 24 from alcohol-related unintentional injuries.[14] Beyond that, an estimated 599,000 students between the ages of 18 and 24 were unintentionally injured because of drinking in 2001.[15] According to campus administrators, alcohol is involved with 38% of the incidents of physical injury, 31% of emotional difficulty, 24% of academic non-success, and 19% of student attrition.[16]

Consequences extend beyond personal use; individuals are affected by others who use substances. This includes children who live with a parent or guardian with drug or alcohol problems, whether or not formally classified as a substance use disorder. It includes others in a workplace setting, whether a supervisor, employee, or work colleague. Consequences are found with relatives, neighbors, friends, acquaintances, and others with whom an individual comes into contact.

The primary issue that comes from the discussion on consequences associated with drug and alcohol use is that many, many consequences result from the use of these substances. Some of the consequences are extreme, and others are relatively minor. The emphasis is upon the negative or problematic consequences, as these are the elements that are sought to be avoided, minimized, or eliminated. The "larger picture" is one of balance – weighing the helpful consequences with those that are not so helpful, so that, overall, the decision to use a substance is a positive or constructive one. With physician-prescribed medications, for example, some include standards for use on an empty stomach, or after a meal; some suggest use while upright and not lying down; some require avoidance of use with alcohol; and some are time-release and are not to be crushed for consumption. The aim is to obtain the positive results without the negative consequences. The intent is to minimize the illicit or inappropriate use of any substance. Further, by identifying specifically the negative consequences, the aim is to identify ways of reducing these to the greatest extent possible.

Dependence Considerations

Another area of concern is dependence. This is a consequence that is not sought, whether it is with drugs and/or alcohol, with gambling, with eating, with spending, or some other outcome with negative consequences typically associated with it. It may not be something that an individual can avoid – but it is something about which greater understanding and attention can be provided, so that factors such as its duration, the extent to which it occurs, and negative consequences can be addressed better.

The issue of dependence is one that is confounded with two distinct yet overlapping factors. One is the nature of the science surrounding dependence; the other is the public perceptions and views about dependence, and particularly about those who are dependent.

With regard to the first consideration, one of the challenges is that the science regarding dependence is evolving. Consider E.M. Jellinek with his "disease concept of alcoholism";[17] he chose the term "concept," as the view of dependence as a disease was relatively new at that time. It appears that he was moving gently into this redefinition of alcoholism. Most recently, with the *Diagnostic and Statistical Manual V* (DSM-5), is the language of "substance use disorder" rather than "dependence" found with the DSM-IV. So the evolution of professional language has moved from alcoholism to drug and alcohol addiction, to dependence, to substance use disorder. That reflects changes in language that are also reflective of changes in our professionals' understanding of the nature and etiology of the disease.

Separate is the second factor that confounds the dependence discussion: the general public. Not only is the average person not kept up to date with the latest science or the most current language for discussing this issue, but the average person has so many perceptions and personal attitudes that are not grounded in current science. For example, the view of dependence or the substance use disorder as a "moral failing" or a "loss of willpower" is not uncommon.

With these factors, it is important to stress that, with the overall emphasis of this chapter on "the nature of the issue from an individual perspective," the aim is that dependence is one of the areas of concern. Many more outcomes are of concern, such as alcohol- or drug-related injuries or deaths, substance-associated crimes or aberrant behaviors, affiliated and non-dependence-oriented consequences, loss of productivity, and inability to maximize potential and performance. With substance use disorders, the aim is to identify ways of reducing its potential to occur or to progress, to minimize its impact, and to maximize successful treatment and recovery. More about substance use disorders and dependence issues is found in Chapter 4.

With data regarding dependence, SAMHSA estimates that 20.2 million Americans can be classified with a substance use disorder. Of these, about 1 million are receiving treatment. It is also well documented that future dependence is more likely when an individual begins use earlier.[18] However, the real "cause and effect" is not established, because earlier use may be due to heightened genetic and/or constitutional factors or vulnerabilities.

Limitations with Data and Information

The information provided in this chapter is intended as an overview, illustrating some of the primary ways that drugs and alcohol have direct effects on individuals. A range of factors is identified in this chapter, from specific data points on injury and death to less quantifiable impacts on self and others. The focus is on drugs and alcohol, and does not include the substance that has the highest number of reported deaths each year – tobacco. For this substance, the estimates are that nearly one-half million people die each year due to tobacco-related causes.[19] Of course, this is a long-term consequence, due to the slow and cumulative impact of tobacco use.

With tobacco excluded from most of the data in this chapter, what remains is data that is extensive and can be confusing. Whether a concerned person is in a leadership position, is a professional in the substance abuse field, or is just interested, a question is whether the focus is on lifetime use or current use of a substance, as well as the consequences and contributing factors. Further attention is needed regarding the source of the information about current or past use, and how accurate the measures are, whether self-reported or other. There will be reviews about how extensive the delineations are among the actual causal factors associated with individual substances, regardless of the consequences; that is, was it alcohol that affected the outcome, or was it the interaction with another substance, whether prescribed or not?

Further, the wide variety of data and data sources can be overwhelming as one seeks to discern specific areas of concern. Some of this is due to the lack of data, such as information that has not been collected. Some of the challenge is with data that is not current (e.g., citing the most recent research or publicly available that is now ten years old). Other challenges are with information that is not reported in an easily understood way. In addition, there are factors that are not well documented, such as the effects of one person's use of a substance on other people; an example would be the consequences of a person's substance use on a family member, friend, co-worker, stranger, or others.

The important message here is that alcohol and drugs have consequences on individuals. These effects are widespread and overlapping; some of the effects are direct and immediate, and others are longer-term. While the specific routes of causation may not be clear or obvious, what is clear is that a myriad of effects are present. Some of these are documented clearly from a quantitative perspective and others are more anecdotal or subjective. However, the consequences are present, and thus raise areas of concern for potential action.

Helpful sources of information about drug and alcohol use are found with long-standing surveys with consistent methodologies. The National Survey on Drug Use and Health (formerly called the National Household Survey on Drug Abuse) provides good information. The data can be mined on numerous variables, whether that be demographics (such as age, gender, education, race, employment), socio-economic characteristics (poverty level, region of country, and type of setting), perceptions of risk and availability, or other surveyed factor. The value of these data is that they provide a "big picture" perspective; the challenge is that these often are cumbersome and overwhelming to find relevant information. A locally developed survey or other assessment may be more helpful, as it can be prepared with local needs in mind; a challenge with these is to maintain quality instrumentation and methodology, as well as to have comparisons with standardized measures at the regional or national level. The ultimate issue is to have data that is useful and appropriate for specific needs at the community, state or national level.

Future Implications

This chapter offers highlights about the overarching construct of how drugs and alcohol affect individuals. While medical, health-oriented, and quality-of-life factors can and often do result from the use of drugs or alcohol, it is the range of problems that can and often result that cause concern. When thinking about future implications, it is helpful to start with the individual and what, ultimately, will improve his/her quality of life. The issues outlined briefly in this chapter dovetail with those covered in the next chapter, which focuses on environmental factors. Overall, understanding the nature of the issue or problem helps define appropriate solutions or strategies.

Several conclusions and implications emerge from this chapter. First, many problems are documented with direct causation by or association with drugs or alcohol. Increasing clarity and shared understanding about these linkages can be helpful for whatever strategies or resolutions are defined. Second, and related to the first item, is that there are many areas where information is not available; research may not have been done, it may be dated, and it may be confounded with other variables or intervening factors.

Third, the data provided in this chapter are national in scope. Individuals seeking to provide leadership may find it helpful and strategic to gather locally relevant data, whether obtaining subsets of the national data, using similar questions and protocols for comparisons, or preparing their own approaches. This data, whether national, local, or combined, help with increasing overall awareness and understanding, and identifying future directions. These include a further research agenda, as well as prioritization of issues, situations, audiences, and more with suspected need.

Fourth, by having greater understanding of these associations between substances and individuals, appropriate strategies can be developed. A clearer delineation of these individually based issues will result in more focused and effective attention that can be provided to eliminate, reduce, or ameliorate the negative consequences.

This foundation helps focus the discussion regarding the results or outcomes to be sought – from the perspective of the individual. While often this is within the context of intervention with those in need regarding their use of substances (see

Chapter 5), the emphasis here is much broader, as it is upon the overall quality of life for individuals. Again, this will dovetail with the relevant outcomes included in Chapter 2 on the environmental context, as well as the importance of one's personal values and experiences (Chapter 3).

Summary

The use of drugs and alcohol affects individuals at the personal level. With a wide range of reasons for use and numerous consequences associated with substance misuse and abuse, foundations are provided to understand better the nature and scope of alcohol and drug problems as well as related problems. This understanding is helpful for clarifying the areas of concern (see Chapter 3, Why Be Concerned?) as well as individual, group, and societal directions for the future.

Notes

1. www.drugabuse.gov/publications/drugfacts/nationwide-trends.
2. www.drugabuse.gov/publications/drugfacts/nationwide-trends.
3. www.drugabuse.gov/drugs-abuse/opioids/opioid-overdose-crisis.
4. Miech, R.A., Johnston, L.D., O'Malley, P.M., Bachman, J.G., Schulenberg, J.E., & Patrick, M.E. (2018). *Monitoring the Future National Survey Results on Drug Use, 1975–2017: Volume I, Secondary School Students*. Ann Arbor, MI: Institute for Social Research, the University of Michigan.
5. Centers for Disease Control and Prevention. (2017). Youth Risk Behavior Survey Questionnaire. www.cdc.gov/yrbs. Accessed December 26, 2018.
6. www.monitoringthefuture.org/data/18data.html#2018data-drugs.
7. www.samhsa.gov/topics/specific-populations.
8. www.collegedrinkingprevention.gov/.
9. www.drugabuse.gov/related-topics/trends-statistics/overdose-death-rates.
10. www.drugabuse.gov/publications/drugfacts/drugged-driving.
11. www.drugabuse.gov/publications/drugfacts/drugged-driving.
12. www.drugabuse.gov/related-topics/trends-statistics.
13. www.drugabuse.gov/publications/drugfacts/drug-related-hospital-emergency-room-visits.
14. Hingson, R.W., Zha, W., & Weitzman, E.R. (2009). Magnitude of and trends in alcohol-related mortality and morbidity among U.S. college students ages 18–24, 1998–2005. *Journal of Studies on Alcohol and Drugs* (Suppl. 16), 12–20. PMID: 19538908 www.ncbi.nlm.nih.gov/pmc/articles/PMC2701090/.
15. Hingson et al., 2009.
16. Anderson, D.S. & Santos, G.M. (2018). *The College Alcohol Survey: The National Longitudinal Survey on Alcohol, Tobacco, Other Drug and Violence Issues at Institutions of Higher Education*. Fairfax, VA. George Mason University.
17. Jellinek, E.M. (1960). *The Disease Concept of Alcoholism*. New Haven, CT: Hillhouse Press.
18. Substance Abuse and Mental Health Services Administration. www.samhsa.gov/disorders.
19. Substance Abuse and Mental Health Services Administration. (2013). *Results from the 2012 National Survey on Drug Use and Health: Summary of National Findings*. NSDUH Series H-46, HHS Publication No. (SMA) 13-4795. Rockville, MD: Substance Abuse and Mental Health Services Administration.

2 Understanding the Nature of the Concern
Environmental Perspectives

Attention to "the environment" brings forth a range of interpretations. What is the environment? What is the nature and scope of its influence? How can this be understood, so as to address more effectively many of its factors? In what ways is "the environment" the same as or different when addressing drug and alcohol issues, when compared with other issues?

For the purposes of this chapter, attention to "the environment" constitutes factors substantively different from those addressed in the first chapter. Chapter 1 focused on the individual, and included a succinct overview of many of the ways in which individuals, as distinct human beings, are affected by their own personal consumption of drugs and/or alcohol. With that, the consequences of death or injury, of thwarted academic achievement or emotional difficulty, and of dependence or financial hardship, were highlighted. In one sense, that chapter focused on the individual in isolation from his or her surroundings.

The reality is that individuals are not isolated, whether from others or their surroundings. Constant interchange and give and take is found between individuals and their surroundings. Individuals affect their surrounding environment, and the environment affects individuals. This interaction is complex, and is the subject of continuous study by sociologists, anthropologists, and others. The complexities of understanding human behavior, from both cause and effect perspectives, are many.

In this chapter, attention is provided to several dimensions of the environment. Following an overview about the environment overall, consideration of some of the consequences of substance abuse is offered. The focus is then upon some aspects of the environment that help shape individuals' and groups' behaviors, with a brief understanding of the "root causes" of substance abuse issues. This chapter does not address issues such as the genetics or constitutional components that contribute to an individual's problematic involvement with drugs or alcohol; rather the focus is on the surrounding culture and cultures that influence, as well as are affected by, individuals.

From the interviews with long-term advocates on substance abuse prevention, a variety of perspectives are provided regarding the environment. These include the importance that the environment can play in creating as well as affecting substance use disorders and related problems. The following quotes are insightful:

The most important things that can be done ... it's using environmental prevention. It's really what's in the environment that contributes to high-risk use. And then addressing those things that you know you can be successful at first, so that there's something you can grab onto and not necessarily pick the one that will have the most resistance.

Deb Thorstenson

I think we did a horrible disservice to what we defined as environment as only being policy and enforcement. Environment is so much more broad, so much more complex, and involves so many more things than just those two elements.

Jeff Linkenbach

We ought to support people who have these kinds of challenges and remove the barriers to achieving goals. I think that's really important as an example, we know that both in the military and on college campuses there are many people who have struggles with addiction.

Robert Lynn

Defining the Environment

As a starting point, think about the environment as a focus on all that surrounds an individual as decisions are made about involvement or non-involvement with substances. The environment influences and otherwise helps shape each individual with information, behavioral norms, attitudes, guidance, and consequences, all of which coalesce to affect the individual and the ultimate decisions and behavior. The environment includes the multiple cultures with which an individual is engaged; the cultures include direct and indirect impacts, dominant and less forceful influences, and strong or light effects. Each individual is a part of, whether active or passive, multiple cultures; some individuals are embedded with many more cultural influences than other individuals. These cultures may include the family, work, social, or recreational, race/ethnicity, language, age, region, and based on affiliation groups that are or are not parallel to the other factors. In fact, there may be additional permutations of culture; for example, the nuclear family may have a culture of traditions, history, symbols, or behaviors drawing from the more extended family; an individual's culture may draw from or diverge from that extended family.

Within this understanding, consider the groups with which one affiliates. Within a community, for example, it may be education groups (e.g., PTA, reading groups), faith community (e.g., leadership, social, educational), recreational, social, or cultural. Within higher education, and focusing on undergraduate students, there may be a residential group, fraternity/sorority membership, recreation or intramural group, academic group, student leadership, athletics, club or organization, employment, mentorship, or social. For those in recovery, a substantive "family" group may be the Alcoholics Anonymous or Narcotics Anonymous group (or groups) for affiliation. Similar affiliation groups will be found with various settings.

When thinking about these groups, sub-groups, and cultures, it is important to understand ways in which these structures affect an individual's behavior. What are the respective cultural norms and standards, and are these stated or implied? In what ways are the standards or guidelines from one group complementary to or competing with those from another group? Further, how does an individual resolve these differences and set priorities, to the extent that they are understood?

The environment includes these various cultures and affiliations, but goes beyond that. The environment also includes laws and policies that occur in the multiple spheres of influence facing an individual – from the local community, state, and nation; from the work setting as well as faith community; within the educational framework as well as the recreational and social settings. The environment includes factors such as rules and regulations, and also includes expected formal and informal behaviors. The various environmental settings include clearly specified norms; they further include those that are implied as well as those less specified or communicated.

What are some of the ways that these environmental influences are evident? One overall strategy is with policies and requirements; these may include prohibitions, limitations, and expectations, whether with a specific substance, conditions of availability, individual access, or other factor. Related to policies are procedures and implementation standards. Also included are enforcement efforts, designed to ensure compliance with the established standards. Affiliated with a policy approach are approaches associated with costs: this may include overall pricing, taxation, and fees. There may be liability considerations as well as licensing standards.

Another is with educational approaches, which may include curricular strategies in organized educational settings or in the community at large. This may encompass training of professionals, paraprofessionals, leaders, employees, parents, or others. Included also are campaigns, whether addressing information or referral sources, best practices, or preferred intervention approaches.

Integral with the environmental approaches, as with other efforts, is the blending of approaches. For example, training programs may be developed to prepare staff members for implementation of a new policy or procedure; similarly, educational campaigns may be offered to inform the public about a change in a law, or to promote the adoption of a helpful practice with addressing substance abuse issues.

Attention to cultural issues from the perspective of the overall society is highlighted by the long-term advocates interviewed. Here are some of their insights:

> *Another important area that currently receives some broad attention is the need to become a culturally responsible counselor and organization. This is an ongoing pursuit. You are never culturally competent. Yet, you can approach the differences of race, ethnicity, and culture with cultural humility – taking the time to be culturally aware of yourself, to be commitment to learning about the clients you are serving, and approaching your clients with an attitude of humility and curiosity.*
>
> Claudia Blackburn

We would probably actually reduce drug abuse for certain people who use it due to stress or discrimination or because they are just lost. In a sense I have always said whenever I've written chapters on drugs and crime that if we could get rid of this economic disparity and racial prejudice, we would reduce a lot of crime in this country.

Helene White

We really need to view this through much more of a cultural lens than we have. We did a great job about a decade ago moving from a focus of only being that of the individual and his or her choices, to looking at and recognizing the incredible role that the environment plays. I believe that it's our mission to look at what is the role and the understanding of culture with these different social ills including substance use.

Jeff Linkenbach

I think we haven't done a terribly good job of figuring out exactly where alcohol fits in our life. Therefore, it is an enigma in many ways in the society. I think the problems have been significant and will continue to be significant as we continue to allow advertising, as we continue to essentially allow unhealthy environments around alcohol to be created.

Tom Griffin

If you look at this statistically it's a little bit of motion versus movement and I think that's because of these issues which are behavioral and cultural. And if you look at Monitoring the Future survey data from one year to the next, you're not going to see behavior change happen in one year's time. And so I think you really have to have the long view and I think you have to be open to being creative and so you have to challenge yourself to have a long view.

Ralph Blackman

Consequences of Drug and Alcohol Abuse

The environment and culture is affected, in demonstrable ways, by the misuse or abuse of drugs and alcohol. Alcohol and drugs have direct as well as indirect effects on various aspects of the environment. Some of the effects are caused only by the abuse or misuse of substances. Other effects are the result of increased susceptibility or likelihood that problems occur; that is, it will be difficult to discern the precise "contribution" of substances to the problematic outcome.

Numerous areas of concern arise related directly or indirectly to these substances. According to the National Institute on Alcohol Abuse and Alcoholism, the cost of alcohol misuse was $249 billion in 2010.[1] NIAAA also reports that three-quarters of the total cost of alcohol misuse is related to binge drinking. From a global perspective, 3.3 million deaths, or 5.9% of all deaths across the world, were attributable to alcohol consumption in 2012. The World Health Organization reports that alcohol contributed to over 200 diseases and injury-related situations in 2014. In 2012, 5.1% of the burden of injury and disease was attributable to alcohol consumption.[2]

Illicit drugs cause problems for the environment, also. For example, the Drug Enforcement Administration cites 28,881 DEA domestic arrests for 2016[3] and 9,338 clandestine meth laboratory incidents in 2014.[4] The National Institute on Drug

Abuse reports that, in 2009, there were 4.6 million drug-related visits to the emergency departments of hospitals.[5] While one-half of these were adverse reactions to pharmaceuticals taken as prescribed, about 45% involved drug abuse. Of the 2.1 million drug abuse visits, over one-quarter (27.1%) involved nonmedical use of pharmaceuticals, over one in five (21.2%) involved illicit drugs, and 14.3% involved alcohol in combination with other drugs. Estimates are that these visits to emergency departments almost doubled between 2004 and 2009 (from 627,291 to 1,244,679).

The costs of the abuse of drugs and alcohol are extensive. These costs are based on effects associated with crime, lost work productivity, and health care. The costs of illicit drugs include the misuse of prescription drugs. With illicit drugs, the healthcare costs in 2010 are estimated at $11 billion, part of the $193 billion overall annual costs.[6] For prescription opioids, the healthcare costs for 2013 are estimated at $26 billion, part of the $78.5 billion overall.[7] Alcohol's healthcare costs match those of opioids, at $27 billion, for 2010;[8] the overall costs of alcohol are significantly higher, at $249 billion.

Additional costs are found with the family members affected by an individual's substance abuse. For example, the NIAAA estimates that more than one in ten children in the United States live with a parent with alcohol problems.[9]

Looking at the college setting, campus administrators report that alcohol is involved with 68% of the incidents of acquaintance rape, 47% of violent behavior, 49% of residence hall damage, and 43% of campus property damage.[10]

Beyond these documented effects are consequences on various environmental and cultural settings for which no financial costs can be specified. For example, what are the emotional or interpersonal costs associated with the family members affected by an individual's substance abuse? In what ways does a family member's substance abuse affect the cognitive functioning of a child, or that child's ability to excel, to relate well with others, and to perform on various functions at the highest levels? It is hard to put a cost factor on these, as well as on many of the indirect or less specified outcomes associated with drug or alcohol misuse and abuse.

As seen with the quotes from the long-term advocates interviewed, as well as with Professional Perspective 2.1, the family and considerations regarding its role as an environmental contributor and consequences are important for understanding.

The strength of the family can't be overlooked in prevention if you really want to have an impact reducing alcohol and drug use problems in teens as well as in treatment where family therapy is the most effective. In my clinical psychology training at the University of Utah, my first course was in functional family therapy taught by Dr. James Alexander, who is the founder of functional family therapy. Hence, very early I learned that to have lasting and positive change in the teens you have to improve the family's communication patterns and assumptions about their relationships.

Karol Kumpfer

You want to see the negative consequences reduced, whether those are medical or social or economic. However you define those consequences, from underage drinking or over consumption and legal consequences, you want to believe that what you're doing is going to contribute to them – either having fewer people experience those negative consequences or those negative consequences being a thing of the past. That's progress and my sense is that there is not a conclusion.

Ralph Blackman

I think substance use addiction is so tied up with sexual violence, and harassment of women, and men too.

Thomasina Borkman

The major violence associated with drug use has to do with the fact that it's illegal; therefore with the legalization of marijuana we may actually see a lot less crime and we might even see a lot less hard drug use. If people can get drugs legally, they may not turn to dealers who also turn them on to other drugs. It will be very interesting to see what happens. But clearly alcohol has a lot of problems that we have not been able to deal with and they will continue.

Helene White

Professional Perspective 2.1

Family Considerations

Jenny Wagstaff, Ph.D.

Alcohol and drug abuse is a complicated issue that not only affects the user, but also affects families, friends, and communities. For family, their involvement in the recovery process improves the prospect of long-term success but also presents a myriad of factors to contend with that merits attention. First and foremost, family members must accept that they did not cause nor can they control the substance use disorder. Instead, it is more important to determine how to help a loved one without enabling the dysfunctional behavior (i.e., making it comfortable for the family member to use substances). When someone loves someone else, it is a natural desire to help during times of need. However, there is a fine line between being helpful and enabling. This is something all families encounter when confronted with a substance use disorder (SUD).

In most families, each family member has a specific role (or more); when someone in the family has a SUD, these roles often become exacerbated, at home, school, work, and social settings. Five common roles are: (1) Hero – the responsible one, class star, workaholic, presenting things in a positive manner; (2) Mascot – the one who makes inappropriate jokes and brings humor; (3) Lost Child – the one who stays silent and out of the way, loner; (4) Scapegoat – the one who acts out, diverts attention, troublemaker; and (5) Caretaker – the one who is a helper, problem-solver, and tries to keeps others happy and balanced. While these roles are often common in families and elsewhere, they can become "survival roles" for those in a family with a SUD; family members often take refuge within these roles, as the roles can help them cope and even find self-esteem. Further, sometimes these roles actually enable the substance abuse behaviors.

Enabling is driven by fear, worry, guilt, and stress. Substance abuse evokes these emotions. The fear and worry that a loved one's substance abuse behaviors will result in harm to self or others leads to a sense of urgency and the need to resolve the problem. This overreaction allows the loved one with the SUD to avoid the natural consequences of their destructive behaviors. Family members believe they are helping, but in fact they are perpetuating the problem. To prevent enabling, family members must avoid taking on responsibilities the loved one is capable of handling alone, and must also continue to promote the option of treatment for the SUD.

Family members must also be mindful of the emotional toll that substance abuse has on the family, both individually and collectively. Anger, frustration, fear, worry, guilt, shame, and embarrassment are common feelings experienced. Typical behaviors include isolation, rigidity, and silence. These feelings and behaviors lead to increased tension and conflict and pose a direct threat to the stability within the family system. Knowledge is power and families are empowered when educated about treatment options, relapse and relapse prevention, recovery, support programs, and coping strategies; this information is readily available. Not only does this information help one make informed decisions about the loved one with a SUD; it also helps address the needs of everyone within the family unit.

It must be acknowledged that family members experience compassion fatigue when the loved one fails to change their substance abuse behaviors. When this sets in, there is a sense of hopelessness which leads to the inability to feel or show empathy. To cope with compassion fatigue, family members must focus on their own needs as much as they focus on the needs of others. Some coping tips include:

1. Practice Self-Care – This means a well-balanced diet, consistent exercise, adequate sleep, and intentional relaxation.
2. Set Healthy Boundaries – Boundaries help establish guidelines for suitable behaviors, responsibilities, and actions within the relationship. It is important to remember that someone can be supportive without taking on someone else's pain.
3. Engage in Activities that Bring Joy – Identify hobbies or activities that promote happiness. It is not selfish to focus on one's own happiness. People are far more effective at helping others when they are happy.
4. Keep a Journal – The process of recording thoughts and feelings is an excellent way to cope with stress. The journal serves as a tool to identify patterns and triggers.
5. Take a Break – Everyone needs time to recharge. A 10–15 minute mindfulness exercise or a short walk in the park can help redirect one's mind off current problems. Be intentional and take a break at least once every day.

6. Learn to Say No – Saying "no" is just as important as saying "yes." It is important to differentiate between essential and nonessential duties. If someone is working harder than the loved one with the SUD, they have failed to say "no." Work smarter not harder.
7. Ask for Help – Talk to a counselor or take advantage of mutual support groups such as Al-Anon or Nar-Anon. There is no shame in asking for help. When people talk to others, they learn how to take better care of themselves and avoid burnout.

SAMHSA's National Helpline is a free, confidential, 24/7, 365-day-a-year treatment referral and information service for individuals and families facing SUDs. SUDs happen in the best of families. A first step toward healing is getting the loved one to agree to accept treatment through a family intervention. When carefully orchestrated and facilitated by a trained professional, this approach can place the entire family on the road to recovery. Family members need to remember that they did not create the problem but they can play a role in helping everyone heal.

Resources

Addiction Resources for Families. (n.d.). Retrieved from www.hazeldenbettyford.org/addiction/help-for-families/family-toolkit.
Berg, B. & Tatkin, S. (2014). *Loving Someone in Recovery: The Answers You Need When Your Partner Is Recovering from Addiction.* Oakland, CA: New Harbinger Publications.
Substance Abuse and Mental Health Services Administration. (September, 2017). Recovery and Support. Retrieved from www.samhsa.gov/recovery.
Substance Abuse and Mental Health Services Administration. (n.d.). SAMHSA's National Helpline. Retrieved from www.samhsa.gov/find-help/national-helpline.
Substance Abuse and Mental Health Services Administration. (n.d.). Treatment for Substance Use Disorder. Retrieved from www.samhsa.gov/treatment/substance-use-disorders.

Jenny Wagstaff, Ph.D. L.P.C., is Assistant Professor in Counselor Education at Campbell University, Buies Creek, NC. Her research focuses on the use of brief motivational interventions to address high-risk substance use behaviors.

The context of this discussion is three-fold. First, this specification of problems helps to focus attention on how substances can and do affect the surrounding environment. While much of this is documented and clear, much more remains unclear and not documented; as identified in Chapter 1, further, more specific, and current factual data and information is needed. Second, is the recognition that lacking specific desired information and data is not a reason for inaction. Many negative consequences are not necessarily quantifiable with "data" in the traditional sense of data (i.e., "numbers"); thus, qualitative information and insights are most helpful as both the primary source of information as well as a complement to any quantitative information that may exist. This calls forth the old mantra "Lack of proof of effect is not proof of lack of effect." Third, it is important to recall that not all consequences of substances are negative. As cited in Chapter 1, helpful results from an individual perspective regarding the appropriate use of substances are found. The focus in this chapter is upon the negative or problematic factors, as these become those elements upon which attention can be brought and, hopefully, some resolution and remediation can be achieved.

Overall, the specification of these issues helps chart an overall course of action for what can be done. With the delineation of these consequences, attention is raised to the need for doing something to address these, and thus reduce the negative impact of drugs and alcohol. The attention is one of viewing many if not all of these consequences as preventable and reasonable for attention. The proximate outcome is one of identifying appropriate action steps for addressing them; the longer-term outcome is that of a healthier and safer environment.

The Environment as a Cause or Contributor

One traditional way of looking at drug and alcohol misuse issues revolves around supply and demand. At its simplest level, this framework suggests that if attention is placed on reducing the supply, then individuals' use would go down. Similarly, if attention is placed on reducing demand, then individuals' use would be reduced. Attention to both approaches is important for a comprehensive approach to addressing substance abuse issues.

It is helpful to use this basic framework, while basic, as a way of looking at the environment. From a traditional perspective, the focus has often been on the supply side of this equation. Reviewing the various aspects of environmental strategies cited earlier, the focus was on approaches such as policies, procedures, enforcement, education, training, campaigns, and costs. The specific strategies incorporated within these and other environmental approaches have, as a primary aim, reduction of supply. With stiffer rules and regulations, limited hours of access, requirements regarding purchase, standards for use, costs, and related specific strategies, the overall aim is to affect the supply. What follows is one interviewee's views on this issue:

> The supply and demand problem is only going to get worse with the decriminalization and we don't have any federal support for training, but we are training specialists at a high rate that we may or may not need at all. So we have more dermatologists than we need and probably more plastic surgeons than we need but definitely not psychiatrists and addiction medicine providers.
>
> Mark Gold

It is within this context that the selected environmental strategies communicate what is important to the organizing community or culture. The establishment of rules or laws, or training or education, of pricing and access points is a way of communicating – and in some cases mandating – what is important to the sponsoring community or culture. Just as with cultures as a whole, these priorities and values may be overlapping among the groups. That is, the standards or rules of one organization (e.g., a workplace or faith community) may be established, and these may be the same as (and also may vary from) those in a different yet similar setting. Further, there may be overlapping or overriding standards, such as state laws; these would take precedence over local ordinances. Further, a particular sub-group or setting may have requirements that are more strict than those found for the surrounding area.

The other way in which the environment can be a cause or contributor to the problem is with respect to the demand part of the basic equation. That means that there are things that the various aspects of the environment do or do not do that influence individuals' demand or desire for substances. There may be acts of commission (what a cultural group or setting does) as well as acts of omission (what it does not do). These environmental influences affect an individual's decisions about drugs and alcohol, including factors such as the quality of information, skills for making a quality decision, and minimizing irrelevant influential factors.

Thinking about the environment and its effects on demand, the focus becomes one of addressing the root causes of substance use and abuse. What is it that contributes to, encourages, or guides an individual to use drugs or alcohol, and are these factors different based on the substance? What is the same, and what is different, when thinking about use versus abuse? What are the reasons someone uses a substance, and what are the reasons someone abuses or misuses a substance?

The reasons an individual uses a substance are an integral part of this "demand" feature. These are summarized in the first chapter, which addressed the nature of the issue from the individual perspective. While the primary focus there was on the effects or consequences of individual decisions, also highlighted were various reasons for an individual using or abusing substances. These were organized within four overall clusters: physical, emotional, cognitive, and social, with the understanding that individuals' behaviors may be a confluence of multiple factors, and that these may evolve over time.

The environmental focus provides attention to these individual reasons, within these clusters, and to understand better ways in which the environment affects these factors, both by what it does and what it does not do. For example, if a reason is to reduce stress, what is the community, work, cultural, or affiliation group doing that promotes a stressful reaction by an individual or group of individuals; similarly, what is that environmental setting doing that will help the individual better cope with or deal with stress, whether caused by that setting or elsewhere. Similarly, if the cognitive reason of "it's not a problem" is present, what is the setting doing that one would reasonably conclude that no problem exists, and what is the setting doing to promote greater problem awareness and sensitivity?

Consider various factors where the environment is a cause or contributor. One way this can happen is with the environment having no or low priority of policies, laws, and procedures. There also may be low or no enforcement of existing policies or laws; similarly there may be limited, low impact, or very mild consequences associated with violation. Another factor may be lack of information among various populations, whether in a leadership or professional role, or as a general member of the community. There may be misinformation, incomplete information, or non-applicable information. Related to that would be the lack of skills for addressing whatever issues may be identified.

On a related note, the communication may be present, and done so with high quality and positive intent. However, what, if anything, is heard by the intended audience? If a target group is new drivers, what messages do they hear about impaired driving? If a target group is older adults, what messages, and what communications channels, are used and what is understood by this audience? Only by understanding the relationship between what is intended and what is heard can a full assessment of the environmental influences be obtained.

How people view and communicate about dependence and related issues is important with some new perspectives. Professional Perspective 2.2 offers some helpful insights.

Professional Perspective 2.2

Sober Privilege – I'm Not Bad. I'm Drawn That Way: The Public Persona of Substance Use Disorders

Thomas Hall, Ph.D.

The public has a complicated relationship with mood altering substances. The media plays a role in creating and reinforcing stereotypes about substance use and abuse. Often stereotypes preserve caricatures of addiction. Ironically, on one hand the media and popular culture stigmatizes substance abuse as a moral failing: the public is familiar with depictions of disheveled, or dangerous "addicts." On the other hand references are easy to find that portray drug users as edgy, cool, or sophisticated. I use the term here because it is a familiar moniker used to describe persons with either a diagnosed or undiagnosed substance use disorder.

Privilege is a sociological construct that examines benefits or rights to certain populations without merit. In other words the advantages enjoyed by a privileged group are unearned. These unearned benefits lead to social, political, and economic advantages. In addition to gender- or race-based privilege, narratives about addiction are also shaped by privilege. Privilege is maintained by unexamined beliefs of a majority group leading to an unearned, collective benefit. Suggesting that the non-addicted population has an unfair advantage or privilege is not without its critics; nonetheless let us consider how blind spots might shape narratives about addiction.

In this context sober does not imply being *in recovery*. The concept of *sober privilege* is based on unexamined beliefs of those who are *not* recovering from or *do not* have a substance use disorder. Many (and perhaps most) people fail to recognize the social and economic disadvantages people with a substance use disorder face—not just as individuals but as a group. Systemic disadvantages of being labeled an "addict" include difficulty accessing healthcare and public assistance, and disenfranchisement in the workplace as well as criminal justice system. It is important to recognize privilege does not imply malice; however, the absence of intent to preserve an unearned advantage does nothing to level the playing field produced by privilege.

For example, a young mother who was being treated for opioid addiction with methadone management – an empirically validated medical treatment – described her feelings of shame after giving birth to one of her daughters. She was "outed" as a heroin "addict" by hospital staff. Despite the fact her daughter was healthy, staff thought her daughter was experiencing withdrawal. As a result of being open about her recovery from heroin addiction and methadone maintenance therapy, this young mother felt less than deserving of respect and support than other mothers on the maternity floor.

As another example, a college student in recovery recently shared his encounter with a primary care provider. He asked his doctor to document his recovery status to warn other medical providers against prescribing him an opioid or benzodiazepine. However, instead of being supported, the student was advised not to disclose his recovery status in his medical record. His provider explained "doctors jump to conclusions and automatically think junkie when they see a drug abuse alert."

Stigma is defined by pejorative attitudes and leads to marginalization of individuals based on group membership. A 2014 study by Johns Hopkins University Bloomberg School of Public Health found survey respondents were more willing to discriminate against persons with drug addiction. Respondents appeared unconvinced that drug treatment works and were more likely to oppose public policy designed to help "addicts" (Barry et al., 2014). Ninety percent were unwilling to support someone with addiction marrying into their family, and close to 80% were unwilling to work closely on a job with someone they perceived to be an "addict." Two-thirds of respondents thought employers should be allowed to deny employment to applicants who disclose an addiction. These attitudes and others influence beliefs about recovery support.

Bias about recovery extends to the type of drug(s) and the context of use. Hierarchies of more or less stigma exist based on the type of drug, the context in which use began, and other demographic factors such as age, gender, and race. Alcohol has less of a moral or criminal undercurrent when compared with illicit drugs. Dependence on prescription drugs is less stigmatized than heroin or cocaine. Improvements in care for opioid abuse became news when white suburban youth became addicted. The suburbanite who becomes addicted to opioids after surgery has an easier path than a public housing resident who is self-medicating due to limited options for medical treatment. Younger people are more "redeemable" than older people. Even self-help groups may have implicit hierarchies. The appropriateness of Alcoholics Anonymous meetings on a college campus or in a community may not be questioned, but hosting

Narcotics Anonymous (NA) meetings could be seen as a problem – ambivalence about recovery from illicit drug use may be nuanced as a safety concern – instead of pejorative attitudes about narcotic use.

Long-term recovery from addiction is built on honesty and courage. Listening to the stories of people in recovery, and trying to understand their experiences through their lens, is not only more supportive but demonstrates efforts to overcome an inherent sense of privilege. All parties benefit when addiction recovery narratives are reframed from a focus on shame to fostering success.

Becoming vocal about privilege starts with a thoughtful examination of our language about and caricatures of addiction. How can we challenge sober privilege when popular culture trivializes, celebrates, or stigmatizes addiction? How can we examine non-inclusive attitudes and beliefs about addiction and recovery when "addicts" are seen as morally inferior to others?

It is timely to set a higher expectation for protecting the dignity of a disenfranchised group – a group that includes friends, and colleagues, mothers and fathers, brothers and sisters. Addressing sober privilege and the bias that follows requires the sober majority to find the honesty to examine stereotypes about addiction – who gets addicted, why punitive policies are supported, how "effective" treatment is defined, and who has access to quality care – and the courage to act. I, for one, will examine my beliefs and attitudes and make a commitment to check my privilege.

Reference

Barry, C. L., McGinty, E. E., Pescosolido, B., & Goldman, H. H. (2014). Stigma, discrimination, treatment effectiveness and policy support: Comparing public views about drug addiction with mental illness. Psychiatric Services (Washington, D.C.), 65(10), 1269–1272. doi.org/10.1176/appi.ps.201400140.

Thomas Hall, Ph.D., serves as Associate Director of substance use disorders, prevention, treatment, and recovery services, Student Health Services at the University of Central Florida, and has over 25 years of experience providing substance abuse and mental health treatment. He frequently partners with university faculty and government agencies to develop, implement, and evaluate evidence, informed prevention, and intervention strategies.

Additional perspectives from long-term advocates include the following:

> *One of the greatest barriers in accessing help is stigma surrounding alcohol and drug use disorders. It blocks those who might need help in asking for it in fear of how others may see them. Besides stigma, health disparities among diverse populations produce some of the greatest barriers to care from limited resources to access care to the quality of care.*
>
> Claudia Blackburn

You can give people all the skills and information in the world but if the environment is permissive, they will use.

Deb Thorstenson

Some of the problems are the stigmatization of addiction and recovery and a lack of education in those areas, where people would say things like "Well we don't want those students on our campus." And or when I tell people what I do professionally, they say things like "Oh, that's so sad." I always found that interesting and surprising; it's not sad, it's exciting and hopeful.

Teresa Johnston

The Environment as a Blockage or Disinhibitor of Progress or Change

Beyond the role of the environment as a causal or contributing factor to substance abuse problems, the environment may be a factor contributing to the lack of change or lack of progress. The previous section highlighted ways in which the environment contributes to problems associated with drugs or alcohol; this section takes a correlated approach, with two primary areas of emphasis. First, the environmental influences and factors can be actual, active blockages of change. Second, the environment can contribute to the lack of progress by being passive or noncommittal, whereby no active stance or public viewpoints exist; in this case, status quo is, by default, the desired status.

How the environment can be part of blockages is different from the environment contributing to change; with this, things are actually done that oppose change. An example would be an organization that has a vested interest in limited regulations, or in fact wants to expand its operations. Consider a bar or tavern, and how its owners may not want further regulation on hours of service, hosted activities, advertising, or other operations. Similarly, with the emerging societal changes surrounding marijuana, there may be entities from both the sanctioned and illicit segments that do not want change, or want change in ways beneficial to their own interests.

Consider also a community that wishes to establish a treatment center, sponsor a halfway house, or offer meeting space for a self-help group. With the NIMBY ("Not In My Back Yard") views that abound, active protests against the specified availability of these services may occur. Similarly, extra procedural requirements may be prepared, whether these involve costs, standards, security, site preparation, or other seemingly neutral or passive deterrents.

With the changes of legislation around marijuana, for example, states or communities may establish standards and other requirements that may make it difficult, if not impossible, for retail establishments to be available for purchase of these newly permitted products. Some of these standards may be based on reasonable and sound information, and others may be simply blockages to implementation of newly established laws or policies. This is how an environment can be part of blockages that occur.

Long-term advocates interviewed had a variety of insights regarding the environment as a potential contributor to problems with substances, as illustrated with the following:

48   Competence

> Alcohol is a drug, and the fact that we continue to separate alcohol and "other drugs" sends a mixed message. One isn't more problematic; both alcohol and other drugs have psychoactive agents that affect the brain and in turn affect behavior. Alcohol is still highly misused but research tells us that marijuana use is rapidly reaching new heights in the young adult population, but I don't necessarily see one more problematic than the other.
>
> Teresa Johnston

> For marijuana, if it is legalized then I suppose there will be more problems to deal with. On the other hand, we might possibly see more people who have a problem with marijuana self-referring for treatment without worrying about getting in trouble. I think it's going to be very interesting to see what happens with marijuana use now with the changing norms in our country and some states making it legal and I will be very interested to see what will happen there.
>
> Helene White

> We as consumers are terrible consumers of the news. We just don't evaluate information that we read in the newspaper or hear; we assume it's all fact. So that what I see is that right now I still see that pendulum swinging out there; that's going to continue to cause us a lot of problems when it comes to policy around alcohol, and it's going to, I think it will manifest itself in some problematic ways that marijuana legalization has dealt with.
>
> Steve Schmidt

The other way that blockages can occur is more passive or neutral; these can be intentional or unintentional. Intentional items may be a blockage prepared in a passive or inactive way ("a wolf in sheep's clothing"). A passive blockage that is unintentional may be based in elements such as lack of awareness or concern. Consider recent changes in knowledge, whether it be science-based findings or changes in legislation. Many community leaders and professionals may not know about these changes, and thus be totally unaware of their implications. Best practices may exist, but dissemination of these or their updates may not have occurred.

Attention to the environment is personalized, when focusing on one's own family. Consider this observation:

> When people are convinced that their kids, there really is a serious risk; there really is a real problem and not just an "oh, everyone's doing it" kind of deal. They show up, and we haven't done a good job of convincing parents that there really is a problem out there, when we get 10% that might show up at any of these things.
>
> Jeffrey Levy

Consider the continued evolution of a solid understanding of addiction or dependence, and how the clinical definitions have evolved. Since 2014, the *Diagnostic and Statistical Manual V* description and definitions associated with substance use disorder has a revised framework that clearly specifies a continuum. Prior to that time, the operational definition had to do primarily with disease and dependence. The "disorder" label appears to change the perceptions of the individual, progression, treatment, and their involvement with substances. With that most recently revised definition, what will the status be with future iterations of the DSM criteria?

Further, professionals typically gain awareness of the most current information through professional journals, conferences, and continuing education. While these professionals may be up to date with the latest science, what is the awareness and understanding by community leaders and others entrusted with making decisions for their various settings, whether in the community, business, education, or other sector? These leaders address policy, curriculum, services, and other resources within their spheres of influence, based on the information and awareness they have. The environmental blockage can thus be unintentional and not malevolent, but just as powerful and impactful as those that are more intentional in nature.

Embedded within this consideration is the lack of current and relevant preparation for understanding substance dependence and related issues. Specifically, to what extent are medical schools preparing soon-to-be doctors in the science of and treatment for substance use disorders? How well are doctors prepared to have discussions about the prevention and intervention with dependence issues, with teens, adults, parents, and senior citizens? How about those who are leading our nation's colleges and universities, particularly within the student affairs divisions; are they prepared with the current science and appropriate strategies for harm reduction, prevention education, problem identification, and referral? With business schools and their preparation of those who aspire to leadership roles in corporate and management settings; what preparation do they have for substance abuse issues, and how to handle problems should they arise? The same is true for law schools, as they prepare individuals to serve in professional roles within the advocacy and client systems for our legal system. The general view with these and other professional preparation programs is that they currently are not addressing these issues. For example, one recent study of higher education master's degree programs shows that none have a required course on drug or alcohol issues; while the topic may be infused in other courses, most student affairs professionals surveyed reported that their primary source of information on this topic (and others) was through self-study.[11]

Also within this larger environmental construct is the view that the status quo is acceptable. This could be based on the view that changes are difficult to achieve, and that a significant amount of work would be required to achieve the desired change. Similarly, there may be limited buy-in by the constituents in favor of the proposed changes. The status quo may, indeed, be accepted; however, the context of this book is that this should be a deliberate and informed choice by concerned individuals as well as by those in leadership roles.

When thinking about governance structures, local authorities may rely on those at higher levels, whether at the national or state levels. Local leaders may rely upon the wisdom and leadership of those at a state or national level, and have the assumption that these individuals and leadership groups have heightened awareness about the latest science, the best practices, the appropriate ways of proceeding, and access to resources. The local leaders' view may be one of waiting for others to take the initiative, rather than relying on their own leadership locally. The view may be that, without a law or a statute, there is no overarching framework or requirement to do anything different. They may hold a perspective that, if there was a need, then a law or policy statement would necessarily exist.

There is also the view that a particular group, institution, and even state may not want to demonstrate leadership. They would rather be led, rather than lead. They would prefer not to be the ones who are out in front, and challenging the current ways of doing things. They would rather follow others' leadership, than taking the initiative and being the initial stimulus or initiator of examinations of current issues, needs, and efforts.

There may be a mindset that precludes changes taking place. Individuals may believe that the issues do not cause any concern. The view may be that "we are no worse than anyone else"; with such a view, they may question the appropriateness of making the effort to implement change. If there is the view that "problems like that just do not happen here," then change may not be considered. Also, if local data or documentation about the need is lacking, then the need for change may be viewed as frivolous or unnecessary. Even if the data is such that it compares favorably (e.g., lower problems) with other settings (e.g., at the regional, state, or national level), change may not be considered. The view may be such that "things are not getting worse," so that might suggest that problems are at least being contained. The challenge may be questions such as how one knows that a certain approach or strategy will be effective, and thus why any change or investment of time or resources should be considered. These and many similar approaches appear to be approaches of resistance, denial, or minimization.

The point in this section is that the environment can be part of the issues surrounding drug and alcohol problems. This can be accomplished by challenges to change, as well as through implementation of approaches that slow things down and promote the status quo. This understanding and specification of the range of environmental factors is important for those committed to making a difference, and to reducing problems associated with drugs and alcohol. Having this background is helpful with determining strategies for making change, and serve as foundations for further development in Chapter 3 (Why Be Concerned?) and Chapter 10 (Leadership and Advocacy). This understanding is most helpful in understanding those factors that are opposing or blocking action, and also those that can contribute to a positive or more productive resolution of the situation; similarly, what is it in our cultures (large and small) that help to guide efforts, and what is it that hinders efforts?

Here are perspectives from two long-term advocates:

> *One of the obstacles to getting increased funding for prevention was getting any kind of interest regarding the rapidly increasing use of substances among teens; it appeared to be that we couldn't get any media coverage about the large increases in teen drug use, such as an 800% increase in heroin and 200% increase in tobacco and alcohol use. The media didn't seem to care to run the story. One thought of mine was that because they used marijuana and alcohol in college, they didn't think or realize that the potency of the new marijuana was much stronger or that teens were now binge drinking to the point of passing out.*
>
> Karol Kumpfer

The most striking observation is how little the general public and specifically parents know about the issue of alcohol and drugs.

Jeffrey Levy

The Environment as a Facilitator of Change

The environment is a critical contributor to decisions ultimately made by individuals, as they move ahead and are involved with various aspects of living their lives. Individuals made decisions, whether consciously or subconsciously, about drugs and alcohol; the range of environmental factors and how they are implemented affect these individuals' behaviors, whether by encouraging or enhancing the behavior, or by restricting, restraining, or altering the behavior. For example, awareness about the enforcement of a law or ordinance may serve as a restraining factor for an individual's decision about use of a substance; similarly, the desire to avoid harsh consequences for driving while under the influence of drugs or alcohol may cause someone to not drive impaired.

With these, many factors are involved, including the establishment of a standard or law, actual enforcement, having consequences of substantive severity, having awareness of the standard and enforcement, having belief that the consequences are severe, and having desire to avoid the negative consequences. This is a systems approach that requires all elements of the organization (e.g., the community, the workplace, the culture) to work together to provide a consistent and coherent strategy and message. An appropriate environmental approach would be to orchestrate this collaboration and consistency, and to identify and reduce loopholes and gaps in implementation.

In thinking of the environment as part of an overall strategy of change, the construct used in this chapter is that of "planned change" (more detail on planned change is found in Chapter 7, Helpful Processes). With planned change, the assumption is that change is desired, and that quality results are more likely to be achieved if proper planning is implemented. The alternative is to have poor planning, poorly executed planning, or no planning at all. Related to this is the view that affecting human behavior is difficult. Helpful will be the reduction of the wide range of individual and environmental factors into more manageable items.

If, for example, the issues and concerns surrounding drugs and alcohol were to be viewed using the Health Belief Model,[12] its six components could be developed within the environmental construct. Perceived susceptibility could be addressed with information campaigns about risk factors, and perceived severity could be implementation and communication about policy, enforcement, and consequences associated with substance abuse. Perceived benefits might promote specific positive action steps (e.g., a wellness approach that directly addresses a root cause of substance abuse), and cues to action could incorporate reminders to engage in the positive behavior. The component of perceived behaviors might be addressed by identifying areas of resistance and creating universal strategies to reduce them, and self-efficacy could promote enhanced rewards that reinforce positive and protective behaviors.

Similarly, the Stages of Change theory[13] is widely used and helpful from at least two distinct perspectives. First, it is helpful when thinking about an organization or community; consideration of where it is, in the overall development process of evolution regarding a topic or issue, is important when determining the best strategies for moving beyond the current state of affairs or the status quo. Second, from an individual or client perspective, this approach is helpful so that the intervention and therapeutic approaches match the individual's readiness to change.

As an example of the application of this theory, as well as the idea of "low hanging fruit," consider the following observations:

> *It's a marvel to watch that the Stages of Change theory adopted in the early 90s, has become the bedrock on how we view the selection of strategies. This theory single-handedly sent a powerful message that approaches need to match the client, rather than the client needing to fit the treatment. It moved the field from blaming the client, to taking the responsibility in how best to approach the client for where they are.*
>
> Claudia Blackburn

> *In our organization's first five years we had 19 deaths, 19 people died of alcoholism in the first five years in New Jersey. They came into our door, we saw them, gave them an assessment, gave them a helping plan, gave them support, sent them to treatment, came out and so on and they just died, horribly. I also think there was a little bit of low hanging fruit there, because we were seeing the people who had no treatment. But in that same period of time we had printed in the newspaper that people were being suspended from the practice of the law for shenanigans or mistakes or negligence and they were the same as our clients for the first five years.*
>
> William Kane

> *It's been fun to watch the policy develop through the years.*
>
> Deb Thorstenson

> *Crazy as it sounds, my kids used me as an excuse. "Are you kidding do you know what my mother does?" Not that they didn't drink like fish in college but no drugs and I would attribute it completely to me being a nut case.*
>
> BJ McConnell

Another way of addressing this, in an organized, planful way and from an environmental perspective, is to use Lewin's Force Field Analysis when thinking about this issue. This process starts with the status quo, and envisions the desired state of affairs. Then, with the status quo, the process looks at those factors that will help move things toward the desired state of affairs (the driving forces); it also looks at the factors that are holding this back, or serve as oppositional factors (the restraining forces). The challenge then is to examine what would help enhance the power and impact of the driving forces, and what would help reduce or eliminate the restraining forces, thus allowing change to occur. More detail is provided on this process in Chapter 7 (Helpful Processes).

As part of the environmental factor, particularly as a facilitator of change, see Professional Perspective 2.3 with attention to the role of engaged community processes.

Professional Perspective 2.3

Coalitions for Impact: Collaboration, Teamwork, and More

Maureen Earley, M.Ed.

Coalition building sounds so easy, but the reality is that it is anything but easy. It takes vision, passion, dedication, commitment, and people, just to name a few of the key factors for success! To transform this group of individuals into a team that will work together, be committed, and move the mission and vision forward takes a significant amount of time and effort. It involves meeting new people who may share your passion, or engaging old friends who have their life story; it is the business partner who has seen the devastation of substance abuse in the workplace; it is law enforcement personnel who witness the destruction; it involves the faith community that tries to catch those that are falling; and it includes people who just know how to tell the coalition story. It is finding these diverse people, building meaningful relationships, and bringing them all to the table. Once they are gathered, coalition building involves helping them step outside their comfort zone, building trust and agreeing on the group outcomes. This partnership of people and organizations can be a driving force within communities to create positive and lasting change.

So what is a coalition? It is a union of people and organizations that forms for a specific purpose or cause. The Community Anti-Drug Coalitions of America (CADCA) defines a coalition as "a formal arrangement for collaboration among groups or sectors of a community, in which each group retains its identity but all agree to work together toward the common goal of a safe, healthy and drug-free community." CADCA determined that a minimum of 12 sectors of the community should be a part of the local substance use prevention coalition and should include the business community, law enforcement, schools, civic organizations, youth-serving organizations, healthcare professionals, local, state, or tribal agencies, faith leaders, youth, parents, media, and others who are passionate about or involved in reducing substance use. It is also important that the membership is culturally diverse and reflects the community demographics. This group of people has firsthand knowledge of their own community and best understands the nuances of the community they live in and the best strategies to address the local problem.

I have led or been a member of various coalitions and responsible for mentoring and training coalitions throughout my career. A main observation is that no coalition looks or operates the same. While many similarities exist, there are many more differences. The differences can be with their organizational structure, by-laws, meeting times, or the composition of their board of directors and is it a non-profit organization or housed in a community organization. None of these differences make it right or wrong; these are what make coalitions unique to their own community. At times the differences can make it difficult for coalitions to move forward. For example, when an original member, who is very well respected, talks about "what they used to do," the fact may be that these approaches are no longer relevant or not science-based; this one member can halt forward movement of the coalition. In helping manage a coalition, it is important to keep focused on the end result and continue to push forward. Various members will either make a decision to jump on board with the coalition membership, or step aside and no longer be a contributing member. This can be difficult and uncomfortable when it is a founding member, a high-profile community leader, or an otherwise valued individual. If someone does step aside, for whatever reason, it is important to recognize their community contributions, whether with the early coalition leadership or other community effort.

Advantages of coalition work can be enormous. By bringing together a diverse group of organizations and people, it will enlarge the base of support for an issue and will provide strength in numbers. Involving a coalition will help accomplish a broad range of objectives and goals that reach beyond the capacity of any one individual or single organization. It can conserve precious resources, whether financial or personnel time, and help eliminate any duplication of effort within the community. By building community concern and consensus, coalitions often gain greater credibility than a single organization or individual could. They provide a wonderful forum to share information and ideas and serve as a place for advice and new perspectives on issues. In addition, coalitions may foster satisfaction, inspiration, and growth for their members either within their job or personally.

In the past, I was responsible for a statewide coalition. This group had meetings throughout the year, but what I found they needed most was a few days as a group, unplugged from phones, the internet, and day-to-day responsibilities, to just sit, talk, share, and reenergize themselves; what better way to accomplish this than at a rustic mountain retreat setting. Those few days not only built trust, but also increased their productivity and renewed their energy for the upcoming months and year. Coalition work is tough work, so a retreat is often a win–win for both the individuals involved and the organization! Plus, a retreat doesn't have to be expensive or overnight; simply having a new location, team building, training, and strategic planning is all that is needed to give coalition members a new burst of energy.

Personally, coalition work can be so much fun. To bring a diverse group of people together to work toward a common goal and have them plan and implement the strategies, and then to see the accomplishments, is so exhilarating. Coalitions have been bringing change for years in communities. It takes patience, particularly since the substance abuse problem isn't going away. With continued efforts, dedicated personnel, working collectively and cooperatively, can continue to chip away and reduce drug and alcohol problems.

Resources

Coalitions Work: www.coalitionswork.com.
Community Anti-Drug Coalitions of America: https://cadca.org.
Prevention Institute: https://preventioninstitute.org.

> Maureen Earley, M.Ed., is a community development specialist with Hanover County Community Services in Virginia, where she provides technical assistance for the local substance abuse coalition. Previously she was coordinator of the Enforcing Underage Drinking Laws program for Virginia and developed the education department within the Department of Virginia Alcoholic Beverage Control, which received various state and national awards throughout her tenure.

Finally, an overall perspective about incorporating an environmental framework for positive change is to identify an appropriate set of guiding principles that will be helpful through the process.

- Acknowledge the extensive, large and long-term nature of the issue. Change will be slow.
- Work in an organized and deliberate manner. Rather than being reactive, or working on standalone elements, have an overall plan that helps guide and shape individual efforts.
- Collaborate with others. This involves bringing others into your framework, and also identifying ways in which your effort can be folded into or promoted by other efforts.
- Make the issue as locally relevant as possible. Gather local data to provide a larger context of the local concern.
- Attempt to identify what it is systemically that affects individuals' decisions around substances. This includes policies, procedures, processes, information, language, services, and more.
- Identify the influencers for, and what messages are heard by, various audiences of interest, whether the ultimate target audience or intermediary audiences (e.g., youth as the target audience, and parents, teachers, or coaches as intermediary audiences).
- Establish reasonable and appropriate outcomes, including long-range aims, intermediate points, and more proximate outcomes. Where possible, establish metrics that help shape decisions along the way.
- When thinking about environmental strategies, consider both those that are proactive as well as those that are reactive or restrictive. Identify strategies that help promote a healthy and helpful setting, as well as those that identify behaviors or situations that are not wanted.
- Acknowledge that whatever is done, whether restrictive laws or standards or positive and rewarding approaches, as well as the processes used to determine and implement these strategies, are making a statement about what is valued and cherished as a nation/group/organization.
- Consider organizational or system readiness. While a longer-term vision may be desired and embraced, much more may need to be done at an earlier time to prepare for more immediate action steps.
- Acknowledge the appropriate sphere of influence, and the larger context within which this operates. Seek to identify what can be done within individual settings

(such as schools or workplaces) or community settings, with awareness that this is within the context of a larger culture within which all reside and work.
- Maintain a perspective of hope and optimism. If change is needed and desired, and if the leaders are not optimistic or don't have a sense of hope, it will be difficult to move forward.

Additional insights about organizational and environmental factors with prevention is found with Professional Perspective 2.4.

Professional Perspective 2.4

The Practice of Prevention: An Ecological Approach

Jim Lange, Ph.D.

Perhaps the most daunting challenge facing those who work within the world of alcohol and other drugs (AOD) prevention is the entanglement of substance use within every level of human experience. From a molecular level of gene expression to geopolitical relationships between nations, there is a place where alcohol and other drugs are playing a role. Even locating concern to merely one's own community can include aspects of multiple intersecting forces: economic, legal, cultural, religious, social services, education, media, medical services, conflicting normative standards, and psychological and developmental aspects.

A typical representation of this multi-layered system is the Social Ecological Model (e.g., DeJong & Langford, 2002). It serves as an easily shared conceptual framework that highlights that the individual is nested within social and societal layers, all playing a role in the resulting behavior. Though having this model does not necessarily guide the practitioner along any specific path of action, it still helps a great deal since it expands the universe of possible actions. Given the breadth of inputs into the resulting AOD misuse, the practitioner can find a place to make improvements at almost every turn: from the local business and its practice of checking IDs, to city policies allowing overnight parking in hospitality zones, to programs for improving parental skills, to substance-free alternative events for teens.

Obviously, this freedom does not mean we are given a "blank check" of programs, with each effort being of equal value toward reaching the identified goals. Indeed, there is a long history of failed prevention efforts that would fit neatly within every level of the ecological model. But staying open to the breadth of possibilities allows for both creativity and also opportunistic flexibility not afforded within many other public health efforts. For instance, focusing solely on educating the individual students, even within the context of an evidence-based program, misses the broader community norms that may be counteracting the efforts.

Taking to heart the ecological model means that prevention work must involve working with the broader community. Here the practitioner is exposed to the diversity of beliefs within society about the nature of AOD issues. Many in this field come from a "public health" orientation toward the topic, so often our concern is health-related harms associated with certain consumption styles or substances, or within certain populations. But that may not be the shared concern of the community at large, or of influential members of the community.

For instance, working to help a European city address underage drinking, an immediate conflict between their low minimum drinking age (perhaps even age 16) and the data on alcohol's impact on developing brains becomes apparent. For many of those in the community who must be counted on as prevention partners, this legal standard sets a community belief that allowing early drinking is actually protective, and not a "problem" regardless of the contrary scientific evidence. So working with these "prevention partners," the first step likely is to specify what, specifically, is being prevented; consider immediate injury or harm, longer-term dependence, specific brain functioning, or other outcome. Regardless of the specific outcome, the likely lists of effective interventions will probably span the ecological levels in similar ways.

Another example of varying perspectives is based on the roles people play with the prevention of drug and alcohol problems. Police, for instance, are necessarily looking for – and spending their time disproportionately with – those whose use causes problems. Thus, they often will have an overestimate of the breadth of the issue and its impact. Emergency medical providers are similarly witnessing only the most serious outcomes. Conversely, those in the hospitality industry may see many drinking alcohol without apparent harm, but fail to see the outcomes that occur after patrons leave their establishment. Thus, they are often surprised to learn of the community-level impact. Or when discussing the spreading legalization and acceptance of cannabis, the expanding list of those with a role in an ecological prevention paradigm becomes apparent.

So, the prevention practitioner needs to work with sensitivity to the community's perception of the environment; not only to the varying conflicting interests of the roles, but also in how an individual's position within the system affects their perceptions of the community norms and problems.

A useful way of approaching the community aspect of this work is employing the same model that has proven useful for individuals: the Transtheoretical Stages of Change Model (e.g., DiClemente et al., 1991). Communities are ready to make change when there is a shared understanding that a social problem exists. How the collective agreement on this problem identification happens is still not fully understood, but it is at least described well in its relationship with drunk driving within the work of J. Gusfield (1984). Essentially, there is a point in which commonly observed and known behaviors become socially agreed upon as a problem. For instance, even though drunk driving was recognized as a hazard prior to the era of mass produced cars (Lange, 2008), it wasn't until the early 1980s that its problem status crystalized among the public.

Thus, the practice of prevention often involves understanding where within the ecological model the community is ready to deploy evidence-based approaches. Assessing this is difficult, but it starts with identifying where there is a shared agreement of the problem, then working to make programs that address it. However, it doesn't stop there. A simultaneous step is finding ways to move the community toward a more complete shared view of the problem. Doing so should allow for a future set of programs that more comprehensively encompass the ecological model's levels.

References

DeJong, W., & Langford, L.M. (2002). A typology for campus-based alcohol prevention: Moving toward environmental management strategies. *Journal of Studies on Alcohol Supplement, 63,* 140–147.

DiClemente, C.C., Prochaska, J.O., Fairhurst, S.K., Velicer, W.F., Velasquez, M.M., & Rossi, J.S. (1991). The process of smoking cessation: An analysis of precontemplation, contemplation, and preparation stages of change. *Journal of Consulting and Clinical Psychology, 59,* 295–304. doi.org/10.1037/0022-006x.59.2.295.

Gusfield, J.R. (1984). *The Culture of Public Problems: Drinking-Driving and the Symbolic Order.* Chicago, IL: University of Chicago Press.

Lange, J.E. (2008). Drunk driving. In V. Parillo (ed.), *Encyclopedia of Social Problems* (Vol. 1, pp. 367–368). Thousand Oaks, CA: Sage Publications.

Jim Lange, Ph.D., is currently Executive Director of the Higher Education Center for Alcohol and Drug Misuse Prevention and Recovery, which is an academic center of The Ohio State University. He is also Coordinator of AOD Initiatives at San Diego State University. He has worked in the prevention field for over 20 years, and has published over 60 scholarly research articles on prevention topics, focused mainly on adolescent and young adult alcohol and other drug misuse prevention.

Two final quotes from long-term advocates are helpful in further examining some of the important factors associated with environmental aspects of drug and alcohol issues.

People wanted easy, society being what it is, give me three doses of something and then I'm going to get all kids to never use drugs or alcohol again.

Bill Modzeleski

What surprised me is that there are factions that are not willing to collaborate, and again I get back to the harm reduction versus zero tolerance. They are not mutually exclusive.

Kurt Erickson

Summary

As elucidated in this chapter, attention to the environment is an important factor for understanding the nature of the issue about drugs and alcohol. The first chapter highlighted the nature of the issue from an individual perspective, and this chapter highlighted the same topic from an environmental perspective. While these are covered in two separate chapters, the relationship between both aspects is of an intertwined nature – each affecting the other, and each being informed by the other.

Notes

1 https://pubs.niaaa.nih.gov/publications/AlcoholFacts&Stats/AlcoholFacts&Stats.htm.
2 https://pubs.niaaa.nih.gov/publications/AlcoholFacts&Stats/AlcoholFacts&Stats.htm.
3 www.dea.gov/resource-center/statistics.shtml.
4 www.dea.gov/resource-center/meth-lab-maps.shtml.
5 www.drugabuse.gov/publications/drugfacts/drug-related-hospital-emergency-room-visits.
6 www.drugabuse.gov/related-topics/trends-statistics#supplemental-references-for-economic-costs. National Drug Intelligence Center. (2011). *National Drug Threat Assessment*. Washington, DC: United States Department of Justice. www.justice.gov/archive/ndic/pubs44/44849/44849p.pdf.
7 www.drugabuse.gov/related-topics/trends-statistics#supplemental-references-for-economic-costs. Birnbaum, H.G. et al. (2011). Societal costs of prescription opioid abuse, dependence, and misuse in the United States. *Pain Medicine*, 12, 657–667. Florence, C.S. et al. (2013). The economic burden of prescription opioid overdose, abuse, and dependence in the United States. *Medical Care*, 54(10), 901–916.
8 www.drugabuse.gov/related-topics/trends-statistics#supplemental-references-for-economic-costs. Centers for Disease Control and Prevention. (2016). *Excessive Drinking Is Draining the U.S. Economy*. www.cdc.gov/features/costsofdrinking/. Updated January 2016. Accessed April 21, 2017.
9 https://pubs.niaaa.nih.gov/publications/AlcoholFacts&Stats/AlcoholFacts&Stats.htm. Substance Abuse and Mental Health Services Administration (SAMHSA). (2012). *Data Spotlight: More Than 7 Million Children Live with a Parent with Alcohol Problems*. http://media.samhsa.gov/data/spotlight/Spot061ChildrenOfAlcoholics2012.pdf. Accessed September 19, 2016.
10 Anderson, D.S. & Santos, G.M. (2018). *The College Alcohol Survey: The National Longitudinal Survey on Alcohol, Tobacco, Other Drug and Violence Issues at Institutions of Higher Education*. Fairfax, VA. George Mason University.
11 Kretovics, M. & Anderson, D. (2013) *Wellness Assessment for Higher Education Preparation Programs*. Kent State University and George Mason University.
12 Becker, M. & Rosenstock, I.M. (1984). Compliance with medical advice. In A. Steptoe & A. Mathews (eds) *Health Care and Human Behavior* (pp. 135–152). London: Academic Press.
13 Prochaska, J. & DiClemente, C. (1983). Stages and processes of self-change in smoking: Toward an integrative model of change. *Journal of Consulting and Clinical Psychology*, 5, 390–395.

3 Why Be Concerned?

The overview provided in Chapters 1 and 2 offers a summary about the nature of the issue. Data abounds about problems associated with drugs and alcohol, for some people and under some circumstances. Again, a widespread claim that "drugs are bad" or "alcohol should be banned" is not what is emphasized; what is highlighted is that many problems have been, and continue to be, associated with drugs and alcohol. More important is that many of these problems can be addressed more effectively, so that reductions in problems can be achieved. The orientation is one of preventing problems – at least preventing their occurrence or minimizing their progression. The perspective is one of doing better.

With the chapters on "The Nature of the Issue," why is it important to have a chapter named "Why Be Concerned?" The simple answer is that it is important to gain clarity about why an individual, an organization, a community, or a larger grouping of people would want to be involved. Through use of the content, strategies, and perspectives in this book, many professionals already involved with substance abuse issues will find support and affirmation for their efforts. They may also learn new ideas or perspectives. Further, it is hoped they will find insights that can be shared with others. Beyond this, individuals for whom drug and alcohol abuse services is not at the core of their expertise or background will be provided more focused perspectives that will help clarify and guide future action.

In this chapter, attention is provided to reasons for being involved, the evolution of science and knowledge, the context of blockages and roadblocks, the role of root causes of substance abuse, and the integration of values at individual, group, and societal levels. This focus on "Why Be Concerned?" is based on the fact that various problems and issues are present, and that these issues call upon us all to address them because improvements can be made, and because of the widespread knowledge that efforts at all levels can be improved. In short, we can do better, and we know that we should do better. To be silent or unengaged with substance abuse issues is not only inconsistent with current knowledge, it is also unfair to those served at the individual, group, or societal levels. Beyond that, it is harmful to these same individuals, groups, and society.

Clarifying the Concern

In understanding why there should be concern about drugs and alcohol, a helpful starting point is to gain as much specificity as possible. This specificity may be general or more specific; it may include overall generic data, or it may be an individually focused or case study situation. Whatever the scope of this, it is helpful to be specific, and to try to understand, as much as possible, any causal linkages.

Reflecting on some of the data from the first two chapters, these represent just a sampling of issues, culled from thousands of studies, reports, and citations. At the most extreme level, consider the deaths associated with drugs or alcohol. The obvious concern with these is that they represent the ultimate or extreme outcome. If the death was acute, such as from an overdose, a poisoning, or a situation (such as drunk driving) directly caused by abuse of the substance, this could have been avoided. If the death was more long-term and gradual in nature, it is likely that that progression could have been addressed earlier, halted, or slowed down. Other concerns are documented with results such as emergency room visits, injuries, harm to others, damage to property, and lowered performance. These specific outcomes are generally not sought or wanted, and thus would be targets for reduction or elimination. The other consideration is a delineation of the causal or contributing factors associated with the substance(s) used. The aim is to reduce the negative consequences of drugs or alcohol and to enhance the quality of life.

Moving beyond this data, it is reasonable to posit that every person has some personal experience with substance abuse issues from their own friendships, family members, work colleagues, community affiliations, acquaintances, and strangers. Consider the exposure of individuals to family members with drug or alcohol problems. Think about the encounters at school, work, neighborhood, or elsewhere, that involved drug or alcohol abuse, whether it be an impaired driver, a colleague or friend with a hangover, or someone staggering or slurring their speech because of over-consumption. The situations abound, and the fact that these may be anecdotal, and for which there may not be concrete data, does not make them any less important.

As part of the specificity of outcomes, it is important to identify other contributing factors that go beyond the specific consequences to an individual or others. Through addressing such contributing factors, it is presumed that the consequences would be affected in the desired direction. As noted in Chapter 2, many graduate preparation programs do not prepare soon-to-be professionals in the higher education setting with substance abuse awareness or skills, whether focused on dependence or prevention. These professionals report learning through self-study; thus, a specific area of concern may be to prepare more thoroughly these professionals, whether through pre-service or in-service education programs. Similar results will likely be found with other professional preparation programs, such as with medical schools, law schools, and business schools.

Another area of concern is topical areas where information, whether current or otherwise, is lacking. Some issues may have never been researched or documented; others may have data that is not current. These become targets for attention, and which will be helpful for preparing specific outcomes.

Additional attention is relevant for higher risk groups of individuals. Some of this concern is based on documented information, and other concerns are based on the risk itself. The concern may also be based on disparities with services and resources, which can be both causal and consequential.

The specification of areas of concern typically focuses on lowering the problem, or reducing the negative factors. A complementary approach is a focus on increasing the positive or enhancing the potential. Thus, the outcome would not be just about reducing harm or minimizing negative results; rather the outcome would be about promoting positive outcomes and potential. As a simple example, consider productivity and work or school; the results may be adequate, and they may be simply sufficient. Could the results be better? Could heightened performance, efficiency, quality, and more be increased? What if the lack of maximum performance was due to drug or alcohol impairment, or based on side effects or after effects, such as a hangover?

The focus on human potential is a different framework to consider "what could be" and moves beyond the mantra central to the medical profession of "do no harm." The "do no harm" approach is essential, as a minimum, as it is helpful for reducing problems. The specific outcomes associated with a parallel or partnering approach of "do good works" can help aid efforts for achieving higher quality results. This complementary approach can help individuals, families, groups, and society live their dreams and achieve their aspirations.

Overall, when the situations or outcomes (whether from data or personal experience) are clarified, a more concrete focus can be obtained. This focus is helpful as plans are made for prevention (Chapter 6), treatment (Chapter 5), and implementation processes (Chapter 8).

The key issue here is that these situations represent areas where change can be made. The view is that the status quo is neither acceptable nor appropriate. The fact that documentation exists, and that there is awareness about these areas of concern, provides the necessary foundation for doing something different, and for trying to accomplish change. The aim is to reduce, modify, ameliorate, and potentially eliminate the problems associated with drugs and alcohol. It is important to stress, however, that while it may be an ideal aim to eliminate certain outcomes or situations (such as death), that goal would not be entirely achievable, and thus it (elimination) alone may not be sufficient as the goal.

The perspectives of several long-term advocates is helpful:

In our summer schools, we had a course for physicians but we included a course for medical students because they were the future and we needed people to see that medical students would give their time to come and learn so that they could be more informed, which they hadn't been previously.

Gail Milgram

Another surprise is the lack of addiction and recovery education provided to the medical profession, how little education they are getting in a time when addiction and recovery science should be on the forefront of medical school curricula.

Teresa Johnston

What we're looking at now is depression in law school where somebody comes in to law school; all of the literature is saying that people went to law school and become depressed because of the enormous demands of the change in thinking and conflict and competition. We have a depressed attorneys group, and there will be about 15 to 20 guys sitting around the table sharing information about how they are inside each other's skin and they welcome the newcomers and talk about meds that work or don't work so, and they are not alcoholic.

William Kane

Consistency and Followthrough

With greater clarity about the areas of concern, whether it is reducing the negative, promoting the positive, or a blend of the two, the next steps are more planning and action-oriented. While future chapters address in more detail specific strategies, the focus here is on clarifying the issue. Within the context of "why be concerned" is the view that many people, whether leaders, practitioners, or others espouse a goal or outcome, yet do not have concrete steps that address this. If an organization, agency, school, community, or government is committed to a certain outcome, then reasonable and concrete steps should be taken to address these.

Consider the mission statements of schools or organizations. These typically include laudatory aims and proclamations, such as to improve the quality of life, to maximize learning, to prepare for the future, to perfect skills, to enhance creative solutions, to inspire excellence, and to encourage greater appreciation of specific aspects of life. More often than not, these mission statements are positive and proactive. An important follow-on issue is what specific steps are taken to help achieve these outcomes. To what extent is attention provided, resources offered, and priority given to strategies that will help the sponsoring group accomplish these aims? If there is clarity about areas of concern, then the decisions and action steps should match that. It is vital that personnel and processes are science-based, up to date, and skilled; leaders must engage with the resources and personnel for planning, monitoring, and follow-up purposes.

Another consideration relates to the lack of documented progress regarding several factors previously described. Specifically, it is documented that some groups, for various reasons, have higher risks for substance abuse problems. Even with this awareness, the attention provided based on their needs may not change. A specific example is with the College Alcohol Survey, where the reported attention by campuses to the unique needs of multiple high-risk groups (women, people of color, LGBTQ) has not changed over the 20 years of data collection.[1] Said differently, if leaders are aware of a problem and report they want to address it, yet have actions that demonstrate no change in effort or priority, then consistency between word and deed is lacking. This could be based on limited resources, low funding, changing priorities, new issues, or other factors; or, it may be based on a genuine lack of caring or concern about the needs of that higher risk audience. It is appropriate to engage in collaborative problem analysis and review to determine the most appropriate steps forward.

Based on the interviews with long-term advocates, numerous different perspectives were expressed about the nature of the concern. Some of these were political, and others reflect changes with what is occurring in the society.

So the big changes in the field would be the number of people using substances, the age of first use, the purity and dose of what's being used and then probably addiction itself has become one of the major, if not the most important health, emerging disease in the United States.

Mark Gold

What surprised me most was the college presidents who quietly patted me on the back and were supportive of what we were doing, who themselves were not willing to stand up and take a strong position with regard to an issue about which I think they have a tremendous amount of potential influence that they were unwilling to exert.

Jeffrey Levy

But I think we came to realize that if you didn't have the bolstering of the community support around the school that anything in the school was just going to be kind of lost because it wasn't going to be consistent.

Darlind Davis

It seems to me that if we've made as much change as I think we've made in the last 50 years, that would suggest to me that we can make that much change maybe in the other direction. I don't know but change is not out of the question.

Jeffrey Levy

There's this brilliant kid, president of the high school class, stoned every day. And all I can say is what could he have accomplished, what more had he quit smoking pot? He is just missing out, you know what potential? Kids always say I know someone who was on the state championship basketball team and they smoke dope all the time. Really? Could they have been All-American? You're never going to know the answer.

BJ McConnell

So I have two hats: Clinician and Scientist. If I was going to be true to my science I would say wait a second in terms of incidence and prevalence data we do not prioritize treatment based on societal needs.

Robert Lynn

These long-term advocates also shared their views about the relative harms and dangers associated with the use of drugs compared with alcohol. Various observations are reflected here:

There are so many more people who drink than use the other drugs, however research is finding an increase in the misuse of prescription drugs.

Kim Dude

There's a tremendous difference between drugs and alcohol how we handle it. There are similarities but there are differences that suggest that alcohol is a different nature.

Jeffrey Levy

I think alcohol is more dangerous; more fatal, creates more problems and is more widespread and by far it's more widespread.

William Kane

I think the problems are very different and probably equally as serious. I think we see more problems with alcohol overuse. When we look at drugs, it seems like we still don't have the number of problems but they are more serious.

Carla Lapelle

Alcohol has been much more problematic in terms of acute effects on violent behavior.

Helene White

I think fundamentally drugs and alcohol are different; they are different culturally because right and wrong, personal opinions aside, alcohol for someone who is over the legal consumption age of 21 is a legal product.

Ralph Blackman

I believe that you have to deal with drugs on each aspect of it in different ways, first of all because one is a legal substance and the other one isn't even an illegal substance. In general, I think when we use the term "drug" you're talking about drugs being heroin, cocaine.

Jeffrey Levy

We know that in terms of incidence and prevalence if we wanted to talk about such issues as morbidity we would be spending much of our money on cigarettes and nicotine rather than other drugs which have received most of our attention.

Robert Lynn

The Evolution of Science and Knowledge

Integral to quality efforts for addressing drug and alcohol issues is being current with science-based and grounded knowledge. This includes incorporating best practices, according to established protocols. It also means attending to emerging approaches and adapting insights and technologies from other fields of study.

Consider the evolution of the DSM criteria; the changing definitions and even the label "Substance Use Disorder" shows a continued quest for documenting and promulgating the best scientific awareness for clinical practice. Similarly, the discovery of neurotransmitters decades ago has been helpful for better understanding specific mechanisms by which drugs and alcohol affect individuals, as well as contribute to dependence issues. Consider also the enhanced understanding of the human brain, through childhood and adolescent years, and ostensibly finishing its development in the mid-twenties; the periods of plasticity for humans have implications for greater understanding of vulnerability as well as interventions. It is reasonable to expect that these scientific discoveries, as well as many others, will continue to generate new knowledge. More insight about substance use disorders is found with Professional Perspective 3.1

Professional Perspective 3.1

The Biology of Addiction: Knowing Fact from Fiction

Michael L. Wenzinger, M.D., and Mark S. Gold, M.D.

Understanding addiction as more than a "moral failing" has been a long-fought battle spanning the very history of what we know as modern medicine. Benjamin Rush, a revolutionary-era physician, deserves due credit as perhaps being one of the most ardent early supporters of a biological understanding toward addiction. In addition to signing the Declaration of Independence and being a founder of American Psychiatry, Benjamin Rush also fought a spirited crusade against truly backward perceptions of alcohol use and pushed for formulation of a medical approach to treating addiction. He understood that the substance controlled the individual, not the other way around – but this was difficult to prove in the 1700s. The more subtle, microscopic underpinnings behind the biology of addiction had been all but invisible to us until the more modern tools of advanced brain imaging and animal models became available. We now enjoy a detailed understanding of neuroscience that drives addiction, but the lag time between the observation of addiction and development of this deep biological understanding was not without its toll. When an illness exists without clear explanation, it invites a variety of speculation as to its cause. The "moral failing" concept has been perhaps the most popular in that regard. That addicts simply are bad or weak people is an easy conclusion for the layman and can preclude appropriate prevention, treatment, and recovery from addiction. Any student of addiction science, no matter their role, must be well informed as to the true science of addiction. This is not only to help dispel the "moral failing" myth and other unhelpful platitudes, but to also reframe it for what it truly is: a medical condition that has real, lasting impacts on the human brain.

In defining any medical condition, one must first understand the organ or system being disordered. Animal models, such as those used by pioneers in behavioral science like Ivan Pavlov and B.F. Skinner, helped form the early but essential framework of understanding how any organism pursues and appreciates rewarding experiences. Thanks also to neuroimaging advances in the past two decades, we now also know that in the brain exist discrete systems. These systems are often called "circuits" due to their interconnected wire-like anatomy, which mediate reward-seeking behavior in all its aspects: motivation for seeking out a rewarding experience, experiencing the joy of reward, or suffering the lack of desired reward. These two forms of scientific investigation together helped us identify and define the target of addiction: the reward circuit. It is intricate, complicated, and involves both ancient brain regions (portions that are very similar across many different species, which is also why animal models have been proven to be so valid) and more advanced brain regions (structures more unique or well defined in humans and other primates). These regions also communicate via use of specific neurochemicals that activate these brain regions, with dopamine being identified as one of the key neurochemicals that drives the reward system. A simple summary would be that the brain uses these regions to motivate us to seek out evolutionarily adaptive activities such as sex, eating, and social interaction. It rewards us for doing so with the pleasurable feeling given by a release of dopamine and other associated neurochemicals, enticing us to seek them out again and again.

The working model of the biology behind addiction is best understood as a repeating, relapsing, multi-step disease pathway that occurs because of disruption of the natural balance of this reward circuit. It is broken down into three major processes: a binge/intoxication phase, a withdrawal phase, and a craving phase. Each process interplays with the other and all undergo dynamic changes as the addict advances through the various stages of severity in addiction (i.e., from the casual user to the severe addict). The binge/intoxication phase mostly involves the ancient regions of the brain – specifically the basal ganglia, which is a structure that provides the pleasing and enjoyable sensation gained through unnatural surges of dopamine often caused by drugs of abuse. This is generally accepted as the flashpoint that kickstarts the entire process. The next phase, called the withdrawal phase, is mapped to another ancient structure called the amygdala. The amygdala has been found to be a key regulator in anxiety and depression, which often serve as potent motivators to spend as little time in this phase as possible. Lastly the craving phase involves our frontal lobe, the part of our brain which is conceptualized as the problem-solving (or executive) portion of our brain, which seeks out whatever substance had caused the pleasurable binge/intoxication phase and thus restart the cycle.

All drugs of abuse, from cigarettes to heroin, foster abuse by finding some point of entry into this cycle through initiating the binge/intoxication phase. Some drugs work more directly (such as cocaine causing increases in dopamine activity) while others operate with more subtlety (such as Xanax through a more roundabout process of dopamine control). Regardless of the initial spark, the fire that results causes these phases and their corresponding regions to then cascade into each other in a vicious, worsening cycle that pushes the addict to compulsively seek out the substances in a manner that completely overrides the reward circuits' usual rhythm in their lives and routines. The effect of more natural rewards (sex, food, etc.) pale in comparison to how much more efficiently and potently drugs of abuse stimulate the reward circuit. As such they are often left unpursued or neglected. As the cycle of stimulation continues, the binge/intoxication phase itself becomes less pronounced as the constant barrage of dopamine release in the basal ganglia overstimulates it to the point where it is desensitized to all but the strongest bursts of dopamine. In its place, the addict then becomes more stuck in the much-less-pleasant phases of anxious craving and dysphoric withdrawal. This change has been repeatedly observed in numerous studies and truly roots the struggle of the addict in medical reality.

What is essential to appreciate is the importance for prevention given the impact of these brain changes as well as an understanding for how medications, therapy, or combinations thereof can specifically intervene and break the cycle of addiction. This conceptualization of addiction as a medical condition, or disease, is not to rob the notion of the role of choice in its development. Few would argue that choice plays no role in the first time someone uses a mind-altering substance. But an impulsive choice does not denote a failing of character. Indeed, impulsivity is a natural consequence of adolescence, which also happens to be one of the most vulnerable populations to the development of addiction. Moments of weakness or impulsivity is something we all experience, but they are not what drive addiction. The more we appreciate it for the biological entity that it most certainly is, the more we can do about it.

Resources

Gold, M.S. & Adamec, C. (2011). *Dr. Benjamin Rush and His Views on Alcoholism*, April 17. Retrieved from www.health.am/psy/more/dr-benjamin-rush-and-his-views-on-alcoholism/.

Plaud, J.J. & Wolpe, J. (1997). Pavlov's contributions to behavior therapy: The obvious and the not so obvious. *American Psychologist, 52*(9), 966–972.

Volkow, N.D. & Koob, G.F. (2016). Neurobiology of addiction: A neurocircuitry analysis. *Lancet Psychiatry, 3*(8), 760–773.

Volkow, N.D., Koob, G.F., & McLellan, A.T. (2016). Neurobiologic advances from the brain disease model of addiction. *New England Journal of Medicine, 374*(4), 363–371.

Michael L. Wenzinger, M.D., is the chief clinical fellow at the Washington University Child and Adolescent Psychiatry training fellowship. He obtained his medical degree from Eastern Virginia Medical School and completed his adult psychiatry training at the Washington University psychiatry residency.

Mark S. Gold, M.D., is Adjunct Professor in the Department of Psychiatry at Washington University in St. Louis. He is also a member of the National Council at the Institute of Public Health at Washington University in St. Louis.

In a similar way, knowledge is increasing about best practices, associated with prevention, intervention, and treatment efforts. Greater attention to documentation and studies on efficacy have moved the science of these overall efforts to heightened levels. While attention by professionals is generally upon doing what is deemed best for the individual, group, or environment, quality research and studies have helped move these efforts to new levels. Consider, for the college setting and a focus on alcohol, the work of the National Institute on Alcohol Abuse and Alcoholism; the CollegeAIM initiative[2] examines published literature on numerous approaches used to address individual or environmental issues; these various approaches are assessed based on criteria of effectiveness, costs, barriers, and quality and amount of research.

Consider also the various documentations of best practices for treatment, highlighted with the SAMHSA-focused Treatment Improvement Protocol publications. What these efforts show is that and current science is moving forward.

Four challenges emerge from this. One is keeping professionals up to date with the latest science. This can be accomplished through professional conferences and journals, training and webinars, in-service education, and collegial mentoring and sharing. The current pre-service education activities, and graduate preparation programs in a variety of fields of study, would be well served to ensure that their curricular efforts are current and appropriate to meet the current and emerging needs of the professionals.

Related to this are the organization or community leaders, and keeping them up to date; these individuals are typically not formally trained in substance abuse issues, whether with prevention or treatment, intervention or recovery. Since they serve as gatekeepers and decision-makers, strategies are needed so they are contributing to (or at least not blocking) the implementation of current best practices.

Third, while the importance of good science and best practices is vital, and should not be minimized, it is also important to consider strategies, styles, and approaches that may not be fully grounded in science or vetted with research. With best practices, all too often individuals are looking for proven strategies. With the CollegeAIM initiative cited above, the strength and importance of this approach is that it takes professional research and blends it with practical considerations (e.g., cost, obstacles); the documentation also cites how extensive the research is, as well as how effective the strategy appears to be. An item in the published listing may not have much or any research, but that could change; there may be items for which no research is available, or for which the research is dated. There may also be effective approaches that are not even listed on the master compilation. These considerations should all be part of the overall decision-making process, so that the actual decisions are grounded in good information and good science. To make decisions based on "feel-good" approaches (sometimes referred to as "coasters and posters") is inappropriate and unwise; however, to limit decisions to only those approaches that have been proven can be limiting.

Fourth, specific substances of concern change over time. The onset of the most recent "War on Drugs" was found in the 1980s, and was linked to concerns about cocaine use. Methamphetamines were drugs of concern in the 1990s, including attention to ecstasy during a short period. More currently, opiates, both prescription and non-prescription, legal and illegal, are of current concern due to their potency and high negative consequences. See more about the origins and nature of the opioid epidemic in Professional Perspective 3.2.

Professional Perspective 3.2

The Opioid Epidemic: How Did We Get Here?

Dana Ripley, M.A.Ed., and Jenny Wagstaff, Ph.D.

The joys and pain of opium have been documented for centuries. Discovered in southwest Asia as far back as 3400 B.C. it did not take long for cultures around the world to uncover the power of the plant and to use it for both medicinal and non-medicinal purposes. Asian countries used the substance to treat ailments including diarrhea, vertigo, headaches, menstrual pain, melancholy, insomnia, and pain while the Greeks and Romans used the substance for religious purposes and spiritual ceremonies. Although America's history with opium is relatively short in comparison to other parts of the world, today approximately 80% of the global opioid supply is consumed in the United States (International Narcotics Control Board, 2018). This vast consumption has led to one of the worst epidemics in history and really raises the question, "How did we get here?" If one listens to the media, the simplest answer is to blame big pharmaceutical companies and illicit drug dealers. While there is no doubt that these two entities have contributed to the crisis, the issue is far more complex.

In his book, *Dreamland: The True Tale of America's Opiate Epidemic* (2015), Sam Quinones described a slow-moving storm that included the combination of pharmaceutical companies, the medical field, and black tar heroin. The initial stage of this storm began in the 1950s and 60s, with Arthur Sackler, a psychiatrist turned marketing guru, who owned a marketing firm and eventually purchased Purdue Pharma (then Purdue Frederick). Sackler and his brothers are credited with altering the way pharmaceuticals are marketed through inundating doctors and their offices with sales people and ads to push their drugs. At the time, this was innovative ad campaigning, which came to influence the aggressive manner in which pharmaceutical companies marketed pain killers (Quinones, 2015).

The second stage of the storm evolved in the 1990s, and appears to have three elements: individual intolerance of pain, non-engagement of holistic approaches, and emphasis on medications. This stage began when medical staff in the VA hospital system concluded that pain was being under treated. This conclusion led to an increased emphasis on the assessment of pain for all patients, making it the fifth vital sign to be measured and treated. The regular assessment of pain led to the expectation that treatment would occur. However, unlike heart and breathing rates or blood pressure and temperature, pain is a subjective measure. Doctors were placed in a position where they must accept and respect patient self-reporting of pain and treat accordingly. Unfortunately, holistic approaches to treating pain were not always covered by insurance; thus pain medicine such as OxyContin was prescribed despite the fact that many doctors were wary due to previously noted addictive qualities. To ease this concern, one study by Portenoy and Foley (1986) published in the form of a brief, five-sentence letter in the *The New England Journal of Medicine* described the treatment of 38 cancer and non-malignant pain patients and concluded that opioid pain relievers could safely be prescribed. Although the evidence was of low quality, the study was frequently cited as a means to support the expanded use of opioids to treat pain (Kolodny et al., 2015). Further bolstering the argument for opiate prescriptions were the more than 20,000 pain-related education programs during 1996–2002 funded by Purdue Pharma touting the benefits of OxyContin (Kolodny et al., 2015).

The third stage of the storm involved the ready supply of black tar heroin as described by Quinones in this manner. Mexicans from a small place called Nayarit found a booming market in the U.S. for heroin, for which poppy is grown and processed in the hills of this region. Innovative sales tactics, involving the driver meeting the consumer (contrasted with the buyer being required to come to a house), and low costs (due to the Mexican supply versus overseas supply), made this heroin desirable and easily obtainable. Also adding to the desirability was that the black tar was pure versus the white powder form that is often diluted several times along the way from growth and processing, to the market. In this case, the drivers delivering the heroin were paid a salary which eliminated the incentive to dilute the drug. This meant that the heroin people were getting was often more potent than what they were typically used to, resulting in increased overdoses.

These three stages are major factors leading to a scary perfect storm. As a culture, Americans are less pain tolerant and often demand a quick fix; the "solution" typically comes in the form of a pill. Today we know that this prescribing epidemic has led to a national crisis of opioid misuse, overdose, and death. In an effort to avoid withdrawal symptoms, those addicted to opioids find themselves "doctor shopping" to refill prescriptions and/or purchasing illicit drugs on the streets – all to moderate their pain.

From a primary prevention perspective, a shift has been made and doctors are in agreement that opioids should not be the first thing used to treat chronic pain. This is a huge step in the right direction. Another huge step is an increase in the availability of treatment and recovery support programs, promoted by the federal government. For example, SAMHSA's Medication Assisted Treatment for Prescription Drug and Opioid Addiction (MAT-PDOA) program is now accessible in areas most impacted by the epidemic (SAMHSA, 2018). To further address the issue it is recommended that insurance companies expand their coverage and access for nonopioid and nonpharmacological pain medications. In addition, harm reduction measures such as needle exchange programs and access to naloxone for overdoses should be incorporated into public health programs. Finally, coalitions that involve diverse sectors of community including medical professionals, department of human services case workers, school administrators, faith community leaders, teachers, counselors, pharmacists, public health officials, law enforcement, and treatment professionals should collaborate to disseminate relevant information, conduct visioning sessions, develop and implement action plans, and implement educational sessions and informational campaigns. While we know that the path to recovery is not always straight forward, hope remains. As a nation, it is important to take the lesson learned from this crisis and take action!

References and Resources

International Narcotics Control Board. (2018). Estimated world requirements of narcotic drugs for 2018. Retrieved from www.incb.org/incb/en/narcotic-drugs/estimates/narcotic-drugs-estimates.html.

Kolodny, A., Courtwright, D., Hwang, C., Kreiner, P., Eadie, J., Clark, T. & Alexander, G.C. (2015). The prescription opioid and heroin crisis: A public health approach to an epidemic of addiction. *Annual Review of Public Health*, 36, 559–574.

Portenoy, R.K. & Foley, K.M. (1986). Chronic use of opioid analgesics in non-malignant pain: Report of 38 cases. *Pain*, 25, 171–186.

Quinones, S. (2015). *Dreamland: The True Tale of America's Opiate Epidemic*. New York, NY: Bloomsbury Press.

Substance Abuse and Mental Health Services Administration. (2018). SAMHSA publishes guidance on clinical best practices using medication-assisted treatment to combat the opioid epidemic. February 15. Retrieved from www.samhsa.gov/newsroom/press-announcements/201802150200.

Dana Ripley, M.A.Ed., L.P.C., is a doctoral candidate in counselor education at Virginia Tech. She has been working in the field of addictions since 2012, and is currently researching counseling interventions for use in MAT models.

Jenny Wagstaff, Ph.D., L.P.C., is Assistant Professor in Counselor Education at Campbell University, Buies Creek, NC. Her research focuses on the use of brief motivational interventions to address high-risk substance use behaviors.

The long-term advocates interviewed offered helpful insights regarding the role of science with a range of substance abuse prevention issues.

> *What surprised me was that the current Western framework of science to action was incomplete. It's not that it's wrong but that it's incomplete, and it's also incredibly pervasive, we build on so many institutions around the gold standard of the clinical experiment.*
> Jeff Linkenbach

> *The difference is that alcohol is acceptable in our society legally; it's acceptable culturally. Illegal substances for the most part are not and that changes the way policymakers think about it. But when it comes to researchers I think the questions in alcohol research are very different than the questions you need to ask in illegal substance research.*
> Steve Schmidt

> *Alcohol use hasn't changed for the last 30 years; it's pretty much the same. We have had this heavy drinking issue among college students forever and we still haven't really put a dent in it.*
> Helene White

I was surprised at how easily professionals in the prevention community would gravitate to the easy programs. I began to get it once I realized how they were being evaluated, by state agencies, funding, or organizations who were saying we need to see stuff get done and that got translated as "How many brochures do I give out, how many classes did I teach, how many trainings did I give?" So I was a little surprised that they were not as science grounded as I thought they should have been.

Steve Schmidt

The prescription drug issue is a big issue we are trying to clamp down on in our community but it's going to take a lot of education too.

Darlind Davis

The research is finally starting to recognize that alcoholism is a chronic disease, because the body of research is growing. And professional treatment is very short, unless people go to AA.

Thomasina Borkman

There is another kind of knowledge and authority, than professional. And that is with experience. And that is the basis of self-help groups. All self-help groups are organized around the lived experience of people with similar experiences.

Thomasina Borkman

With the legalization of marijuana we may be able to reduce some of the crime associated with the drug markets and the violence associated with that crime. On the other hand, I don't know what effect it's going to have on increasing problematic use among young people. I think it is a progressive move but I won't know until we see what happens.

Helene White

It is a fact that we have never been questioned upon delivering one of our programs out into the public domain where somebody has said either this is just plain wrong or this is just plain self-serving. I think at the end of the day having an open process, and being true to the data and the substance we see out there, is really how we have tried to overcome that obstacle of being industry funded.

Ralph Blackman

Drug use has certainly changed a lot with the different epidemics of what's popular and so I think drug use is more interesting to study.

Helene White

One was really counterintuitive, it was a basic science project but then turned out to be highly relevant to medicine in general. This is when you learn something in one state, your maximum recall is when you are in the same chemical state; so if you learn something on amphetamine the challenge for you is to take the test almost at the same amphetamine level.

Mark Gold

We really do not have a scientific basis for understanding the impairment caused by drugs at this point.

Jeffrey Levy

What I believed earlier, that I no longer believe, is that people need information only, or the values clarification. If you can get the information great, but I think some other things need to be set up first. And for me policy enforcement is just a cornerstone of what we do, then everything else wraps around it.

Deb Thorstenson

And considering client presentation combined with research that allowed us to achieve quality care with case managed treatment systems. I think we've bumped it up a notch and we are developing more bench to trench and trench to bench models that inform care and I'm pretty excited about that.

Robert Lynn

It's extremely difficult to move that needle, to have the change with use of drugs and alcohol.

Bill Modzeleski

The Context of Blockages and Roadblocks

Another factor with the consideration of approaches is with the range of challenges faced by one seeking change. This is not a focus on an individual within a clinical setting, but rather upon the systems, leaders, and priorities of an organization or group. These are relevant in this segment because an awareness of these challenges helps one understand the larger perspective of areas of concern. It is the mindset of those who serve as leaders, decision-makers, and gatekeepers that is helpful to understand as preparations are made to effect change.

One major obstacle is with lack of awareness by those in leadership positions. Since many of these individuals do not have the background or experience with substance abuse issues, it is not surprising that they are not aware of the nature and scope of the issues. They may know some of the basics, but may actually have misinformation or hold as true some commonly held myths. While they may have some working knowledge, they may not understand the overall context. Further, it is not surprising that they are not aware of the various idiosyncrasies affiliated with substance abuse issues. They may not be aware of the complexities of the continuum of use or substance dependence, as well as the factors associated with substance use disorder and its progressive nature. Equally important, they may not understand how both individual and environmental factors are relevant for understanding and addressing substance abuse.

As with various other issues, a challenge with substance abuse issues is that the guiding frameworks and paradigms may be outdated. For example, the disease concept of alcoholism was a new approach nearly a century ago; prior to that, this "disease" view was neither understood nor respected. With alcohol problems, there were eras based on the public health model elements of agent, host, and environment; the U.S. had a period of time where alcohol problems were based on concerns with the host; then it was more of an issue with the agent of alcohol itself; and more recently a more holistic or environmental approach is acknowledged.[3] This dovetails with the moralistic view about drug or alcohol problems, which suggests that use of substances is wrong, and that it is primarily a problem of the individual. There were periods of time when knowledge alone was seen as sufficient to make a difference. Alternatively, attention to just enforcement has been viewed at some times as the only appropriate approach for addressing substance abuse issues. For an overview of paradigms over time, and how they can affect current thinking, see Chapter 4, which includes a Professional Perspective.

With these old paradigms, two things are important. First, many of these noted are outdated and invalid, from the current perspective of substance abuse professionals. While these professionals may be up to date, many others working with substance abuse issues, as well as the general public, will not have been educated on current paradigms, and may very well have their thinking guided by old frameworks or approaches, many of which had been discounted and discontinued decades and decades earlier. Second, different paradigms do exist, and may very well be valid for the specified audiences. With the various professional entities addressing substance abuse issues, from educators to counselors, from enforcement personnel to treatment providers, it is not surprising that different professional affiliations have different frameworks or paradigms. Even within the specific counseling profession, counselors in general use different theories and modalities, each with their own levels of efficacy.

Turning to an individual's role in an organization, there may be issues associated with having a shared vision. One or more individuals may have what is deemed to be an appropriate and helpful perspective regarding substance abuse issues; this may not be shared more widely, for any of a variety of reasons. For movement to occur within an organization or group, the decision-making must be such that approval by whatever power structures exist is central.

Also within a group or organization, it is often found that change is difficult. The issue of changing direction or creating inertia around a new issue can be challenging. With limited resources of time, personnel, and funding, priorities need to be established. With different perspectives, backgrounds, awareness, paradigms, experiences, and needs, it is not surprising that challenges exist for reaching consensus on a shared vision surrounding substance abuse issues.

As highlighted in Chapter 1, attention to approaches such as a Force Field Analysis can be helpful for better understanding the roadblocks and obstacles, and to identifying appropriate courses of action for addressing these issues. Chapter 8 (Resourceful Approaches) will further examine specific ways of moving forward in appropriate and reasonable ways for attending to current needs and issues, and not relying on the status quo. A specific overview of roadblocks at various levels of society is found in Professional Perspective 3.3.

Professional Perspective 3.3

Reflections on Substance Abuse Prevention Strategies: Overcoming Obstacles

Gail Gleason Milgram, Ed.D.

Many factors play a role in substance abuse prevention. Some are extremely well-intended but not necessarily effective and others are punitive, which also are often ineffective. To understand the roadblocks to reducing alcohol and drug use, it is vital to consider all the factors that have an impact on the use of alcohol and drugs, particularly in our youthful population.

Primary is the *community*, as its attitudes and values reflect its members. The members often don't know what's really happening within their borders, even with awareness of surrounding towns struggling with issues such as underage drinking and heightened opium use. This mindset covers up issues that need to be addressed. Years ago, when opioid addiction was rising, it was suggested that naloxone (i.e., Narcan) be available in the community with a trained person (e.g., a school nurse). Many communities viewed this as unnecessary as they didn't understand the need for action.

With a societal priority of minimizing pain, members of the *medical profession and hospitals* (with motives of keeping a patient comfortable), gave pain killers before requested; further, Tylenol was often much harder to obtain than OxyContin. With time limits for painkiller prescriptions, individuals became addicted and sought other sources to eliminate pain. Some individuals turned to heroin, extremely cheap and more potent than previously found. Doctors and dentists were told that painkillers were not addictive and weren't advised to initially prescribe a small quantity of the drug.

Our *legal system* also impacts the community through laws. Previously marijuana was considered more dangerous than alcohol and many people, particularly youth, were arrested for possession. Though it's clear that both substances can cause problems (e.g., driving under the influence), it's critical to identify rational ways of preventing problems related to any substance use. Local police are charged with enforcing laws as well as local edicts. As one example, a local police department previously had the right to enter a home if it was reported that two or more underage youth were there alone, to make sure they weren't consuming alcohol or using drugs: a call from a neighbor obligated police to check this out.

The *police*, with an aim of being a positive influence on youth, founded DARE and other programs, thus bringing police into classrooms to discuss alcohol and drugs as well as problems related to substance use. Some school systems had a teacher or another important school person (e.g., nurse) remain in the classroom, demonstrating that school people were available to handle questions or situations that arose later. One often cited positive outcome was that the students became more comfortable with police which led them to reach out to them for assistance if needed.

Similarly, some *school systems* do not allow students to participate in extracurricular activities (e.g., athletics, chorus, theater), after discovering they had used alcohol/drugs during non-school hours (sometimes including the summer). Some mandated that students in violation had to receive counseling before returning to school. While these policies may have been well-intended, the ramifications on students and parents were overlooked. Suspending students from school not only removes them from the learning environment but also provides time for drinking/drugging. Since the majority of parents work, they are faced with having to choose missing work or leaving their child unsupervised. A more enlightened approach is offering classes on alcohol and drugs in school.

The *local school system* also reflects the community's attitudes and values. Teachers are encouraged to present the facts, an important approach. However, they are also encouraged to refrain from personalizing the information, thus making important information almost unusable to students. Discussions with students typically revealed that they had not thought about and/or prepared for drinking at a party, such as considering alcohol quantity, impact based on body weight, and resulting BAC (blood alcohol concentration) and behavioral effects. The same discussions regarding marijuana and other substances need to occur, demonstrating that personalizing the information has a vital role.

Parents play an important role in their children's perception of what is acceptable and appropriate. Alcohol and drugs should be discussed in the home to prepare children to make responsible decisions about using alcohol and drugs in the future. Role modeling by parents and their guests might result in children learning that it's OK to drink to the point of intoxication and then drive home. Similarly, with marijuana use in states where this is legal, young people may watch impaired friends of their parents leave and drive, implying (inaccurately) that an individual's ability to drive safely was not affected by marijuana use.

What can be done to eliminate roadblocks to implementing necessary change? Leadership on all levels is needed, as various aspects of society are now experiencing a crisis. Our communities need to discuss how the pattern of substance use and related problems can be diminished. The recent innovation of having Narcan available in a community library makes great sense and should motivate consideration of other venues (e.g., athletic games, community pools, dances, malls).

National leadership along with financial support of treatment programs is vital. It's not enough to say that addiction to alcohol and drugs is treatable, when it's almost impossible for individuals to afford treatment. Providing help to treatment centers is needed.

Partnerships need to be created with society and our communities, so that substance abuse prevention strategies are effective. Further, measures of effectiveness for all strategies are critical. Guiding principles to support substance abuse prevention strategies follow:

- Remain aware of what's taking place in the community, for example vaping of marijuana is increasing among the young.

- Encourage community input by inviting a broad cross section of the community to attend local meetings.
- Develop partnerships between all sources of influence on young people.
- Keep programs relevant and related to young people.
- Have young people provide guidance to what will work and what won't.
- Understand that programs supported by the community and the school are critical to prevention.
- Support programs for individuals who are experiencing alcohol/drug problems.

Gail Gleason Milgram, Ed.D., is Professor Emerita, Rutgers, the State University of New Jersey. She served as Director of the Education and Training Division, Center of Alcohol Studies for over three decades, and has authored books, articles, and pamphlets.

The interviews with the long-term advocates were instructive about the various roadblocks and challenges regarding substance abuse and making progress with reducing negative consequences.

So we know what we want, and as you turn into a science such as prevention, you turn to alcohol, there's so many variables, and so you ask "What is it that we want?" and "What is success?" Is it getting everybody not to use drugs? Is it getting 50% of the kids to use drugs less? Or is it success if we go from heroin down to marijuana, and from marijuana to alcohol? I mean some parents will say that's a success, but is it?
Bill Modzeleski

We have had more progress on the treatment side than on the prevention and education side. This is just the new paradigm.
Mark Gold

One of the obstacles or concerns, I think that sometimes what I see is that we live in what I call a whack-a-mole society. What I mean by that, like the game called Whac-A-Mole, where you have a kid with a mallet and the mole sticks its head up and then you need to whack it quickly, and then the other one sticks up and then whack, whack. So I think we have a whack-a-mole approach and we call it prevention but really it's just reactive movements for the issue du jour.
Jeff Linkenbach

What surprised me is how little people know or may be interested in addiction until it happens to them and then they realize they know nothing and how little they do know.
Teresa Johnston

The average person is exposed (through cable TV and movies and other places) to the fact that they probably know more than ever before about alcohol and drugs. They see people in public life being confronted with it so it's out there. It's just a matter of whether or not they understand how they can play a part in reducing it in order to have a better quality of life.

Darlind Davis

When you sit down and you get a parent and provide a working knowledge of human brain development, and about consequences, and you find that they have no idea what you're talking about.

Jeffrey Levy

Dealing with resistance – communities don't want to deal with these issues. Parents say "not my kid." Schools say "leave us alone, we are only concerned about grades."

Darlind Davis

Other efforts have met with such adversity or such hurdles that we couldn't get over so we tried forever to get some kind of social host policy or law; we have tried to do something about the crime around our bars, and we have pretty much met with so much resistance that nothing's happened.

Carla Lapelle

What you're up against all the time is people who are argumentative and hit heads or they just don't want to try anything new or they are just uncomfortable with the topic. The barriers were always just attitudinal.

Darlind Davis

The obstacles tend to just be individuals who are in powerful positions who are not going to budge on their decisions.

Kim Dude

I suppose one of the other obstacles is diversity of partnership and it's never easy. It's a tightrope walk just about every day to do this.

Kurt Erickson

The perceived obstacle was that the alcohol industry was the opponent, the foe, and that the alcohol industry was out to kill all of our kids. When you got down to the senior most people in the alcohol industry, almost every one of them was a family man with kids of their own, and were pretty hard-nosed about their kids' behaviors and did have the best interests of kids in general at heart. And I found it to be kind of a conundrum, that I am absolutely totally against drunk driving, and totally against underage drinking, and I am your greatest ally; yet you won't talk to me because I'm talking to people in the alcohol industry.

Jeffrey Levy

I think, the elephant in the room is that our efforts are funded by the distilled spirits industry. So I would be remiss if I didn't point to that being an obstacle in some people's minds.

Ralph Blackman

We need to address that rite of passage issue; it's been around forever and it continues to be an obstacle.

Carla Lapelle

For me it is just about moving forward. It was always looking at the barriers and challenges. As an example there were often funding barriers such as the unholy alliance between funding agencies and treatment programs that said we will fund you as long as you keep the beds filled but little attention was paid to exactly what happened to people with addiction. So for me it became crucial to develop systems where research and outcomes could inform care, such as collecting information on the last thousand people we treated, because that might be really useful in treating person #1001.

Robert Lynn

Root Causes of Use and Abuse

Attention to the root causes of substance abuse is an important aspect within this chapter on "Why Be Concerned?" as this helps to address part of what is known as the "cycle of addiction." With multiple factors contributing to an individual's harmful involvement with drugs and/or alcohol, these factors will continue if not addressed. If it were as simple as a single factor or reason, and that reason was not addressed, the outcome would likely not be sustained for that individual. Similarly, with factors or reasons not addressed, other individuals will likely be affected. Further, as will be seen with recovery issues in Chapter 5, a central component for success in recovery is that individuals change their settings, friends and acquaintances, and expectations; this helps change some of the elements contributing to their dependent use of substances.

Chapter 1's summary of why people drink and use drugs is a helpful starting point. If many of those contributing factors were better addressed, then substance abuse would likely be decreased. Similarly, if some or many of the risk factors associated with an individual's use are addressed, then s/he would be less likely to become harmfully involved with substances.

The biopsychosocial disease model of addiction helps encapsulate the variety of causes of dependence.[4] This acknowledges the fact that individuals may end up at the same place, within the progression process articulated in the DSM-5 criteria of Substance Use Disorders, and for different reasons. The model documents the genetic and constitutional factors associated with the disease; similarly, individual psychological factors play an important role, as do sociological and sociocultural elements. An individual may have a very high genetic risk for dependence, thereby requiring few psychological or sociological factors to promote progression along the DSM-5 scale. Alternatively, an individual with very little genetic predisposition for dependence may have strong sociocultural influences, and limited psychological coping skills, and their progression occurs nonetheless.

What happens in the broadest sense is that an identification of root causes for harmful involvement with drugs and/or alcohol can be helpful. This can help prevent harm or other problems, it can help halt a progression along the DSM-5 scale, and it can help promote greater resilience and overall quality of life. Beyond the individual, attention to root causes can be helpful for others in similar situations; this may include an affiliation group based on family background, culture, or choice. Common risk factors for a group can be addressed more globally, helpful for overall prevention globally, or based on selective factors (see the Institute of Medicine Model in Chapter 4).

In review of the root causes, anticipated outcomes would be two-fold if these are addressed well. First, this attention would result in a reduction of the issue that contributes to substance abuse, thus reducing substance abuse itself. This would be the case, as noted above, for the individual affected as well as others in similar circumstances. Second, this attention would help with the issue itself, and for its own benefit. For example, with root causes on the individual level, consider those such as stress, time management, anger, loneliness, comfort talking with others, and anxiety; if these were addressed, at least to some level, the result for individuals could include enhanced quality of life. With root causes at the environmental level, consider those such as misleading advertising, lower cost, or lax regulations; if these were addressed, there may be spinoffs for other areas of concern, such as respect for the law generally, belief in marketing and advertising, and followthrough with regulations and procedures.

Addressing the root causes of substance abuse issues is designed to not only reduce negative consequences associated with substance abuse, but to have a positive effect due to the specific nature of the elements themselves. It is clear that professionals and program planners working with substance abuse issues do not want the negative consequences; it is also quite desirable that these same people want the positive outcomes. As the issue of substance abuse is addressed, understanding more about the root causes becomes an opportunity to provide healthier and more productive people and settings.

An example of addressing root causes comes from an adaptation of a think-tank process conducted in 1994 at the University of Notre Dame. During this national conference, over 200 attendees participated in Vision Groups, where they discussed ways of better addressing substance abuse issues among young adults. During their report-out process, overall strategies and recommendations were shared; these tended to cluster around seven themes. The view of attendees was that if these themes were better addressed, then young adults would be less likely to become harmfully involved with drugs or alcohol. For example, with optimism, the view was that if individuals were more optimistic, they would be less likely to have problems with drugs or alcohol; if they had a clearer sense of their own values, they would be less likely to be problematically involved with substances. Through the publication of a book[5] that built upon these seven themes, and subsequent funding to operationalize these themes, COMPASS: A Roadmap to Healthy Living was developed. These seven themes were operationalized into 31 topics, which become specific items that link to many of the reasons for use, both from a negative (problem reduction) or positive (proactive resiliency) perspective (see Figure 3.1).

These clusters and topics help illustrate one way for addressing the root causes of substance abuse. Similar processes of vision groups, whether through a conference setting or through ongoing planning efforts, can be used for various settings. The

82 Competence

Cluster	Specific Topic
OPTIMISM	Attitude
	Self-Esteem
	Self-Responsibility
	Creativity
VALUES	Spirituality
	Human Respect
	Cultural Competence
SELF-CARE	Nutrition
	Exercise and Physical Fitness
	Body Image
	Sleep
	Time Management
	Financial Management
	Stress and Relaxation
	Mental Health
	Writing and Study Skills
	Alcohol
	Tobacco
	Drugs
	Personal Safety
RELATIONSHIPS	Interpersonal and Family Relationships
	Assertiveness
	Anger Management
	Conflict Resolution
	Sexual Decision-making
	Etiquette
COMMUNITY	Social Life and Activities
	Campus Involvement
NATURE	Natural World
SERVICE	Volunteering
	Career Planning

Figure 3.1 COMPASS Topics

essential consideration with this is that attention to root causes be provided, with attention to the specific audience and setting.

With the in-depth interviews conducted with long-term advocates, many had backgrounds that help inspire and propel them in their work with substance abuse issues.

> *I was an elementary school teacher in the early 1970s and I began to be interested in the impact that alcohol and other drug use had on students' ability to learn because I realized that some students were just having difficulty adjusting to the school environment, the classroom. It did not seem to be a question that they were not able to learn because of their intellectual capacity but they were distracted. Therefore, I started learning more about the role of substance use in families and actually was appointed by my principal to a drug education committee.*
>
> Tom Griffin

I used to believe that comprehensive is enough and that it is attainable. I now believe comprehensive is important but we need to look at something that is holistic. Holistic brings in that element of balance and spirit and culture. I used to believe there is a dogma that says we just need to be more comprehensive and so I spent about 20 years going to meetings where, irrespective of the issue, the solution was we need to be more comprehensive. And I used to think that that was being proactive but then I realized that comprehensive is actually quite reactive, it is always trying to be comprehensive enough and yet there's always a sense of inadequacy, of deficit, it's a deficit-based approach. It doesn't mean we forgo it but it does mean there is something more that needs to emerge and that it's not just more, it's different.

Jeff Linkenbach

The most important things that can be done ... we have to change the way young people deal with stress, that seems to be the biggest reason. Also, for the young people to find some acceptance in whatever social groups that they are in, so it's that social acceptance and then that contributes to stress.

Carla Lapelle

The most important things that can be done ... Wellness, because it's a product, if you want to improve your life, you have to make those daily decisions to improve physically, mentally, emotionally, socially, and spiritually for your life; and that's not something that you think about but you do it, you have a plan.

Mary Hill

So having a social justice bent and wanting to work with those who are struggling the most I would move beyond looking at drugs use alone to include all of the quality of life challenges that impact on recovery.

Robert Lynn

The Importance of Values

Central to this chapter on "Why Be Concerned?" are values. These are most relevant at the individual, group, and societal levels. Individually, values can be helpful in preparing plans of action regarding prevention, as well as within the construct of clinical activities. Similarly, at the group or organizational level, as well as at the societal level, the question of values arises with delineation of what is important and what the entity stands for. The previous chapter was on the environment; one of the guiding principles highlighted there was that what the community can do regarding this (and other) issues is a statement or reflection of priorities, and thus its values. This is true for an organized or ad hoc group, an educational setting, an organization, and a government.

At any of these levels of understanding, the values can be what is stood for, as well as what is stood against. This is similar to reducing the negative, as well as promoting the positive. They are similar to what we want to prevent, which may complement and be distinguished from what we want to promote (see Chapter 6 on Prevention and Education). For example, what we want to prevent can be seen as what do we not want to see or do; what we want to promote can be viewed as what it is that is desired or wanted.

Further, at any of these levels, the focus can be on outcomes or results, as well as processes. The outcomes or results are the specific behaviors, knowledge, attitudes, and more that we want to see; some of these will be increases in the desired results, and others will be decreases in the unwanted outcomes. The processes are also important, including who is involved and levels of engagement, nature of approaches used, technical and other information needed for decision-making, time factors, impact assessments, public awareness, and ultimate authority.

For those involved in substance abuse issues, the answer to the question of "why be concerned?" is often based on prior personal experiences. This background helps shape a world view, and thus personal values, to help define what is wanted as the desired outcomes and processes. So many professionals begin their careers with substance abuse issues because of concerns with an individual or a situation in their past; some of these come from personal or a family member's involvement, and others emerge because of a traumatic situation involving others. Ultimately, for many professionals, the motivating factor for involvement is based on reducing the negative circumstances or conditions with an individual, and ultimately helping others have healthy and productive lives.

With the values, an initial question is how the issue is defined. One factor would be on the results, and specifically on reducing the negative – what are the specific negative items that are identified for reduction? Is it death? Injury? Harm to self? Harm to others? Property damage? Automobile crash? Accidental overdose? Suicide?

Another factor is based on the audience. This may be due to any of a variety of demographic or socioeconomic factors. This may be age, gender, race/ethnicity, setting (urban, rural, suburban), education, work status, or more. The issue of different standards or services for an audience based on one or more of these factors – health disparities – can result in a deliberate review for potential modification.

Within all these considerations is the factor of extent or quality – of excellence. While most professionals would agree that high standards are important, they would probably also agree that perfection will never be achieved. Can all problems with the illicit use of prescription drugs be eliminated? Is it reasonable to expect that all instances of alcohol problems will be reduced, including impaired driving and teen drinking? Can occurrence of substance use disorders actually be prevented? The point is that the specified outcome must be reasonable; while the ideal outcome may still be sought (e.g., no deaths), having such a goal can be viewed as a set up for perceived failure if "success" is specified as having such a goal.

The other consideration within a group, organization, community, or beyond is with the positive or human potential perspective. So much attention is provided to "reducing the negative" or "eliminating the problem"; this complementary approach is one of "promoting the positive" and "enhancing potential." The proactive approach can also be viewed as one of promoting resiliency skills, such as was addressed in the previous section on root causes.

As noted in the first two chapters, drug and alcohol abuse and misuse can get in the way of individuals living their lives in a safe and healthy way, and achieving their dreams. With the negative consequences identified, the ways in which productivity and performance can easily be found. Beyond that, however, the results are somewhat more elusive. For example, in what ways would an individual's performance be enhanced if s/he was not affected by a family member's problems with substances? How would their productivity be affected if they were not suffering the effects of a hangover? If they were not thinking about an upcoming social event, or focused on their finances associated with substance use? The question is, what would their life be like if drug and alcohol issues were not a central part, or even a part, of their life? These questions may be based on elements such as the quality of life overall, their creativity, their ability to think through a problem, their perseverance, their satisfaction, their happiness, or more. The focus here is on the more positive items, and reflects those that may be viewed as "less essential" or "superfluous."

The balance between reducing the negative and promoting the positive is central to the discussion of values. The attention to the former – "problem reduction" – is generally found because of the public nature of these problems, and the desire to remove them. The attention to the latter – "enhancing potential" – is more of a feel-good approach, which may also help in reducing the problems. Values can help determine what is important to address, and how to make this determination. One community may value attention to a specific audience or to the disparities found with a grouping within their purview; another group or organization may focus on a specific substance or type of outcome.

This is not to suggest that one priority is better than another, or that one group or community's approach is more favorable than that found in another setting. It just highlights the importance of clarifying and specifying the outcomes and processes in a clear way. This clarification process is helpful with the allocation of resources, which are all too often limited and thus need to be focused. The process also helps with the specification of reasonable outcomes, so that appropriate metrics can be established to aid with understanding the results, and assessing the cost-effectiveness of the investments of time and funding resources to achieve the outcomes.

Interviews with long-term advocates provide some summative insights regarding the values held by individuals as well as society overall:

Substance Use Disorders all have similar processes and characteristics, but vary in intensity, physiological risks, patterns of use, etc. Yet, alcohol is so accepted in the U.S. that we normalize the effects. This makes it more difficult for folks to see it as a serious problem for themselves or others.

Claudia Blackburn

It is the one public issue which is completely preventable. With every drunk driving fatality, crash, injury, arrest being 100% preventable, we really should be able to lick this.

Kurt Erickson

> When AA people end up being ornery – it is for good reason. They have to think out all sorts of things for themselves, rather than being told what to do. Which is so ironic, when AA is sometimes called a cult.
>
> Thomasina Borkman

> I don't want to say resolve an issue but resolve a problem.
>
> Jeffrey Levy

The Integration of Values

Building upon the clarification of the values at individual, group, and societal levels is ways in which the leaders at all levels can be effective. This involves moving beyond personal clarification and moving toward agreement or consensus. This includes how to engage others with a leader's own values.

The factors associated with awareness of the problem (Chapters 1 and 2) is the necessary first step. It incorporates gathering good, current information. It also means gathering information that may not have been done to date.

Related to that is thinking about the organization and its mission statement. As noted earlier, many of these mission statements have aspirational goals, both broad and narrow. It is essential to acknowledge what the statement really says, and what its intent is. For example, central to the medical and healthcare professions is the Hippocratic Oath, which is "first do no harm." This is essential to these medical professionals, and it is upon this that many procedures and protocols are built. Other organizations and groups have mission statements that are lofty, and are both positive and proactive; these share aspirations and visions that help project what it is that the group seeks. These elements are often attractive to potential and current members.

For those who are drawn to a group or organization based on its publicized vision and mission, these statements can be seen as a statement of their values. If these individuals truly believe in these elements, they would want to have clear assessments of the performance of attainment of these factors, including those aspects that contribute to their attainment and those that repress or challenge the outcomes. Leaders and invested individuals will want to know how the priorities are being established, and ways in which the monitoring of outcomes and processes are achieving desired outcomes. This can be helpful to current and future decision-makers regarding the expenditures of funding, as well as time and resources.

All of this is espoused within the context of leadership. Regardless of the role of an individual, whether as a designated leader or not, each individual has an opportunity to help shape the organization or group. Simply put, if those in leadership roles or with leadership opportunities are not leading, then who will? If those who have awareness and knowledge do not attempt to make a difference by sharing that knowledge, then who will? It is not sufficient to assume that others will lead; with that, the silence can be deafening. It is the moral responsibility of those with knowledge and leadership roles to speak up and speak out to attempt to affect change.

This does not suggest that, because of this values-based leadership, change will occur. Nor does it suggest that, because of the leadership, attempts at change will occur. What is important is that the effort be made. This involves some reasonable efforts, and with incorporation of some skills to enhance the likelihood of success, to try to influence the change process. Individuals come to positions of responsibility with varying backgrounds and orientations; their views may be different, and their values for themselves and for the groups being served may vary. It is a matter of working together, and sharing these values and perspectives, that will help with obtaining a clearer understanding of desired future outcomes and potential steps for moving forward.

The specified reason for this chapter titled "Why Be Concerned?" is that the status quo is not acceptable. It is an important statement, for the individual, the group, the organization, and the society at large, that there be efforts to improve toward achievement of the specified outcomes. While an advocate does not need to know all the details, having a general, fuzzy plan at the outset is acceptable, reasonable, and appropriate. The specific ways of moving forward will become clearer, through various visioning and strategic planning approaches. More specific approaches on this will be addressed in later chapters of this book (see Chapters 7, 8, and 10).

Overall, it is important to think about the "Public Good" that is often espoused. Some of this is incorporated in organizations' mission statements, and other foundations are noted with the funding provided through public dollars, targeted budgetary items, charitable giving, and volunteering of time. While much attention is provided to an individual benefit perspective (e.g., "What's in it for me?"), the larger framework is to look more broadly to the outcomes associated with the investment of the resources for the sponsoring group, organization, or society. Many organizations look at the return on investment (ROI) for funding provided. This can be a helpful discussion, as long as the determining factors are not all focused on a financial construct. Specifically, much of the ROI will be on elements that are more qualitative in nature, such as the quality of life, civic engagement, human respect, and the ability to pursue greater potential. The results of such discussion on values must transcend the personal and individual-focused ROI, and help describe how the specified efforts contribute to the larger group, including the society as a whole, that extends beyond the individual. It will be helpful to not only have discussion about these factors, but to attempt to move toward some type of metrics that can be helpful in documenting progress toward them.

Summary

This focus on "Why Be Concerned?" is based on the fact that various problems and issues are present, that these issues call upon us to address them, because we can do better, and because we know that we should do better. To be silent or unengaged with substance abuse issues is not only inconsistent with our knowledge, it is unfair to those served at the individual, group, or societal levels. Further, inaction is harmful to these same individuals, groups and society.

Notes

1 Anderson, D.S. & Santos, G.M. (2018). *The College Alcohol Survey: The National Longitudinal Survey on Alcohol, Tobacco, Other Drug and Violence Issues at Institutions of Higher Education*. Fairfax, VA. George Mason University.

2 www.collegedrinkingprevention.gov/.
3 Rorabaugh, W.J. (1979) *The Alcoholic Republic: An American Tradition*. New York, NY: Oxford University Press.
4 Havelka, M., Lucanin, J.D., & Lucanin, D. (2009) Biopsychosocial model: The integrated approach to health and disease. *Collegium Antropologicum*, 33(1), 303–310.
5 Coleman, S. & Anderson, D. (1995) *Charting Your Course: A Life-long Guide to Health and Compassion*. Notre Dame, IN: University of Notre Dame Press.

4 Foundational Factors

When addressing drug and alcohol issues, having a strong foundation is essential. When building a quality home, strong foundations are prepared, appropriate design and materials are used, and necessary time and skilled application are vital. With substance abuse issues, numerous elements of the foundation are critical for having "competence," which is why this chapter is included in this section of the book. Not only is actual competence vital, but also necessary are the requisite skills for grounding the competence seen by others. Regardless of whether the planned effort is prevention-based, intervention-focused, treatment-oriented, or recovery and support in nature, it is vital to have a good understanding of the range of frameworks and paradigms.

Initially, the topic of "foundations" may seem confusing or daunting in nature. One might ask whether it would simply be easier to have a single framework or set of standards. That is, "isn't there one standard approach"? The answer is both "yes" and "no." With the range of professionals involved, social workers have standard guidelines that may differ from those of a nurse or of a doctor, for example. Those involved with prevention in high school have different standards from those so involved in higher education settings. Further, it is helpful to be aware of the different frameworks and paradigms; some of these may be widely used, yet have been supplanted by advances in science or quality practice. Others may be valued by the audiences served, yet are known by professionals to be dated, ineffective, or inappropriate. Overall, so much depends on factors such as the role in which one serves, the intent (prevention-based, intervention, treatment, recovery), the individual circumstances and idiosyncrasies, and culture, and the history.

This chapter provides an overview of many of the relevant frameworks and paradigms. In preparation for professional activity, each individual needs to sort through these and make the best judgment for the specific courses of action. As with so many issues, there is no one best solution, and no single effective strategy, that works for all people. The professional will use his/her best judgment. Even with sound planning, professionals may find that those approaches did not achieve the desired results; thus, there may be a need to return to the contents of this chapter to draw upon different or complementary approaches for subsequent efforts. This perspective is a precursor for the third overall section of this book – Commitment – as that is the theme of perseverance throughout the efforts.

Paradigms

A paradigm is a framework or construct; it is helpful for understanding and guiding the specific efforts. Having a proper and effective paradigm is essential for making sound decisions about appropriate courses of action. For example, when the paradigm was that the world was flat, how could circumnavigation of the globe be considered? If the paradigm is that left-handed people are evil (see the source of the term "sinister"), what is reasonable to conclude about these individuals? With the issue of drugs and alcohol, consider the major shift in this field with the publication of Jellinek's book *The Disease Concept of Alcoholism*;[1] certainly, just the words of the title, and the overall paradigm shift, was then and remains significant for how alcohol dependence is viewed and how professionals treat and interact with those who are dependent.

An old paradigm, yet still believed by many non-professionals, is that *knowledge* is what is needed to make a difference regarding drugs and alcohol. The assumption is that knowledge, alone, is sufficient for making a difference. This is not to suggest that knowledge is irrelevant; it is to suggest that holding onto this paradigm alone is not appropriate. Knowledge may be helpful for some or many individuals, but knowledge or information alone is not sufficient for the ultimate aim of behavior change.

A similarly old paradigm, yet still accepted by many in the general public, revolves around the *"moral failing"* associated with substance use. While there may be moral issues associated substance use, to hold the view that a person is immoral when using drugs or alcohol, or when she/he is dependent or in recovery, does not take into account the current science surrounding drugs and their effect on the human body.

Helpful views and insights are provided with Professional Perspective 4.1 as well as some observations from the long-term advocates interviewed.

Professional Perspective 4.1

On the Prevalence of Old Paradigms or Knowledge

Allan Cohen, Ph.D.

Importantly, historical paradigms surrounding substance abuse have driven the nature of community responses to address drug and alcohol problems. When this author entered the field in 1966, American professionals had already moved beyond the early characterization of alcoholics and addicts as sinners, those who should be shamed for moral transgressions. The "sin" orientation morphed slightly into a paradigm of defective character, suggesting the dismissal of users as "bad people," entirely responsible for their dilemmas. Moral and social castigation was found to be insufficient to control abuse. So, from the Prohibition period through the mid-1950s, a paradigm of criminality emerged strongly, with users and addicts considered as lawbreakers, generating a priority on law enforcement and custodial punishment, still evident to this day.

However, in the last decades of the twentieth century, the medical or disease paradigm emerged, allowing alcoholics and addicts to be considered "sick" or "diseased," a conceptual model that now dominates the treatment of alcoholics and addicts. In the last decade, the disease model has accelerated its focus on issues surrounding the central nervous system, specifically labeling chemical dependency as a "brain disease." Whatever its limitations, the medical model did lead to the inclusion of substance abuse disorders in medical practice and health insurance. Also, the emergence of a "brain disease" framework has generated more sophisticated approaches to medications used in detoxification and rehabilitation.

Paradigms of substance abuse prevention and early intervention also evolved historically from concepts involving sin and defective character. Arguably, beverage alcohol paradigms evolved differently from other psychoactive substances. After Prohibition in the United States, although many counties remained "dry" and some religious traditions held firm against drinking, the concept of moderate and responsible drinking among adults as permissible became more dominant. Perceived and actual dangers of nonmedical psychoactive substances (such as heroin, marijuana, and cocaine) generated strict attempts to limit use through robust enforcement of laws. The misuse of prescription medications (most recently opioids) has only recently received national and legislative attention. Again most recently, scientific data on adolescent brain development has buttressed the rationale of controlling underage drinking and drug use.

Current paradigms for youth are still quite diffuse. Theories about risk and protective factors, the role of peers, media, socioeconomic forces, and family dynamics all appear to have some merit, but none alone can account for the near majority of youth in developed countries who experiment with alcohol and psychoactive substances, nor the significant minority who are regular "social" users. The historical lack of clarity of specific directions may come from scientists and policymakers applying a disease or deviance model to a population that is neither diseased nor deviant. The failure for researchers to prioritize the study of youth motivation has thwarted the ascendancy of the most promising paradigm, focusing on individual motivation with a consumer-based model. Paradigms that include consumer motivation such as curiosity, risk-seeking, pleasure-seeking, or social bonding, have not been well explored. Thus, promising intervention strategies, such as positive and competing alternatives to psychoactive substances, spirituality, and consumer-relevant drug information, have not enjoyed substantial attention. The most fruitful science examines what works. However, many promising strategies have never been examined because of the unblinking "requirement" of having laboratory-based evaluation methodology (e.g., expensive random controlled trials) for preventive interventions in order to qualify as "evidence-based."

In general, the plodding progress of paradigmatic change has been fueled not only by the relative failure of earlier intervention strategies but by the contributions of knowledge from social science, public health, and the biological sciences. Although advances in the neuroscience of drug effects are accelerating dramatically, the resulting findings appear not to translate easily to the public or to policymakers; this may be due to lack of awareness of these findings, lack of understanding, not believing them or some other reason. For example, substance abuse personnel consider it shocking that some consumers still do not know that nicotine is an addictive substance. Also, marijuana legalization occurs with profound ignorance among policymakers and the public about the effects of THC, the primary psychoactive ingredient in cannabis, despite thousands of studies citing serious neurologic, teratogenic, behavioral, and addictive sequelae.

In sum, in the domains of substance use and abuse, paradigms matter. They influence policy and the public health. Science has influenced the evolution of paradigms toward greater effectiveness in societal response, but only slowly. Too often, especially about youth, the prevalence of scientific arrogance discounts the credibility of clinical experience, field-based practitioners, and individual reports of life experience. Whatever future policy decisions emerge, the most promising paradigm shifts will come from the grass roots, extracted from the positive results of preventive, interventive, and treatment success. Hopefully science will be able to communicate relevant discovery to this process. One way or another, we can hope that sensitive and compassionate paradigms, buttressed by evidence, will begin to reflect social and personal reality.

Allan Cohen, Ph.D., after earning his doctorate at Harvard, spent almost four decades in substance abuse prevention and education, teaching at Harvard, UC Berkeley, and Kennedy University and supervising research at the Pacific Institute for Research and Evaluation. He has managed some of the largest prevention program evaluations at SAMHSA, written extensively, and earned a lifetime career achievement award from the National Association of State Alcohol and Drug Abuse Directors.

I believed earlier in my career that if we produced good materials and that if we worked with credible people that some in the field of underage drinking, drunk driving, alcohol abuse, whatever you want to define the field to be, would see beyond the funding source and would look at the substance of what we do. And I think there are still way too many people who, though they can't find anything to criticize, are still rooted in the belief that it can't be good.

Ralph Blackman

It is very clear that the field is finally shifting. Physicians and major treatment professionals are realizing that alcoholism is a chronic disease. AA has known that since 1935.

Thomasina Borkman

I thought that law enforcement was the answer. Then I thought education was the answer. Then I thought policy was the answer. Then I thought parents were the answer and you know what ... it's all of them, with a lot of luck. Every one of us as parents know how close we've probably come to that awful phone call. Good parents, good people, well intended, attentive, involved.

BJ McConnell

The most important thing that can be done is not enforcement, it is education. And enforcement needs to take place; you are not going to solve this problem by arresting kids. This drugs and alcohol problem has got to be resolved by educating people as to what the true consequences are in getting buy-in on the solution as opposed to making it in opposition – where it's the cops versus the students.

Jeffrey Levy

Take it out of the realm of being a legal issue but rather a health and/or safety issue.

Helene White

It's not a moral issue. It's a health and safety issue.

Deb Thorstenson

One thing that surprised me is that AA members are sometimes wrong. For example, from AA meetings, I would have inferred that if anyone at age 18 is addicted, then they are going to be a lifelong alcoholic. The research on adolescents shows that for some of them, "addiction" is only temporary, and that they grow out of it.

Thomasina Borkman

We have to find other ways, be it community service, be it courses, be it practicums, there has to be a better way. Otherwise we will see more drug abuse because what do you do with them, you don't put them in jail. You just know they used something, it just kind of makes everything a little bit crazy.

Gail Milgram

When I started teaching, I basically was saying that there is no genetic basis to alcoholism. Now I have completely turned around 100% in that.

Helene White

Supply and demand is an important construct. This is important for a range of economic and trade issues, as well as for drugs and alcohol. There's a constant tension between these two overall factors. If supply is curtailed or reduced, prices tend to rise; if demand is reduced, prices may be adjusted downward to make the purchase more attractive. If supply is reduced yet demand remains, alternative sources of the supply, or substitutes for the supplied substance, will likely be sought. Consider the proliferation of designer drugs, synthetic marijuana, and heroin or morphine adaptations or substitutes. These often get produced to meet the need (the demand) of individuals, as well as to create a demand for a "new" substance. Looking at the balance of supply and demand, if demand were reduced, it may not matter what substances appear on the market since the demand would not be present.

Related to this and worthy of attention are *proactive and reactive* approaches. This is a common distinction made, and which has been highlighted in Chapter 3 (Why Be Concerned?). The reactive approach is one that is more reactionary and addresses problems as they appear. Responses are made as situations arise and while the responses may have been thought through or planned, the situation has already occurred, and the attempt is to reduce the impact of the consequences. Proactive approaches, on the other hand, are those that seek to prevent or avoid the occurrence of the problematic situation. These can be environmental or individual in nature, and seek to create skills or settings that reduce or eliminate the likelihood that negative outcomes occur.

Very popular among health-oriented professionals are two frameworks or models. The *Public Health Model* encompasses three elements: Agent, Host, and Environment. Within the context of substance abuse issues, the "agent" refers to the substance itself, such as beer, marijuana, or a pill. The "host" is the individual who consumes the substance, and "environment" refers to the setting or surroundings. The *Health Belief Model*[2] has six elements, starting with perceived susceptibility (likelihood of being affected with negative consequences) and perceived severity (how bad the effects would be, if they occurred). The model also has perceived benefits (related to positive, health- or safety-oriented decisions), and perceived barriers to these health- or safety-oriented approaches. Finally, the model includes cues to action (internal or external triggers) and self-efficacy (perception of one's own competence).

More recently, the *Stages of Change* (or *Transtheoretical*) *Model*[3] is helpful with understanding an individual's or group's placement with regard to behavioral changes. In short, this model suggests that movement from one place to another is somewhat sequential, so knowing the current status is essential for determining future action. The model starts with pre-contemplation, where someone may not know the facts, consequences, or effects; the individual may not know that options or choices exist. This is followed by contemplation, where consideration of options are accomplished. Then come preparation (actually making a decision) and action (which is implementing the decision). Once the decision has been implemented, the individual (or group) goes into the stage of maintenance, which ideally occurs over the long term and includes monitoring the decision and its impact. Following the maintenance phase is either termination (no continuing need for monitoring) or relapse (the resumption of the problematic behavior that was previously changed). Ideally maintenance of the change will sustain the decision; however, relapse is not an uncommon experience with many who are affected by substance use disorders.

Harm reduction approaches are designed to reduce any of a range of consequences associated with substance abuse; these may include needle exchange programs, opioid replacement therapy, and designated drivers. These may be viewed as controversial, as some argue that their existence or sponsorship implies endorsement of the problematic behavior whose negative impacts their implementation seeks to reduce. *Zero tolerance* is another approach, which involves strict enforcement of rules and regulations. These may include bans on illicit drugs and strong consequences for possession of drugs or alcohol.

Finally, the *biopsychosocial disease model* is an important construct. This has two broad elements: the "disease" part and the "biopsychosocial" part. The disease element refers to a medical condition that restricts or harms the normal functioning of the body; it is a disorder of structure or function, and includes various signs and symptoms. Within the context of substance abuse, the "disease" suggests that drug and alcohol dependence should be viewed as a disease, and that treatment is appropriate. The term biopsychosocial emphasizes that three separate yet overlapping thrusts are operational with substance abuse issues: there are biological elements (including genetic, biochemical, and constitutional factors), psychological elements (such as coping skills, personality, attitude), and social elements (e.g., family, affiliation groups, culture, socioeconomic). No single one of these elements is the cause of substance use disorders, nor should a single element constitute treatment or other approaches for addressing problems. These three, and their individual components, work together to promote, reduce, or address problems associated with drugs and alcohol.

The intent of this brief overview is to provide some basic exposure to several of the dominant frameworks or paradigms. This is not to suggest that one is better than another; it is also not to endorse, necessarily, any single one of these. Some (e.g., the moral failing view) are more dated and not viewed positively by professionals dealing with substance abuse issues. Others (e.g., the Health Belief Model and the Stages of Change Model) have been adapted and updated over time. Different individuals, whether through training, background, experience, setting, population, or professional role, will have preferences for different paradigms or frameworks.

Most important, this attention is designed to provide greater awareness to the various approaches that exist. Some approaches are more appropriate for a particular setting or audience based on the culture, background, age, history, or current status; other approaches may be more appropriate with other factors. Blending multiple approaches (e.g., parts of the Health Belief Model with aspects of the Stages of Change Model) can aid with achieving more consequential results.

The importance of understanding paradigms is related to having an effective framework for the audience and setting being addressed. Having appropriate paradigms is critical to developing appropriate strategies. Having this awareness is important for the professional or community leader to make sound, informed choices for the desired outcomes.

Brain Health

One of the frameworks highlighted in the previous section – the biopsychosocial disease model – incorporates attention to the confluence of three general considerations when thinking about the prevention and treatment of substance abuse as well as substance use disorders. The "bio" part of this framework emphasizes the genetic and biochemical aspects of the body. Since much of this can be viewed as being housed in the brain, this overarching view is often relabeled the "neurobiopsychosocial disease model," thus emphasizing the neurological and neurochemical aspects of the brain.[4]

Attention to the brain and brain health is important when dealing with substance use and abuse, as well as the propensity for the existence and progression of substance use disorders. At its simplest levels, the brain controls basic and critical body functions, such as blood circulation, blood pressure, and breathing. The body is continuously adjusted to internal and external changes in the environment, seeking homeostasis. The brain is extremely complex, with thousands and thousands of different sites for the communication of messages. Neurotransmitters help by traveling across synapses, and targeting cells of other neurons or cells. The central nervous system (CNS) has the capacity to change in response to experience, known as plasticity; the CNS's ability to undergo plasticity can be modified by chemicals, whether consumed for medical benefit, recreational purposes, or other reasons.

The importance of neurotransmitters is that many drugs (including alcohol) can affect their activity; the use of substances can enhance, restrict, or alter their activation or deactivation. With hundreds specifically identified, neurotransmitters are typically linked to specific drugs. While not a one-to-one relationship, a drug may affect more than one neurotransmitter, and a neurotransmitter may be affected by different substances.

The linkage of drugs and alcohol to brain health is several-fold. First, the natural state of the brain can cause deficiencies or increases in the amount or renewed production of specific neurotransmitters. This increase or decrease of neurotransmitters can ultimately affect an individual's behavior, depending on what the neurotransmitter's functions are. Second, and related to the first, is what happens with the constitutional nature of the brain. These are not directly genetic in origin, but result by factors such as diet, exercise, stress, or sleep. These constitutional factors, which may emerge over time, can result in similar deficiencies or increases with neurotransmitter production. Third, a deficiency may result in an individual's satisfaction (even enhanced craving) when experiencing the effects of a substance. Fourth, introduction of a substance may result in reduced internal production of specific neurotransmitters, thereby setting up a cycle for increased use of the substance. This may result in dependence or addiction, which is ultimately caused, to a large extent, by biochemical changes in the brain.

The most important consideration with "brain health" is to have respect for the brain and the body that supports it. Since the brain controls so much, since it is so delicate with finite spaces, and since it can be compromised, its role with maintaining health and overall balance in one's life as essential cannot be overstated. Monitoring ways of promoting its health and effective functioning are worthy of close attention.

Further insights about the brain and the role of genetics with substance use disorders and individualized effects of various substances are found with the Professional Perspective 4.2 and comments from the long-term advocates.

Professional Perspective 4.2

The Brain Disease Model of Addiction Should Be Reevaluated

Christopher Medina-Kirchner, Kate Y. O'Malley, M.A., and Carl L. Hart, Ph.D.

Since the 1990s, health professionals and trainees specializing in substance use disorders have been increasingly indoctrinated with the belief that addiction[1] is a brain disease. This perspective purports that because psychoactive substances exert their actions through specific brain mechanisms, distinct brain differences must exist between those who meet criteria for a substance use disorder and those who do not. These differences are then seen as the *cause* of drug addiction and potential targets for treatment.

Apparently, some of the most compelling evidence underlying the brain disease model of addiction comes from research that investigated the neurobiological and behavioral consequences of amphetamine administered to laboratory animals. Large amphetamine doses administered to drug-naive animals have been shown to produce behavior disruptions and neurotoxic effects to monoamine neurons. However, close examination of these studies shows that the usual dosing regimens employed do not correspond with those typically used by humans. For example, human recreational drug users tend to increase their doses gradually as they become more experienced with the drug. Under this type of human dosing regimen the development of tolerance is likely to occur, which can be protective against drug-related neurotoxicity. Indeed, amphetamine-related neurotoxic effects in laboratory animals are attenuated when escalating amphetamine doses are administered over several days.

In humans, a common strategy used to examine whether drug addiction produces neurotoxicity is to compare the brains of drug addicts with those of non-drug users. Currently, positron emission tomography (PET) imaging is the most suitable technique used to detect neuronal element damage in the living human brain. With this technique, a radioactively labeled chemical that binds to specific receptors or transporters is injected into the bloodstream, then a computerized scanning device maps out the relative binding of the chemical in various brain regions. In the case of neuronal element damage, one would expect to see less receptor or transporter binding in specific brain regions. Indeed, one consistent PET imaging finding is lower dopamine transporter binding in the striatum of methamphetamine addicts compared with non-drug users. Some researchers have interpreted these differences to indicate neuronal damage caused by methamphetamine, and thus, a diseased brain *caused* by drug addiction. Receptor binding potential differences, however, may simply reflect the downregulation of receptors due to tolerance, not toxicity. In addition, these differences could have existed prior to the initiation of drug use. In other words, PET imaging data alone are insufficient to determine whether neurotoxicity has occurred. Importantly, neurotoxicity among human drug users has yet to be definitively demonstrated.

The clinical relevance of any observed brain differences is difficult to determine because oftentimes cognitive (or any behavioral) testing is absent or limited. Furthermore, when statistically significant differences on cognitive tasks are found, they are frequently interpreted as cognitive pathologies caused by the illicit drug of interest. Incidentally, control groups in these studies frequently have a significantly higher mean level of education than the drug using comparison group, and individuals with more education have been demonstrated to outperform those with less. Moreover, simply knowing that a statistically significant difference has been observed between groups does not provide enough information to determine whether the observed difference reached clinical significance (i.e., pathological levels or marked behavioral disruptions). For this reason, it is important for researchers to compare cognitive scores to those from a normative database. Normative data, which are obtained from a large, randomly selected representative sample, incorporate important variables such as age and education. They establish a baseline distribution for measurement. Unfortunately, this basic requirement is often ignored. Notably, when cognitive scores of individuals with a methamphetamine use disorder (or any other use disorder) are compared to those from a normative database, the scores overwhelmingly fall within the normal range. In other words, on average, the cognitive abilities of people with methamphetamine addiction are normal.

Despite a lack of evidence indicating a diseased brain in addiction, this model remains appealing and influential. One reason for the attraction to this perspective is the belief that it offers straightforward treatment approaches. For example, if brain differences can be identified, then they can be targeted for treatment. Another reason for interest in this view is that, in theory, treating addiction as a brain disease shifts the cause of the disorder from the person to the brain thereby reducing the blame attributed to the addicted individual. In practice, people who meet criteria for substance use disorder are still being sent to jail at high rates for engaging in drug use regardless of their moral culpability.

A major concern is that beginning with the assumption that addiction is a brain disease minimizes the role of psychosocial and environmental factors in contributing to drug addiction and in treating this condition. There now exists a large database demonstrating the fact that alternative reinforcers can be used to effectively treat substance use disorders. Therefore, the brain disease model should be reevaluated to formulate a more accurate view of drug addiction, one that emphasizes a prominent role for psychosocial and environmental factors. This reevaluation might result in empirically based treatment approaches such as contingency management becoming more welcome and widespread in drug addiction.

Notes

1 The terms "addiction," "addict," and "dependence," as they are used throughout this review, conform to the *Diagnostic and Statistical Manual of Mental Disorders* (5th ed.) (DSM-5).
2 The American Psychiatric Association (2013) made the decision to switch from using Roman numerals to identify the manual to Arabic numerals [5] making future revisions easier to document.

Christopher Medina-Kirchner is completing his Ph.D. in the Psychology Department at Columbia University under the mentorship of Professor Carl

Hart. He is interested in the neuropsychopharmacological effects of psychoactive substances in humans.

Kate O'Malley is Coordinator of the Neuropsychopharmacology Laboratory at Columbia University, researching combined effects of recreational drugs. She holds an M.A. in Forensic Mental Health and is completing her Ph.D. in Psychology from Swinburne University, Australia.

Professor Hart is Chairman of the Department of Psychology at Columbia University and Ziff Professor in the Department of Psychiatry Columbia's College of Physicians and Surgeons. He is also an award-winning author who has published extensively in the scientific and popular literature.

I think we are making progress on getting rid of some of the myths about alcohol and drug use. We're starting to realize now that drugs have a genetic basis and an environmental basis. So it really is a disease of lifestyle and not just a religious personality deficit. I think there's optimism or hope because at least we are now better able to understand the causes of drug use and what programs work.

Karol Kumpfer

Before brain imaging proof I, with a colleague, wrote a series of papers postulating that the literature was wrong and that rather than cocaine increasing dopamine it might do that acutely but in chronic use it burns out or depletes the brain of dopamine causing a dopamine deficiency. And that was the basis for brain imagery work, and the Dopamine Depletion Hypothesis.

Mark Gold

Biologically, scientifically the youth brain is still evolving, and among the last areas to develop are those that control judgment and impulse control and inhibitions.

Jeffrey Levy

Different people definitely are attracted to different drugs. Whether it's their personality or genetics or whatever causes that, I'm not quite sure.

Helene White

Principles Defining the Effects of a Drug

An important and helpful framework is that named "Principles Defining the Effects of a Drug." For example, consider the effects of a drug on a person – why does the person behave or react a certain way? Why do two people react in different ways? This framework helps with understanding the physical effects of substance use. Seven factors constitute this framework, and can help with understanding a substance's effects.

The first factor is *Properties of the Substance*. This has to do with the chemical composition of the substance ingested. While often confounded with how the drug or alcohol is taken into the body, those particular elements are considered separately. For example, this factor helps distinguish a substance as a stimulant versus a sedative, as well as considering a mixture of substances. With prescription drugs, these are more easily known; with illicit substances, a legitimate question exists about what is in the substance, as they are often prepared or altered with unknown ingredients. The concept here is that "the body doesn't know what a person is putting into it, or why, or whether it was medically prescribed; it is just responding to what it receives."

Second, the factor *Characteristics of the Individual* includes factors such as gender, weight, age, body metabolism, body composition, and other genetic aspects that can affect the processing of substances. It also includes prior experience, expectations, mood, and the presence of food or other substances. With genetic and constitutional factors, these are central to brain health and the body's neurotransmitters, including neurological deficiencies and susceptibilities.

Setting is the third factor, involving the circumstances under which drugs or alcohol are taken or consumed. These circumstances affect the ways in which a person experiences a substance, and can dovetail with the previous factor about the individual's characteristics (such as mood or expectations). This can involve substance use alone or with others, and it can be in a location viewed as safe as contrasted with one that is susceptible to risky circumstances including legal interventions. Another important factor is homeostasis or system equilibrium, when one's brain responds to environmental cuing.

The fourth factor is *Dosage*, with includes the amount of the active ingredient of the substance that is ingested. Prescription and over-the-counter drugs report different amounts or concentrations (e.g., milligrams or milliliters); with alcohol, consider the actual concentration combined with the volume (ounces) consumed. With marijuana, different concentrations of tetrahydrocannabinol (THC) will result in different effects; the same will be true with other active ingredients in cannabis.

The next two factors go hand in hand. *Means of Preparation* emphasizes how a substance is prepared; that is, whether the substance is in pill form, powder, liquid, or ready to be chewed and digested. Some drugs are of a time-release nature. The complementary factor is *Method of Use*; it is this preparation of the substance that helps define the appropriate way for it to be used. The standard view is that liquids are to be drunk, pills are to be swallowed, leafy substances are to be smoked, chewed, or eaten, and edibles are to be eaten. Consider also substances used in unintended ways (e.g., crushing pills and snorting, vaporizing, or injecting), as well as the ways in which many illicit substance are used (e.g., injecting or snorting heroin or methamphetamine).

The final factor is *Distance from the Plant*, which emphasizes that substances in nature are generally less potent and less addictive. Typically, when a plant from nature is processed, its active ingredient gets more concentrated; it may also have synthetic materials added. With the opium plant, for example, its primary active ingredient is morphine, used for pain management; its strength can be enhanced with combinations of other additives, and one resulting product is heroin.

The blend of these seven principles helps with understanding how strategies for addressing drug and alcohol issues benefit from the individualized approaches. Blending environmental and individual approaches is important for effectiveness, within the overall understanding that the same approach will not work for every person, yet some efficiencies of scale and cost-effectiveness can be achieved with global or environmental strategies.

A helpful perspective about the way that substances affect individuals is provided by the following quote from an interviewee; this illustrates how the principles cited in this section can be helpful for understanding drugs' effects.

> *I think there is a double stigma for dry drugs, and I think that when the chemical gets to the brain, the brain doesn't know whether it's legal or illegal, it only knows whether it's up, down, or sideways. Then you have the idea of being a lawbreaker, when you're having an affliction that's illegal. And there's so many more, every day a thousand people still die of tobacco-related disorders, 400 die of alcohol, and less than 50 die of dry drugs.*
> William Kane

Continuum of Use

The ways in which individuals use substances can be helpful for preparing individual, group, and environmental approaches. The Continuum of Use can be construed in different ways, similar to how the Continuum of Strategies is described in the next section. It is helpful to view an individual's use as a continuum. Just as the DSM-5 description of Substance Use Disorder shows the progression of dependence along a continuum, so also can an individual's pattern of use be seen along a continuum.

An important thing to know is that individuals do not necessary automatically "progress" through the continuum; that is, while an individual will typically arrive at higher or more problematic levels after being in a lower or initial level, this movement is not "automatic." Many individuals will remain at the abstinence level throughout their lives, and most individuals who do use substances will remain at the low-risk point for most of the time. There may be occasional forays into higher risk classifications. Another factor is that an individual's use of substances is not universal across substances; that is, s/he may be a low-risk user of alcohol, but be an abstainer with all other drugs. A person may be involved with high-risk or problematic use of one substance, but not with alcohol or other drugs. Finally, an individual who experiences problematic use of drugs of abuse may, indeed, be in the progression of substance use disorder, according to the DSM-5 criteria; it is also possible that this individual may not be diagnosed in that same progression, which is something more appropriate for a clinical assessment and diagnosis. A detailed review of the DSM-5, and some of its historical context, is provided with Professional Perspective 4.3.

Professional Perspective 4.3

Understanding the DSM-5

Diane Rullo, Ph.D.

The current tool for diagnosing mental disorders including substance use is the *Diagnostic and Statistical Manual*, Fifth Edition (DSM-5) (American Psychiatric Association, 2013). This version of the manual was 14 years in the making (Blashfield et al., 2014). The first *Diagnostic and Statistical Manual* (DSM-I) was published in 1952 and included three categories of psychopathology. Formulations of diagnostic criteria for alcoholism, developed by E.M. Jellinek in 1940 (Kelly, 2018), were included in the DSM-I and DSM-II (1968).

In the earlier versions alcoholism was categorized as a subset under the category "Personality Disorders and Certain Other Non-Psychotic Mental Disorders," along with homosexuality and neurosis. The DSM-III (1980) replaced "alcoholism" with two distinct categories: "alcohol abuse" and "alcohol dependence." The DSM-III also specified alcohol abuse and dependence within a new category "Substance Use Disorders" rather than as subsets of personality disorders. DSM-III-R (1987) described dependence as including both physiological symptoms (e.g., tolerance and withdrawal) and behavioral symptoms (e.g., impaired control over drinking). Abuse became a residual category for diagnosing those who never met the criteria for dependence, but who drank despite alcohol-related physical, social, psychological, or occupational problems, or who drank in dangerous situations, such as in conjunction with driving. This conceptualization allowed the clinician to classify meaningful aspects of a patient's behavior even when that behavior was not clearly associated with dependence. Like its predecessors, DSM-IV (1994), followed by the DSM-IV-TR (2000), included non-overlapping criteria for dependence and abuse. In a departure from earlier editions though, DSM-IV provided sub-typing of dependence based on the presence or absence of tolerance and withdrawal (physiological and psychological). The criterion for abuse was expanded to include drinking despite recurrent social, interpersonal, and legal problems as a result of alcohol use. DSM-IV highlighted the fact that symptoms of certain disorders, such as anxiety or depression, may be related to an individual's use of alcohol or other drugs. The changes were made in keeping with the growing need for reliable and valid diagnostic criteria.

Several significant changes took place in the DSM-5;[2] it refers to classifications as disorders rather than diseases. When verifying a disease one would turn to lab tests, brain scans, X-rays, or chemical imbalance tests. No such verification exists for mental illness, thus using "disorder" to indicate a "conceptualization of a clinically significant behavioral or psychological syndrome or pattern" (Telles-Correia et al., 2018).

The DSM-5 is directly correlated with the World Health Organization's (WHO) International Classification of Disease-10 (ICD 10). This change from previous versions makes it easier to measure and compare disease throughout the world. DSM-5 incorporates the ICD-10 diagnostic codes which are alphanumeric (e.g., F34.1).

The chapter organization of the entire DSM-5 volume is in a lifespan approach; this includes early developmental disorders first (i.e., neurodevelopmental and schizophrenia spectrum and other psychotic disorders), followed by diagnosis more common in adolescence and young adulthood (i.e., bipolar, depressive, and anxiety disorders), to adulthood and later life (i.e., neurocognitive disorders).

The DSM-5 moves away from disorders being considered "on or off" like a light switch (i.e., a patient has a disorder or does not have a disorder); the DSM-5 utilizes a continuum in many diagnostic categories (this is also termed dimensional approach). A continuum recognizes that symptoms are not perceptibly different but the extremes are distinct. This gives the practitioner the ability to diagnose disorders that may be less severe in some patients but nevertheless present, causing challenges in the patients' lives. Using a continuum format gives the diagnostician the choice to identify disorder as mild, moderate, severe, or extreme. The continuum thus helps with treating patients individually based on the severity of their disorder, and with identifying best practices in interventions.

A component not to be minimized when using the DSM-5 is the assessment of culture (i.e., systems of knowledge, concepts, rules, learned practices transmitted across generations including language, religion, spirituality, family structures, life-cycle stages, ceremonial rituals, customs) on the patient's behavior. Diagnostic assessments must consider whether an individual's experience, symptoms, and behaviors differ from sociocultural norms and lead to difficulties in adaptation from the patient's culture of origin, referring to the distinct ways people live in different parts of the world represented by their experiences.

One's cultural background can greatly influence how an individual perceives and presents with psychiatric symptoms, as well as impacting diagnosis and treatment. The DSM-5 includes an assessment tool entitled "Cultural Formulation Interview" which helps provide an in-depth cultural assessment (American Psychiatric Association, 2013), evaluating the patient's sociocultural norms.

Three significant changes took place in reference to substances within the *Diagnostic and Statistical Manual* (DSM-5). First is the chapter title – "Substance-Related and Addictive Disorders." Second is the elimination of the diagnostic categories of substance abuse and substance dependence; substance use disorders are now a single disorder measured on a continuum from mild to severe. No longer used are terms like alcoholism (removed in 1980 from DSM-III), abuse, dependence, or addiction (although "addiction" is in common usage in the substance use treatment field).

The third significant change is the addition of the only behavioral, non-substance disorder to this chapter. Gambling Disorder was added due to evidence that gambling behavior activates similar reward systems (American Psychiatric Association, 2013) as do other substances in this chapter.

This chapter is organized by class of substances. The practitioner is required to use the code in the particular category of the substance being diagnosed and specifically identify the substance used, e.g., F15.10 Mild Methamphetamine Use Disorder. There is no longer a category for polysubstance use. If one meets the criteria for several substances, each substance needs to be diagnosed separately.

In summary, the DSM-5 reflects the current status of scientific understandings of substance use disorders. The evolution over time demonstrates ways in which the scientific and clinical communities seek to ground helpful clinical strategies on the latest knowledge. As further discoveries and understanding of substance use and other disorders occur, additional modifications with the DSM will undoubtedly help with clinical efforts.

References

American Psychiatric Association. (2013). *Diagnostic and Statistical Manual of Mental Disorders* (5th ed.). Arlington, VA: American Psychiatric Publishing.

Blashfield, R.K., Keeley, J.W., Flanagan, E.H., & Miles, S.R. (2014). The cycle of classification: DSM-I through DSM-5. *Annual Review of Clinical Psychology*, 10, 25–51.

Kelly, J.F. (2018). E.M. Jellinek's disease concept of alcoholism. *Addiction – Society for the Study of Addiction*, July 31, 2018. doi.org/10.1111/add.14400.

Telles-Correia, D., Saraiva, S., & Gonçalves, J. (2018). Mental disorder: The need for an accurate definition. *Frontiers in Psychiatry*, 9(March), Article 64, 1–5.

Diane Rullo, Ph.D., is a core faculty member at the Barbara Solomon School of Social Work and Human Services, Walden University. She has been teaching master's level students for 28 years, as well as in the clinical treatment field for 38 years and has a private practice in Orlando, Florida.

Abstinence means no use of the substance. Abstinence may be a lifetime decision, or it may be for a particular point in time (e.g., while pregnant). This may be the case for all substances, for all substances except those prescribed by a physician, or for select substances. *Experimentation* is when a person first uses a substance. Once a person has used a drug or alcohol, at least a few times, then experimentation is no longer the classification. That is, a person can not be experimenting for months and months.

The next step on the continuum is *low-risk use*. This is when a person is using alcohol or drugs, and for which no or only a few negative consequences are occurring. This is typically viewed when use is within the standard guidelines. For example, with alcohol, standard drink guidelines exist for men and women, for consumption at any one setting as well as for over a specified period of time. *Higher risk use* is when a person is using more than what is recommended; it can also occur when negative consequences start to occur. This is an opportunity for individuals and groups to review these negative consequences, and to determine ways that they can be reduced or eliminated.

Problematic use of drugs or alcohol involves problems with oneself or others, as a result of the substance use. Many of these were highlighted in the first two chapters of this book. Some individuals who experience problematic use will rationalize it, or minimize the linkages between the problems and their personal use of the substance(s). *Abuse* is when a person continues use in spite of problems that occur.

Some people continue to use drugs or alcohol, and then enter another stage, which is *addiction* or *dependence*, and more recently *substance use disorder*.

This continuum is helpful in discussions with individuals, as well as for an understanding with a larger group or community, and will be helpful in determining the specific and personalized "nature of the problem" (if any) with that audience. The individual focus is found within the clinical or counseling segment (see Chapter 5); understanding of group level behaviors can help with prevention and education approaches (see Chapter 6).

Further understanding about the nature of usage patterns is found with the Professional Perspective 4.4 describing the continuum of use. Further insights are excerpted from the interviews with long-term advocates.

Professional Perspective 4.4

Continuum of Use

Randy Haveson, M.A.

While most people who use drugs or alcohol do so without significant life problems, there are many people for whom problems do occur. For many of these people, the problems get worse over time – something known as progression. Helpful for understanding this is the most recent clinical diagnostic framework found with the *Diagnostic and Statistical Manual* (DSM-5). The DSM-5's formal label is a Substance Use Disorder (SUD), and acknowledges the importance of a continuum. This section describes, in a less clinical way, the various stages of the continuum of use. By defining the various stages in this way, those who wish to help others, in whatever capacity as a professional or volunteer, can get a better idea of where a person of concern is on the continuum.

1. Abstinence – Someone who has never had the substance, whether it is alcohol, marijuana, cocaine, nicotine, or opiates. They have no personal experience with the drug and don't know how their body would react if the drug was present in their body.
2. Experimentation – Someone who does a drug for the first few times (one to three). The experimentation comes from wondering how their body will react to the drug/alcohol. Some people use a substance one time and realize it is not for them. They experimented and realized they do not want to use the substance again. Others do use a second or third time to see what the drug or alcohol will do multiple times, but then stop for a number of reasons and don't continue to use.
3. Social or "low-risk" use – The vast majority of people fall into this category. These are people who have a drink after work, a glass of wine at dinner, or a beer or two at a ball game. They drink for the social aspect, where alcohol is not a focal point. They tend to have a "take it or leave it"

attitude about drugs or alcohol. A main aspect of low-risk drinking is that the person drinks without the feeling of intoxication; those who drink for the result of intoxication do not fall in this category. This is also why it is impossible for people who use drugs other than alcohol to be in the low-risk category, since drug use is primarily for the intoxicating effect. Since there are so many factors that go into how the body will respond to drugs other than alcohol (e.g., stress level, stomach content, medication use, tiredness, illness, body type), it is impossible to use drugs other than alcohol in a low-risk way.

In order to help define social or low-risk drinking, the 0-1-2-3 formula is helpful. Even for people who drink in a low-risk way, there are times when they realize that not drinking, or having 0 drinks, is the best option for them. If a person does choose to drink, having no more than 1 standard drink per hour is the low-risk guideline since that's what your body and liver can handle at any one time. The low-risk guideline also means drinking no more than 2 times per week since those who drink 2 times or less in one week tend to have fewer problems with alcohol. Finally, it is important to have no more than 3 drinks per day, since those who drink four or more drinks in a setting tend to have more problems with alcohol than those who have 3 or less.

4. High-risk use – A person who goes over the low risk guidelines or uses drugs other than alcohol. Since this is a continuum, some people go back and forth between high-risk and low-risk use. They might engage in low-risk use most of the time, but periodically engage in high-risk use.
5. Problematic – Someone who experiences a problem in their lives directly related to their alcohol or other drug use. Whether it is a hangover, a DUI, an accident or fall, a fight with a friend or loved one, or anything else that causes trouble in their lives, this is problematic. Many people experience a problem in their lives as a result of drinking or other drug use and say, "Wow, I'm never doing that again." And they don't. They go back to low-risk use and they stay there.
6. Abuse – Someone who continues to drink or use in a high-risk way even though they experience problems in their lives as a result of their use. This is where the term "drug abuse" or "alcohol abuse" comes from. At this stage people use defense mechanisms to explain their behavior and hide from the fact that their alcohol or other drug use is having a detrimental effect on their lives.
7. Addiction – Someone who continues to drink or use in an abusive way and crosses the line into addiction. This is a one-way line. Once a person crosses this line, they can never return to low-risk drinking. The only way to tell if someone is addicted or an abuser is their inability to stop or control their use. A good test is to have someone abstain for a month or have them stick to the 0-1-2-3 low-risk guidelines, and see if someone has control or not. A good definition of addiction is "The inability to *consistently* control how much or how often you drink."

While clinical assessments exist for many ailments or diseases, which may include how advanced these are, no simple test exists for drug or alcohol dependence. This is why it is such a tricky disease. This continuum helps provide a general idea of which stage someone is in, and how severe a problem someone might have. This continuum offers a guideline helpful for reinforcing good choices and better defining if someone is starting to engage in dangerous behavior. The formal assessment by a trained clinician, using the DSM-5 criteria, is the most grounded approach for diagnosis.

Resource

Haveson, R. (2016). *Party with a Plan: The Guide to Low-Risk Drinking.* n.p.: RISE Publishing.

Randy Haveson, M.A., has worked in the substance abuse field since 1986. He has worked on four college campuses as the coordinator of AOD and health education. As a professional speaker, he has worked with over 100 campuses, speaking about harm reduction, self-esteem, leadership, and supporting students in recovery.

> *So many of the ideas in AA, like the concept of addiction as chronic disease, are implicit; they don't go around talking about it as a chronic disease. But it is implicit in the idea that you are supposed to stay forever in the organization. Because you could go back to drinking. That's another way of saying "chronic disease."*
> Thomasina Borkman

> *I think there is much confusion in the psychological and counseling communities as to whether you call addiction a disease or disorder or whatever term you like to use. The major challenge should be treating the patient as they present.*
> Robert Lynn

Continuum of Care

Correlated with the continuum of use, although not a direct relationship, is the continuum of care. This includes prevention, intervention, treatment, and recovery and support services. These elements are related in fairly straightforward ways, as prevention would be appropriate to keep an individual or group of people from progressing to a more harmful status, and something like treatment and recovery approaches would be appropriate for those who need or have been in treatment. Also, because of the content details for each of these, more information and foundational materials are found in Chapters 5 and 6.

Prevention refers to approaches designed to keep problems or negative consequences from occurring. As will be specified in Chapter 6 (Prevention and Education), it will be important to clarify, both generally and specifically, what it is that counselors and leaders seek to prevent. This may include impaired driving, injuries, harm to self or others, property damage, and many of the other outcomes identified in the first two chapters of this book. Prevention focuses on keeping something negative, harmful, or bad from happening. Prevention is often discussed when problems are found, as the question is often "How could this have been prevented?" or "What can be done to prevent something similar from occurring in the future, with this person or others?"

Intervention includes strategies that are instituted to keep a negative consequence from continuing or from getting worse. Intervention involves individualized, group, or societal approaches to halt a problematic behavior. Ideally, interventions are done as early as possible, when the situation isn't as bad as it would be if left unaddressed. The challenge is one of awareness of a problem, which may not occur until there is some progression. Intervention is appropriate for individualized events or situations (such as impaired driving or domestic violence), as well as for those that have grown and require some therapeutic process (i.e., treatment). Many more details on intervention, including a distinction between "Small i" and "Big I" interventions, are found in Chapter 5.

Treatment is appropriate when an individual or family has reached a point where multiple approaches are needed to halt the problematic behavior. Treatment for substance use disorders typically includes a variety of approaches, as a single strategy (e.g., medication, group therapy, individual counseling) will not be sufficient. As will be described in Chapter 5, quality treatment includes numerous approaches, can vary in length, and involves family members. Treatment is not, in fact, a simple solution and a cure-all.

Recovery and Support Services – following treatment efforts, individuals are in recovery from drug and/or alcohol dependence. This lifelong process generally cannot be done alone, and requires engagement in various services that will support the outcomes of treatment, primarily that of being abstinent. The aim is to not just avoid a relapse, but to engage in a positive and healthy life. Typically included in recovery are involvement in self-help groups and engagement of a sponsor; other support services, whether counseling or life skills development, may further enhance the likelihood of success in recovery.

The overall context with this Continuum of Care relates to the point of Chapter 3 (Why Be Concerned?); that chapter helped clarify that the aim of being involved with leadership for substance abuse prevention is not just about problem reduction, but also about promoting human potential. Because of the inclusion of treatment and recovery as distinct elements of this continuum, the assumption may be that the focus is on substance use disorders and reducing their presence and impact. While that is important, the larger issue is how to maximize healthy living. Many people will not use substances, and most people will not have many negative consequences associated with drugs or alcohol. Some people will become harmfully involved, and some will become dependent. The continuum of care is envisioned to help keep all people as far toward the prevention end as possible. This continuum also acknowledges that some people will move, through their behavior, toward the elements that need intervention, with some of these people requiring treatment and/or recovery and support services.

Further explanation about the Continuum of Care is found within the context of a comprehensive initiative. Whether a comprehensive approach is envisioned for a community, a school, a university, a state, the nation, or another setting, the important perspective is that a variety of strategies are included, and involve a wide range of individuals and organizations. Professional Perspective 4.5 provides further insight on this, as well as the content found in Chapter 8 (Resourceful Approaches). In addition, insights from long-term advocates are provided to further illustrate the nature and complexity of having a fully-constituted continuum of care.

Professional Perspective 4.5

Comprehensive Approaches to Prevention

William DeJong, Ph.D.

All health-related behavior – including alcohol, tobacco, and other drug use – is determined by several interacting factors, and therefore prevention efforts to reduce substance use and its negative consequences will be more successful if they address these multiple influences in tandem. This requires an intervention plan that weaves together several evidence-based strategies into a comprehensive and integrated whole.

The first step is to conduct a thorough analysis of the problem that answers the following questions: Which population groups are most affected by the problem? What factors cause or contribute to that problem? Whose behavior needs to change to address the problem, and what exactly do they need to do differently? What interventions have already been attempted to affect the desired behavior change, and what can be learned from those efforts?

The scope and direction of this analysis is best guided by the social ecological framework (Golden et al., 2015), which goes beyond the individual level and interpersonal factors that influence behavior to include environmental factors that operate at institutional, community, and societal levels. In turn, this same framework can be used to organize a strategic planning process for addressing the identified determinants.

At the individual level, there are several behavioral determinants outlined by behavior change theories, including the Health Belief Model, the Theory of Planned Behavior, and Social Cognitive Theory (National Cancer Institute, 2005). These theories are best applied in combination so that all of the individual-level determinants listed below are considered during the planning process (Eldredge et al., 2016). Behavior change is more likely to occur under the following conditions:

- Knowledge – People know basic facts about the health problem (its seriousness, warning signs, who is at risk, their personal susceptibility) and the behavioral alternative's key features.
- Beliefs and Attitudes – People have beliefs and attitudes that are consonant with and support the behavioral alternative.

- Perceived Outcomes – People believe that the behavioral alternative provides benefits they personally value and can expect to receive if they change their behavior, and that the alternative presents more advantages than disadvantages.
- Social Norms – People perceive social pressure to perform the behavioral alternative, based on what they observe other people do (descriptive norms) or what they think other people expect them to do (injunctive norms).
- Personal Norms – People believe that, compared to their current behavior, the behavioral alternative is more consistent with their self-image, values, standards, and goals.
- Behavioral Skills – People have the skills necessary to perform the behavioral alternative at specific times and places (e.g., self-assessment, self-management, refusal skills, relapse prevention).
- Perceived Behavioral Control – People believe they are capable of performing the behavioral alternative and can overcome any barriers that might stand in their way (that is, they hold "self-efficacy" beliefs) (Bandura, 1986).
- Cues to Action – There are environmental stimuli (engineered by oneself or others) that trigger the new behavior or remind people of their behavior change objective.

Factors operating at the interpersonal level are family, group, and peer influences: their expectations for other people's behavior, the behavior they model and reinforce, and the social support they can provide, especially when those they care about are trying to change their behavior. Where appropriate, people should be encouraged to seek out social support to help them initiate and then sustain their behavior change efforts.

At the institutional level, interventions to influence health behavior can address organizations' policies and their enforcement, as well as whether they make available educational programs, products and services, incentive programs, and other resources that can inform, motivate, and facilitate behavior change.

At the community level, interventions can address the availability and quality of education, public safety, and public health and medical services provided by governmental and nongovernmental agencies; opportunities and supports for civic participation; and improved local laws and their enforcement. An additional option is to focus on the "built environment" through land use and tax policy, zoning regulations, and infrastructure investment.

At the societal level, interventions can focus on changing state or national policy through new laws and regulations. To be effective, a policy change has to be accompanied by a funding appropriation and an enforcement mechanism, which in turn needs to be publicized to produce a deterrent effect (DeJong & Hingson, 1998). Interventions can also be designed to address media influences on behavior, including entertainment programming, news coverage, commercial advertising, and social media content. Other societal level factors – for example, demographic trends, economic cycles, and income distribution – are also important influences, but addressing those is beyond what a substance use prevention program can accomplish.

To illustrate how applying the social ecological framework can be used to organize a strategic planning process, consider some of the many program and policy options for addressing underage drinking. While this example focuses on youth alcohol use, the framework can be applied to animate the planning process for preventing any type of substance-use-related problem.

At the individual level, among other topics, school-based education programs and brief interventions could provide data to correct students' exaggerated beliefs about how much alcohol their peers are actually drinking (Perkins, 2003) and outline the latest research on alcohol's effect on brain development, which continues until young adults reach their mid-twenties (Hermens et al., 2013).

At the interpersonal level, parents, guardians, and other adult caretakers could be taught how to initiate and sustain an ongoing dialog with their children, beginning at age nine and continuing until they reach the legal drinking age (21 years in the U.S.) (Kuntsche & Kuntsche, 2016). These conversations should focus on family rules in support of the minimum legal drinking age, the importance of obeying the law, and how to recognize and respond appropriately to peer influences, as well as on the developmental challenges their children are facing so as to mitigate the root causes of youth substance use and other risk behaviors. Parents could also be guided to monitor their children's activities more effectively, ideally in concert with other parents, most of whom believe that discouraging underage drinking is a priority concern (Fairlie et al., 2015).

At the institutional level, a responsible retailing program could work with owners and managers of bars, restaurants, and alcohol retailers to train staff to check ID and refuse sales to minors and patrons who seem to be intoxicated, followed by the use of "mystery shoppers" to monitor and improve staff performance (Grube et al., 2018). Similarly, colleges and universities could require student organizations to follow guidelines for reducing alcohol availability at social events (e.g., requiring a bartender certified in responsible beverage service, enforcing limits on the types and amount of alcohol present, restricting the invitation list to students of legal age) (Zimmerman & DeJong, 2003).

At the community level, community leaders could explore imposing zoning restrictions to decrease the number and density of alcohol outlets and pass local ordinances to prohibit "happy hours" and restrict the hours of sale. Local law enforcement efforts could also be enhanced, with compliance checks at retail establishments to enforce the minimum legal drinking age and stricter enforcement of social host laws to penalize parents or others who allow minors to drink alcohol on their premises (Hingson & White, 2014).

Finally, at the societal level, state officials could pass laws to increase alcohol excise taxes, which would influence minors more than other alcohol consumers (Elder et al., 2010); impose greater penalties on minors who are in possession of alcohol or use a fake ID to make an illegal alcohol purchase, and on persons who provide or serve alcohol to minors; mandate responsible beverage service training for alcohol servers; and reduce the per se limit that legally defines alcohol-impaired driving to 0.05% BAC (blood alcohol concentration) or lower (Golden et al., 2015).

There is research that demonstrates that each of these measures would help reduce alcohol-related harms among youth, but their impact on changing youth alcohol use would be even greater if resources were available to enact many or all of them in concert as part of a high-profile, comprehensive campaign.

The social ecological framework can be applied in this way to address the full range of public health problems related to substance use. Doing so will help intervention planners identify a complete set of behavioral determinants, consider multiple program and policy options to address those determinants, and identify opportunities for creating a synergistic and comprehensive prevention effort.

References

Bandura, A. (1986). *Social Foundations of Thought and Action: A Social Cognitive Theory*. Englewood Cliffs, NJ: Prentice Hall.

DeJong, W. & Hingson, R. (1998). Strategies to reduce driving under the influence of alcohol. *Annual Review of Public Health*, 19, 359–378.

Elder, R.W., Lawrence, B., Ferguson, A., Naimi, T.S., Brewer, R.D., Chattopadhyay, S.K., ... & Task Force on Community Preventive Services. (2010). The effectiveness of tax policy interventions for reducing excessive alcohol consumption and related harms. *American Journal of Preventive Medicine*, 38(2), 217–229.

Eldredge, L.K.B., Markham, C.M., Ruiter, R.A.C., Fernández, M.E., Kok, G., & Parcel, G.S. (2016). *Planning Health Promotion Programs: An Intervention Mapping Approach* (4th ed.). San Francisco, CA: Jossey-Bass.

Fairlie, A.M., DeJong, W., & Wood, M.D. (2015). Local support for alcohol control policies and perceptions of neighborhood issues in two college communities. *Substance Abuse*, 36(3), 289–296.

Golden, S., McLeroy, K., Green, L.W, Earp, J.A., & Lieberman, L.D. (2015). Upending the social ecological model to guide health promotion efforts toward policy and environmental change. *Health Education & Behavior*, 42(Suppl. 1), S8–S14.

Grube, J.W., DeJong, W., DeJong, M., Lipperman-Kreda, S., & Krevor, B.S. (2018). Effects of a responsible retailing mystery shop intervention on age verification by servers and clerks in alcohol outlets: A cluster randomised cross-over trial. *Drug and Alcohol Review*, 37(6), 774–781.

Hermens, D.F., Lagopoulos, J., Tobias-Webb, J., De Regt, T., Dore, G., Juckes, L., ... & Hickie, I.B. (2013). Pathways to alcohol-induced brain impairment in young people: A review. *Cortex*, 49(1), 3–17.

Hingson, R. & White, A. (2014). New research findings since the 2007 Surgeon General's Call to Action to Prevent and Reduce Underage Drinking: A review. *Journal of Studies on Alcohol and Drugs*, 75(1), 158–169.

Kuntsche, S. & Kuntsche, E. (2016). Parent-based interventions for preventing or reducing adolescent substance use: A systematic literature review. *Clinical Psychology Review*, 45, 89–101.

National Cancer Institute. (2005). *Theory at a Glance: A Guide for Health Promotion Practice* (2nd ed.). Washington, D.C.: National Institutes of Health, U.S. Department of Health and Human Services.

Perkins, H. (2003). *The Social Norms Approach to Preventing School and College Age Substance Abuse: A Handbook for Educators, Counselors, and Clinicians.* San Francisco, CA: Jossey-Bass.

Zimmerman, R. & DeJong, W. (2003). *Safe Lanes on Campus: A Guide for Preventing Impaired Driving and Underage Drinking.* Washington, D.C.: U.S. Department of Education, Higher Education Center for Alcohol and Other Drug Prevention.

William DeJong, Ph.D., is presently an adjunct professor at Tufts Medical School, in Boston, Massachusetts, and formerly a professor at the Boston University School of Public Health. His primary interests are alcohol, tobacco, and other drug prevention, health communications, intervention planning, and program evaluation.

We need to integrate alcohol and drugs, particularly treatment, into that kind of a comprehensive approach.

Darlind Davis

I think you really need to understand how complicated trying to deal with these issues, and again whether it's drugs, alcohol, tobacco, unsafe sex, again risky behaviors in the recesses of the teen mind, how really complicated that is.

Ralph Blackman

But I think a lot of the education that we do now is actually called prevention but it's actually after-the-fact. We could learn a lot from those in recovery – what worked for them and what was useless even as they become dependent.

Teresa Johnston

The workplace was a major player, the family was a major player, the community was a major player. Brink Smithers believed wholeheartedly in education about alcoholism, which at this point was the National Council on Alcoholism and he felt it needed a larger presence.

Gail Milgram

Professionals should know that there is a resource. How are they going to access knowledge about Alcoholics Anonymous? AA treats more people than all professionals in the United States, put together, in one year. It's free. It's a gigantic volunteer effort that is practically unrecognized. It's a recovery-oriented system of care that the professionals in addiction are now starting to talk about more regularly. They should know about the value of self-help/mutual aid groups such as AA, use it, and respect it. It is kind of invisible, and complicated by the traditions of AA.

Thomasina Borkman

> It almost has to be a public health model. It has to be from the pediatrician to the classroom teacher to the science teacher to health education to PE, just like we are trying to deal with obesity.
>
> BJ McConnell

Nature of Strategies

This final section of Chapter 4 on Foundations provides a brief overview of strategies appropriate for addressing the range of issues associated with substance abuse. Strategies are appropriate for individuals at all places on the Continuum of Use. Similarly, strategies will be appropriate for all aspects of the Continuum of Care. Regardless of what approaches or overarching design is undertaken, the overall perspective is that, to address substance abuse issues appropriately and adequately requires a comprehensive approach. As will be outlined in more detail, "comprehensive" essentially means doing a variety of different things using a variety of different individuals, groups, and organizations.

These strategies are seen with the broad perspectives of "what" and "how": the specific approaches to be considered (e.g., policy, program, training, service, activity) as well as the processes used to prepare and implement these (e.g., planning activities, task force, organization, engagement of others). Specifics on the "what" are found in Chapters 5 and 6, and details about many of the "how" elements are included in Chapters 7, 8, and 9.

With a focus on the strategies themselves (the "what"), consider the framework used to distinguish the first two chapters of this book: the individual and the environment. Strategies can be viewed in much the same way: individually focused and environmental based. A current example with the college and university setting is found with the CollegeAIM resource; this reviews current scientific literature and incorporates reviews based on cost, obstacles, and other factors. Overall, CollegeAIM offers two distinct designations based on the professional, scientific literature: individual and environmental.

Finally, the Institute of Medicine has developed a helpful framework for strategies considered for implementation, particularly from a proactive or public health perspective. This approach is useful for targeting messages and approaches, and provides the contextual framework of *universal*, *selected*, or *indicated*.[5] *Universal* approaches are those designed for everyone – these include policies, public awareness, procedures, and any approach that offers a "broad sweep" in a community, region, or the entire nation. *Selected* approaches represent one way of narrowing down the strategies; these can apply to a school or community, a work setting or a region, or nationally. They are based on a circumstance or set of factors, such as a group based on high-risk factors or demographics (e.g., college fraternities and sororities, children of alcoholics, those with a family member with a drug or alcohol dependence pattern). *Indicated* approaches are those based on individualized or personalized issues, concerns, or needs. These are focused because of specific issues that arise with a person, and perhaps triggered by legal offenses, medical situations, or other risk behavior.

Summary

Having helpful foundations is an important part of substance abuse prevention work, just as it is important for most areas of study and work. This chapter was designed to provide a broader perspective on many key factors associated with the range of specialty work found. Professionals with preparation and training in treatment may not typically see the prevention considerations, nor will those with a public health or community education background see the range of factors associated with treatment and recovery concerns. Beyond this, most of the people with whom professionals working on substance abuse issues come into contact are not informed or current on the science surrounding substance abuse prevention and substance use disorders.

This chapter is designed to provide some common perspectives and approaches, while acknowledging that increased depth is provided in other chapters, and significantly greater depth is found only with extensive study, research, and experience. Three overarching points help summarize this chapter. First, no simple answer or approach exists; there is no magic bullet for substance abuse issues. Second, it is important to acknowledge that a comprehensive approach is what is needed to address substance abuse issues; that means doing as much of this as possible. Third, this vital work best occurs within a "systems approach" and an organized plan to coordinate the range of strategies and services; all elements must work together and seek consistency to achieve the desired, shared outcomes for individuals, groups, and society.

Notes

1 Jellinek, E.M. (1960). *The Disease Concept of Alcoholism*. New Haven, CT: Hillhouse Press.
2 National Cancer Institute. (2005). *Theory at a Glance: A Guide for Health Promotion Practice* (2nd ed.). Washington, DC: National Institutes of Health, U.S. Department of Health and Human Services.
3 Prochaska, J. and DiClemente, C. (1983). Stages and processes of self-change in smoking: Toward an integrative model of change. *Journal of Consulting and Clinical Psychology*, 5, 390–395.
4 Silbersweig, D.A. (2015) Bridging the brain–mind divide in psychiatric education: The neuro-bio-psycho-social formulation. *Asian Journal of Psychiatry*, 17, 122–123.
5 Springer, J.R and Phillips, J. (2007). *The Institute of Medicine Framework and Its Implication for the Advancement of Prevention Policy, Programs and Practice*. Washington, DC: Institute of Medicine, U.S. Department of Health and Human Services.

5 Skills for Intervention, Treatment, and Recovery

This chapter focuses primarily on issues associated with substance use disorders. The specific portions of the chapter that address treatment and recovery definitely go hand in hand with this clinical assessment. The intervention segment, which typically links to treatment, can be viewed in a broader context, as it also addresses situations that may not be tied to a clinical diagnosis. This includes those that are more acute, such as violence and drunk driving. In brief, this chapter addresses three out of four of the elements of the Continuum of Care described in Chapter 4.

At the outset of this chapter, a central point is a reminder about its overall context, particularly based on the nature of the chapter's focus. It is important to recall that, typically, the progression toward later stages of the substance use disorder assessment has taken a long time – many years – to develop. First, these types of services and strategies must be individualized; there is not a "one size fits all" perspective. Related to this is the second point: there is no "magic answer" for addressing substance use disorders; even with personalized approaches, typical strategies involve a range of modalities. Success with addressing these disorders is not easy nor is it simplistic; however, best practices and protocols do exist. Third, the role of the professional is vital for success with these efforts. While many of the components with intervention and recovery can be accomplished without formal professional services, the involvement of trained and competent professionals throughout this process is vital.

While none of the chapters in this book are designed to provide an in-depth understanding of the specified topic, that caveat is probably more relevant for this chapter due to the personalized nature of appropriate services. A parallel to the legal environment may be helpful; in that setting, the standard of "due process" is widely espoused and respected. The corollary question is "what process is due?" with the response based on various legal and situational factors. For this chapter on intervention, treatment, and recovery, typical standards include quality care, effective approaches, desired outcomes, and helpful processes. The related questions focus on defining these within the context of current science-based knowledge, best practices, and individualized needs. This context serves to undergird the chapter's contents within the three broad topics of intervention, treatment, and recovery.

Intervention: The Response Process

In its basic sense, intervention is the process used to halt a harmful behavior. However, the typical impression of "intervention" when talking about drugs or alcohol is that its purpose is to get an individual into treatment. This section takes a broader view of intervention, and includes its role with substance use disorders as well as problematic situations that may be localized and one-time in nature.

As a starting point, consider the word "intervention"; when using this term with the general public, the typical reaction is two-fold: "It's about treatment" and "I can't do it." For whatever reason, the phrase conjures up these common reactions; and these reactions are accompanied by various perceptions, attitudes, stereotypes, myths, and more about substance abuse, dependence, and related issues. What would others' reactions be like if the term was different, such as "respond," "attend to," or another phrase? Thus, if someone was describing the substance use behavior of a person about whom they were concerned, the reaction by others would likely be different if the language talked about the need to "respond" or "attend to" rather than the need to "intervene." Thus, this section on "intervention" can easily, and perhaps more appropriately, be named "the response process."

Two additional elements are important regarding interventions. Again, the typical view about intervention is that it is designed to get a person involved with appropriate treatment services. While that is true, interventions can be used for acute as well as chronic situations. First, consider a situation involving drugs or alcohol with a person on the verge of harmful involvement for self or others; this could be with situations such as driving, use of machinery, assault, property damage, or harassment. An intervention to halt that activity could be deemed very appropriate (except, perhaps, by the individual on the receiving end of the intervention). Second, intervention at earlier stages of the progression found with a substance use disorder is appropriate. There is no need to wait to do an intervention until treatment is urgent; interventions are appropriate at earlier stages along the continuum of use, at earlier stages of the progression of the substance use disorder. While it may be more difficult to ascertain the extent of progression at earlier stages, and while the resistance and denial of the person of concern may be higher, the progression of the disease within the entire biopsychosocial life of this person will be less.

Finally, it is important to consider intervention more as a process rather than as an event. With many interventions, especially at various stages along the progression with substance use disorders, the outcome will not be what is desired. Interventions ultimately seek a change in behavior, as that is what is sought by the concerned individual(s). Some desired changes may be achieved for a short period of time. However, to achieve sustained results, the necessary treatment and support services that are due must be implemented. Further, multiple interventions may very well be required to achieve the appropriate results.

The view of intervention as a process is directly relevant to individuals for whom progression is occurring, a central aspect of the Substance Use Disorder diagnosis included with the DSM-5. If the progression is viewed along a continuum (such as specified in Chapter 4 with the Continuum of Use), then behavior will be getting increasingly worse for the individual who is progressing with the disease. If the Continuum of Care (from Prevention to Recovery) is overlaid on the Continuum of Use, the activity of "intervention" takes place when problems start to occur, and continues with increases in the nature and scope of problems. While initial interventions may be short and targeted to focused problem behaviors, later interventions would appropriately be directed toward treatment services of some nature. Consider interventions as a process, with a series of interventions that grow in nature and scope. In a simplistic way, consider initial interventions as a "Small i" type of intervention, and later interventions as a "Big I" type of intervention. With that continuum, as problems associated with a person's drug/alcohol use grow, the interventions move from the "Small i" interventions to larger and larger ones, and ultimately toward the "Big I" intervention, whose goal is to get the individual into treatment. The aim of any intervention is to halt the problems associated with drugs and alcohol; thus, the model provided here works across various different situations, both acute and short-term situations, as well as long-term ones.

To help understand the intervention process, a four-part model is offered; this includes Awareness, Concern, Contact(s), and Follow-up(s). The model is appropriate for any individual problems with drugs or alcohol, whether acute or chronic. While initially considering these steps for short-term, immediate, and acute situations, the model is also appropriate for individuals seeking to address their concerns about another person's increasing problems and progression along the continuum of a substance use disorder. The concerned individual does not need to be clinically trained, as the process works for a wide range of areas of concern.

The model is appropriate for any of a range of settings and individuals; this can be helpful with family members, work colleagues, friends, acquaintances, and others. Attention to each of these steps is important for adequately completing the process of an intervention. For example, without the first step of awareness, there would be no acknowledgment of a situation that would even warrant attention; similarly, with awareness but no concern, it is unlikely that any further action (the contact) would occur.

Finally, it is important to acknowledge the anxiety or nervousness often underlying any involvement with another person, particularly when this has to do with that individual's abuse of drugs or alcohol. Much of this has to do with the aura surrounding the term "intervention"; reframing this as a "response process" may help with some of those feelings. The concerned individual may seek support or guidance from trained professionals, before or after involvement with this process. Similarly, it is important to manage one's own expectations regarding the likely outcomes associated with such an intervention or series of interventions; while important to do, interventions often do not result in the desired outcome. This is not a reason to not engage in the process, but rather to persevere (thus, the steps called "Contact(s)" and "Follow-up(s)" with an emphasis on the plural form of each of these steps).

Awareness: The first step is awareness of some behaviors associated with problematic use of drugs or alcohol. Some of these are immediate or acute, such as an individual preparing to drive a car or operate a boat while under the influence of substances. This may be an immediate hazard or problem, and may or may not result in legal consequences. Others may be based on changing patterns over time, such as tolerance, blackouts, withdrawal, work performance, interpersonal skills, or responsibilities. To help with awareness, consider using as an organizing structure the four areas identified in Chapter 1 for the reasons why people use drugs or alcohol: Physical, Social, Emotional, and Cognitive. If individual issues are extreme or become progressively worse, or if a variety of different issues becomes evident, these contribute to "awareness" of a problem or area of concern.

Some examples within these areas are helpful. For the physical area, this could include injuries, sleep disturbances, lowered energy levels, withdrawal symptoms, use of increasing quantities, use over longer periods of time, lowered effects of substances, and lack of control over decision-making about use. Emotional issues include decreased emotional control, mood swings, lack of self-care, withdrawal, self-condemnation, anxiety, and use to address emotions. With cognitive factors, this may include forgetfulness, blackouts, poor judgment, lack of attention to detail, lowered quantity and quality of performance, lack of followthrough on a commitment or obligation, and decreased attention and concentration. The social area includes personality change, physical aggression and fighting, argumentativeness, lowered involvement in leisure time interests, engagement with others who are heavy users or abusers of substances, and deterioration of interpersonal relationships.

The essential part of "awareness" is that signs and symptoms are present, and that they can be seen. A caution is that some of the signs may have nothing to do with drugs or alcohol, but may be reflective of some other underlying area of concern, or may be of concern in and of themselves. Awareness represents the cornerstone of an appropriate response or intervention, and its specifics will be used in the third component of this process.

The framework provided with the DSM-5 (see Professional Perspective 4.3) comprises the items included with the Substance Use Disorders diagnosis. With this, the items include two or more of 11 items: Hazardous use; Social/interpersonal problems related to use; Neglected major roles to use; Withdrawal; Tolerance; Used larger amounts/longer; Repeated attempts to quit/control use; Much time spent using; Physical/psychological problems related to use; Activities given up to use; and Craving. While these are clinically assessed criteria, an understanding of their nature and scope can be helpful for all when attempting to ascertain whether interventions are appropriate. However, the key point is that if an individual's behaviors or lifestyle are becoming problematic or of concern to others, then having an intervention is likely to be warranted.

Some of the long-term advocates provided insights regarding intervention and treatment services. Among their insights are the following:

Certainly screening, brief intervention, and referral to treatment are now the soup du jour, but they are still underutilized.

Teresa Johnston

I think what I'm most known for is the Rutgers Alcohol Problem Index, the RAPI, that I developed with Erich Labouvie 30 years ago. It's kind of a fluke really; he and I just had this list of alcohol problems and we did some factor analysis (not even sophisticated stuff) and we came up with this short little list of problems related to alcohol use. Then Alan Marlatt used it in one of his studies as a screening instrument when he was doing one of the first big prevention programs and after that it became used throughout the world.

Helene White

Concern: The second component of the intervention or response process is "concern." The issue of "concern" is personal, and is based on several factors, such as an individual's level of information and understanding, his/her values, an assessment about whether to become involved with the life of another person. Just as this book's Chapter 3 is titled "Why Be Concerned?," this "Concern" element of the intervention process is included to emphasize the perspective that there are choices regarding whether or not to get involved.

To place this in context, the first step – Awareness – is a necessary precursor in this process; without awareness, there is no need to be concerned. However, with awareness comes a decision point: what is appropriate to do, with this situation, with this person, and at this or another point in time. Some considerations within this context include the following:

- How clear it is that the behavior is drug- or alcohol-related, or that drugs or alcohol are the cause of the behavior
- Based on the relationship with the individual, what obligations exist
- What implications might involvement place on the relationship
- How the behavior compares with others' behavior
- The extent of the problem and its impact on the individual and others
- How long the problem has been occurring
- A general view of whether or not to get involved with anyone else's life
- How much time it might take, and other priorities of the intervener
- An assessment of personal safety or risk.

These and many other items factor into an individual's decision about whether to get involved. Through personal assessment, self-reflection, discussion with others, and potentially consultation with a professional, the individual intervener decides whether to become involved. To not get involved may actually be part of the enabling process, which thus allows the person's drug or alcohol problems to continue unabated and unaddressed. The factors involved in the decision may be excuses, rationalization, or minimization of the issue and/or person of concern. That is precisely the point of having this element of Concern specified clearly as part of the decision-making process. It is ultimately an individual's values that determine this, based on many personal factors, prior experiences, and the assessment of the situation.

A similar calculus of decision-making occurs throughout one's life, with all types of situations. When driving a car on a high-speed highway, for example, the driver is constantly making assessments about how to handle various situations, based on speed, weather, road conditions, and more. If another driver, bicyclist, or pedestrian appears to be in distress, the decision about whether to stop and help may include factors such as the setting and safety issues. Similarly, with substance abuse, having an impaired individual seeking to drive a car would require an immediate response, based on the concerned person's assessment of the situation and personal values.

Related to this topic of Concern is the common self-perception that a potential intervener does not feel qualified to do this. An individual may believe that an intervention is appropriate, but not know how to proceed. Based on this lack of confidence, the specific approaches identified in the next step – Contact(s) – will be helpful. In addition, it is appropriate for the potential intervener to seek professional consultation to gain clarification about and support for proceeding; the professional may also provide further tips and suggestions to maximize a quality process.

Perspectives of long-term advocates regarding the intervention process are helpful:

> *I was intervened upon by four non-alcoholic attorneys and it was a classic Johnson Institute intervention. And what I liked about having been intervened upon is that I was so eloquent in saying "Oh thanks very much for coming out, I appreciate it you guys, I have a gourmet dinner so I don't have time to go right now, thank you very much." And I was articulate and eloquent and I was pitting them one against the other, "I drove you home drunk" and so on, and it was working, I was breaking them down and at the same time there's a tape running in the back of my head saying "Could this be the end? Could this be it? I hope they don't stop. I hope I can't convince them." So the words are coming out and I am winning, I am dividing and conquering and in the meantime I have this voice in the back of my head saying "I hope they nail you, I hope you can put the plug in the jug, I hope this will be the end." And I have these two things I will always remember, the two competing debates and so then one of them said "Listen, you are going and you are going voluntarily, and if you don't go voluntarily don't ever ask any of us to do anything for you ever again." So I let that sit for a while, and they thought I was going to walk, and I said I'd go and they were surprised. So I went to a detox in Paterson, New Jersey, Straight Street and Narrow Street.*
> William Kane

> *People are trying to adapt the alcohol brief intervention programs to marijuana use and it will be interesting to see whether those are going to be as effective or if they're going to need something different.*
> Helene White

> *What contributed to our success? The timing was right and ready and open, and New Jersey is kind of open to things, they don't scoff at innovation. It's an active state, they have attitudes and they are in your face but they hit the ground running and they are kind of pleased about that, and not always amicable that is the case, there is energy here.*
> William Kane

Contact(s): This next step is the actual "how" of the intervention. Once the awareness is identified, and the concern is clarified in the mind of the intervener, the focus turns to the intervention itself. As identified in the beginning of this section, having the actual discussion about an individual's drug or alcohol abuse is often viewed as scary, intimidating, inappropriate, and something to be avoided. Thus, it can be helpful to reframe the intervention with other descriptive labels, such as "response process," "conversation," "confrontation," and "carefrontation."

This process of having "the contact" can be organized within five basic steps. These are general parameters and a broad framework. What is most important in making the contact is for the intervener to make the conversation personal by using his/her own language, and sharing his/her own "heart" or spirit. The precise wording is not what is critical, and the conversation does not need to be long or elaborate.

The five steps include:

1. *I care about you.* This seeks to establish a safe place and a context for the conversation; it suggests that the intervener is committed to the individual's wellbeing and overall health and safety. It is this specific foundation that can be returned to throughout the conversation, to remind the person of concern about why the intervener is having the conversation.
2. *Here is what I see.* This focuses on the behavior of the individual, as well as what may be observed with the impact on other people or situations. It builds directly upon the first part of the intervention model (Awareness), so specific examples and observations are important to cite. Since some of the awareness and concern is due to patterns of behavior or changes over time, these should be specified clearly.
3. *Here is what concerns me.* This step shifts the focus onto the intervener and emphasizes his/her personal feelings. It emphasizes why this conversation is occurring, and reflects back on the first statement of expressing caring. This can incorporate the intervener's views about the individual's future potential, consequences associated with continuation of the problematic behavior, or other factors. It may also include personal feelings such as embarrassment, neglect, or hurt, as well as concerns and feelings due to prior similar conversations with this person. This step may also include personal consequences, such as those involved with the intervener (e.g., loss of friendship or relationship).
4. *What do you think can be done?* In this step, the focus is on potential next steps. This may elicit a commitment to change, and it may generate a discussion about ways in which the intervener's concerns can be addressed. It is appropriate here for the intervener to share specific strategies and approaches.
5. *I will help in any way if you would like.* With this step, the message is one of a partnership or shared responsibility. This does not leave the person of concern alone or "stranded"; nor does it put the entire responsibility upon the intervener. The locus of control is with the individual, and the intervener is offering a commitment to be involved to help resolve the areas of concern. This step also has a linkage to the "Follow-up(s)" element of the overall intervention framework.

With the conduct of the intervention, the intervener should be clear about his/her expectations. The aim is one of success; however, for various reasons, many interventions are not successful. The key points are to maximize the opportunity for success, and to acknowledge that this is a process; thus, the label for Contact is specified in the plural form with an "s" provided. This means that an intervener should be prepared for an outcome that may not be fully satisfactory: the individual of concern may not agree to the desired behavior, or s/he may agree and start to change but not continue that changed behavior. The fact that an intervention may not be successful (or is likely to not be successful) should not be the reason for not pursuing it; an individual who is concerned should make the attempt and demonstrate his/her caring. For a broader perspective, it is not clear what, specifically, makes a difference with an intervention, and what might make it successful. It may be due to the specifics surrounding the intervention (e.g., problematic behavior), how long the problems have been occurring, how many prior interventions have occurred, who is doing the intervention, what the consequences of no change might be, or simply that the individual doesn't want to experience future interventions.

This factor of the potential or probable need for multiple contacts dovetails with the progression of the substance use disorder, and the view of intervention itself along a continuum from "Small i" to "Big I" interventions. Some interventions will be repeated, and others will morph into different formats and intensity over time. The key elements with the five steps identified still work, and the incorporation of consequences for the intervener (perhaps modifying or ending the relationship) may become increasingly incorporated.

Some additional aspects of the Contact(s) element are relevant. First, the discussion can be short or long, depending on the individual circumstances associated with the behavior and the person of concern. This is also based on the extent and nature of previous interventions. Second, and related to this, the five steps can be blended together in whatever way the intervener deems appropriate. Each of the steps highlights important aspects of the conversation, from personal values to behavior to next steps. Third, interventions may involve more than one person. This is particularly the case as the interventions move along the continuum from "Small i" toward "Big I"; more individuals, whether family members, work colleagues or supervisors, friends or acquaintances, may become involved in the discussion. The aim with these is to emphasize how many people are concerned, and to impress upon the individual of concern the importance of behavioral changes.

Finally, the nature of the "Big I" intervention, with the goal of the person of concern getting treatment services, warrants additional attention. Typically, these are conducted with the leadership and assistance of a trained interventionist. The key individuals for a person's life are involved with this planned event. Each of these individuals will, ideally, have prepared written remarks to share with the person of concern. The professional will guide the discussion, and will incorporate the five steps cited in this intervention model. The professional will structure the process in a caring and loving way, but also stress the importance of the event and the consequences for non-compliance with the group's requests. The intervention itself will likely be a surprise to the individual of concern, and the outcome of treatment services will be clearly specified.

Follow-ups: The final element of the intervention model is that of following up with the individual of concern. After the intervention, it is all-too-easy to avoid any reference to the conversation that occurred about the individual's drug or alcohol abuse. It is not sufficient to have an intervention, and then assume that everything is taken care of. To demonstrate the importance of the first step of the Contact ("I care about you"), the intervener should check in with the individual and reflect upon the conversation. While this can be awkward, it is important to show that genuine caring was present. The important thing is that, in the days and weeks following this discussion, some reference is made to the conversation that reinforces the overall themes provided by the intervener. This is not to belabor "the conversation," but to demonstrate genuine caring for the individual, and to stress the importance of the individual getting appropriate assistance to modify the behavior.

No formal structure is offered for this; this may be part of regular discussions or meetings, or it may be scheduled simply to provide awareness that monitoring of the drug or alcohol-related situation and discussions will be occurring. This may be a query about whether any questions remain, as well as clarifying ways of moving forward. This places the previous intervention(s) into the context of the Continuum of Care, providing reinforcement for the behavior in a healthy context.

The details associated with any intervention are necessarily personalized to the specific issues and problems associated with the person of concern. These will vary based on setting as well as the nature of the issue as being more acute or long-term and progressive in nature. Dovetailing intervention activities is critical to occur with an understanding of the nature of the issue as well as the progression of the substance use disorder. Further guiding intervention activities are personal, group, and cultural values associated with the interventions themselves as well as substance abuse issues. More specific insights about intervention and using this type of "response" to problematic situations is found with Professional Perspective 5.1.

Professional Perspective 5.1

Redefining Intervention: Altering Trajectories to Reduce Harms

Jason R. Kilmer, Ph.D., and Shannon K. Bailie, M.S.W.

Intervention. People who have watched any movie or television show portraying a person whose family or friends perceive that their behavior seems out of control (or who have watched 1–2 hours of reality television) instantly have a stereotype of what "intervention" means. They tend to picture a person entering their home, walking into a room finding themselves surrounded by friends and loved ones, being assured that everyone loves them and is there for them before they are confronted about a problem they are presumed to be in denial about. Fear of that type of intervention could lead people to avoid or be reluctant to engage in an intervention, but an intervention can and should mean so much more.

When we consider interventions in a community or work setting, these can be brief, non-confrontational, non-judgmental conversations that focus on eliciting personally relevant reasons to change when a person is ambivalent about change or perhaps hasn't yet begun to think about change. Most efficacious brief interventions are informed by or directly utilize Miller and Rollnick's (2013) *Motivational Interviewing*. In settings with a clearly designated population being served, such as a college campus, screening can formally take place in campus counseling or health centers, and, when a score from a screening measure suggests reason for concern, a provider can explore this further and/or deliver a brief intervention or make a referral when indicated. Informally, this can come up in conversations in academic advising, residential life, peer-to-peer, or elsewhere on campus. In work settings, formal interventions may occur within human resources departments, and informal interventions may occur with supervisors, managers, or work colleagues. In the community, screening can formally occur in health, medical, or counseling settings; informally, this can occur in a manner similar to other informal approaches identified.

So often, people say, "well, they haven't hit 'rock bottom' yet, so is there anything to do?" Why would we want anyone, whether a 15-year-old, a late adolescent or young adult, or anyone for that matter, to hit "rock bottom?" The key to an intervention can be to alter a trajectory – if a student is going in a direction associated with academic struggles, health concerns, impacts to relationships, or other unwanted outcomes, the student may choose to make changes to reroute where they are heading.

In a conversation with a student, a concerned student affairs professional can describe what they are seeing rather than making assumptions about the cause (e.g., "the last three times we've met, you mentioned you were coming off of a rough weekend … what's been making it rough?" or "At the start of the quarter or semester, you were handling all of your responsibilities; how are you doing?"). Then, see what concerns the person shares about their substance use, if any. You don't have to be the person to deliver additional services; instead, referral can be made to a provider who can provide a more formal brief intervention. For one audience – college students – Brief Alcohol Screening and Intervention for College Students, or BASICS (NIAAA, 2015) – is a helpful and effective in-person option; similar resources exist for other settings and can even be accessed via the internet (e.g., the National Institute on Alcohol Abuse and Alcoholism's "Rethinking Drinking" website, accessible at: www.rethinkingdrinking.niaaa.nih.gov/). If they are not concerned, barring a life threatening situation, let them know that whatever they choose to do is ultimately up to them, and that you're there for them if they want to discuss things in the future.

Know that you can "plant seeds" during a caring, empathic conversation with a person, and that research shows a "sleeper effect" of brief interventions even 15 months later when the door to potential change isn't closed (White et al., 2007).

Realize that much of what scares people about interventions (e.g., an angry reaction from the person being addressed) can be minimized when labels are avoided. Miller and Rollnick (1991) suggest that "denial" is much more a by-product of an interpersonal exchange that didn't go so well than a characteristic of an individual. For example, a person says to someone, "I'm worried about you and am here for you, but think you're an alcoholic, have a problem, and need help … you should go to treatment." If the person reacts negatively, they're considered to be "in denial." But how should they react when they are labeled (i.e., "alcoholic"), diagnosed (i.e., "problem"), and told what they need to do (i.e., "you should go to treatment")? Do what you can to meet the person where they are in terms of their readiness to change a behavior – if they're unsure about what to do, suggestions about what to do, even when well-intended, can cause a disconnect between where they are and what they are being asked to do. Be careful not to label behavior (e.g., avoid terms like "alcoholic," "addict," "problem," or "negative").

Understandably, this can feel heavy or intimidating – you're talking with someone about content that could be life changing. But remember, just opening the door to the conversation, reserving judgment, and expressing empathy can help facilitate or set the stage for students to consider changing their behaviors. It is always good to consult and connect with other professionals, including a supervisor or service providers. In the spirit of taking care of yourself, be careful not to take on too much, and know that there are resources available for support and consultation.

References

Miller, W.R. & Rollnick, S. (1991). *Motivational Interviewing: Preparing People to Change Addictive Behavior*. New York, NY: Guilford Press.

Miller, W.R., & Rollnick, S. (2013). *Motivational Interviewing: Helping People Change* (3rd ed.). New York, NY: Guilford Press.

National Institute on Alcohol Abuse and Alcoholism (NIAAA). (2015). *Planning Alcohol Interventions Using NIAAA's CollegeAIM (Alcohol Intervention Matrix)*. NIH Publication No. 15-AA-8017. Bethesda, MD: NIAAA.

White, H.R., Mun, E.U., Pugh, L., & Morgan, T. (2007). Long-term effects of brief substance use interventions for mandated college students: Sleeper effects of an in-person personal feedback intervention. *Alcoholism: Clinical and Experimental Research, 31*, 1380–1391.

Jason R. Kilmer, Ph.D., works at the University of Washington in both a student affairs and a research capacity. As Associate Professor in Psychiatry and Behavioral Sciences, he serves as an investigator on several studies evaluating prevention and intervention efforts for alcohol, marijuana, and other drug use by college students; as Assistant Director of Health and Wellness for Alcohol and Other Drug Education in the Division of Student Life, he works with different areas across campus to increase student access to evidence-based approaches.

Shannon K. Bailie, M.S.W., is Director of Health and Wellness at the University of Washington, a holistic program that addresses the overlap of multiple issues on college campuses through education, prevention, intervention, and strategic outreach. Prior to this position, Shannon worked as a sexual assault and relationship violence information specialist, providing both response and support to survivors of assault, as well as being actively involved in prevention efforts in the college setting.

Treatment

Treatment involves the services, activities, and processes designed to help an individual with a substance use disorder end their dependence on alcohol and/or other drugs. Treatment is individualized to address a person of concern's specific and general needs. It consists of a wide range of approaches and therapies. Beyond that, treatment is designed to address some or all of the underlying needs and issues that contributed to the substance use disorder. Its aim is to help the individual be "clean and sober," and for this to be maintained for the rest of the individual's life. Within that context, the individual, upon completion of treatment, will be "in recovery" for the rest of his/her life; they will not be seen as "being cured."

As emphasized by the National Institute on Drug Abuse, addiction to drugs and/or alcohol can be treated; however, as is also known by many substance abuse professionals and those in recovery, it is not simple. "Because addiction is a chronic disease, people can't simply stop using drugs for a few days and be cured. Most patients need long-term or repeated care to stop using completely and recover their lives."[1] They further note that "Addiction treatment must help the person do the following: stop using drugs; stay drug-free; be productive in the family, at work, and in society."

For many people, treatment is often viewed as synonymous with a "28 Day Program," popularized in the film *28 Days*.[2] While month-long, inpatient treatment programs do exist, professionals have a much a broader view of treatment. As with various medical, mental health, and psychological issues, professionals working with these areas of concern have different philosophies and strategies for treatment. With substance use disorders, different service providers use and promote different strategies. This section provides an overview of common considerations and elements.

Treatment insights are provided from several long-term advocates

> *We were still having the debates about whether everyone in the field should be a recovering person.*
>
> Gail Milgram

> *I think we got to the point where it was very important to have academically trained individuals and also to have people who were coming along with their own recovery and going to school. That turn probably happened with the dawn of the recovering people deciding that they wanted to be certified, respected, looked at maybe not as an academically trained person but someone who had a background and was worthy.*
>
> Gail Milgram

> *What is AA? It is long-term chronic care, aftercare. So these people are finally recognizing that addiction is a chronic disease that needs recovery-oriented systems of care.*
>
> Thomasina Borkman

> *An important development, or as I would like to add, reinstitution, is the integration of peer providers. When the field began, most providers were peers – a person in recovery. Then, standards, certifications, and educational requirements came along*

that made it difficult for those in the field to move with the field. The field made it difficult for those in recovery to play an active role – a role that included a living wage. This continues today. It saddens me because the field was born on the backs of those in recovery. While we are inviting them back to the table, and this invite is often from those that don't know the history, it saddens me that we have treated those in recovery with minimal respect – it is one way that the field itself continues to create stigma – not valuing lived experience.

Claudia Blackburn

Core Principles of Effective Treatment

The National Institute on Drug Abuse has identified 13 principles of effective treatment.[3] Their documentation, based on sound research over the past four decades, provides the following principles that should be understood and built upon for the treatment program to maximize its effectiveness:

- Addiction is a complex but treatable disease that affects brain function and behavior.
- No single treatment is right for everyone.
- People need to have quick access to treatment.
- Effective treatment addresses all of the patient's needs, not just his or her drug use.
- Staying in treatment long enough is critical.
- Counseling and other behavioral therapies are the most commonly used forms of treatment.
- Medications are often an important part of treatment, especially when combined with behavioral therapies.
- Treatment plans must be reviewed often and modified to fit the patient's changing needs.
- Treatment should address other possible mental disorders.
- Medically assisted detoxification is only the first stage of treatment.
- Treatment doesn't need to be voluntary to be effective.
- Drug use during treatment must be monitored continuously.
- Treatment programs should test patients for HIV/AIDS, hepatitis B and C, tuberculosis, and other infectious diseases as well as teach them about steps they can take to reduce their risk of these illnesses.

Foundations for Treatment

Overall, five basic considerations serve as foundations central to appropriate treatment services for substance use disorders. First, treatment should be based on individual needs. This will include the substance(s) of concern, length of dependence issues, nature of harmful or problematic consequences, and family context. Second, the approaches used should be culturally appropriate. This is especially true for race and ethnicity, but also may include factors such as primary language, age, and gender. Third, a clinical assessment will garner many of these individual needs and history. It will also include an assessment regarding the presence of other mental health conditions or disorders. Through this process, the most appropriate treatment plan will be developed. Fourth, attention to cost-effectiveness and cost-appropriateness will be made. This may include a sliding payment scale, and what services are appropriate based on the clinical assessment conducted. Finally, a blend of approaches is typically incorporated as part of the treatment plan. These may include large group therapy, small group therapy, individual therapy, self-help groups, life skills training, family involvement, education about substance use disorders, medical care and medications, and assignments.

To help prepare the specific course of action for a client, based on his/her individualized needs, understanding some of the factors that constitute clinical assistance is helpful. Professional Perspective 5.2 provides many of these insights.

Professional Perspective 5.2

Assessment and Diagnosis of Substance Use Disorders

Michael E. Dunn, Ph.D., and Jessica N. Flori, M.A.

Those who assess and diagnose Substance Use Disorders (SUDs) are in *helping* professions. It is important to begin with that reminder because it is the basis for working effectively with people suffering from alcohol and substance use problems. Many people seeking SUD treatment are motivated and forthcoming, but many others are less so for a variety of reasons (e.g., being mandated for assessment and treatment). Regardless, clinicians who use the model we describe will be most effective in helping those who suffer from SUDs.

Effective assessment relies on an appropriate psychosocial interview. Content will vary with assessment setting and patient population; however, the most effective method across settings and populations relies on Motivational Interviewing (MI) techniques. Developed specifically for working with SUDs (see Miller and Rollnick, 2013), MI has become a staple in many disciplines. The focus is to "meet people where they are at," encourage "change talk," and use various techniques for dealing with resistance that redirect interviewees and encourage rapport and engagement.

Screening measures provide a starting point for a more detailed interview and most include questions that address diagnostic criteria including impaired control, social impairment, risky use, and pharmacological criteria (tolerance and withdrawal). The most widely used and well-validated measures include the Alcohol Use Disorders Identification Test (AUDIT; Babor et al., 1992), the Cannabis Use Disorders Identification Test (CUDIT; Adamson & Sellman, 2003), and the Drug Abuse Screening Test (DAST-10; Skinner, 1982).

The diagnostic interview will focus on symptoms associated with problematic use of a particular substance. As described in the DSM-5 (*Diagnostic and Statistical Manual of Mental Disorders* (5th ed.); American Psychiatric

Association, 2013), diagnosis of a SUD must be specific for one of nine types or categories of drugs (Alcohol, Cannabis, Hallucinogens, Inhalants, Opioids, Sedatives/hypnotics/anxiolytics, Stimulants, Tobacco, or "Other"). Diagnostic criteria are essentially the same across substance classes, although some symptoms do not always apply (e.g., phencyclidine, hallucinogen, and inhalant use disorders do not include withdrawal).

Diagnosis of a SUD requires a problematic pattern of substance use leading to clinically significant impairment or distress, as manifested by at least two symptoms within a 12-month period. Eleven symptoms are listed, including tolerance, withdrawal, problems associated with use, inability to control use, craving, and risky behaviors associated with use. Current severity is determined based on number of symptoms (two or three symptoms is considered "Mild," four or five is "Moderate," and six or more symptoms is "Severe").

If assessment and diagnosis were as simple as asking questions based on diagnostic criteria and noting the number of symptoms endorsed, no further direction would be needed. The process, however, is rarely that simple. By definition, assessment involves quantifying symptoms and capabilities to inform diagnosis and intervention, and most information gathered in the assessment process is self-report data. There are many reasons an individual might be motivated to distort their self-report of symptoms related to any disorder. They may exaggerate or minimize symptoms, or their self-report might be influenced by their culture, demographics, or legal problems (e.g., a recent arrest for driving under the influence). Regardless, practitioners must focus on being helpful rather than seeking truth. We do not accept answers to questions at face value, but expressing doubt about someone's responses is usually counterproductive by damaging rapport, preventing engagement, and motivating the individual to repeat the same inaccurate responses. We need to be aware of factors that can influence self-report and consider them carefully in making diagnostic decisions, always keeping in mind the fact that our goal is to help, and focusing on "truth" will often do more harm than good. People tell you what they can, and a skillful clinician, by meeting them where they are and promoting engagement, makes it possible for them to tell you what you need to know to help them.

The following example illustrates the process. During a traffic stop, a 20 year-old woman we will call "Jane" had a blood alcohol concentration (BAC) of 0.16. Jane was given the option of assessment and intervention in our clinic rather than being arrested. During her interview, Jane stated that she had never consumed alcohol prior to the evening of the traffic stop, but the pharmacology of alcohol makes it clear that Jane is unlikely to be telling the truth. Had this been her first drinking experience, it is unlikely that she would be fully conscious with a 0.16 BAC, let alone able to operate a vehicle. Rather than confront Jane with this information, the interviewer focused on other aspects of Jane's life, thus building rapport and engagement. It was explained that information Jane revealed would not be used to make things more difficult for her because our purpose was to help Jane in putting the event behind her. As trust was established, Jane revealed that alcohol use had been a regular part of her social life and that she had experienced problems. Jane met criteria for Alcohol Use Disorder, Moderate Severity, and was scheduled for treatment in our clinic.

Although Jane's case was a success story, we have individuals who refuse to be forthcoming despite our best efforts. In those cases, we do our best to build trust and encourage the individual to contact us in the future if they have concerns. The goal in those situations is to reduce the barriers to intervention and increase motivation to seek help.

References

Adamson, S.J. & Sellman, J.D. (2003). A prototype screening instrument for cannabis use disorder: The Cannabis Use Disorders Identification Test (CUDIT) in an alcohol-dependent clinical sample. *Drug and Alcohol Review, 22*, 309–315.

American Psychiatric Association. (2013). *Diagnostic and Statistical Manual of Mental Disorders* (5th ed.). Arlington, VA, American Psychiatric Association.

Babor, T.F., De La Fuente, J.R., Saunders, J., & Grant, M. (1992). *AUDIT: The Alcohol Use Disorders Identification Test: Guidelines for Use in Primary Health Care, Revision.* WHO Document No. WHO/PSA/92.4. Geneva: World Health Organization.

Miller, W.R. & Rollnick, S. (2013). *Motivational Interviewing: Helping People Change* (3rd ed.). New York, NY: Guilford Press.

Skinner, H.A. (1982). The drug abuse screening test. *Addictive Behaviors, 7*(4), 363–371.

Michael E. Dunn, Ph.D., is a licensed psychologist (FL PY5502) and a founding faculty member of the Clinical Psychology Ph.D. program at the University of Central Florida. He has worked in the field of substance use research and treatment of Substance Use Disorders for over 30 years.

Jessica Flori is a clinical psychology doctoral student at the University of Central Florida. Her background includes work on research projects focused on treatment for Opioid Use Disorder and development of alcohol expectancy-based interventions for high-risk drinkers.

In addition to these observations, some quotes from long-term advocates provide additional perspectives on treatment services.

> *I thought that taking somebody's history in an hour would be the most impactful thing in a person's life. Because there's a chance you won't see them ever again and so you had to maximize your screening and assessment and blend it all in, all the while eliciting their symptoms. I always say that they have to prove their alcoholism to me, I refuse to accept anybody's self-diagnosis or anybody else's diagnosis. I asked people what kind, what was their drink of choice, what was their second drink of choice, what was their third drink of choice, what size bottle did they buy it in, what size glass do they drink it in. And I would go down and say scotch, vodka, rum, whiskey, and so on, have you*

ever tasted it, would you taste it again, or would you not taste it? So I want a picture of this person's life with alcohol in it and every flavor they've ever had, and sometimes they would say no I'll never drink gin, it tore my stomach up. Well then they think they are into controlled social drinking because they exclude one kind from their diet. I used to think that social histories should be the most impactful thing; it doesn't work for everybody. When un-peeling the onion, un-peeling the onion in every respect in the tiniest details to get to know the person, have them disclose these things they've never disclosed before, and even today people who have gone to treatment in several places, when I do the social history they say nobody has ever asked me those questions before.

William Kane

Remember that each person is an individual. The need for AOD and addiction services can be relentless. With all of the education and work we do, people keep coming. It's easy to get weary and for judgment and criticism to become the order of the day.

Teresa Johnston

And the other interest of mine has been developing systems around the world that were able to meet client needs as they presented. My niche has been developing care – coordinated, client-driven treatment systems based on research, outcomes, and client needs.

Robert Lynn

I think that if we had a better understanding of the specific aspects of certain drugs that people are drawn to, we might be able to do better in treating people for their addictions and preventing problems from developing.

Helene White

An initial part of treatment, if needed, is medically supervised withdrawal; also called detoxification, this incorporates approaches, including medication, to help the individual's body adjust to the lack of presence of the substance(s) to which the person had become dependent. Withdrawal from different substances varies in nature, based on the substance and the individual; these range from life-threatening and other dangerous conditions to hallucinations, extreme discomfort, or mild withdrawal. Through this process lasting several days to a week or more, attention is provided to minimize negative and harmful conditions and help the individual move toward a substance-free life. This part of the treatment, while potentially harmful, is typically viewed by many professionals and patients as the easiest part of treatment.

Following any necessary detoxification services, the treatment program can be implemented. Different types of programs are available, including two broad types of intensive programs: inpatient treatment and residential programs. The inpatient treatment programs are hospital-based or included in a medical clinic. These are particularly useful for those with other co-occurring disorders and those for whom intensive medical services may be needed. They are also more likely with adolescent treatment where closer monitoring and structure is required. The residential programs are a setting separate from a person's normal day-to-day life where they can focus entirely on their substance use disorder and many of the life skills necessary for full functioning. Different types of programs exist, and with different periods of stay. Some adolescent programs include a school-based curriculum, and some adult programs incorporate school certificates and job and career preparation activities. Specialized programs based on cultural or personal needs exist; examples are those for Spanish-speaking men and for women with children.

Three other types of programs are partial hospitalization or day treatment, outpatient programs and intensive treatment programs. With the partial hospitalization or day treatment programs, the individual lives at home but participates in the treatment program for half a day or more. These may be located in a hospital or a separate clinic facility. Outpatient treatment is provided in a variety of settings, whether a mental health facility, counselor's office, health clinic, or health department; the individual lives at home or on his/her own. Participation may be daily, several times a week, or once a week. The intensive treatment program, lasting from two months to a year, includes treatment services up to 20 hours each week.

The actual composition of the treatment program will vary based on the priorities and specialties of the service provider. The linkage of an individual's needs and the appropriate services will be based on a clinical assessment and the other factors identified earlier in this section (e.g., cost-effectiveness, cultural considerations). Some of the basic components are summarized here:[4]

- Assessment – A clinical assessment of treatment needs and involves the development of an effective treatment plan.
- Medical Care – Screening and treatment for HIV/AIDS, hepatitis, tuberculosis, women's health issues.
- A Treatment Plan – Written guide with goals, activities, progress monitors, timeframe; this is reviewed and adjusted over time to meet changing needs.
- Group and Individual Counseling – Group therapy offers facilitated discussion and interaction to provide support and encouragement from others affected by substance use disorders; this helps motivate people to remain drug/alcohol free.
- Individual Assignments – Readings, written assignments, challenges to adopt new behaviors.
- Education about Substance Use Disorders – Readings, videotapes, audiotapes, lectures, activities.
- Life Skills Training – Social skills, communication, stress management, time management, anger management, financial skills, goal setting, leisure activities, employment and job-seeking skills.
- Testing for Alcohol or Drug Use – Urine samples, breathalyzer tests.
- Relapse Prevention Training – Identify relapse triggers, coping with cravings, plans for handling stressful situations; preparation for what to do if relapse occurs.
- Orientation to Self-Help Groups – Understanding of Twelve-Step programs and self-help groups.
- Treatment for Mental Disorders – Attention to emotional issues such as depression, anxiety, post-traumatic stress disorder (PTSD).

- Family Education and Counseling Services – Lectures, discussions, activities, group meetings. Family counseling and parental involvement are included.
- Medication – Prescribed as needed to help stay abstinent.
- Follow-up Care / Continuing Care – Individual and group counseling, halfway houses, supportive living and transitional apartments.

As noted, families are an important consideration throughout the treatment process. Some insights regarding their important role are found in Professional Perspective 5.3.

Professional Perspective 5.3

The Role of the Family

Randy Haveson, M.A.

Being in a family system with a practicing addict or alcoholic is traumatic. You never know who will be walking through the door at any given moment. Sometimes it's predictable when the cyclone will hit (Friday night after 9 p.m., Sunday around half time, during a holiday gathering, or after an argument), but most of the time the damage comes at unexpected times. Family members become exhausted from always being "on guard." Children growing up in alcoholic households learn three common rules, "don't talk, don't trust, don't feel."

Often, families get into patterns of enabling the alcoholic or addict. Either consciously or unconsciously, they engage in behaviors that keep the pattern going. Attempts such as pouring out bottles that are found, watering down bottles of alcohol, making excuses for the addict to employers or friends, cleaning up after them if they vomit, putting them in bed if they pass out on the floor, confronting the person while they are drunk or high, or making idle threats to leave if the behavior doesn't change, all don't work. While the alcoholic or addict might make promises to change, it is their behavior, not their words that matter most. Enabling can be subtle too, such as: staying silent after an outburst, getting in the car with the person after they've been drinking or drugging, or avoiding the kids after they were yelled at.

Here are some tips to help families effectively confront an alcoholic or addicted family member:

1. Never, ever confront the person while they are drunk or high. It is much better to confront them the day after an episode, earlier in the day before they start up with drugs or alcohol again.
2. Confront behaviors, not attitudes. Saying "Last night when you were drunk you said some very hurtful things to me and the kids" is much more effective than "last night you were a total jerk."
3. Use the word "concerned" rather than other words like worried or scared. "Last night you drove drunk and you said you wouldn't do that again. I'm

concerned you have an alcohol problem." That is more effective than "I was really worried about you last night because you drove drunk." Or "You really scared me last night."

In my years as a therapist, some of the most traumatized people with whom I worked were those who grew up in alcoholic or drug-affected family systems. They typically didn't realize how much the alcoholic/addict affected them until later in their lives. Some become dependent themselves and often use drugs or alcohol to hide from the painful memories. Others become over achievers and nearly kill themselves staying busy. When they do take a breath and ask for help, they see how their behavior is a result of not wanting to deal with the feelings. They believe that if they stay busy, they don't have to feel.

Just as traumatic for many people is living in a home with a newly recovering addict or alcoholic. While you wish, hope, and pray that the person will turn things around and stay sober, it can be unnerving every time they leave the house, and you wonder if they are going to relapse. Family members feel like they have to walk on egg shells around the person, hoping they don't say or do anything that will set them off on another bender. The most important thing to remember is: *You are not responsible for their drinking and you are not responsible for their recovery.*

Learning appropriate boundaries is vital for the health of the family. Finding support for family members is as important as finding support for the alcoholic. Programs such as Al-Anon, Ala-Teen, ACoA (Adult Children of Alcoholics) and CODA (Co-Dependents Anonymous) are there to assist family members. It is best to go to a few different meetings to find one that fits you best. Just like shopping for a new outfit, you should shop around for the one that fits you best because not all meetings are alike.

When dealing with a newly sober addict or alcoholic, it is also important to remember that recovery takes time. It's a process, not an event. They didn't become addicted overnight and they won't magically get better overnight either. Be patient. Remember that the family members need to heal too; they will go through a process themselves. Things that can help in recovery are therapy, journaling, meetings, and removing yourself from old, dangerous activities and people.

Addiction is insidious. It is cunning, baffling, and powerful. The good news is that, particularly during recent years, issues of dependence, addiction, and recovery are talked about more often. Families dealing with dependence issues with a loved one, as well as people in recovery, are speaking out and making it more acceptable to get help. If you or someone in your family is an addict or alcoholic, it's more than OK – it's healthy – to ask for help.

Resources

Beattie, M. (1986). *Co-Dependent No More*. Center City, MN: Hazelden Foundation.

Al-Anon: www.al-anon.org.
Co-Dependents Anonymous (CODA): www.coda.org.
Adult Children of Alcoholics (ACoA): https://adultchildren.org.

Randy Haveson, M.A., has worked in the substance abuse field since 1986. He has worked on four college campuses as the coordinator of AOD and health education. As a professional speaker, he has worked with over 100 campuses, speaking about harm reduction, self-esteem, leadership, and supporting students in recovery.

Family issues are identified as very important by numerous long-term advocates; what follows are several insightful comments.

> *The most important things that can be done ... it starts in the family, it starts with dinner time, it starts with shared values. But in an experimental culture where experimenters are in their own experiment we need to provide safety and treatment in ways for people to be evaluated, treated, and recover.*
>
> Mark Gold

> *Involving families in treatment began with psycho-education, including showing films. It moved from this to more focused family approaches that address the psychosocial and the emotional issues that evolve in living addiction.*
>
> Claudia Blackburn

> *More resources need to focus on early childhood prevention, and prevention within the family and community context. Considering the alarming statistics in the U.S. regarding opioid overdoses, the delivery of interventions need to occur on each systemic area: communities/municipalities, schools, physician offices, workplace, etc.*
>
> Claudia Blackburn

With the continued evolution of strategies for addressing the range of needs and issues associated with substance use disorders, the need for updated materials, resources, and protocols is needed. As cited in Chapter 3 (Why Be Concerned?), and Chapter 4 (Foundational Factors), increased scientific understanding and new knowledge has occurred. For example, many of the biological foundations associated with substance use disorders were not known several decades ago. Further, the understanding of the brain and its functioning continues to unfold. Thus, the need for current information and compilations of best practices for addressing these issues and specialized aspects of substance use disorders and populations is warranted. To help with this, the Center for Substance Abuse Treatment, within the Substance Abuse and Mental Health Services Administration, has prepared a series of publications to help with treatment services. These publications are organized as TIPS (Treatment Improvement Protocols) and are widely available. These resources combine clinical, research, and applied findings and expertise to help them offer quality services. The titles of many of these help illustrate the range of issues and needs, and further document the need for individualized and culturally appropriate services for treatment. Sample titles, among the dozens available from SAMHSA, include:

- *Medications for Opioid Use Disorder*
- *Trauma-Informed Care in Behavioral Health Services*
- *Addressing the Specific Behavioral Health Needs of Men*
- *Behavioral Health Services for People Who Are Homeless*
- *Improving Cultural Competence*
- *Clinical Supervision and Professional Development of the Substance Abuse Counselor*
- *Substance Abuse Treatment: Addressing the Specific Needs of Women*
- *Addressing Suicidal Thoughts and Behaviors in Substance Abuse Treatment*
- *Incorporating Alcohol Pharmacotherapies into Medical Practice*
- *Managing Depressive Symptoms in Substance Abuse Clients During Early Recovery*
- *Substance Abuse: Clinical Issues in Intensive Outpatient Treatment*
- *Substance Abuse: Administrative Issues in Outpatient Treatment*
- *Detoxification and Substance Abuse Treatment*
- *Substance Abuse Treatment for Adults in the Criminal Justice System*
- *Medication-Assisted Treatment for Opioid Addiction in Opioid Treatment Programs*
- *Substance Abuse Treatment for Persons with Co-occurring Disorders*

The long-term advocates interviewed had helpful insights regarding treatment services.

> *There is an age-old battle across treatment approaches about what is more important – insight into your presenting problems or gaining coping skills that you haven't developed to support change. In SUD treatment, a counselor needs to balance these. You can have all the insight into your addiction, but never learned coping skills that could help in managing recovery or other life issues. Equally important, the client needs to have confidence that they can do it and use their coping skills.*
>
> Claudia Blackburn

> *But fascinating when you think about, and thus the interaction that might have come about at night, people sitting around talking about well do you think this is a good way to treat. One time during the Rutgers Summer School a student who came in believed very strongly in acupuncture as a way for treatment; I think the field for a long time was very open to discussion of varying views, it wasn't this "it's my way or the highway"; it was "well maybe there's a point to that, maybe we should try it, but I'm not so sure" and that was acceptable. I think as politics and other things changed, it got more rigid and was no longer as open.*
>
> Gail Milgram

> *So one thing I know for sure is that essentially treatment has not changed and whether that's good or bad and without outcomes I don't know.*
>
> Robert Lynn

138   Competence

Regretfully we have not made many changes in treatment over 40 years. Regretfully, because it would appear that treatment should have evolved; on the other hand, without outcomes we really do not know much about the quality of treatment. We know more about an appliance we want to purchase than a treatment program we want to send a loved one to.

Robert Lynn

I think the changes that I have seen improved some modalities of therapy, for example motivational interviewing being one of them, how do you get people to stop.

Teresa Johnston

From a therapeutic standpoint, I don't feel like a whole lot has changed. It has still stymied a lot of folks because it is complicated; alcohol and drug use patterns are interdisciplinary; social, behavioral, physical, mental, spiritual, it's not just one thing.

Teresa Johnston

Experiential knowledge is a valuable and authoritative source of knowledge, and a central part of self-help groups.

Thomasina Borkman

I have some optimism or hope that we are going to get funding eventually that is going to help people, it's no longer going to be that insurance agencies can not cover alcoholism treatment and that there should be more emphasis on prevention so I'm hopeful that that will happen, and I hope that within this approach that we can start bringing down these rates.

Karol Kumpfer

As a provider, you have to be resourceful. Your organization will not have all the services that your client and their family need. You are not only working on building a connection with your client, but developing connections with other community services so that you know how to access the services when your client presents needs that you and your agency can't fulfill. You are more than a counselor or administrator – you are also a resource broker.

Claudia Blackburn

I'm thinking about treatment because at the end of the run, after everyone, we get all the education, all the laws, and all the enforcement, we're still left with a huge number of people that require treatment. And the price tag is unbelievable, and I don't know who's going to cough that up, and I do see where the government is not going to be willing to cough that up.

Jeffrey Levy

Three final considerations are important for an understanding of treatment services. First, the role of self-help and mutual aid activities is essential. While these were noted in the summary of typical treatment services, as well as the attention to the importance of others facing substance use disorders in the group therapy setting, further details were not provided. The larger discussion about self-help groups is provided in the next part of this chapter with attention to recovery issues. However, self-help groups are an important part of treatment, and this includes much more than an initial introduction to them. Greater insight and understanding about self-help approaches, and ways they can be helpful, are provided with Professional Perspective 5.4.

Professional Perspective 5.4

Self-Help/Mutual Aid Groups for Sustained Recovery from Substance Use Disorders

Thomasina Borkman, Ph.D.

Many models about helping individuals assume that an expert who has not had the problem should be in control of the interaction in exchange for fees (directly or indirectly through insurance) and deference. In contrast, the self-help ethos places the *person with the problem in charge*[1] of the helping and the running of the group. The person with the problem is both a recipient and a provider of help with *no fees* or deference involved. Relationships are personal, egalitarian, and *reciprocal* and the *lived experience* of recovery is authoritative knowledge. Above all, participation and extent of involvement is *voluntary* and there is some *personal change goal* such as abstinence from substance use and living a more productive lifestyle.

Self-help/mutual aid groups are also known by a variety of names such as self-help groups, recovery support groups, or mutual aid groups. I will use mutual aid group (MAG). The "self-help" refers both to taking self-responsibility and to using inner resources; the "mutual help" conveys the reciprocal helping and the group context. A circle of sharing the individual's "experience, strength, and hope" in and around meetings constitute MAGs' primary activity but they also facilitate friendships, social activities, and helping events.

MAGs are a critical component of the substance abuse treatment system in the United States and probably assist more individuals with Substance Use Disorders (SUDs) in a cost-free manner than do professional treatment resources. Regrettably, their predominant role in substance abuse services is not always recognized or understood. Internationally limited research on MAGs has been conducted which has found them used in 50 countries, but probably less extensively than in the U.S.

Alcoholics Anonymous (AA), the 12-step, 12-tradition group is by far the largest and most influential MAG and has been extensively studied. The 12 steps are a philosophy and a complex program of personal change and the 12 traditions are guidelines for group functioning.

AA and other 12-step anonymous MAGs are abstinence-oriented, spiritual but not religious programs. Members are asked to conceptualize "God" or "Higher Power" for themselves – an approach unimaginable to a religion;

atheists are less likely to attend 12-step groups but those who do actually have similar outcomes.

AA became the model for 80–100 other groups, not only for other substance use disorders such as Narcotics Anonymous (founded 1953) and Cocaine Anonymous (founded 1982) but also for process and other addictions (such as Gamblers Anonymous and Overeaters Anonymous). Al-Anon for family members and friends of alcoholics was initiated in 1953 as a 12-step anonymous program similar to AA. Non-12-step MAG alternatives to AA developed in the 1970s and were primarily abstinence-oriented but opposed to 12-step spirituality or the male orientation of early AA.

It is important to note, however, use of the 12-step philosophy, 12-step treatment, and the Minnesota Model of treatment in various kinds of professionalized treatment programs are all significantly different from and should not be confused with the voluntary, member-run mutual help groups that operate in civil society outside the marketplace and the government.

Effectiveness: Scientifically rigorous validation of AA's effectiveness was scarce until the 1990s when an increasing number of research studies confirmed that (1) professional treatment followed by AA involvement was effective in higher rates of abstinence and psychosocial functioning; (2) AA involvement alone was effective in higher rates of abstinence and better functioning especially because members created larger social networks of abstinent friends who supported abstinence and not only attended meetings but worked the steps, used sponsors, and helped others; (3) AA involvement was cost-effective not only for reduced costs for substance use treatment but for general healthcare utilization.

Myths and Misconceptions: Professionals who favor professionally controlled interventions *only* are likely to be unaware of their biases against MAGs (those who maintain that no scientifically adequate studies of MAG effectiveness exist or misrepresent MAGs). The most prevalent misconception is the spiritual but non-religious aspect of AA. MAGs are also puzzling to many attendees with their lack of hierarchy, bureaucracy, or membership lists, and peer helping with no strings attached.

Professional Cooperation with MAGs: Recent research shows that when clinicians in treatment programs introduce MAGs in some detail and intensively refer clients to MAGs, clients are more likely to attend and become involved. The large national randomized MATCH trial had as one experimental condition, TSF (Twelve-Step Facilitation), which involved training professionals to introduce clients to 12-step programs; TSF clients did as well or better than the two professional conditions (cognitive behavioral therapy and motivational enhancement therapy) and became one of SAMHSA's evidence-based practices (Project MATCH Research Group, 1998). Making AA Easier (MAAEZ) also introduces relapsing clients to AA very effectively (Kaskutas et al., 2009). MAGs, especially 12-step groups, are valuable not only for long-term recovery but they are also helpful as supplements to free professionals to focus on specialty treatments for complex and difficult cases.

Note

1 The italicized words or phrases refer to the universal elements that define self-help/mutual aid groups.

References

Kaskutas, L.A., Subbaraman, M.S., Witbrodt, J., & Zemore, S.E. (2009). Effectiveness of Making Alcoholics Anonymous Easier: A group format 12-step facilitation approach. *Journal of Substance Abuse Treatment, 37*, 228–239.

Project MATCH Research Group. (1998). Matching alcoholism treatments to client heterogeneity: Project MATCH three-year drinking outcomes. *Alcoholism: Clinical and Experimental Research, 22*, 1300–1311.

Resources

Borkman, T. (1999). *Understanding Self-Help/Mutual Aid: Experiential Learning in the Commons.* New Brunswick, NJ: Rutgers University Press.

Humphreys, K. (2004). *Circles of Recovery: Self-Help Organizations for Addictions.* New York, NY: Cambridge University Press.

Kurtz, L.F. (2015). *Recovery Groups: A Guide to Creating, Leading and Working with Groups for Addictions and Mental Health Conditions.* New York, NY: Oxford University Press.

Thomasina Borkman, Ph.D., is Professor of Sociology Emerita, George Mason University, Fairfax, Virginia. She has studied MAGs including AA for 50 years and is best known for her concept of experiential knowledge or lived experience as authoritative in MAGs.

In addition to these perspectives, the long-term advocates offered the following observations:

> *That reminds me of Mark Keller's conversation of sitting with Bill W and trying to talk through, Bill W, when he first taught at the Rutgers summer school in 1943, used his full name, William Wilson. Because he thought educationally there would not be an issue, that anonymity didn't go into that area that he sat and he would chat for hours with faculty and students and after a year or two decided that he should be anonymous in all aspects of life when he was talking about alcoholism and recovery. So the first year he was William Wilson the second year I believe he was William W, the third year he was Bill W.*
>
> Gail Milgram

> *AA is a distinctive, unusual organization.*
>
> Thomasina Borkman

When I teach I sometimes say "I need to tell you that I believe that the 12 steps are the way for the most people to stop drinking, to stay stopped, and to develop an interesting and fascinating growth style of life." And that is what keeps us going, it is exhilarating to see people recover.

William Kane

What I am seeing in society and across globally, that self-help is becoming front and center as an idea, in many different ways. It is the value of telling your personal story. In self-help groups, that is obvious; that is the way that people heal. We are finding that with veterans affected by post-traumatic stress syndrome, and with South Africa with the creation of reconciliation; the process of telling your personal truth. I see that as an emerging recognition in the larger context of the value of sharing your personal story; and the value of how that has been nurtured in self-help groups.

Thomasina Borkman

AA forces people to come up with their own definitions of a higher power, no one is going to do that for you. It forces you to think for yourself.

Thomasina Borkman

Second, the terms "counseling" and "therapy" are often used interchangeably when describing treatment services. In fact, there may be differentiation between the two, particularly among those specialists and service providers. Typically, counseling is more short-term in nature, and therapy is of a longer duration. Therapy is often seen as getting more in depth with individuals' backgrounds, attitudes, and other factors that have affected various aspects of their lives. Within the context of treatment, both counseling and therapy may be appropriate, in both the individual and group settings. Reflecting upon the Continuum of Use, counseling may be more appropriate for lower risk use, and for moderating patterns of drug and alcohol use and incorporation with harm reduction strategies; therapy may be more appropriate with a focus on abstinence following the treatment services.

Third, and essential to the following section on recovery, is a reflection on the ultimate purpose of treatment programs and services. While treatment will be for a limited period, it is not a program of a set of services and protocols that is designed to "fix" a person. Treatment is designed to help a person, and to provide participants with skills, attitudes, tools, and perspectives that will aid them in their lifelong efforts to remain drug and alcohol free. Part of the perspectives associated with treatment is that individuals do, in fact, have so many gifts and talents. Drug and/or alcohol abuse has caused harm to them and often their families, friends, co-workers, and others. Treatment is designed to help them with their lifelong journey, and for some a lifelong struggle, to maximize their own human potential.

As a final issue associated with the choice of treatment components, as well as with the transition to healthy recovery, attention to the issue of medication-assisted treatment is warranted. Professional Perspective 5.5 illustrates some of the controversy surrounding this.

Professional Perspective 5.5

Medication-Assisted Treatment ... A Drug to Treat a Drug?

Dana Ripley, M.A.Ed., and Jenny Wagstaff, Ph.D.

There has long been debate in the world of addiction treatment about abstinence only versus a harm-reduction approach. Bringing this issue to the forefront for health professionals and those in recovery is the increasing use of Medication-Assisted Treatment (MAT), especially for those with opioid use disorders. MAT is defined as the combination of medication to treat the physical symptoms of addiction, and counseling to treat the psychological components of addiction. MAT is most commonly used for opioid and alcohol use disorders. Even with its effectiveness, it is widely misunderstood. How can replacing one substance for another be part of the recovery process? The intent of MAT is to treat the "whole person"; the medication aids with the physical symptoms of addiction including detoxification, withdrawal, and correction of the neurobiological processes that contribute to relapse, while counseling helps to build healthy coping skills, treat underlying mental health concerns, and assist in relapse prevention.

Buprenorphine: A Viable Option

Several medications are approved for use in MAT for alcohol and opioid use disorders. Each medication works differently in the body and has different considerations for treatment that need to be taken into account with client needs when choosing a medication. While multiple options exist and still more will undoubtedly be developed, the focus here is on buprenorphine to illustrate how MAT can be an appropriate strategy. Buprenorphine is one type of medication commonly prescribed within MAT. Approved for use with opioid addiction in the United States in 2002 by the Food and Drug Administration, it is an opioid partial agonist. It works by attaching to the same brain receptors as full agonist opioids, but, as a partial agonist, it does not usually cause a high. It is believed that a part of heroin's addictiveness is the intense, immediate gratification, which does not occur in buprenorphine when used as prescribed (Gerra et al., 2009). This prescribed drug thus reduces cravings, but allows the user to function normally. For many, this means they are able to shift their focus from needing and seeking drugs, back to the important aspects of life such as family and work. Buprenorphine has low abuse potential and is difficult to overdose on, making it preferable, in some cases, to the more strictly controlled methadone, which is a full agonist. It is metabolized and reacts differently in the body than short-acting opioids like heroin and oxycodone. A large part of the appeal of buprenorphine is that it can be prescribed in office-based settings (Center for Substance Abuse Treatment, 2004), as opposed to specialty clinics (methadone), making it more easily available to those in need. In addition, buprenorphine, along with methadone and naltrexone (opioid antagonist used for alcohol and opioid disorders), have been seen to reverse the negative effects of illicit opioids on the brain, such as changes in reward pathways and stress responses (Bart, 2012; Kosten & George, 2002). In short, buprenorphine, in the context of MAT, has been accepted as an evidence-based standard for treating SUD.

Counseling: The Other Half of MAT

It is important to remember that the medication is not a standalone treatment (and thus the importance of the word "assisted" within the MAT descriptor). MAT includes the use of counseling, which is necessary so clients can address the psychological issues that accompany addiction. Although it is required by law for those in MAT to also receive counseling, the amount and type may vary. As the aim of MAT is to treat the "whole person," it is necessary to base decisions about frequency and type of therapy on client needs and goals. No matter how similar two clients appear, treatment needs to be tailored to the individual.

In conclusion, MAT is one option for viable treatment of SUD, with advantages over other approaches. This includes the research that support its efficacy, its accessibility to clients, and its contribution to reduced transmission of disease and overdoses. Unfortunately, adoption of MAT has been slow due to concerns about substituting one drug for another, as well as negative views by some health professionals. The inclusion of MAT is essential for consideration with an integrated behavioral health approach to treat SUD effectively.

References

Bart, G. (2012). Maintenance medication for opiate addiction: The foundation of recovery. *Journal of Addictive Disorders, 31*(3), 207–225. DOI:10.1080/10550887.2012.694598.

Center for Substance Abuse Treatment. (2004). *Clinical Guidelines for the Use of Buprenorphine in the Treatment of Opioid Addiction.* Treatment Improvement Protocol (TIP) Series, No. 40 (Report No. SMA 04-3939). Rockville, MD: Substance Abuse and Mental Health Services Administration.

Gerra, G., Maremmani, I., Capovani, B., Somaini, L., Berterame, S., Tomas-Rossello, J., Saenz, E., Busse, A., & Kleber, H. (2009). Long-acting opioid-agonists in the treatment of heroin addiction: Why should we call them "substitution"? *Substance Use & Misuse, 44,* 663–671. DOI: 10.1080/10826080902810251.

Kosten, T.R. & George, T.P. (2002). The neurobiology of opioid dependence: Implications for treatment. *Addiction Science & Clinical Practice, 1*(1): 13–20.

Dana Ripley, M.A.Ed., L.P.C., is a doctoral candidate in counselor education at Virginia Tech. She has been working in the field of addictions since 2012, and is currently researching counseling interventions for use in MAT models.

Jenny Wagstaff, Ph.D., L.P.C., is Assistant Professor in Counselor Education at Campbell University, Buies Creek, NC. Her research focuses on the use of brief motivational interventions to address high-risk substance use behaviors.

A final observation from a long-term advocate follows:

> The field continues to move toward biomedical interventions – pharmacotherapy for addressing cravings, blocking physiological reactions, and preventing overdose. This area, I believe, is in its infancy.
>
> Claudia Blackburn

Recovery

After the treatment services an individual receives, what follows has been called "aftercare," "ongoing treatment," or "recovery." For this volume, recovery is used as the operational word that encompasses all that is post-treatment. Essential within this context is that recovery is a lifelong process, and one that will go through various phases and elements over time. As defined by SAMHSA, recovery is "a process of change through which individuals improve their health and wellness, live a self-directed life, and strive to reach their full potential."[5] The emphasis on helping individuals reach their full potential is consistent with the entire Continuum of Care, and the thrust of this book, as the focus is not just on "problem reduction" or "symptom relief," but on enhancing the overall quality of life.

Within the context of recovery, SAMHSA's Recovery Support Strategic Initiative identifies four dimensions that command attention for recovery.[6] First, *health* includes informed choices regarding physical and emotional well-being. Second, one's *home* should be stable and safe. The third aspect is *purpose*, including employment, education, and other elements for full societal participation. Finally, *community* engagement includes social networking and quality relationships.

Just as with treatment, no single approach or path for recovery is most appropriate for any one individual. As cited in the previous section, treatment services must be based on the personal history and needs of the individual, and a variety of approaches and strategies are included. Perhaps even more valid with recovery, no single approach, regimen, or content is found. Further, because recovery is much more self-directed and occurs in an unstructured setting, its components and considerations can be less clear. What is important in this process is that attention to SAMHSA's four dimensions be maintained. Through this, the need to maintain hope by the individual and those significant people in his/her life, and support by these key people, is vital.

The "content" of recovery may, in fact, include many of the elements essential for the treatment services. Just as treatment is personalized, so also is recovery. The recovery efforts may include professionally guided group counseling, individual counseling, and medication. It will likely include attention to life skills, many of which may have been neglected during the individual's period(s) of substance abuse. Attention to life skills, such as management of stress, time, financial, or anger issues, and also with quality relationships with family, friends, acquaintances, and oneself, are central to these efforts. This focus upon the whole life within a wellness construct includes maintaining a balanced approach to life's challenges and opportunities.

Involvement in mutual aid support groups, such as Alcoholics Anonymous and Narcotics Anonymous, is central to a sound recovery. Individuals with a substance use disorder genuinely need and often rely upon the assistance of others to aid in their recovery. The Twelve Steps and Twelve Traditions embodied within these organizations help provide the basis for moving forward with individuals' lives. The belief is that a person with substance abuse issues cannot "make it alone" easily, if at all. The need for support and perspectives about the journey of recovery, from the experiences and lives of others' recovery, is most helpful. The term "self-help" implies to many that an individual can manage recovery alone; in fact, the focus is upon mutual aid, with attention to the support from others involved with similar journeys of recovery, and without the leadership or facilitation of a trained professional.

With mutual aid support groups, many additional issues are embodied in understanding what contributes to their role, as well as to their success. Many misconceptions as well as different points of view are embodied in these group approaches. Some include the differences between open and closed meetings, whether mandated attendance is helpful or appropriate, the role of a higher power, the use of sponsors and chips, funding, the Big Book,[7] and more.

Through the recovery process, what is important is that the themes of "hope" and "support" are maintained, as emphasized at the start of this section. Slips and relapses are not uncommon; these are part of the transition of the recovering individual into a life without the use of substances. With so many factors and often lengthy times that contributed to the process of an individual becoming dependent through the process of developing a substance use disorder, it is not unexpected that emerging into a life without substances will provide its own challenges. Thus, a strong support system, encompassing family and work environments, and recreational and social settings, and addressing trigger issues and cues, will be essential for having an appropriate, personalized strategy for recovery.

Further insights regarding the importance of these mutual aids as well as about recovery overall, and how others can be supportive of these integral processes, is highlighted in the Professional Perspectives 5.6 and 5.7.

Professional Perspective 5.6

Steps Toward Effectively Supporting Recovery

Jenna Parisi, M.S.P.H.

Just as there are myriad avenues to recovery from substance use disorders, there are multiple ways to approach recovery advocacy. This segment will identify specific strategies to lead others toward an appropriate understanding of recovery as well as allyship techniques to help our respective communities become more recovery ready.

What does it mean, specifically, when you say you work to support people in "recovery"? As a foundation, it is critical to specify recovery from substance use disorders. Folks who work around the topic of alcohol and other drugs will often know what this means; health promotion and community health folks will get on board easily. However, the average layperson, community leader, or businessperson might need a little more of an introduction.

Another helpful foundation is to connect others to recovery. So many people have a personal connection to this issue; when I show a video of my sister and then I unveil her identity (and her relationship to me), the audience truly knows why I care about this topic. But why should they care, if they are one of the few who do not know someone in recovery? For starters, it is a social justice issue.

People in recovery should not have to choose between their recovery and something else important in their life (like family, an education, a job), but that can be a challenge if folks feel like they have to compartmentalize their experiences. For example, it may be critical for an employee to leave work on time to make a regular mutual aid support group meeting. If they are frequently asked to work late or otherwise adjust their schedule to take on important assignments, and they do not feel comfortable disclosing their recovery and communicating this need with their employer, their recovery and personal well-being could be at risk. Thus, we need to work on creating more recovery-friendly environments.

Also consider the receptivity of the environment. For example, imagine you are feeling confident about laying the groundwork for a major behavior change, such as drastically altering your diet or pledging to exercise daily. You are coming from a setting that was supportive – where people understood how hard it was for you to make that change, where they wanted to make it easier for you to understand yourself, and how to succeed and follow through on your commitment moving forward. Then you leave that environment, and surround yourself with all new people, places, and things that might not reinforce your new change. That is what it can be like for a person new to recovery to leave treatment. Moreover, a young person in recovery, whose brain is still developing, may be primed for risk taking while still in the process of learning self-regulatory strategies to cope with life stressors. They may find it incredibly challenging to continue to work on their recovery if their peers and the adults in their lives are unsupportive. So what can we do to make it easier for people in recovery?

Here are three specific recommendations. First, understand recovery, even at a very basic level. There is not one definition, and it could refer to different things. So if you are conducting a training, get your audience on the same page quickly while recognizing there are multiple pathways to recovery. It is helpful to address some myths. One example is that people in recovery are not trying to convert you; they figured out what works for them, and as members of a society that includes people in recovery, we have a responsibility to respect that. Congregations, worksites, recreational settings, and neighborhoods could all be places where people in recovery demonstrate community membership without the intention of "recruiting" others into recovery. Another example is that people in recovery cannot only be friends with each other. Being in recovery does not preclude individuals from making decisions about those with whom they do and do not feel comfortable socializing. And you certainly cannot spot a person in recovery just by looking at them.

Second, create some ground rules for how to talk about recovery. The language we use is of utmost importance, so part of being an effective supporter or ally of recovery involves carefully selecting the words you use to talk about this topic. Person-first language focuses on the person, not the disorder, and helps discontinue harmful negative stereotypes that inhibit help seeking. For example, say "person with a substance use disorder" instead of "substance abuser" or "addict" and say "person arrested for a drug violation" as opposed to "drug offender"; also refer to "positive" drug screens, instead of "dirty" or "clean" ones. Some recovery advocates even discourage use of the word "relapse" because that is not used in reference to other chronic diseases. You can use helpful research (Kelly & Westerhoff, 2009), blogs (White, 2014), or posters from the local behavioral health agency to reinforce why language matters.

Third, generate ideas about how to make your space more recovery-friendly. For example, a university setting is a well-documented high-risk environment for young people in recovery, thus creating an obligation to help protect the recovery of students. A high-stress work environment, with deadlines and perfectionist standards, can be a challenge for those in recovery. And a family setting, with drug or alcohol patterns long established, can test a recovering person's perseverance. What helps is to engage others in thinking about what might make it easier, versus harder, to be a person in recovery in that setting. If there are many events or activities where alcohol is being served, that makes it harder. If there are many fun, free events that neither involve nor advertise drinking, that makes it easier. Recovery-friendly environments are more oriented toward health and well-being, so be the one to spearhead questions about how all members of the community or space can make it beneficial for all of us.

References

Kelly, J.F. & Westerhoff, C.M. (2009). Does it matter how we refer to individuals with substance-related conditions? A randomized study of two commonly used terms. *International Journal of Drug Policy, 21*(3), 202–207.

White, B. (2014). Language abuse. [Blog post]. Retrieved from www.williamwhitepapers.com/blog/2014/02/language-abuse.html.

Jenna Parisi, M.S.P.H., CHES, is Director of the Office of Health Promotion at Gonzaga University. She previously served as Director of Collegiate Program Development at Transforming Youth Recovery.

Professional Perspective 5.7

Mutual Aid Groups' Contribution to Recovery-Oriented Systems of Care

Thomasina Borkman, Ph.D.

The addiction treatment system evolved since the 1970s and was designed by professionals to involve providers treating acute illness; this system involved short lengths of treatment, "graduation," brief aftercare, and an emphasis on abstinence and symptom reduction. Increasing scientific evidence of the ineffectiveness of this approach combined with evidence of the consistently good outcomes over long time periods for treated individuals who maintained deep involvement with mutual aid groups (MAGs) created a transformative space for a new paradigm.

CSAT (the Center for Substance Abuse Treatment) developed in 2005 an expanded, consensus-based definition of Substance Use Disorder (SUD) recovery: "recovery from alcohol and drug problems is a process of change through which an individual achieves abstinence and improved health, wellness and quality of life." In this definition, new Recovery Oriented Systems of Care (ROSC) are proposed that emphasize the enlarged and holistic concept of abstinence and recovery over the long run: recovery within a chronic disease model of continuing supportive care from multiple stakeholders – professional providers, peer supports, MAGs, family, and community recovery supports.

My home state of Maryland has been undergoing a transition since 2008 from the acute pathology model of addictions and an equivalent model of mental health conditions into a combined behavioral health unit that focuses on ROSCs for both. Many other states and localities are likewise experimenting. Central ideas of this enlarged view of recovery that apply to MAGs include:

- Recovery is an individual, self-directed journey, using the help and assistance of family, peers, professionals, and the community. "You alone can do it but you cannot do it alone," which sums up the seeming paradox of self-help and mutual aid.
- Many paths to recovery exist and include use of spiritually oriented MAGs, non-spiritually oriented MAGs, medication, professional treatment, religion, and no external help.
- ROSCs should include the ubiquitous 12-step MAGs and alternative MAGs such as Women For Sobriety, Life Ring, and SMART.
- ROSCs should include housing, transportation, and other practical assistance.

Non-12 step MAGs developed by rejecting AA's spirituality or other features. Women for Sobriety (WFS), founded in 1973, accepted spirituality but rejected the then overly male orientation of groups. SOS (Secular Organizations for Sobriety) founded in 1986 rejected spirituality; in 1999, an

SOS affiliate separated with its own name, Life Ring. A hybrid group with some professional elements is SMART (Self-Management and Recovery Training), founded in 1994, which defines SUD as self-limiting bad habits. These major alternative MAGs are small and geographically limited. A large (N=9341) national and fairly representative online study of individuals recovering from SUDs found that only 8% had attended WFS or SMART, only 2–3% had attended Life Ring or SOS meetings, while 73% had attended 90 or more 12-step meetings. Other smaller alternative MAGs are specifically Christian or Jewish. Two 12-step groups dealing with the dual issues of SUD and psychiatric disorder were founded in 1989: Dual Recovery and Double Trouble in Recovery (now a SAMHSA-certified evidence-based practice). Moderation Management (founded 1994), created for non-dependent problem drinkers, is an exception to abstinence-oriented groups and supports moderate use as a goal.

MAG effectiveness outside of AA has rarely been scientifically studied, but a recent exception is a longitudinal study following participants from WFS, Life Ring, SMART, and 12-step groups for 12 months to determine if the outcomes of the first three were similar to the 12-step groups. Researchers found that involved members of WFS, Life Ring, and SMART, measured as more than attending meetings, were as likely to be abstinent with as few problems as 12-step members.

Drug-free safe recovery residences are developing for people with SUD disorders as part of ROSCs. An early, well known, well researched, and large organization of recovery residences is Oxford House, founded by AA members in the late 1970s; a self-supporting, autonomous, democratically peer-run sober-living environment and a SAMHSA-certified evidence-based practice, Oxford House had about 1500 rental houses in 2015. Other recovery residences with or without MAG inspiration are available.

AA members began a journey of recovery in 1935 that has blossomed into many MAGs, Oxford Houses, and other vehicles of recovery that contribute nearly cost-free services to the public health system throughout the U.S. AA and other MAGs are found to varying extents in 50 other countries but information is limited due to lack of research. Before ROSC, the professional treatment system seemed to ignore the experiential knowledge of recovery practiced by hundreds of thousands of abstinent and well-functioning recovering persons in AA and other MAGs. AA and the 12-step anonymous model of addiction recovery exemplify the principles of recovery promoted by SAMHSA, and warrant expanded attention and support. As this journey of recovery approaches its one century mark, its contribution to countless lives is deserving of heart-felt respect, understanding, promotion, and enhanced research.

Thomasina Borkman, Ph.D., Professor of Sociology Emerita, George Mason University and affiliate scientist at the Alcohol Research Group in Emeryville, California, has researched mutual aid groups since the 1970s and is known internationally for her work.

To round out the observations from long-term advocates, the following are insightful views:

> I think that there's still an awful lot of work that could keep people from having problems with drugs and alcohol, and thus needing treatment and recovery.
>
> Carla Lapelle

> What was significant for me was learning from those struggling to find quality in life and working with them to develop care plans that met their needs and were sustainable. It was about community empowerment and leveraging resources that supported long-term recovery.
>
> Robert Lynn

> We have a recovering women attorney group; they call it women attorney peer counseling. That's also been around for 20 years because men interrupt women at meetings. And so these women have been together and then what they have done, they have blended depression and other problems into the women's group, it's kind of a unitary support group for women.
>
> William Kane

> Rehabilitation became accepted almost fashionable in some circles, but recovery was something that was not unusual and became something to be pleased of and proud of, you know, and it was a positive. There still remains the stigma and so on there's lots of denial, but I think that the acceptance of treatment has happened.
>
> William Kane

Summary

This chapter addresses three broad elements essential for understanding and addressing substance abuse issues. The segments on intervention, treatment, and recovery as a whole, as well as the important role of self-help mutual aid groups, each served as a targeted focus on the aspect within the Continuum of Care. While research has been long-term, and numerous articles and books have been published, what remains are varying strategies, no "magic answer," and the importance of individualized approaches. Further, while those dealing with substance abuse issues professionally have a broader and deeper understanding of the intricacies and idiosyncrasies associated with the identification and treatment of substance use disorders, these grounded perspectives are typically not seen or understood by others. The challenge is one of continuing the quality approaches, supporting further research for best practices, and promoting the hope and support for sound and productive lives.

Notes

1 National Institute on Drug Abuse. www.drugabuse.gov/publications/drugfacts/treatment-approaches-drug-addiction.

2 The film *28 Days* was released in 2000.
3 National Institute on Drug Abuse. www.drugabuse.gov/publications/drugfacts/treatment-approaches-drug-addiction.
4 U.S. Department of Health and Human Services (2014). *What Is Substance Abuse Treatment? A Booklet for Families.*
5 SAMHSA's *Working Definition of Recovery: 10 Guiding Principles of Recovery.* PEP12-RECDEF, First printed 2012.
6 SAMHSA's *Working Definition of Recovery: 10 Guiding Principles of Recovery.* PEP12-RECDEF, First printed 2012.
7 Alcoholics Anonymous (1939). *Alcoholics Anonymous: The Story of How Many Thousands of Men and Women Have Recovered from Alcoholism.* New York, NY: Alcoholics Anonymous, World Services.

6 Skills for Prevention and Education

Prevention is widely espoused, highly valued, frequently discussed, and emphasized for numerous health and safety issues. Consider heart disease, crime, emphysema, traffic safety, life longevity, violence, obesity, and more: each of these has epidemiological information that can be useful to identify risky situations as well as higher risk individuals. Each of these also has strategies helpful to affect outcomes such as their incidence, prevalence, severity, and affiliated consequences.

With substance abuse issues, initial questions focus on what to prevent and how to do it. All too often, attention is placed on the "how" or "what" aspect of prevention, such as the strategies, activities, services, and other approaches to be used. These may sound fun and engaging; they also may be perceived as superfluous and unconnected to the true purpose of prevention. Thus, prevention as a whole may sound easy to accomplish; however, it is not particularly simple. The level of attention to prevention, with science and grounding, is limited yet evolving. Further, the prioritization of resources, funding, action, and science-based strategies with substance abuse prevention are all limited.

This chapter provides structure around prevention issues. The perspective offered is broader than what has been traditionally emphasized, as it includes a focus on health promotion and wellness. This chapter addresses reasonable outcomes for prevention, including what should be prevented and promoted, both from the high-level perspective as well as from a more focused viewpoint. The chapter provides a framework to guide planners' thinking about specific prevention strategies. The role of education as part of prevention is highlighted, with attention to content and desired approaches. Also included is the training of professionals, paraprofessionals and peers.

Defining Prevention

Prevention of substance abuse issues is generally understood as reducing (or ideally, eliminating) problems and negative consequences associated with drug or alcohol use. Prevention has traditionally had a focus on those harmful, illegal, or inappropriate outcomes that occasionally or often come from the use of drugs or alcohol. The focus has been on the negative, and on things that are not wanted; this is in contrast to the positive, or what is wanted. Prevention's aim is to have any use of substances done in ways that do not bring harm to the user or others; this harm can be physical, social, emotional, cognitive, legal, financial, or other. The Center for Substance Abuse Prevention (CSAP) has organized prevention around different substances:

- Alcohol use is acceptable only for those of legal age and only when the risk of adverse consequences is minimal;
- Prescription and over-the-counter drugs are used only for the purposes for which they were intended;
- Inhalants, such as gasoline, glue, and aerosols, are not abused and are instead used only for their intended purposes; and
- Illegal drugs are not used at all.

As emphasized throughout this book, the larger perspective is one of maximizing the quality of life: the focus is on both reducing the negative or "bad" things, and also promoting the good, positive elements, thereby increasing human potential. While the word "prevention" does not specify this clearly, the intent for prevention efforts is to focus on both ends of this spectrum: both risk reduction and health promotion. One reason for this, to be specified further in this chapter, is the role of resiliency and protective factors. Another is that the focus on the positive is about what one wants to promote, and what is desired "to do"; this is in contrast to the reduction of the negative, and what "not to do." Not only do both aspects of the spectrum have validity for impact, but also many involved with addressing substance abuse issues find the proactive and positive approach to be more rewarding.

Another way of looking at prevention is from the perspective of the often cited medical model, which has three components. With *primary prevention*, the aim is to keep an individual from using substances at all; its aim is to keep any problems from occurring, and to intervene to halt this at the earliest possible time. It may focus on higher risk groups or situations, as well as risk factors. *Secondary prevention* helps keep negative consequences from continuing or progressing; this dovetails with intervention and treatment activities. Its focus is to help the individual return to the earlier behavior that was without problems. *Tertiary prevention* is for someone who has received treatment; its aim is to keep them from relapsing or returning to their drug- or alcohol-abusing behavior.

The long-term advocates have each had a role with prevention, whether primary, secondary, or tertiary prevention. Their insights regarding changes in the drug and alcohol abuse prevention field, as well as some of their successes and challenges, are illustrated by these quotes:

> We realized that there had been some real shifts and drug education efforts, prevention efforts over the decades from the 1960s. We went through the period of scare tactics and then factual information, and then we really emphasized self-esteem, and then we emphasized alternative activities, alternatives to substance use, and we got into the social influences model of prevention and then probably in the 1990s we started to look much more into policy-level interventions and environmental approaches. And I think the shifts have been based on limitations, the limited success of each of the earlier

efforts and I think now we are recognizing the importance of policy, the importance of structure, of environmental influences, focusing much less on individual capacity building and much more on community building. And I think that's a trend that will continue and should continue an emphasis on population health rather than individual health.

Tom Griffin

I think that's been important to really learn from past experiences and the kind of prevention that I did in the early 1970s was vastly different than the kind of prevention work I was involved with in 2000. Therefore, I think a common thread was a willingness to learn from our successes and a willingness to learn from our mistakes and to change our minds.

Tom Griffin

One of the things that I was never able to do was to define in simple terms for educators what effectiveness is.

Bill Modzeleski

All of that really misses the primary deliverable which is "how do you get better public health?"

Kurt Erickson

The most important things that can be done ... substance abuse education, and where they are going to get it from, that's a concern that I have. It's how do they get straight up information that's made palatable for their understanding and that's not either biased or tinged with scare tactics so that they can have a clear understanding of what the consequences are. To that end, I shouldn't say students, it's parents as well. For parents to understand the same risks. Studies show time and time again that parents can have an integral if not the most integral role to whether their kids engage in risky behaviors including alcohol abuse.

Kurt Erickson

And we did a lot of community meetings with prevention people all across the state to develop these standards that were fairly simple but yet we felt that these were the building blocks of what has now become the promising practices and, you know, evidence-based model. All of that stuff which we talked about in the mid to late 70s but it took a long time for it, for the research to be done to show that yes in fact you have to be culturally competent, and that you had to have some baseline information and that kind of stuff.

Darlind Davis

Substance abuse prevention, though it is identified as an important issue, it does not take priority because of some other higher risk issues that we deal with on health and safety.

Mary Wilfert

156 Competence

Prevention Outcomes

Having clearly defined results for prevention is an essential foundation for quality efforts. This aim is helpful for the process of collaboration and consensus, as well as for the specification of appropriate strategies to address the desired outcome. Consider, for example, the most effective strategies to reduce death due to drinking and driving. While typical initial responses might be sobriety checkpoints, harsh sanctions, and quality education, the answer is that these are not as effective as airbags and safety belt use. Why? The initially cited responses will help with the incidence of drinking and driving, but greater effectiveness for "reducing death" (the specified outcome) is found with airbags and safety belts. Clearly specifying the desired results helps narrow the outcomes and also points toward the appropriate strategies. This specification is also helpful for conducting meaningful evaluation, and for identifying potential attribution of causal factors.

It is also vital to be reasonable with the desired outcomes for prevention efforts. While the vision may be to eliminate all drug and alcohol abuse, a more reasonable aim would be to reduce the harm or incidence by a certain amount, and among a certain population. With the "War on Drugs" espoused so often, the implication with this language is that the outcome is either winning or losing; thus, if the war hasn't been won, then it must have been lost. A more helpful aim or goal, and thus language, would be to *manage better* the problems associated with drugs; with that focus, attention can then be placed on what defines "better manage the problems" and what outcomes would be associated with success. Thus, attention to what is reasonable to prevent, among whom, and over what period of time, is the recommended focus.

In a broad and general sense, some items for consideration are helpful with what substance abuse professionals or community leaders might want to prevent, and what they might want to promote. The specificity necessary will follow, but the essential starting point is to determine, at a broad level, what to address. Considerations for what to prevent include the following; for each of these the association with drugs and/or alcohol is implied if not specifically stated:

- Substance use
- Starting use of drugs or alcohol
- Violence
- Injury
- Death
- Automobile crashes
- Family problems
- Child abuse and neglect
- Perceptions of drug/alcohol abuse as "fun" or "acceptable"
- Distribution of unregulated drugs
- Diseases associated with drug/alcohol abuse.

Associated with this are considerations for what to promote, each with a linkage to drugs and alcohol (whether stated or implied):

- Current and accurate knowledge
- Parental skills with communication
- Resistance and refusal skills
- Skills for intervention, engagement, and speaking up
- Awareness of effects of substances
- Consistent enforcement
- Engagement with positive activities
- Accurate parent awareness of youth behavior
- Development of clear personal guidelines
- Use of designated sober drivers
- Stress management skills.

These are broad considerations for what to prevent and what to promote. Important with prevention, however, is to be much more specific and focused. Consider some reasonable outcomes with prevention:

- Reduce the overall percentage of high school seniors who report getting drunk from consuming alcohol to a level of 4% below its current level, each consecutive year for five years.
- Reduce the percentage of 8th grade youth who report having used marijuana for the first time by 5% per year.
- Increasingly decrease, by 3% each year, the desirability of using any substance that causes a "high" among high school students.
- Increase, to 75%, the percentage of parents who report a level of comfort as "high" or "very high" regarding having frank conversations with their son/daughter about drugs and alcohol.
- Reduce the prevalence of violent family disruption associated with drugs or alcohol by 3% a year, for three years, in a designated area of the community.
- Increase by 2% each year, for five years, the percentage of adults over age 75 who report extreme honesty with discussions about their personal alcohol use and their medications with their physician.

The point with these outcomes is that they provide the basis for being focused and measurable. Part of the emphasis is upon a specific population or audience, and inclusive of specific substances or outcomes. Each of these will benefit from even further specificity regarding the setting (e.g., a particular school or region of the locality). Helpful with this process (and described further in Chapter 7, Helpful Processes) will be some designation about the appropriate evaluative measures. For example, with the item above about "reduce the prevalence of violent family disruption," it will be important to state further "as measured by …" to identify the ways that "violent family disruption" can be documented in a reasonable way.

In the process of preparing prevention approaches, it is important to have a clear logic model to demonstrate how the activities and strategies link to the desired outcomes. Vital is having a clearly specified logical chain of events that shows how various strategies are affiliated for achieving the desired outcomes. For example, if knowledge acquisition is identified as an important outcome, it will be important to specify if the ultimate outcome is knowledge itself, or if knowledge is presumed to be essential, although not sufficient, to achieve the desired outcome of a specific change in behavior. If the latter is the case, the linkage between these various elements must be clear.

Overall, the importance of specificity with prevention is important. Related to this is the emphasis on risk and protective factors. With prevention, the aim is to reduce the negative, and thus address the risk factors. The companion aim is to promote the positive, and thus increase the protective factors.

The long-term advocates provide some views about prevention, from changes in what they believed to some general observations:

All that grew out of this was the original principles that we all agreed were necessary to having good outcomes and having some behavioral changes in attitudinal changes. And we still have to keep incorporating new information into this because the researchers are still coming up with better stuff, better approaches.

Darlind Davis

I think my key accomplishment was pushing the whole issue of results-oriented programming.

Bill Modzeleski

I call it "foofoo prevention" where it might feel good and look good but it really doesn't do anything.

Deb Thorstenson

What I believed earlier, that I no longer believe ... is that we can approach prevention by strengthening individuals, and I'm not opposed to strengthening individuals, but that's not sufficient. So I think I did believe that we could construct classroom environments and have activities in schools that could bolster an individual child's capacity to resist substances and I don't think that that's the case now. I think the environment has so much of an influence that we really do need to address that more fully.

Tom Griffin

What I believed earlier, that I no longer believe ... education does work. That's what we're all about. If education didn't work we wouldn't be in the business of education. It's how you define effective education and I think what people mean when they say that they mean that just providing the facts about drugs or, you know, the impact of drugs alone does not change behavior. So that certainly is something that early on that's how we would've trained you, you know. You provide information and they'll take that information and make good decisions. Well we know there's all kinds of other forces around individuals that impact their behaviors and their choices and we have to address all those other forces and not just provide the information.

Mary Wilfert

The Role of Health Promotion

As highlighted at the start of this chapter, an important part of prevention efforts surrounding substance abuse issues is on what to promote. This can be viewed as a wellness approach and addressing resiliency. The emphasis here is ultimately upon behavior, but also includes attitudes, skills, knowledge, and perceptions. The essential part of this approach is two-fold. First, by addressing these positive or health promoting attributes, the risks associated with the harmful use of drugs or alcohol become lessened. Second, addressing these positive issues can be valued in and of itself.

An example of this emerges from a conference in the mid-1990s, where attention was provided, using a think-tank format, to identify ways of reducing substance abuse among young adults. Also important to address in this process was attention to the root causes of individuals' substance abuse. Emerging from this process were seven themes, described below. The premise of this process was that with stronger attributes in these seven areas, individuals would be less likely to become harmfully involved with drugs or alcohol. That does not suggest that they would be guaranteed to not be harmfully involved; it does suggest that they would have reduced risk or exposure.

The first theme was *optimism*; the belief was that having a sense of hope and of a better future was an essential first step for reducing harm associated with substances. This can be valid regardless of where an individual is situated on the Continuum of Use. Further, even a modicum of hope is appropriate for moving forward. Second, the issue of *values* was identified as essential. Having one's personal values clarified can be helpful for maintaining healthy decisions regarding drugs and alcohol. Some values may be encapsulated with family members, work settings, communities, or the larger society. The Professional Perspective on setting guidelines for chemical health provides a way of clarifying these. *Self-care* is the third theme; this encompasses many skills that can help individuals make responsible choices. Consider stress management, time management, exercise, nutrition, and sleep. For each of these, quality skills, knowledge, and attitudes around the issue are as important as its own outcome; each one also has linkages to reducing risks for harmful substance use.

Relationship health is the fourth theme, encompassing skills of assertiveness, anger management, sexual decision-making, conflict resolution, and communication. With this, attention to quality relationships with family, significant others, supervisors, mentors, neighbors, friends, acquaintances, and oneself can help with the quality and engagement in life. *Community health* complements relationship health, and addresses ways in which individuals interact in work, social, and group settings. This involves intact affinity groups as well as the general societal network. The sixth theme is *nature*, which involves one's respect for the environment and the natural world; it incorporates an awareness of how people interact with the larger setting and can draw inspiration and insight from their surroundings. *Service* is the final theme, with an emphasis on volunteering and leadership. The premise is that by giving back, an individual becomes strengthened and increasingly self-motivated.

With these seven themes, attention is focused on the positive and the proactive. The aim with the think-tank process was to address, at least somewhat, the root causes of substance abuse. As noted, the proactive approach is helpful for its own merits (e.g., reducing stress or promoting quality relationships). Further, it is helpful for substance abuse prevention initiatives, complementing the traditional approaches of policies and education efforts.

Having a positive, proactive, results-oriented approach is something important to the long-term advocates. As they focus primarily on children and youth, these interviewees provide some helpful observations.

> *You have to give kids a reason to say "no" like "I'm not doing this because I'm a scholarship recipient."*
>
> BJ McConnell

> *Ultimately they have to decide what is an acceptable level of behavior on their own. There are programs, there are activities, there is enforcement, but at the end of the day you've got two worlds colliding. You've got the teen world that wants to spread its wings; at the same time you've got the administration world that wants to, by virtue of safety and adult thinking, do everything in its power to avoid the real tragic things that can be outcomes, and that we know are outcomes.*
>
> Ralph Blackman

> *The most important thing that can be done ... is to reduce stressors for everyone, which will help to bring down alcohol and drug use, delinquency, inherited health problems, etc.*
>
> Karol Kumpfer

> *I think helping our students make healthy choices mentally, physically, emotionally, socially, and spiritually. If we can do that, to me that's a do-do program, and we would not have to do so many of the don't-do programs because it would be giving them skills so that they can succeed in life.*
>
> Mary Hill

> *I believe that we are in a much better place than we were back in the 70s just from my own experience as a student but also some of the efforts that I was engaged in early on and even then back in the 90s when we were on campus; even though the effort was growing I think we are in a much better place where we understand the factors that contribute to behavior. And that's where we are putting, that's where we are focusing our effort is on that, that understanding of what is going to support positive behaviors and positive environments rather than wagging our fingers at kids and telling them "just say no."*
>
> Mary Wilfert

> *Kids do best what they do the most.*
>
> BJ McConnell

> *When you try to educate children you don't know when it is they're going to need those new skills. They may not need them for years, they may not need them that year you*

are teaching them, and they may forget them by the time they need them, and they may need them this weekend.

BJ McConnell

Helping distinguish some views about prevention are insights provided with Professional Perspective 6.1; this illustrates much of the difference between problem resolution and promoting assets.

Professional Perspective 6.1

Promoting Health/Preventing Problems

Thomas M. Griffin, Ph.D., and Jennifer Griffin-Wiesner, M.Ed.

Efforts to establish and encourage use of guidelines for low-risk-substance-use decisions (see Professional Perspective 6.2) emerged during an era in which responses to problem behavior, substance-specific prevention strategies, and broader health promotion and youth development efforts were largely siloed. There was growing recognition among researchers and practitioners, however, that separating these endeavors was not only inefficient, but also very often ineffective.

Our three-component model (see Figure 6.1) aimed to blend for practitioners, a focus on response to problems, prevention of high-risk behavior, and health promotion in a way that led to comprehensive and multi-faceted approaches. This was designed to not just prevent problem behavior, but also promote chemical health as part of overall healthy human development. In 1984, Griffin et al. wrote in *Chemical Health: A Guide for School Officials in Responding to Alcohol and Other Drug Issues* (1984):

> The concept of chemical health is a new, positive, and comprehensive response to chemical use issues and problems. Chemical health contributes to general health and is defined as a state of spiritual, physical, emotional, and social well-being which results in responsible decisions about chemical use and nonuse.

Substance use problem prevention includes both individual and environmental approaches, with the goal of decreasing the likelihood of specific problems such as death and injury caused by substance-use-related incidents, addiction, poor academic performance, and fetal alcohol effects. Health promotion and youth development approaches emphasize personal, social, physical, and spiritual well-being, reflective of the understanding that, as Karen Pittman (1999) began saying in the early 1990s, "Problem-free is not fully prepared."

Our model guided the field and specifically the efforts of the Hazelden Foundation and the Minnesota Institute of Public Health through the 1980s,

162 Competence

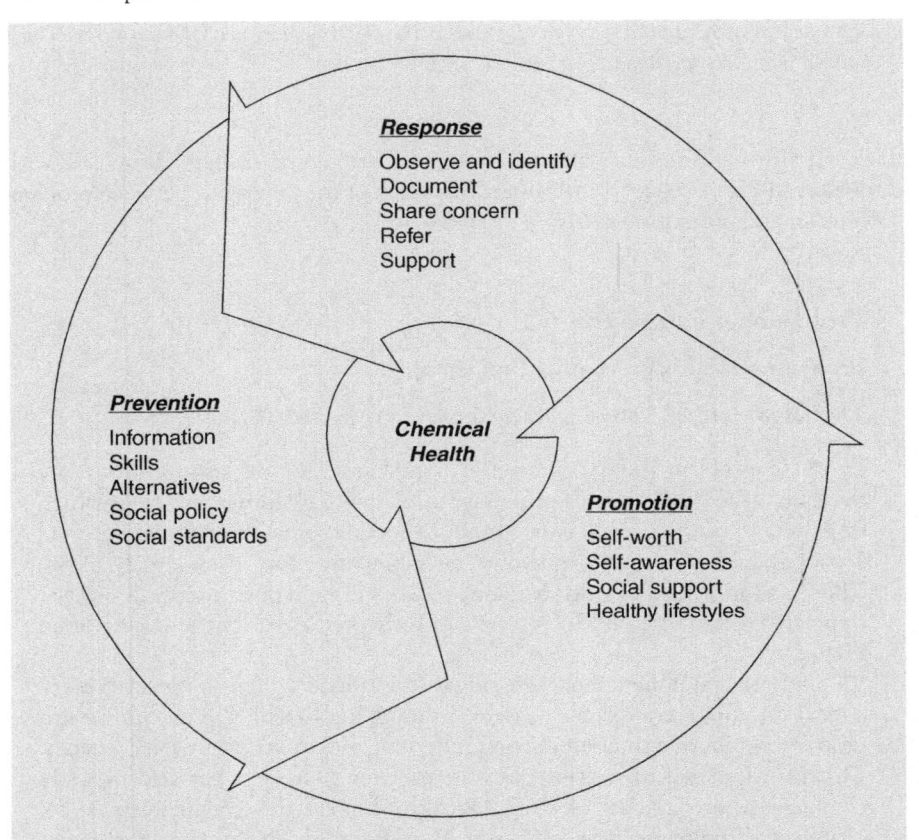

Figure 6.1 The Role of the School in Responding to Chemical Health Issues and Problems

[Figure 6.1 content:
- **Chemical Health** (center)
- **Response**: Observe and identify, Document, Share concern, Refer, Support
- **Prevention**: Information, Skills, Alternatives, Social policy, Social standards
- **Promotion**: Self-worth, Self-awareness, Social support, Healthy lifestyles]

1990s, and early 2000s. This provided community groups with an evidence-based, evaluable way to balance problem-specific prevention and referral efforts with broad health and human development approaches. Evaluation of the effectiveness of various ideas and initiatives that aligned with the approach led to the evolution and growth of various other frameworks and research-driven strategies. Perry and Jessor, for example, proposed a model that included efforts to strengthen health-enhancing behaviors and weaken health-compromising behaviors within a construct that included four dimensions: physical, psychological, personal, and social (Perry & Jessor, 1985). Hawkins, Catalano, and colleagues from the University of Washington presented similar research that emphasized identifying risk and protective factors that included contextual as well as individual and interpersonal components (Hawkins et al., 1992). Somewhat simultaneously, Search Institute identified first 30 and then 40 positive supports and strengths that help young people survive *and* thrive. Half of these *Developmental Assets* focus on external relationships and opportunities within families, schools, and communities; the other half focus on internal social-emotional strengths, values, and commitments that are nurtured and grow within young people (Benson et al., 1999).

The refining, expanding, and continued relevance of this work have depended on attention and commitment to ongoing research and evaluation, communities of practice, and creativity. In the years to come we will understand even more about factors such as brain development, social determinants of health, Adverse Childhood Experiences (ACES), and other factors with implications for health promotion and problem prevention. Some changes we can anticipate, some we cannot. New laws regarding marijuana use, for example, will affect norms and behavior. Opioids and other prescription drug use is an issue and a challenge we're just beginning to understand. We know too that the research base regarding effective environmental strategies will increase in depth and breadth. And as our nation's population ages and diversifies in myriad other ways, so too will societal norms as well as personal decisions regarding chemical health. What will remain constant is the need for rigor, inquiry, innovation, and, perhaps most important, a willingness to humbly leverage our knowledge and experience without attachment to "the way things were," so that we may respond and adjust to the way things are with an eye toward how they will be.

References

Benson, P.L., Scales, P.C., Leffert, N., & Roehlkepartain, E.C. (1999). *A Fragile Foundation: The State of Developmental Assets among American Youth*. Minneapolis, MN: Search Institute.

Griffin, T.M., Svendsen, R., & McIntyre, D. (1984) *Chemical Health: A Guide for School Officials in Responding to Alcohol and Other Drug Issues*. Center City, MN: Hazelden Foundation.

Hawkins, J.M.D, Catalano, R.F., & Miller, J.Y. (1992). Risk and protective factors for alcohol and other drug problems in adolescence and early adulthood: Implications for substance prevention. *Psychological Bulletin, 112*(1), 64–105.

Perry, C.L. and Jessor, R. (1985). The concept of health promotion and prevention of adolescent drug abuse. *Health Education Quarterly, 12*(2), 169–184.

Pittman, K. (1999). The power of engagement. *Youth Today*, September. Washington, D.C.: The Forum for Youth Investment.

Tom Griffin, Ph.D., M.S.W., entered the field of prevention in the early 1970s, working in the public and private sectors during a time of rapidly emerging knowledge about the effectiveness of prevention and health promotion approaches.

Jennifer Griffin-Wiesner, M.Ed., is Tom's daughter, and currently runs her own consulting practice based on bridging research and practice in youth development. Prior to that she spent a decade working at Search Institute during the emergence of the Developmental Assets framework and the related national Healthy Communities • Healthy Youth initiative.

Risk and Protective Factors

A helpful way of looking at prevention is with the construct of risk and protective factors. This dovetails with the data provided in the first chapter, documenting the issue of higher risk individuals and groups. With this construct, understanding both of these can help guide the prevention efforts so that individuals' and groups' likelihood of harmful consequences associated with substances are reduced. By reducing the risk factors, and by enhancing the protective factors, the likelihood of negative consequences is lowered. Attention to both risk and protective factors complements the important balance with "prevent" and "promote," or with "problem reduction" and "health promotion" stressed in this chapter.

Six clusters of factors are included in this construct. *Individual* risk factors include lack of knowledge, favorable attitudes, early experimentation, genetic predisposition, psychological disposition, sensation seeking, and antisocial behavior. *Family* risk factors include poor parenting skills, conflict, lack of engagement, lack of healthy communication or support, economic hardship, parental, sibling or family member substance use, substance approving attitudes, or abuse. Risk factors with *peers* include time spent with peers with favorable attitudes toward substances, participation with substance-affiliated activities, and peers' experimentation or use of substances; particular attention is provided to older peers. The *school* risk factor includes a negative school climate, nonexistent or lenient policies, lack of school bonding or spirit, poor grades and disconnectedness with school. *Community* risk factors include lack of awareness of substance issues, norms favorable to substance use, lack of enforcement, problem minimization, insufficient resources, and lack of attachment or bonding. *Societal* risk factors include overall norms tolerant of use, nonexistent or lax policies, poor or inefficient procedures, inappropriate sanctions, and lack of awareness of problems.

With each of the clusters of risk factors are protective factors, encompassing specific interventions and strategies designed to enhance their viability. For example, with the individual domain, interventions focus on increased knowledge and more positive attitudes. Family approaches include parenting skills, including communication, family activities, and parental knowledge and skills on substance use. For peers, approaches include skill-building activities, positive youth development, youth leadership and peer education, and recreational events. With the school cluster, attention is provided to curricular content, school climate, positive school bonding, clear and consistent policies, and adult resources. With the community, numerous groups are involved, such as the workplace, faith community, service organizations, coalitions and media; attention is provided to service activities, volunteering, positive activities, overall planning and communication, mentoring, policies and enforcement. The societal factor involves overall media strategies and campaigns, community engagement, laws and policies, regulations and enforcement, education, training, and leadership development,

The long-term advocates offer varied viewpoints on prevention, including the overall construct of risk and protective factors, as well as other ways of examining and conceptualizing prevention efforts. Their perspectives and insights are very helpful:

We are dealing with people who are invincible in this demographic and prevention work often falls on deaf ears. Students think "It's not going to happen to me," and they are balancing the costs and the benefits of the decision all the time, so I think prevention should always include risk analysis and cost benefit. that's what prevention is to me.

Teresa Johnston

To better understand the causes of drug use, we tested a Social Ecology Model of pathways to substance abuse. The model also pointed out what all of the other models had shown that peer influence was the final pathway to drug use. However, this model collapsed parent and peer influence into the same factor because they were so highly inter-correlated, so the final pathway is both family and peer influence.

Karol Kumpfer

I think that what we didn't realize is that strongest for kids, as they go in to adolescence, teenagers' strongest influence is their peer group.

Bill Modzeleski

Give them challenges and tools and say if not this then what? And why would you want to consider that? And make it their decisions not mine, because I'm already old, I know my decisions, they haven't made theirs.

BJ McConnell

How important it was for parents to say to their children if the person that's been driving you has consumed alcohol or if you have consumed alcohol you will call for a ride, we will not argue or fight with you, we will discuss it the next day but we will pick you up. And I had people in the audience saying that is encouraging young people to drink. And some in the community were saying we are not going to tolerate underage drinking. And I certainly don't think we should be encouraging underage drinking but I think we should come up with plans to figure out what we do if underage people drink and how do you deal with it.

Gail Milgram

But it also missed the point and it shows what our society is missing in that young people are learning to consume alcohol at home and that maybe a small amount of alcohol is not against the law.

Gail Milgram

Really understanding how we educate people to some extent in the preventative disease model, the obsessive compulsive behavioral component of addiction alongside the brief intervention or referral to treatment models.

Teresa Johnston

Prevention Framework

In preparing approaches within prevention, broadly defined, seven items are identified as helpful considerations for this planning. Rather than move quickly into the activity, policy, or strategy, it is important that these areas be actively considered, as each one has implications for achieving the desired outcomes.

1. Substance – What is the specific substance? Strategies will vary based on whether it is alcohol, illicit drugs, illegal drugs, prescription drugs, tobacco, inhalants, or a combination of two or more. Further, within the nature of the illegality it is important to consider marijuana versus other illegal drugs, and how marijuana is viewed legally in different states.
2. Population – With whom is the attention to be focused? Higher risk groups (such as young drivers, college students, older adults) have unique needs and behavior patterns that warrant different strategies.
3. Focus – What is the scope of concern? This may be with an individual (or group of individuals), an organization, or the larger environment. The scope of attention and strategies will vary based on this factor.
4. Concern – What, specifically, is the concern? As noted in the section on outcomes above, what is envisioned as the result? Use, misuse, and abuse may each have different strategies. Attention to negative consequences and an emphasis on unmet potential may generate different approaches.
5. Personal Factors – What are unique, individualized considerations with individuals? These may include age, gender, genetic predisposition, family background, language, sexual orientation, and more.
6. Sociopolitical Context – What is the setting within which the strategies will be planned and implemented? Different states, regions of the country, and setting (urban, rural, suburban) will affect these efforts. Also important are overall social norms and perceptions of these norms, as well as the current dialog about these issues.
7. Theoretical and Planning Grounding – What theory or theories guide the planning? Related to the theories undergirding the proposed efforts is the logic chain identified earlier. These underpinnings are essential for addressing the critical question "why?" For example, which aspects of the Health Belief Model, and/or the Stages of Change Model, are relevant for anchoring the efforts. Other theoretical or research foundations from Chapter 4 or elsewhere will be helpful. Having this grounding clearly specified is an important aspect of the planning efforts.

The purpose of having these seven considerations is to firm up the likelihood of success with the desired outcome. That is in contrast to implementing a strategy because it has been used elsewhere, because it seems to be interesting, or because it is in the realm of initiatives called "coasters and posters." Rationale that is limited or lacking is not helpful or appropriate for a quality initiative.

Once the planning and careful considerations are done, the organizers can then focus on two elements of the prevention approach:

- Methodology – What are the specific strategies? This focus is on the prevailing conceptual planning for interventions, and what planners seek to do. Included here may be items such as a policy, procedure, educational curriculum, skill-building, campaign, poster, discussion, public service announcement, and more.

- Message – What is the planned message, linked to the desired outcome, about what is desired for the audience to know, to feel, or to do? Messages such as "Just Say No," "Don't Drink and Drive," "Friends Don't Let Friends Drive Drunk," and "If You See Something, Say Something" are widespread, for different purposes and with different outcomes.

It is these final elements – methodology and message – that serve as the visual, concrete elements of prevention. It is these that, all too often, program planners and well-intended professionals ascribe to without the desired and appropriate considerations cited in this section.

To help illustrate some of the practical applications associated with prevention efforts, the long-term advocates provide insights and observations based on their years of experience:

Inclusion might be the word, of the individual treatment kinds of approaches that have been able now to be expanded to a little bit more small group interventions.

Mary Wilfert

It is really a question of creating as many "aha" moments as we possibly can. It's all about the stages of change, trying to move people through the stages of change. But unfortunately as a profession we have put all of our eggs in a behavior-change basket saying if you do not show behavior change then you have failed, when in reality we are trying to move people down those stages of change and with each of these interventions we hope we are moving them to ultimately change their behavior, but that may not even happen soon.

Kim Dude

Come from where you've come. Those were the best words I'd ever heard because "come from where you've come" I could go back to my coaching, I could design my training based on that model, tell them interactive activities, let them do it, let them go through it being involved, so most of my training I used "come from where you've come," as my past coaching background and found that it has been successful because you do let the people, you ask them what they want, then you try to design their program, let them do it, and then you walk through it with them on it.

Mary Hill

I think that we've certainly grown in our understanding and appreciation of student development and how that impacts the kinds of messaging or strategies that work on changing behaviors. I think we learned a lot over the years and we learned maybe to apply some of the things that we learned back in the 1970s about behavior change, we learn better how to apply those and how to recognize whether what we are doing is effective or not, how to measure what we are doing so that's a trend that certainly I have seen over the years that we've become more proficient in being able to identify things that don't work.

Mary Wilfert

Having to do a lot more investigation as to the best approaches and the best messaging to influence various demographics; some things work for some kids, some students, some groups.

Mary Wilfert

Prevention Methodologies

The strategies used in prevention efforts range from large-scale to small-scale, direct to indirect, individual and environmental, and personalized and group. This section highlights some of the major approaches that have been included within prevention efforts. The important factor is to be clear and intentional in planning and execution, and not to simply implement a strategy. As will be highlighted in Chapter 8 (Resourceful Approaches), planning frameworks and matrices can be helpful with a planned process.

Common approaches in prevention include the following:

- Policy – Rules and regulations, pricing and taxes, licensing, hours of operation, service standards, advertising and marketing, food, alcohol-free bans at settings/events, amnesty, drinking age, beverage industry/pharmaceutical company sponsorship standards.
- Enforcement – Consistent implementation and followthrough of existing policies; clear procedures
- Information Dissemination – Facts about substances, body processing, short- and long-term effects, consequences of misuse and abuse, normative re-education
- Affective Approaches – Values clarification, personalized feedback
- Campaigns – Topical issue, event/season initiative, policy change, social norming
- Curriculum – Structured setting/school, information and resources, scientific grounding
- Skills Training – Blood-alcohol concentration assessment, expectancy challenge, goal-setting, self-monitoring, life skills
- Skill-Building – Stress management, time management, assertiveness, exercise,
- Peer Approaches and Mentoring – Outreach to peers with education, advising, support, connecting older and younger youth and adults, safe places
- Programming – Social and cultural events, substance-free activities, "alternative events"
- Training – Skills training of vendors and service providers, bystander intervention
- Community Engagement – Leader training, public commitment
- Media Involvement – Media relations, media advocacy
- Support Services – Brief screening protocols, motivational interviewing, individual and group counseling, mutual aid/self-help groups, medications for substance use disorder
- Needs Assessment and Evaluation – Quantitative and qualitative assessments, process and outcome measures, planning and monitoring.

With this compilation, two overarching concepts are important. First, prevention efforts are best implemented within the context of a comprehensive approach. This means that no single approach (e.g., policy or curriculum or programming) is sufficient for making a difference; an orchestrated variety of approaches is what is needed. Second, for any of the individual approaches used, blending different approaches or having a hybrid is appropriate. For example, consider information dissemination using a campaign; using media relations to highlight the enforcement efforts associated with a policy; or doing skills training on bystander interventions.

Central to effective prevention is attention to the processes used to plan, implement, and review the strategies undertaken. Chapters 7 (Helpful Processes) and 8 (Resourceful Approaches) will emphasize these in greater detail. A vital aspect of these processes is the Strategic Prevention Framework developed by SAMHSA; this is a helpful process aiding individuals, groups, and communities address substance use and misuse.

Additional attention to the strategies used with prevention effort are two things. First, Professional Perspective 6.2 offers a resourceful approach, grounded with self-examination and personalized values clarification efforts. Second, the long-term advocates offer their insights about prevention methodologies and activities based on their experience.

Professional Perspective 6.2

Choices and Guidelines about Alcohol and Other Drugs

Thomas M. Griffin, Ph.D., and Jennifer Griffin-Wiesner, M.Ed.

Societal norms about drug and alcohol use have been difficult to discern since the inception of the United States (Anderson, 1976). At various times throughout U.S. history, segments of the population have viewed alcohol use as moral transgression, personal foible, public health crisis, or all of the above. Alcohol has, in the not-so-distant past, been outlawed. Conversely, the drinking culture today is normalized and even glorified through advertising and sponsorship of sporting events and other entertainment. A vast majority (86%) of American adults have consumed alcohol in their lifetimes (SAMHSA, 2015). More than half have consumed in the past month, and 24% report having had five or more drinks in a row in the past month (SAMHSA, 2016).

Mixed messages and confusing discrepancies in societal attitudes make establishing and maintaining personal norms challenging, especially for young people. Relatively easy access combined with pervasive positive messaging leaves many without clear standards for decisions about substance use.

Further muddying the already murky waters are illegal drugs, as well as legal drugs used in an illegal manner. Particularly confusing is marijuana, which is often touted as less harmful than alcohol or other drugs, and is now legal in some states recreationally, medicinally, or both.

In the late 1970s and early 1980s, our work related to setting personal and/or community alcohol-use guidelines began to take root. Our aim was to try to mitigate the confusing and often conflicting context, and empower individuals and groups to establish their own standards and norms.

While the focus was on individual decision-making, the backdrop was a desire to create a common foundation that would minimize public health risks and costs for institutions, systems, communities, and society at large. Initial efforts were implemented where there was obvious benefit gained from the well-being of a population sub-group: the workplace, school campuses, and athletics teams (see, for example, Svendsen & Griffin, 1990). The motives were both humane, wanting to promote health and safety, and practical. In 1983, Griffin wrote in *Prevention Is Everybody's Business* (1983):

> We have long realized that it is less costly to provide treatment for a chemical use problem than to allow a person's problems to get increasingly worse. We are now beginning to realize the cost effectiveness of prevention services as well.

At their core, guidelines start with the premise that illegal drug use is inherently high-risk and therefore simply not advised. The composition and dosage of illicit drugs is unknown by the user and the unsupervised use of prescription drugs presents risks of unanticipated effects including overdose. Low-risk choices about alcohol are more nuanced and emphasize the following:

- It is a *personal choice* to use or not to use alcohol;
- *Alcohol use is not essential* for enjoying social events, and;
- If a person chooses to use alcohol, then it is important to *establish low-risk limits of moderation* before beginning to drink.

The guidelines-setting process underscored the added critical health risks of substance use that leads to impairment or intoxication. Additional components included learning how to avoid or get out of situations when someone else's use may put one at risk and minimizing overall health and safety risks, for example when serving alcohol or driving while impaired by alcohol, prescription, or illicit substances.

In the decades that have followed, the guidelines-setting process has been used by athletics teams, in schools, and in workplaces toward a goal of minimizing potential performance problems due to alcohol consumption or other drug use. Examples include:

- Self-enforced athletics team standards such as no illicit drug use, no alcohol use on game days, and a maximum of two drinks on any day during the season.
- No alcohol or other drug use during the work day and no alcohol or other drug use while interacting with clients at any time.

- Positive messaging campaigns in schools, focused on actual data on percentages (usually higher than students think) of young people who choose not to use substances and their reasons for doing so.

In each example, members of teams, worksites, and school communities engage in conversation about possible guidelines and establish their own standards so that they are willing to personally adhere to them and encourage others to do so as well. As we know, choices about substance use are ultimately individual and personal. However, by encouraging conversation and reflection and providing a framework for decision-making, we can support and encourage choices that benefit both the individual and the common good.

References

Anderson, D. (1976). *A History of Our Confused Attitudes Toward Beverage Alcohol.* Center City, MN: Hazelden Foundation.

Griffin, T.M. (1983). *Prevention Is Everybody's Business.* Anoka, MN: The Minnesota Institute of Public Health.

Substance Abuse and Mental Health Services Administration (SAMHSA). (2015). *National Survey on Drug Use and Health.* Washington, D.C.: SAMHSA.

Substance Abuse and Mental Health Services Administration (SAMHSA). (2016). *National Survey on Drug Use and Health.* Rockville, MD: SAMHSA, Center for Behavioral Health Statistics Quality.

Svendsen, R. & Griffin, T. (1990). *Alcohol Choices and Guidelines for College Students.* Mounds View, MN: Health Promotion Resources.

Tom Griffin, Ph.D., M.S.W., entered the field of prevention in the early 1970s, working in the public and private sectors during a time of rapidly emerging knowledge about the effectiveness of prevention and health promotion approaches.

Jennifer Griffin-Wiesner, M.Ed., is Tom's daughter, and currently runs her own consulting practice based on bridging research and practice in youth development. Prior to that she spent a decade working at Search Institute during the emergence of the Developmental Assets framework and the related national Healthy Communities • Healthy Youth initiative.

I think that they should invest resources into prevention and those kind of brief motivational interventions.

Helene White

Over the years a tight funding stream that has never really given prevention sufficient resources to explore new ideas.

Tom Griffin

I've seen a big shift, and in a sense there is some caution there because some of the folks that are involved in individual intervention may not fully understand or appreciate prevention science. I think more and more of them do because their work has contributed to it but you will find professionals who are trained in counseling and individual interventions that get put in positions of primary prevention and they may not have that skill set or that understanding of the breadth of the field to be able to effectively provide those kinds of effective primary prevention strategies.

Mary Wilfert

There are all sorts of really good practices in high schools, such as on prom night. There are pockets of good practice like alternative practices that are fun.

Thomasina Borkman

We had wonderful little programs and things like that but some of this we just said that's good but that is not the meat and potatoes here. We need all of these pieces but unless we have many of these elements working simultaneously we are really not going to show a lot of difference. And I can remember requiring them to keep data on their programs and what they were doing on a day-to-day basis.

Darlind Davis

I think there needs to be a recognition on law enforcement's part, they need to start to follow what is good policymaking.

Steve Schmidt

The most important education and intervention that can be done … to a large extent is parent training. You've heard that you have to get a license to fish but anybody can become a parent. Helping new parents at any age to understand what it means to raise a child, what a healthy family system can look like and understand that addiction prevention should be taught at home.

Teresa Johnston

At the end of the day my sense is that if you are 18, 19, and 20 years old, sooner or later you have to look at your own culture around you and decide that there are people who are counterproductive to the kind of life that you want to lead. And so somewhere along the way I think we have to put the power into the hands of those youth to address the culture. And so we as adults looking in on that environment can certainly provide some tools, but ultimately I think until young people come to the conclusion that they are not happy about property damage in the elevator, that they are not happy about the bathroom, that they are not happy about violence, whatever that is. Ultimately I don't think you can enforce a cultural change on others, I think that culture has to decide that it needs to change or should change, or there are benefits of changing and I think that's a little bit of a philosophical shift going forward.

Ralph Blackman

Prevention Messages

The importance of helpful messaging is central to prevention efforts. While the effort may be of a quality nature, it is important that the recipient of the prevention efforts (that is, the audience or participants) are obtaining the messages that are intended. The planner must be very clear about what is wanted for the recipient to "know, feel or do"; also, the recipient should clearly understand what that outcome is. Further, these two must match!

To be effective, six steps are offered. Some of the elements within these are reminders of other content described elsewhere in this chapter.

1. Clarify Outcomes – It is important to be clear with what you want the audience to know, feel, and/or do. Be focused and specific. Make sure your communication points to a next step. Don't be ambiguous with your suggestions or guidance.
2. Build a Plan – In the process of designing the message, be clear, focused, deliberate, and planful. Know your theoretical underpinnings, and what logic sequence guides your efforts. Distinguish clearly between what you want to prevent and what you want to promote. Identify ways in which the message and its delivery will be culturally relevant.
3. Identify Strategies and Channels – This includes methods such as brochure, poster, banner, television or radio public service announcement, use of social media, or fact sheet. It includes postcards, letters to the editor, newsletter content, resource guides, speech, workshop, or public presentation.
4. Gather Tools and Resources – Consider the use of examples or testimonials, social marketing, data and facts, expert opinions, "what if" scenarios, creative epidemiology, positioning, linking and pairing, and more.
5. Make It Persuasive – To do so make sure the content is current, credible, and attention-getting. Make it clear and understandable, as well as personally relevant and actionable. It should be visually engaging, consistent, and free of errors. Through this, make sure to blend facts and emotions.
6. Review – In the planning process, build in an evaluation plan starting at the beginning (to measure the achievement of desired outcomes). Assess the messaging itself, to see whether it was heard or seen, whether it was understood, whether it was believed, whether it encouraged someone to act or think, and what message was heard. It is this assessment process that helps with examining whether the message received or heard matched the sent message, and what, if any, resulting impact was achieved.

This messaging is an important aspect of prevention, so that what is communicated is consistent with the other elements of the strategy. Quality prevention efforts without quality communication will likely not be effective.

More detailed insights about specific wording and its importance is provided in Professional Perspective 6.3; this can be helpful in being clear and respectful, and also helping move forward the overall public awareness of and sensitivity to many of the issues in the substance abuse prevention field.

Professional Perspective 6.3

Words Matter

Barbara E. Ryan

Those in prevention communication need to carefully consider the words they use in conveying messages to a variety of audiences, from young people and college students to policymakers and the general public. But competing perspectives, purposes, and imagined "audiences" running throughout the "give and take" in developing prevention practices and policies make it difficult, if not impossible, to come to even some basic agreement. For example, one might be concerned about the precision of any term (e.g., "risky drinking") in light of attempts to measure drinking in standardized instruments. On the other hand, one might be less interested in "scientific" use of language and more concerned about the "message" that use of a term might have for drinkers. Likewise, if communication is directed to policymakers or administrators, a different set of concerns might be salient, such as public problems associated with drunkenness rather than levels of consumption by individuals.

Nevertheless, the dogged efforts to find common language (see Professional Perspective 9.2) underscore the impulse in the alcohol and other drug problem prevention and treatment fields to get agreement on terminology and language to meet a number of objectives, not the least of which is to improve communication among researchers, administrators, policymakers, practitioners, and the public. However noble that objective, the ongoing debate over the term "binge drinking" illustrates the difficulty in coming to agreement on a common terminology for developing prevention communication messages.

In 1984 the Harvard School of Public Health College Alcohol Study (CAS) published a survey that labeled drinking by college students at levels of five or more drinks on an occasion for men and four or more drinks for women as "binge drinking." Subsequently the National Institute on Alcohol Abuse and Alcoholism[1] and the Substance Abuse and Mental Health Services Administration[2] added additional nuances to the definition of "binge drinking." However, throughout the twentieth century, binge has been a workhorse in speech and literature where the subject is drinking. American dictionaries define binge in no uncertain terms: "a drunken celebration or spree," "a riotous indulgence," "an uninhibited and usually excessive indulgence, especially in alcoholic beverages." Webster's Third International Dictionary cites as possible synonyms: orgy, rampage, and splurge. Bat, toot, and bender are other words used interchangeably with "binge." The term has been closely associated in the public's mind with the periodic alcoholic drinking (and not the scientific definitions) depicted in films such as *The Lost Weekend* and *Leaving Las Vegas*.

College students, themselves, quickly rejected the term "binge drinking" as applied to their drinking behavior, prompting a spate of articles and papers promoting professionals' use of alternative language to describe such high levels of drinking when crafting prevention messages. High-risk drinking, dangerous drinking, and heavy episodic drinking are just some of the terms proposed in lieu of binge drinking. But language is not likely to be changed by fiat. The popularity of the term binge drinking remains ubiquitous, as evidenced by a recent headline "Young People Who Binge Drink Could Increase Risk of Stroke, Study Suggests."[3]

Another terminology conflict came to a head when the Office for Substance Abuse Prevention (OSAP) – now the Center for Substance Abuse Prevention (CSAP) – was created through the Anti-Drug Abuse Act of 1986 to address a resurgence of illicit drug use and provide federal leadership for prevention. The very name of the Office was the subject of lively and often contentious debate in the field, with a number of organizations and individuals lobbying unsuccessfully for using the phrase "alcohol and other drug abuse" in the agency's title in order to emphasize in the public's mind that alcohol is indeed a drug. Needless to say, the alcohol industry strongly resisted that association.

In addition, over the past three decades, prevention research has found that measures such as altering the social, physical, economic, legal, and cultural environments surrounding individual drinking and drug-taking decisions can, in fact, reduce a range of alcohol and other drug problems. Be that as it may, the language of prevention, for the most part, continues to focus on individual decisions and behaviors. While there is a greater understanding by the public and policymakers about the role that the environment plays in contributing to and reducing the magnitude of alcohol and other drug problems, if real advances consistent with prevention research are to be made, the language of prevention needs to come up with ways to communicate evidence-based messages about the efficacy of environmental change in reducing problems at both the individual and societal levels.

Notes

1 www.niaaa.nih.gov/alcohol-health/overview-alcohol-consumption/moderate-binge-drinking.
2 www.niaaa.nih.gov/alcohol-health/overview-alcohol-consumption/moderate-binge-drinking.
3 *Newsweek*, August 13, 2018.

Barbara E. Ryan has over 40 years of experience in the alcohol, tobacco, and other drug prevention field as a writer and editor. Among numerous publications, she edited the quarterly magazine *Prevention File: Alcohol, Tobacco and Other Drugs* (1990–2009). She currently works as an editorial consultant at the University of California-San Diego.

As part of appropriate messaging is a specific audience – youth and young adults. With the legal age of purchase being 21 in the United States, and also the age of majority being 18, different messages and ways of addressing alcohol and other drugs are seen. The various long-term advocates, each with varied backgrounds and settings, offer a wide range of perspectives and approaches that may be helpful for individuals or groups as they formulate guidelines and messages. First, from an overall, global perspective, some of the interviewees have generalized remarks.

> We endeavored to take the language of prevention from each agency and tried to put it into common terms into common English. That product ended up becoming evidence-based principles of prevention.
>
> Darlind Davis

> The field has not come as far in recognizing how youth, and we are not talking about youthful parents, communicate.
>
> Ralph Blackman

> I've had acquaintance with therapeutic communities, they help people who nobody else will help and whatever they are doing, but they talk about ex-addicts rather than recovering addicts. Now the word spiritual I think is the wrong word, it's a very difficult word just to share with anybody. There's got to be another word for wellness or whatever it is something metaphysical or cosmological, our value system is precious and there are certain things we don't have words for, words are feeble, they don't work.
>
> William Kane

> And we always know that when perceived risk decreases, substance use can increase.
>
> Mary Wilfert

> I think communication and education are critically important. But to expect that that's going to help clients make a behavior change just isn't enough.
>
> Steve Schmidt

Long-term advocates were asked about specific advice they would give to a 21-year-old. They were also asked what advice they would give to an 18-year-old, and whether that would be the same or different from that with a 21-year-old. These are distinguished in the following illustrative quotes:

> The advice I would give to a 21-year-old is ... not to use drugs at all and alcohol probably very little, very little. Not to use at all if you think you could be getting pregnant and just because of what can happen in terms of date rape. For an 18-year-old just no drugs or alcohol at all. And I think they need a lot more education about the damage that alcohol and drugs do to the developing brain. So the advice that you give to a 12, 13, 14, 15-year-old about how their brain is still developing and they are not really thinking entirely clearly about consequences because of executive functioning, prefrontal cortex is not developed fully until about 25 to 30 years of age. We need to help youth understand the decisions that they are making right now really do impact the rest of their lives. I want them to have a good time but poor decision-making or risky decision-making could destroy the rest of their life or could destroy their dreams. So just think about what they are doing and just know that anything is possible if they set their mind to it unless they misstep and end up, they could end up obviously getting

into really bad legal trouble or have physical issues or end up with a disability or whatever the case may be. Really what they do now is going to have an impact on the rest of their lives. So that would be one thing – for them to be cautious, but also be willing to never quit, to always try to fulfill whatever their dreams are.

Karol Kumpfer

The advice I would give to a 21-year-old would have to do with healthy stress management to avoid alcohol and other drugs. An 18-year-old, probably something fairly similar. They, even three years earlier than 21, they are going to have a little less mental capacity to get those long-term goals that just seem more and more, we just don't see 18-year-olds that have set long-term goals for themselves, so my message would probably be different but I would still be pushing for healthy rather than popular.

Carla Lapelle

Then for the 18-year-olds I think they're at an age now that they can understand that there's got to be better ways to have fun than to go get drunk.

Jeffrey Levy

The advice I would give to a 21-year-old is to know your family history as it relates to alcohol and drugs, and addictive behavior, mental health. And I would give the same advice to an 18-year-old.

Teresa Johnston

Look into your genetic heritage. If you have alcohol or drug abuse in your past, you could have a propensity to drink or use drugs that you could fall down in a hole or ruin your life before you know it. Is it different for 18 versus 21-year-old? I think the advice is to some extent ageless.

Thomasina Borkman

The advice I would give to a 21-year-old is be thinking of today's consequences but if there was a way to help them understand the quality of life and how it's impacted by the choices they make at 18 and 21, the advice I would give to a 21-year-old is to avoid the regrets or the sort of lingering negative impact that some of those choices have on our health as we mature. On our cognitive health, on our physical health, those kinds of thing. Think about what you do today really will impact the quality of your life later on.

Mary Wilfert

If you are 21 and you choose to consume alcohol, that obviously you do it responsibly and responsibly has to be defined by you, defined by your own social network, defined by your family, defined by your culture. If you are 18 I think you are still in a situation where obviously have your eyes open to responsible consumption, hopefully on the part of adults who are over that legal age, and at the same time you are obviously witnessing, especially if you're on a college campus, you are obviously witnessing irresponsible consumption and hopefully you're making the value judgments that are required to guide you in terms of how you want to behave, how you *want to model behavior for others especially. For an 18-year-old I don't think it's as cut and dried as we would all like it to be. I think it's a matter of developing your values, understanding the consequences, deciding what's right for you and being empowered enough to make those good decisions.*

Ralph Blackman

The advice I would give to a 21-year-old and 18-year-old is ... I would probably give them the same advice and that is be sure you understand what the impact of any drug intake, any alcohol you drink will have in your life. Make informed decisions. I would probably send exactly the same message to both of them.

Tom Griffin

Long-term advocates with advice for the 21-year-olds include the following:

The advice I would give to a 21-year-old is ... People are terrific, life is curiously interesting, and if you need chemicals to make it okay, then what was the question you're asking if that's the answer?

BJ McConnell

Always be thinking about things critically and evaluating what you read and what you hear and always be questioning that. Also, think through what you think you want to do and if you have a passion for that. I think you have to pursue that passion and if it changes don't sweat it. I do think it's valuable to do a couple of good basic things and that's got to be a good writer, build those skills and I think one of the ways you build those skills is reading whether it's newspapers, magazines. That's another thing I think, stay current with what is going on in the world, critically important.

Steve Schmidt

We need to think carefully about what we're doing and say how these future leaders can learn from this, and by promoting the behaviors that they themselves participate in, it's not going to get any better. The advice I would give is that if we would just ask what their long-term goal is and that they really need to get drunk in order to have fun, most of them would say "no."

Jeffrey Levy

If you are engaging in a dialog and you're becoming emotional or you're being drawn into a conflict of some kind to step back. And that will help you in your mind to distance yourself from it so that you can retain your cerebral skills in order to use your brain to help solve the problem. And it will serve you well for the rest of your life.

Darlind Davis

Have courage to believe in yourself and take a deep breath and trust yourself while looking for mentors. Experience life, don't rush through it and find your own strengths. Take the opportunity to learn as much as you can academically and professionally.

Robert Lynn

Wouldn't you rather look back on your college experience and say that you helped build the Cumberland Trail, as an alternative spring break project? Or did environmental work in Costa Rica? There are other ways that you can have "fun" experiences in your life. The expectations of many people is that young people have to sow their wild oats and there are parents reinforcing that as well.

Deb Thorstenson

Make sure when you drink you are protected. I'd teach protective behavioral strategies.

Helene White

Honor the law, the law matters and there really is some good science coming out in terms of brain development that you need to look into. You need to examine and create personal guidelines and ask questions about whether, when, and how much. And to know there are times when everyone needs to abstain.

Jeff Linkenbach

Really try to work on how they are doing this and the dangers that could be involved. Help them to reach their potential in life.

Mary Hill

Lay the facts before them, that's really how WRAP has distinguished itself, rather than scare tactics, rather than the crashed car, is knowledge, get them back to education, give these folks what they need without being biased and without being influenced in any way except that here is evidence-based material on what the consequences are, and here is how your body processes alcohol.

Kurt Erickson

Get the best education that they can and that they should continue in their education until they find something that they would like to pursue.

Mark Gold

Education and Training

Throughout this chapter, the emphasis has been upon prevention as a whole. Attention has been provided to education as a part of prevention, and also to training as a part of prevention. This final segment highlights some additional perspectives regarding these two aspects of prevention strategies.

Regarding education, all too often this is viewed as synonymous with prevention. As illustrated throughout this chapter, prevention is much more complex and sophisticated than simply education. Education is typically that of an information focus, providing others with facts and figures, and often with scare tactics. Also, education is often seen as relegated to the classroom setting, and focusing on youth. While education and information are central to prevention efforts, they are not sufficient.

In reviewing the various components of prevention, education will likely be incorporated throughout these, whether through campaigns or media efforts, skills training or support services, or peer training or policy implementation. Also with education, consider that different audiences, whether by age, setting, language, or prior education, have different learning styles and preferences.

With prevention overall, it is important to move beyond a basic, information-focused, education approach. As noted, one important factor is that any single approach will not be sufficient for making a difference. Another factor is that because of all the education that has gone before whatever education is planned currently, new approaches are essential. The vast majority of people (excluding those working professionally with substance abuse issues) have misinformation about the basic facts about drugs and alcohol, substance abuse, dependence, and more. Further, significant personal experience serves as a factor in attempting to make a difference with them for their own lives and the lives of those around them. Thus, current best practices call for grounded thinking and new strategies for making a difference.

Hand in hand with the education efforts is training. Just as with education, training is essential throughout the prevention efforts. For example, with new policies and procedures, training is needed for those enforcing these standards and for those educating about the standards (whether teachers, trainers, media personnel, or community leaders). Training is important for those in the school setting, for example. Not only is this vital for those directly involved with the curriculum on drugs and alcohol, but it is also important for other topic areas where misinformation could be shared unintentionally, and where opportunities for inclusion can be used.

Training among various professionals is vital, whether for substance use issues as well as for other related topics linked to the proactive approaches recommended. Training of professionals preparing to work in various settings will be helpful and important; consider the medical profession, the legal profession, the business administration field, and the student affairs profession in higher education. With medical schools, how much attention is provided to substance use disorders, and how well prepared are doctors for having conversations about drugs and alcohol from a prevention and early intervention perspective? To what extent are law schools preparing those entering the legal profession to understand the nature and scope of substance abuse involvement with their clients and their cases? How much attention is provided in business schools for those seeking to manage others, lead organizations, and inspire quality and productivity? And for college higher education graduate programs, how much attention is provided to preparing professionals to lead and address substance abuse and other wellness issues? The answer to all of these is virtually nothing. Specifically, with higher education preparation programs, none of 180 has a required course on substance abuse issues, and only three have a requirement addressing wellness issues.

Training is essential throughout the spectrum for prevention efforts, not just on how to execute effectively the various strategies identified, but also on the facts, attitudes, perceptions, and skills surrounding substance use. This includes substance use disorder, as well as drugs and alcohol and their specific consequences.

As efforts to organize prevention activities can take shape in different ways in different settings, it is helpful to examine some processes that can be helpful in helping get other individuals and groups to collaborate. These processes can be helpful for worksite, secondary school, higher education, community, state, and national initiatives. Professional Perspective 6.4 offers some succinct steps about this effort.

> **Professional Perspective 6.4**
>
> **Building Capacity for Community Change**
>
> *Joseph Espinoza, M.S., and Kelly Schlabach, M.A.*
>
> Communities comprise various entities, shared problems affect all entities, and efforts for change and improvement are more effective when these entities work together. All members of a community are affected by substance abuse and its various outcomes; so how can they stand together to prevent or better address these issues? This can be accomplished through building capacity such as increasing the knowledge, skills, and ability to plan, undertake, and manage initiatives related to substance abuse issues (CADCA, 2010). Building capacity in a community is an initial step; as such, it does not speak to sustaining, enhancing, or revitalizing capacity.
>
> Robbers (2004) states that social support includes one's "network of friends, family, acquaintances, and other resources" (p. 546). Robbers further emphasizes that social support serves primary functions of integrating individuals into society and helping serve as a buffer when faced with stressful events. Essentially, various networks and social support groups make up communities, and building capacity for change within communities can lead to more widespread and sustained change.
>
> One particular theory useful for conceptualizing how to build and organize community capacity is the Self-Determination Theory (Deci & Ryan, 1985). This emphasizes that autonomy, competence, and relatedness increase motivation. Deci and Ryan (1985, p. 56) state that one increases autonomy through "acquisition of competency in dealing with its environment." Thus, by increasing competency in substance use prevention and intervention efforts, social group members will eventually feel more autonomy (and subsequently motivation) with these efforts. Relatedness is defined as feeling connected to others through group membership, and being emotionally invested with and for that group (Baumeister & Leary, 1995). By increasing relatedness within a social group, there is more motivation and accountability for sustained behavior such as the reduction or elimination of substance abuse.
>
> Beyond this theoretical foundation, "effective collaborations highlight cultural issues and integrate them as core aspects of building communitywide support" (CADCA, 2012). Not only is this culturally appropriate, but it also helps localize the strategies identified to meet issues of relevance. By creating drug and alcohol abuse prevention initiatives guided by, at a minimum, these factors, individuals can increase the motivation of community members – both individuals and organizations – to engage in this work.

To illustrate the application of these theoretical constructs, consider having an educational program or campaign. To be effective, this strategy will educate members about the impact and warning signs of drug and alcohol abuse (*competence*), bring awareness to the effects of substance use in various social groups through facilitated discussion (*relatedness*), and create a plan for other members of the community to intervene when there is a concern about drug or alcohol abuse (*autonomy*). Specific elements within this strategy may incorporate the following:

- Create a brief presentation including the warning signs and impact of substance abuse to build the competency of participants.
- Separate larger groups into smaller social groups and networks of approximately 3–10 individuals to better facilitate discussion and build relatedness.
- Create specific discussion questions aimed at strengthening connections and understanding the impact of substance abuse on communities. Sample questions include:
  - How often do you think your social group engages in substance use?
  - What do you think the rates of substance use in your region are? (Then compare these views with previously-collected regional results.)
  - How has substance use affected your life, whether personally or with friends, family, colleagues, or neighbors?
- Facilitate a discussion among social group members to create an individualized plan for strategies relevant for members of the group. These plans may include:
  - A list and schedule of substance-free events in the community of potential interest to social group members.
  - A specific code word or phrase for use when a certain environment is unsafe, uncomfortable, or activating further substance use.
  - Encouragement of bringing concerns of substance abuse up in a private setting, preferably a home environment.
  - Having each person acknowledge feelings of defensiveness and discomfort and being willing to listen.

While the work of prevention can often fall on one person, it is important to engage multiple people across varying skills, training, experience, and competencies to create a more unified and connected leadership body. By doing so, the capacity of the community is strengthened and the breadth and depth of knowledge and issues addressed can be expanded.

Building capacity for community change begins with individuals strengthening the relations within their communities. An intervention program grounded in Self Determination Theory, involving building competence, autonomy, and relatedness, can increase motivation to reduce substance and alcohol abuse, while also strengthening communities even further.

To truly create change, it takes participation from individuals of all backgrounds to come together and address the prevention of drug and alcohol abuse at the community level. Most, if not all, individuals in the United States are affected by substance abuse and by building capacity within communities, many of the desired outcomes can be achieved.

References

Baumeister, R. & Leary, M. (1995). The need to belong: Desire for interpersonal attachments as a fundamental human motivation. *Psychological Bulletin, 117*, 497–529.

Community Anti-Drug Coalition of America (CADCA). (2010). *Capacity Primer: Building Membership, Structure and Leadership*. Alexandria, VA: National Community Anti-Drug Coalition Institute.

Community Anti-Drug Coalition of America (CADCA). (2012). *Cultural Competence Primer: Incorporating Cultural Competence into Your Comprehensive Plan*. Alexandria, VA: National Community Anti-Drug Coalition Institute.

Deci, E.L., & Ryan, R.M. (1985). *Intrinsic Motivation and Self-determination in Human Behavior*. New York, NY: Plenum.

Robbers, M. (2004). Revisiting the moderating effect of social support on strain: A gendered test. *Sociological Inquiry, 74*(4), 546–569.

Joseph Espinoza, M.S., serves as Case Manager for the Office of Student Outreach and Support at the University of Denver; his background includes working in health education and prevention services, advocating for mental health promotion, and behavioral health among college students. He holds a Bachelor of Science in health and exercise science with a concentration in health promotion from Colorado State University.

Kelly Schlabach, M.A., is Case Manager at the University of Denver. She earned her bachelor's degree in social work at Ohio University where she also gained experience in developing, presenting, and analyzing bystander intervention trainings focused in harm reduction techniques.

Some final views of long-term advocates are helpful for an overall prevention perspective:

> What I believed earlier, that I no longer believe ... that the deliverables of prevention have been a tough sell. I believed that education can have a positive impact on behavior. I think it's important to have information out there to use as a primary strategy to change behavior.
>
> Kurt Erickson

> My optimism is absolutely hitched to education and I'm concerned that a lack of education will continue.
>
> Kurt Erickson

I think we got most of the people to realize and understand that there are some programs out there that are more effective than others so let's adopt them.

Bill Modzeleski

Summary

Prevention is a lot of different things, with a variety of messages and strategies. It is not as simple as education and information. It is not just policies and procedures. It is more than training and alternative activities. And certainly, it is not just "posters and coasters." In fact, prevention is more than a litany of strategies. To be done well and to achieve the desired results, it is important to have a sound plan with clearly defined outcomes. The process of designing prevention is becoming more robust and organized, and this represents a lot of hard work. It is moving toward becoming more and more scientifically grounded, with quality approaches. Prevention requires a lot of time and effort; however, it is important to recall the context of doing prevention. One part of this is to address, more effectively, much of what was outlined in the first two chapters of this book regarding the nature of the issue. The other is to recall the importance of doing so, as discussed in Chapter 3 (Why Be Concerned?) This context will be helpful for sustaining and improving prevention initiatives at various levels of society.

Part II
Confidence

Confidence is the second component included in the *Pyramid of Success*. This is based on people believing in themselves, and having the perspective that they have something of value to offer or share. Confidence allows the individual to move ahead and share insights, expertise, experiences, and understandings. It is helpful with sharing viewpoints when addressing controversies or helping establish priorities. The individual believes in his or her perspectives, and seeks to share these for the larger good of individuals, groups, communities, or beyond.

With this element, skills can be improved upon so that one's knowledge and expertise can be shared more comfortably and skillfully. To have someone who is highly competent, yet does not believe in their own knowledge, experience, or background, can result in limited exposure of this expertise. The individual may not feel the self-esteem to share their perspectives, thereby thwarting or not advancing the cause of reduced drug and alcohol problems. Thus, confidence is an essential part of the *Pyramid of Success*, as it helps the competent person share insights and wisdom with others.

7 Helpful Processes

This chapter is the first of three within the Confidence section of this book. The section as a whole builds upon the Competence chapters which emphasize the importance of current knowledge and skills regarding various dimensions of substance abuse issues. This chapter directs attention to processes helpful for developing and promoting positive outcomes at the organizational, community, and societal levels. This chapter highlights foundational processes for collaborative and engaging planning processes. The next chapter "Resourceful Approaches" addresses a range of strategies and actionable approaches; the final chapter in this section, "Personal and Professional Strategies," offers specific strategies and tips regarding persuasive communication and advocacy efforts.

This chapter is organized around a planning model, within the overall constructs of planned change and strategic planning. The importance of this is that a process be implemented to provide structure and organization to the efforts undertaken at the group level, whether large or small. This is consistent with the themes of early chapters in this book, where the nature of the issue and reasons for concern may extend beyond problems and problem reduction. That is, while it is important to be reactive and address problems, it is equally (and perhaps more) important to be proactive and not just prevent problems, but also enhance the quality of life.

Planning processes can be helpful with achieving these outcomes. The old mantra of the seven Ps (Proper Prior Planning Prevents Pathetically Poor Performance) summarizes the context of planning efforts. This chapter begins with attention to Planned Change, and why this is vital. This is followed by the construct of Force Field Analysis, to help leaders conceptualize the issue and where the planning efforts fit. The remainder of the chapter addresses an overall Planning Framework that can be helpful for organizing and orchestrating these efforts. While strategic planning processes are described in many different ways, this framework provides a way of implementing these efforts throughout various settings.

Planned Change

When thinking about ways of addressing drug and alcohol concerns, the key premise is that change is needed. The nature of the issue, from both individual and environmental perspectives, was summarized briefly in the first two chapters of this book. Based on those factors, and many more documented with research studies, government reports, and personal experiences of so many, change is essential. That was the essence of Chapter 3 (Why Be Concerned?); just having the knowledge that problems exist, and having a desire for not having these problems, constitutes the foundation for change.

Simply put, to not change, or to not even examine whether change might be needed or valuable, is to accept the status quo.

If the aim is to change, then the approach to achieve that change is, ideally, one that is planned. The alternative is "unplanned change" which could also be named "disorganized efforts," "chaos," or "movement without direction." Ostensibly, all those committed to change efforts would desire approaches that are planned, organized, thoughtful, and well orchestrated. In the legal world, attention is provided to "due process," with the follow-on question of "what process is due." For planned change, the parallel question is what process is appropriate, or what planning elements are central, for a sound process to occur and to maximize quality results.

The focus upon planned change does not suggest, however, a specific process. As noted, numerous strategic planning frameworks exist, and one may be more appropriate or more beneficial in one situation when compared with other approaches. The Planning Framework offered in this chapter is certainly no guarantee for success; it represents a composite of numerous approaches and strategies that will increase the likelihood for the desired outcomes as well as sustainability over time.

Similarly, engaging in an organized, orchestrated strategic planning process will help reduce the presence or impact of unanticipated consequences. By specifically identifying and planning for the likelihood of challenges or obstacles, efforts can be undertaken to reduce their impact. By actively considering these challenges, strategies can be identified to reduce their influence, as well as to increase, strategically, the protective or resiliency factors with individuals, organizations, and society at large. It is within this context that the Force Field Analysis approach is helpful for conceptualizing and planning for localized strategies.

The interviews with the long-term advocates were helpful for providing a range of perspectives regarding the importance of planning efforts. This type of grounding is vital for having meaningful efforts.

> *Being able to incorporate current research into everyday practice is a key ingredient in being a good clinician.*
>
> Claudia Blackburn

> *I think my biggest regret is pushing the field, the research field into doing what I think the education field wanted, not what research wanted. And that's still one of my problems, is that I don't see researchers doing enough applied research, doing enough research that is one of my schools.*
>
> Bill Modzeleski

> *I think two factors – collaboration and an ability to learn from the past – were common characteristics in all of those accomplishments.*
>
> Tom Griffin

I think tobacco has had something to do with it, in fact, whatever we have done with tobacco, if we can pick that apart, see what elements went into the tobacco revolution and apply that to other social problems, somebody has got a Nobel prize there if they can figure that out. What combination of Surgeon General and public policy and so on, what combination of those things overturned the magnificent powerful tobacco industry? That was your main opponent. So whatever we did with tobacco, if we can replicate that we could solve other problems in our society I think. And I think that just getting clean from tobacco helped people in recovery too, I think it showed that that sort of abstinence was a favorable thing.

William Kane

So we spent a lot of money on stuff, there wasn't a real careful, thoughtful process for trying to figure out how to solve a problem. It wasn't done in any strategic way.

Bill Modzeleski

I believe in ready, aim, fire. An awful a lot of people are ready, aim, aim, aim, aim, aim, and they don't fire because they are waiting until they have everything absolutely perfect. I think we do ready, aim, fire, and then we ready it again and aim, and fire, and what is the worst thing that can happen?

Kim Dude

We focused primarily on how we could create systems that would assist those, whether it was in dealing with underage drinking or those dealing with responsible alcohol beverage service in the licensee community, where our agency was a catalyst for bringing groups together to deal with that as well as to create "train the trainer" programs.

Steve Schmidt

Force Field Analysis

This approach can be viewed as both an overall construct as well as a planning process. Essentially, Force Field Analysis[1] examines opposing forces (driving and restraining forces) and attempts to identify strategies to make progress with addressing problems or issues. It presumes that these opposing forces are temporary in nature (although they may have existed for long periods of time), and that change is possible. From the perspective of an overall construct, Force Field Analysis helps organize general thinking and perspectives. For the planning process, Force Field Analysis can be used to identify specific obstacles and challenges, as well as assets and resources. It can help identify ways to reduce or eliminate the former, and enhance or improve the latter. Further, this same process can be used with the review of each obstacle and asset.

The overall intent of Force Field Analysis is from a systems perspective, useful for groups, organizations, and communities. It can be adapted from an individual or clinical view, although that is not its general use. Specifically, the process involves six steps:

1. Problem Specification – State the nature of the problem or issue as it currently exists. This should be as clear as possible. For substance abuse, this may be the existence or increase in opioid deaths, emergency room visits, automobile crashes, underage drinking, or substance-related overdoses.
2. Desired Results – This addresses the endpoint or change that is desired. It may be the achievement of a specific level or quantity, or it may involve a change of a certain percentage (e.g., 20% reduction). It is also helpful to include any specific information on the current state of affairs; this allows for a review of achievement or lack thereof when comparing with the status quo.
3. Driving Forces – This is the first of the opposing forces, and addresses what forces can help in the movement from the current state of affairs, toward the goal of achievement of the desired state of affairs. These include currently existing factors, such as resources, personnel, awareness, strategies, or other forces; they may also include some "what if" elements, such as proposed or future factors.
4. Restraining Forces – This is the other opposing force and identifies those factors that hinder or block movement toward the achievement of the goal. These include policies, approaches, resources, or other issues that impede or restrict goal attainment.
5. Prioritization – Rate each of the identified forces in terms of importance. This can be done in priority order (according to which has the greatest influence) or by rating each one from low (limited impact on the factor) to high (major impact).
6. Strategy Development – Using the prioritization, identify which driving and restraining forces will be addressed; this does not necessitate addressing all the forces, but rather emphasizes selecting which ones should be addressed at this point in time, based on various local and current factors. The decision will be based on the decision-makers' assessment of factors such as importance, urgency, feasibility, and availability of resources. For each Driving Force selected, identify what can be done to increase its strength or potency. With each Restraining Force selected, look at what strategies would help reduce its potency. The same "driving and restraining forces" assessment can be done for each of these. For example, if a driving force for change was the existence of a local coalition, identify what would help strengthen its capacity, membership, influence, and role; also identify risks or problems that might ensue so these can be minimized.

The Force Field Analysis process can be helpful as an overall construct by thinking about the overall endpoint, what will help achieve this, and what is in the way. The specific planning process can be adapted, shortened, or expanded to help identify clearly various options and opportunities regarding where things are currently, what the desired future is, what will help, and what is in the way. With processes such as engaging in a planning process that incorporates some or all of the concepts incorporated with Force Field Analysis, the desired outcomes are more likely to be achieved.

The long-term advocates talked about ways of balancing their assets and their constraints. Some comments are helpful in this regard:

> *We were in the business of having people look at that block in the Johari Window that was like what I don't know and what no one else knows about me. What you don't know you don't know. It's just if you can bring it up to the surface and you can face it, then you have a chance to maybe do something about it.*
>
> Darlind Davis

> *I think it's probably to be more aggressive, overall I think we are an aggressive group but I suppose that we are also cognizant of the politics that are involved, that are involved with such.*
>
> Kurt Erickson

> *The most important things that can be done … Everybody is still doing their thing and I'm not saying it's easy but my sense is that there are most likely resources out there that if you could break down some of those barriers you would find our resources that are usable in very creative ideas.*
>
> Ralph Blackman

> *There was a mismatch then, and there continues to be a mismatch. Until we get to the time where the researchers realize that the customers are not themselves, customers are people who are in schools, they are teachers, they are parents, until we get their input and have a better idea of what they want and tailor our research to what they want we're not going to be successful.*
>
> Bill Modzeleski

Planning Framework

Building upon the construct of the Force Field Analysis, a seven-step Planning Framework is offered. Strategic planning, action planning, systematic planning processes, and similar approaches all encompass the important emphasis upon planning. The aim of planning is to be organized, thoughtful, and timely. The aim is to be prevention oriented; while reactive responses will be necessitated, the focus is on trying to avoid a crisis mode as the standard procedure. The Planning Framework detailed in this chapter is a compilation from various tools and approaches used. It is offered as a starting point, as a reminder, or as an alternative for professionals, community leaders, and advocates with organizing efforts in their respective settings.

It is also noteworthy that the U.S. Center for Substance Abuse Prevention has developed and promulgated the Strategic Prevention Framework (SPF).[2] By design, this SPF was developed to help individuals, groups, and communities address substance use and misuse. Professional Perspective 7.1 offers some additional insight about this framework and how it can be used.

Professional Perspective 7.1

Strategic Planning: The Power Is in the Process

Dave Closson, M.S.

A strategic plan is the formalized road map that describes how your organization identifies and executes the chosen strategy. The plan spells out where an organization is going and how it's going to get there. It is a tool that serves the purpose of helping an organization do a better job, because the plan focuses the energy, resources, and time of everyone involved. The plan keeps the group on track, helps them develop and implement efforts and activities that are meaningful to their community, and outlines what everyone involved should be doing to move toward the goals. Strategic planning is an approach that embraces teamwork, promotes outcomes-based initiatives, and data-driven decision-making.

As you start off on the journey of creating your strategic plan it is important to have a framework to guide the process. Many frameworks are available to help you through the strategic planning process. The framework I use most often is SAMHSA's Strategic Prevention Framework. It provides a clear and comprehensive process for addressing the substance misuse and related behavioral health problems facing a community. This framework is not just for communities, as it can be adapted for large and small settings, worksites and schools, and with paid staff and volunteers. Ultimately, the power and effectiveness of a strategic plan comes from the process that built it. The process is what will ensure everyone is on the same page and that no key tasks are missed. Further, this framework's "prevention" emphasis encompasses primary, secondary, and tertiary prevention, or the entire continuum of care.

Here are five questions to guide your strategic planning process.

1. What is the problem, and how can I learn more?

As professionals you will need to identify the pressing substance use, related problems, and the contributing factors. Take time to gather and assess data from a variety of sources to ensure your prevention, treatment, and recovery efforts are appropriate and targeted to the needs of your community. The data gathered will help you identify and prioritize the substance use and related problems in your community. It will help to clarify the impact of these problems community members and the resources needed. Be sure to engage the key stakeholders in gathering and assessing the data. Not only will this increase their buy-in and understanding of the problems, it will also aid substantially with the sustainability of the efforts.

2. What do I have to work with?

Moving forward you will need to identify, build, and mobilize local resources and readiness to address the specific needs of your community or setting. You will need to assess the community resources and readiness. This includes both human and structural resources to establish and maintain your efforts. A few resources to consider are the people (staff, volunteers, experts), community connections, supplies, and existing efforts to meet the identified needs. When the motivation and willingness to commit local resources are high, your prevention programs are more likely to succeed.

3. What should I do and how should I do it?

As you answer this question you will be creating the detailed plan for addressing the priority problems and achieving your goals. In developing your plan, you will link risk and protective factors, select effective interventions, and build a logic model linking problems, factors, interventions, and outcomes. This approach helps link what you are doing with the local needs and local resources; it keeps your efforts focused and targeted. This will increase the effectiveness of your efforts by ensuring you select and implement the most appropriate strategies for your community. An effective plan will have input from key stakeholders and community members. Following a strategic planning framework built on a collaborative process is more likely to address the community's needs and be sustained.

4. How can I put my plan into action?

At this point, things are starting to come together. You have a well-developed plan with effective interventions that will meet your community's needs. Your plan (building on the logic model from Step 3) includes efforts with prevention and education, with treatment and recovery, and with related efforts that help address substance abuse issues. The next step is to put the plan into action. It is important to describe the specific steps to be taken and who is responsible for each step; also helpful are timelines to help ensure accountability. This overall plan will help ensure everyone is on the same page and no key tasks fall through the cracks. Further, reviewing the plan periodically (before, during, and after key tasks) can help ensure quality with current as well as future efforts.

5. Is my plan succeeding?

This isn't just about collecting information. It is about using that information to improve the program and strategies. Knowing how well the programs or services were delivered and how successful they were in achieving the desired outcomes will help leaders decide whether or not to continue the program or whether modifications are appropriate. The evaluation results – both outcome and process in nature – are typically reported to stakeholders and community members which can increase support, interest, and long-term sustainability for the program.

Remember that the effectiveness of a strategic plan is derived from the processes that built it. Use this planning process to build your team, promote outcomes-based prevention and data-driven decision-making. The process will ensure no key tasks are left out and that everyone is moving toward the same goals. The power is in the process.

> **Resources**
>
> Substance Abuse and Mental Health Services Administration. Applying the Strategic Prevention Framework. www.samhsa.gov/capt/applying-strategic-prevention-framework.
> Substance Abuse and Mental Health Services Administration. Understanding Logic Models. www.samhsa.gov/capt/applying-strategic-prevention-framework/step3-plan/understanding-logic-models.
>
> Dave Closson, M.S., is a national expert on substance misuse prevention and law enforcement. He is the author of *Motivational Interviewing for Campus Police* and brings a unique experience to substance misuse prevention, having served as a campus police officer at Eastern Illinois University.

The Planning Framework embodied in this chapter has seven steps, illustrated by Figure 7.1. These steps are envisioned as a sequential process, whereby each step follows the previous one. The framework is also a cyclical process, whereby at the conclusion of Step Seven, the process begins again. Central to each of these steps is the engagement of key individuals and groups with the process. These include

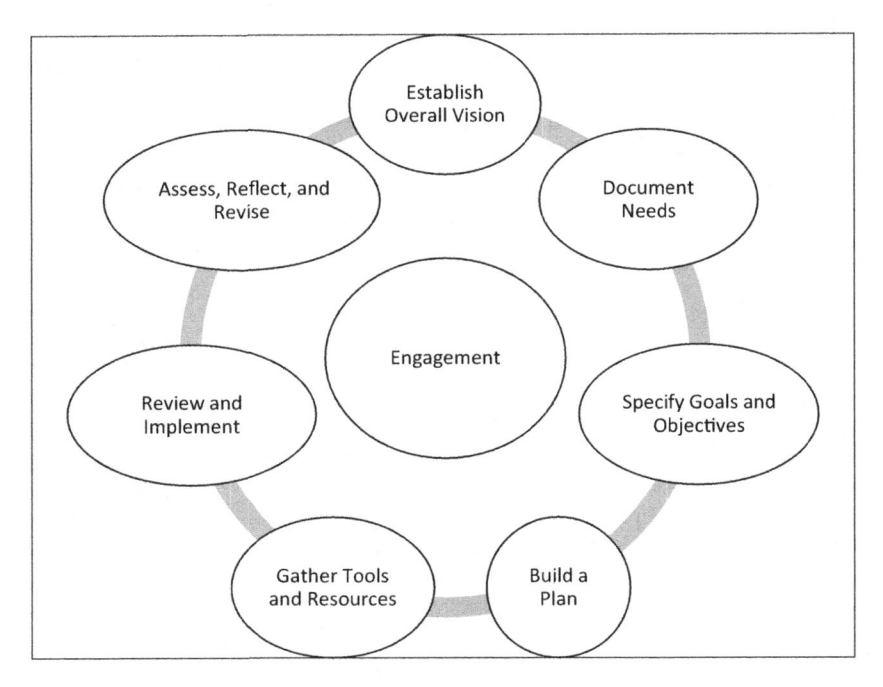

Figure 7.1 Planning Framework

stakeholders, decision-makers, experts, affected individuals or groups, and others. More detail on those are provided in the following section of this chapter.

Step One: Establish Overall Vision

This first step is an important one. It begins with an individual or group believing something is not the way it should be. This could be a problem situation, or it could be the fact that there is not satisfaction with the current state of affairs. It may be triggered by something internal to the group or community, or by an external source. It may be just to take a "pulse check" to assess where the community is, to be sure that behavior, attitudes, knowledge, or other areas of consideration are where the leaders and planners want them to be. This step may initially be general and not articulated well; in fact, it may be "fuzzy" and nondescript in nature. The intent with this step is to have some general agreement that a change is wanted, and that the status quo (whether a long-term feature or something that is relatively new) is not acceptable.

In establishing this vision, it is helpful to move toward some type of specificity. For example, while the initial general view may be that "the community has too many drugs," the discussion processes may then focus on what helped drive that belief. The narrowing of the overall vision may address youth (and specifically the 14 and 15 year olds, for example), the substance (marijuana, for example), and the setting (after school, for example). Just having some discussions to determine the nature of the concern can be important in determining the rest of the process.

As part of the overall vision process, and grounding with essential background, blending research and practice is an important guiding principle for organizations and groups. Professional Perspective 7.2 provides some practical suggestions regarding how to accomplish this, and why this is not only helpful, but essential.

Professional Perspective 7.2

Blending Research and Practice: Recognizing the *Question* in Program Design

Jim Lange, Ph.D.

No matter where along the prevention continuum (primary, secondary, and/or tertiary), and no matter the use-continuum being addressed (abstinence, low risk, and/or dependence), from any prevention practitioner's perspective, research is a necessity. How else can they actually know what problems to prevent, which populations to serve, or how to best elicit the sought-after changes in behaviors? But just *using* research, as though it's a roadmap to program success, is limited. First, across the breadth of the prevention topics there are often too few studies to form a clear guide. Second, the individual research studies that form our evidence base tend to have enough contextual and individual variables that program designers must always be ready to adapt what has been previously studied to fit local circumstances. For those reasons confidence in the program planners' desired results is never assured and should therefore be evaluated so assure program progress. So during both the planning and evaluation, research plays a critical role.

But even that planning and evaluation orientation toward research's role is limited for it places it as an outside (almost alien) part of the process. This can lead to unfortunate experiences with research. Evaluators are often brought onto the scene after program development (and even implementation) has occurred and asked to divine if the program worked. The evaluator becomes the forensic investigator, reconstructing the motives and actions of the program team from clues left behind. Often, there is no specified program model for change, no baseline or outcome measures, nor other critical clues. It is frequently left to the evaluator to frame the program's theoretical model of change, and to do so in a post hoc way (akin to preparing an outline for a manuscript after writing the manuscript). It's sometimes impossible for the evaluator to succeed, and a potentially important opportunity to advance the field of prevention is lost because of the disconnect between program practitioner and researcher.

It is far better if research is thought of as an integral part of the process of prevention. And while many would agree with that sentiment, actually implementing it is often seen as daunting. But it need not be.

Research – broadly speaking – means *asking questions* and then *seeking answers*. Of course, we usually use notions of scientific methods when attempting to find those answers, but the *how* of research does not play into integrating it into prevention until later in the process. Thinking about the simplistic sketch of *research* (question and a quest for answers) points us toward integration of research and prevention programming and other strategies. It is not about "fitting" research into our prevention program, but instead, viewing our prevention programs through a research lens; in other words, as a question.

By their nature, the prevention work we do can easily be described in question form: *Can we change X to produce Y?* This may require a change of thinking, but it's not complicated; we must merely change our typical declarative statement (e.g., *We will implement a program to produce an outcome!*), into a question (e.g., *Can we effect change to produce a desired prevention outcome?*). For example, we might ask *Can we change the ID checking practice of local businesses to produce less underage drinking?* Note all the elements in that stated question that can potentially be answered with research:

Is it possible to change the business practice?
How will the program accomplish this?
Does the way you've chosen actually produce change in business practice?
Does that change in business practice affect the drinking of young people?

Essentially the program question forces the prevention designer to consider the model of change that they are perhaps implicitly using and make it explicit. And most importantly, it allows for the follow-up question: *How will we know the answers to these questions?* That question can easily guide the program evaluation planning and will almost certainly mean integrating formal research methods into the program's implementation design. And voila – integration of research into program design, implementation, and evaluation will have been accomplished.

Research need not be daunting, scary, or alien; it's merely asking questions and seeking answers. It can start with a consumer mindset: what evidence or literature can be drawn upon to guide the prevention work. But then, by framing the prevention activity as a set of steps, acknowledging that each step seeks, but is not certain of a particular outcome, the steps can therefore be the basis for a question. If need be, seek assistance from professionals with research and evaluation expertise who can help assure your initiative's questions are answered. When done well, this is all part of the planning process. Allow for enough time to be thoughtful and thorough. With these perspectives, you'll be more grounded and, ultimately, more effective.

Jim Lange, Ph.D., is currently Executive Director of the Higher Education Center for Alcohol and Drug Misuse Prevention and Recovery, which is an academic center of The Ohio State University. He is also Coordinator of AOD Initiatives at San Diego State University. He's worked in the prevention field for over 20 years, and has published over 60 scholarly research articles on prevention topics, focused mainly on adolescent and young adult alcohol and other drug misuse prevention.

Step Two: Document Needs

Once the initial activity of visioning has been done, the effort should focus on documentation. This is the needs assessment and data collection phase. It is where concrete information is gathered. While the initial phase may have come from some casual observations or anecdotal data, or even from some data collection processes, this step is crucial for further substantiating the need. This may indeed validate the earlier concern; or, it may turn out that no specific needs are identified or documented. Further, additional issues may emerge from this process.

When documenting the needs, several considerations should be kept in mind. First, the priority with any needs assessment is to document why there may be concern, and to serve as the foundation for making plans to address these concerns. This documentation should be sufficient to determine whether or not to move forward, and to help inform the design of the intervention strategies. If the documentation is incomplete or flawed, the basis for addressing the current needs may not be substantiated.

Second, it is helpful to conduct this process using both quantitative and qualitative approaches. Each of these can complement the other. Gather numbers to the extent possible, whether through surveys, online polling, incident reports, or other concrete data sources. Some of these data may already be available, and others may need to be designed for the current purpose. Qualitative approaches may include observations, interviews, discussion groups, and other strategies. Both approaches are required, as this reflects on the primary aim of needs assessment of documenting the need: the numbers (quantitative) are concrete and address more of the logic, and the stories (qualitative) help illustrate the issue and speak to the heart. Each benefits the other, and one without the other is often not sufficient.

The third consideration with the documentation of needs is to think, to the extent possible, of gathering information that will be able to serve as a type of baseline or marker from which to track progress and to make comparisons in the future. While needs assessment processes won't necessarily be in precisely the same form as the ultimate evaluative approaches, there may be some data sources and content that can be replicated over time to help with the ongoing monitoring of progress and impact.

In moving through the background and planning activities, it is important to be both research-based and scientifically grounded. Some specific strategies for accomplishing this, and for keeping an eye on the important factors associated with the needs, is found with Professional Perspective 7.3. In addition, some insights from the long-term advocates are found with selected comments and observations based on their experience.

Professional Perspective 7.3

Rising above Politics in Alcohol and Drug Abuse Prevention[1]

Richard Lucey, Jr., M.A.

To paraphrase Benjamin Franklin, there is nothing certain in life except death and taxes. I think the same can be said for politics with a small "p," which I loosely define as the dynamics that occur relative to an organization's people, policies, and procedures. Whether you work in education, health care, law enforcement, business, or media – some of the more common sectors of drug-free communities – you are hard pressed to find any setting in which politics do not exist. In this segment, I offer three guidelines on how to rise above politics in drug abuse prevention efforts.

Follow the Science

Community coalitions, elementary and secondary schools, colleges and universities, and other groups are involved in drug abuse prevention efforts. They benefit from nearly three decades of intensive research on evidence-based strategies, thanks in large part to projects funded by the National Institute on Drug Abuse and the National Institute on Alcohol Abuse and Alcoholism.

Admittedly, you might encounter critics – even within your own organization – who will challenge you and claim that the prevention approaches you want to implement are based solely on your opinion. Fortunately there are easily accessible online resources that have compiled research-based prevention strategies in easy-to-follow formats, to which you can point your potential detractors.

Another important resource is the Surgeon General's report on alcohol, drugs, and health that was published in 2016. This landmark publication, which includes a comprehensive chapter on research-based prevention policies and programs, can be found online at https://addiction.surgeongeneral.gov.

We are no longer at a point in time when we can say we don't know what works, or more importantly, what doesn't work. Approximately 30 years of solid research have helped to form prevention science, so it is relatively easy to rise above politics when drug abuse prevention activities are rooted in evidence-based strategies.

Identify Your Prevention Allies and Champions

Mobilizing a coalition has long been recognized as a key element of successful drug abuse prevention. In fact, it is nearly impossible to achieve any form of measurable and long-lasting success in preventing drug abuse in a school or community by going it alone. Therefore it is important to identify prevention allies and champions, two roles that I view as distinct.

Allies are individuals who actively participate in a drug abuse prevention coalition, and they represent a wide range of interests, including education, health care, law enforcement, and the media. Undoubtedly the coalition members' respective agencies will have distinct and seemingly disparate missions, and yet they can come together on a regular basis through the coalition's efforts to prevent drug abuse. Effective leaders can help coalition members rise above politics when they put aside their personal or agencies' agenda and instead collaborate to focus on the coalition's shared goals.

Champions are individuals who not only support a coalition's efforts, but also are vocal and visible in that support. These are the leaders in business, education, government, and civic groups – just to name a few – who clearly recognize that drug abuse prevention is a nonpartisan issue that transcends any type of politics. These champions also have an innate ability to promote the importance of drug abuse prevention across a variety of platforms, including social media, and explain why your coalition's efforts are essential and having a positive impact on individuals, families, and communities. Since prevention champions' schedules are often quite full, demands of them should be simple and realistic.

Be Strategic in Your Efforts

Drug abuse prevention is not random. It must be intentional, purposeful, and most of all, strategic. Unfortunately, one of the struggles we face in prevention is impatience. Here is where rising above politics can be most difficult, because sometimes the pressure to produce results quickly comes from politicians who want to demonstrate to their constituents that they are making a difference.

Due to political or other pressure you face to demonstrate results, you might be tempted to rush to replicate programs implemented elsewhere, without regard for whether those programs are a good match for your setting or can actually produce positive outcomes. As challenging as it will be, it is imperative to rise above politics and follow a strategic planning process.

That process will help you and your colleagues determine which drugs are having the most negative impact on your school or community, which evidence-based programs will be most helpful in your prevention efforts, and the best way to proceed with implementing and evaluating that program in your particular setting. While the strategic planning process probably will not eliminate anyone's impatience to produce immediate results, it will help you develop reasonable short- and intermediate-term outcomes, which you can explain are the necessary foundation to achieve long-term change.

In summary, politics of any kind are inevitable in our field. But if you follow the science, identify your prevention allies and champions, and are strategic in your efforts, you will be well positioned to rise above those politics.

Note

1 The contents of this book represent the scholarship and professional opinions of the editors and chapter authors. The Drug Enforcement Administration nor any other federal or state agency cited in this book neither states nor implies any endorsement, association, or recommendation with regard to George Mason University or Routledge Publishers or their products or services.

Richard Lucey, Jr., M.A. in Liberal Studies, is Senior Prevention Program Manager in the Drug Enforcement Administration's Community Outreach and Prevention Support Section. He formerly served as a special assistant to the director for the Center for Substance Abuse Prevention in the Substance Abuse and Mental Health Services Administration, and as an education program specialist in the U.S. Department of Education's Office of Safe and Drug-Free Schools.

They were very, very concerned about outcomes and whether or not we were showing that we were moving in the right direction on these things.

Darlind Davis

We spent an awful lot of time and an awful lot of money just doing things, without any understanding about whether or not those things worked. I think the further we dug into these things, the more we realized that we were wasting a lot of money because these things had no efficacy, they had no results, and some of these things had negative consequences rather than positive consequences. I think the one thing that I was able to do was to stand ground and basically say even though a program is popular, if it doesn't work we need to either change it or get rid of it.

Bill Modzeleski

I think because we are data-driven, try to do best practices and are student driven, we have witnessed measurable successes.

Kim Dude

I have to admit that I'm still a little disappointed today that there still seems to be a focus on what is politically expedient.

Steve Schmidt

People in the field sometimes do not seem to be willing to pay attention to evaluation findings in emerging data, emerging evidence. That is a bit of a surprise because I think that most of us are thoughtful people, but I guess I am surprised occasionally when people seem to be locked into their perspectives and unwilling to change. I guess another surprise as I think back on it is the power and the influence of money, and I shouldn't have been surprised; I have but I guess I didn't give full credit to the power and the influence of advertising.

Tom Griffin

Step Three: Specify Goals and Objectives

Presuming that the needs are documented at some level, the focus of the planners can now be upon what is reasonable and appropriate to address. As with the Force Field Analysis cited in the previous section of this chapter, multiple forces may be at work and thus some prioritization will be necessary and appropriate. Similarly with the needs assessment process, the organizers will need to determine, based on the results, what is appropriate to address. This may include immediate and achievable results (so-called "low hanging fruit") as well as the intermediate or longer-term outcomes. All are important.

What is important in this strategic planning process is to gain greater specificity, based on the extent of the need, the level of interest, and the resources available to address the issue. As with most issues, no quick fix exists with substance abuse issues; plus, the issues are deep-seated, long-term, and quite varied in nature. The organizers will determine what is reasonable to seek to accomplish, for this setting at this particular point in time.

The purpose of goals and objectives is in part to help organize the planning efforts; this helps provide focus. Another purpose is to gain specificity that will be useful in the design of the evaluation efforts, thus helping to document the results obtained and processes used.

Simply put, goals are the overarching aims that are sought, and the objectives provide structure for results that are measurable and achievable. For example, a goal may be to increase the functioning and well-being of young adults; several objectives could be focused on increasing the skills of stress management, interpersonal relationships, and drug and alcohol guidelines by 10% each year, over a three-year time period. These would be structured more precisely, so comparisons could be made to assess the progress that is being made. With this simple example, it is important to note that the aim is not perfection on those elements, but rather improvement (as demonstrated by achieving increases of 10% a year).

Once the goals and objectives are specified, activities or strategies are defined to help achieve the objectives. The aim is for all of these to hang together, with objectives supporting the attainment of the goal, and activities or other strategies helping to bolster the attainment of the objective. To have an objective with no supporting activities or strategies means that it likely would not be achieved; similarly to have an activity or strategy that is not linked to an objective means that it really has no purpose.

The long-term advocates have additional insights regarding some of their experiences, and some guidance that can be helpful for current and emerging professionals working in this area.

> *What surprised me is how we were willing to say things, do things, support things, because it is what we thought people wanted to hear, rather than based upon science.*
>
> Bill Modzeleski

> *We are very data-driven and make our decisions on what areas to focus on, based on data. We evaluate everything we do and follow an extensive strategic plan. We look at best practices and, if appropriate, try to replicate it on our campus.*
>
> Kim Dude

> *And the measurable, marked increase in awareness, education, fearing getting caught drunk driving (which was ultimately the goal of the campaign), but also action-wise. We had as many as 10% of persons saying they changed their behavior as a result of this campaign; that may not sound huge but in a state like Virginia with 8 million people, that is 800,000 people that could right now be using a designated driver or some alternative transportation rather than driving home drunk. So it's moving the needle in a measurable way.*
>
> Kurt Erickson

Step Four: Build a Plan

This step of the planning process is where specific strategies are defined. Once noted above, specific approaches are necessary to help an objective be attained. A helpful starting point with the planning efforts is a review of best practices and grounded approaches. Whether this is with current registries of evaluated programs or strategies, or with various organizations' guidelines and standards, the important thing is that the approaches chosen be due to some knowledge or basis that they are helpful – that they work. While the intent of personnel organizing community or organizational efforts is excellent, the need for evidence-based efforts (whether from documented efforts elsewhere or theoretically grounded approaches) is vital. These efforts must go beyond the "feel-good" approaches all too common with many initiatives, whether with substance abuse efforts or elsewhere.

It is at this point that an overall implementation design is prepared. This addresses the strategies, the personnel or resources needed, the timeline, and what needs to be done to assure smooth execution. Further, it specifies what communications plans are being made for the targeted audience, as well as for any stakeholders or others with a vested interest in the outcomes. GAANT or PERT charts, contingency plans, partnerships with others, and similar resources are helpful with this planning segment.

Also essential with the plan is the design of the evaluation. Completing issues associated with the needs assessment processes documented earlier, the evaluation should incorporate both quantitative and qualitative approaches. It is important that the evaluation address the impact or outcomes associated with the effort (what results were achieved?), as well as the processes and strategies used (how was it done?). Both of these are useful in the review of findings and results, for potential future refinement or replication.

With the evaluation, the key question is that of documenting, to the extent possible, the results. With the overall vision established, and the documentation of the need, the question will be whether the effort achieved what it set out to achieve. In this part of the planning effort, with building the plan, the focus should be on this question: "What documentation or evidence is needed to assess whether what was done actually made a difference?" This is where it is critical to have stakeholders and decision-makers involved in the discussion and buy-in process. If their aim is to have no incidents of a specified nature, it must be argued at the onset that, while desirable as an aim, this may not be reasonable as a result. Just as outlined early in this book that the phrase "War on Drugs" suggests winning or losing, and if there is not a win then it must be a loss, similarly a result of "zero usage" may not be reasonable. The outcomes of a certain level of increase or decrease, or a reasonable endpoint of a specified target, and with a defined audience, would be appropriate. The key point is to obtain clarity of reasonable and appropriate outcomes at the onset, and to get buy-in and understanding as appropriate.

Insights from the extensive experience of long-term advocates is found with some additional comments emerging from their in-depth interviews:

> *The three Ps: one is prevention, one is policies, and the other is price. Price is where we are the most vulnerable because our state has the lowest alcohol tax and the lowest tobacco tax in the entire country.*
>
> Kim Dude

> *I have a high sense of optimism and hope because of the response we've had, that's probably, that's part of this answer too, the response we get from students. You know, we've done empowerment programs, step up bystander intervention, and there are other things that we've done to engage others as change-makers. I think that's where that optimism is ... Because then you see the response, you see that they are interested and they are feeling differently about it than if you are lecturing them about all of the negative consequences of use.*
>
> Mary Wilfert

Step Five: Gather Tools and Resources

With the overall plan in place, the next step is to gather whatever is needed to accomplish the goals and address the identified needs. As part of the implementation design, the identification of needed resources includes assets within the community, group, agency, or organization. Some of these will need to be created or developed, and others can be adapted from what has been done in similar or different settings or for similar or different issues.

The strategies identified in Chapters 8 and 9 of this book will be helpful in the design and implementation of the process. These can aid in not having to design everything from scratch, as well as to identify the evidence-based approaches to be used.

The communication plan for the effort needs special attention, so that information is clear and appropriate regarding the strategies. Further, documentation can be helpful with the preparation of the effort as well as the follow-up after the strategies.

The aim is to not have to do it all alone, and to identify ways of being cost-effective, grounded, and effective concurrently. Further, the engagement of others in the planning and implementation can help in the success as well as sustainability of the effort, due to their resource investment and ownership.

Part of the process of gathering "tools and resources" is the preparation of good relationships with individuals and organizations that can help with accomplishing specified goals and objectives. Sometimes these individuals or groups have a voice, sometimes they have a unique appeal, sometimes their stories and their own experiences are influential, and sometimes it's a matter of collaboration and having shared voices. Professional Perspective 7.4 provides insights about the role of youth with an important national initiative. In addition, various perspectives from long-term advocates are helpful in moving forward these efforts.

Professional Perspective 7.4

When an Adult Organization Needs to Engage Young People to Drive Change

Robert Heard, M.B.A.

Mothers Against Drunk Driving (MADD) was founded in 1980 after the death of Candy Lightner's daughter at the hands of a drunk driver. The creation of MADD spawned a national movement that not only drove public policy, but it ushered in a culture change that made drinking and driving intolerable. MADD and its members have been credited with significant legislative victories, including raising the legal drinking age to 21 and reducing the legal allowable blood alcohol level for drivers to 0.08. These two accomplishments are credited with significantly reducing the number of alcohol-related fatalities and injuries in the U.S. and saving countless thousands of lives.

In 1996, MADD expanded its focus, incorporating language into its mission statement that addressed the prevention of underage drinking. The organization understood that to prevent current and future drunk driving, their efforts would need to expand to include working with and on behalf of young people. With a rightful reputation of angry mothers shaking fists on the steps of Capitol Hill, MADD realized that a partnership with young people would be difficult and there would be significant challenges in their persuading a generation of young people to change their attitudes and behaviors regarding underage drinking. The organization's leadership knew that they would need to take drastic measures to enlist young people and train them to become their own champions to shift the underage drinking culture.

The first step was repositioning the organization in the eyes of teens, branding themselves beyond the stereotypical emotional mother. A range of programs were identified and rolled out, beginning with the development and production of a multi-media school assembly program called *Take the Lead*. The MTV-style production used Top 40 music and celebrity interviews in combination with dramatic, real-life stories of teens devastated by the impact of underage drinking and impaired driving. These traveling shows were presented in high schools across the country and featured in all 50 states. Their messages reached millions of middle school and high school students, communicating with them on their own terms and inviting them to be a part of the solution.

At the same time, MADD began recruiting school groups and community-based teams of young people interested in leading the charge to prevent underage drinking. Week-long leadership camps were offered in several states that connected students with other like-minded teens. During these summer sessions, young people were encouraged to identify issues that they were interested in addressing and then helping them to plan and implement school-based prevention programs once they returned home.

Out of these outreach efforts MADD would launch a community-based program for youth activists called Youth in Action. This program was designed to help young people identify the challenges in their communities and to train them to use their voices to drive policy and increase enforcement of underage drinking laws. Youth in Action (YiA) members were trained to draft and deliver testimony to local city councils on underage drinking policies. They were coached on speaking to law enforcement leadership and state alcohol beverage commissions, advocating for the enforcement of the 21 minimum drinking age law and encouraging police to crack down on the use of fake IDs and penalize retailers known for selling alcohol to underage youth. YIA members were encouraged to work in partnership with law enforcement to conduct sting operations identifying adults who were willing to purchase alcohol for illegal use by minors as well as establishments that were not properly and consistently checking an ID before alcohol sales.

MADD used this local moment to rally young people to address national policy. In 1997, MADD hosted a National Youth Summit to Prevent Underage Drinking in Washington D.C. Through a competitive application process, one high-school-aged young person was selected from each of the 435 U.S. Congressional districts to attend the event at the nation's Capitol. A four-day agenda included delegates interacting with influential policy leaders such as the U.S. Surgeon General, the Drug Czar, and members of Congress. With their newly developed policy recommendations in hand, these students marched up the steps of the Capitol to meet with their legislators. Their visits resulted in the funding of a national $25 million underage drinking initiative through the U.S. Department of Justice's Juvenile Justice and Delinquency Prevention arm.

MADD took its success with adult constituents and translated its lessons learned into a powerful partnership with students. MADD provided a forum for those concerned with or impacted by underage drinking and impaired driving and invited them to be part of the solution. MADD provided a platform for young people to use their own voices to make a difference in their cities and nation.

Seven lessons emerge easily from this partnership; these are directly relevant to many of the wide range of challenges and opportunities surrounding drug and alcohol issues. First, think big. Second, focus on actionable items. Third, make it locally appropriate. Fourth, engage the constituency affected. Fifth, include a training component. Sixth, partner with established organizations. Seventh, identify ways to link to policymakers and those with influence. While no guarantee of the specified desired results can be made, the probability of positive impact will be much more likely.

Robert Heard, M.B.A., CAE, serves as Associate Executive Director, Membership and Education Division at the American College of Emergency Physicians.

I see the really big money is that consolidation, the producers have the resources that they can make tremendous inroads and it doesn't seem to me that they are doing anything about that right now but that seems something that is a concern and that needs to be addressed downstream.

Jeffrey Levy

We are beginning to learn how to operationalize data, how to bridge the gap between research and treatment while breaking down some of the treatment silos that do not allow for comparative data. Some of those silos are being broken down around the country and around the world and I think that's pretty significant.

Robert Lynn

One of my accomplishments was to honor the perspectives of the alcohol servers themselves. There was a lot of policy flying around and including mandatory service training, but nobody was asking the alcohol servers about the key issues that were somehow going to affect them and they were going to need to act on.

Jeff Linkenbach

I had to become that bridge between the Tavern Association and big government entities that were funding it, in terms of research. So a significant accomplishment for me was learning as a researcher how to become that bridge and bring together different entities that don't always play nice together.

Jeff Linkenbach

So it seems that there is a whole lot more out there for younger students, and not so much out there for college students. The other thing that has really seen change though is the way that we in higher education partner with our local communities.

Carla Lapelle

Step Six: Review and Implement

With all the planning and gathering of resources, it is appropriate to review the processes. This review process can easily include pilot testing, to the extent possible. That pilot testing may be a walk-through with various audiences and constituencies, looking for areas that may not work well or may not be clearly specified. Essential with these is the communications aspect, so that the desired outcomes from the initiative are clear. Specifically, the audience should be very clear about what the organizers want them to know, to feel, or to do.

Some of this review process may not be completely feasible. For example, if a strategy is the implementation of a policy, it would be appropriate to talk this through with a representation of those who may be affected. Similarly, with a new procedure, it may help to test this in a small setting, whether a specific community or workplace; it may be that the procedure is fine but the communication about it is lacking. The aim is to have a review of as many aspects of the planned implementation efforts as possible. This saves from embarrassment, inadequacies, or problems as the initiative is undertaken.

It is with the actual implementation that the careful planning activities pay off. The implementation will, ideally, go smoothly. The back-up plans, redundancies, and contingency plans will be present and useful if needed.

During the implementation process, attention should be paid to both how the processes functioned and how they were received. This is the case whether the strategies were a policy or procedure, an event or a curriculum, training or social media initiative, or other approaches. This is helpful for the final step for any necessary modifications. It is also helpful for documentation for replication with other settings.

Step Seven: Assess, Reflect, and Revise

With the good planning efforts throughout the process, the evaluation activities (both outcome and process evaluation) will be helpful in providing insight. With clearly defined objectives and measures that capture the attainment of those objectives, data will be helpful in assessing the extent to which the objectives were and were not accomplished. Other evaluative approaches will help the organizers understand what may have contributed to the accomplishment, or lack thereof, of the objectives. These evaluative efforts may be focus groups, interviews, observation, or other targeted approaches.

With whatever results and insights are achieved, the program planners now review and reflect upon these findings. This is done within the context of the overall initial vision and assessment of the needs that were to be addressed. The results may show that efforts were appropriate and sufficient; however, the insight may also be that these same efforts need to be nurtured and reinforced so that the results can be sustained over time. The results may show that the efforts were partially successful, perhaps with one audience (e.g., boys) yet not with another audience (e.g., girls). Or the results may reveal that some confounding factors (e.g., a local incident that occurred) or interference (e.g., conflicting messages from a parent or a teacher) may have affected the results.

The important thing is to have sound evaluative processes in place so that a reasonable and appropriate review can occur. The findings, both quantitative and qualitative, will help provide insights about what can be done next. This may be to continue, to revise, or to go in a totally different direction.

One observation from a long-term advocate is particularly helpful in this context; it resonates with other points made elsewhere in this chapter from other interviewees. This summative view is helpful for prioritizing the evaluative and review processes.

> I think that was for the first time saying you need to know what the problem is, you need to measure the problem, you have to have some results coming out, if you don't have results or don't do an evaluation, then it's not worth it. And so the whole push towards results-oriented programs, towards evaluations, towards research, I think that I had a significant role in pushing.
>
> Bill Modzeleski

Engaging Others

The entire Planning Framework described in the previous section of this chapter is a process. As illustrated in the figure, it can be best accomplished through the process of engaging others. While the planning can, indeed, be done alone, whether by an individual or a core group, the attainment of the desired results is best achieved when done in a collaborative way.

Central to this is the process of partnering with others. This can be for overall planning efforts as well as with the specific elements of the process. For example, specialists with evaluation and needs assessment can be helpful with those processes; this may include professionals or agencies, academic settings, or organizations with this interest and expertise. Some of these may occur at no cost through a cooperative agreement or partnership. Another example is with communications efforts: engage those with knowledge and expertise to help with different aspects of this, such as media campaigns, news organization initiatives, social media, advertisements, and more. This could be volunteers, organizations, retirees, students, or others.

The important role of coalition building, partnerships, and negotiation of shared approaches and resources can be helpful. Thinking about ways of accomplishing the overall aims and vision, and who else might benefit from achievement of or participation in these efforts, can make the process more manageable. While it requires more careful planning and coordination, it can also help get others on board with the process and reduce some of the challenges and obstacles. Further, this type of collaboration and partnership can be helpful with the longer-term sustainability of the effort. Not only is one group or organization interested in the effort, but, with partnerships, other groups will be supportive for the longer-term institutionalization of these efforts.

What do the long-term advocates have to say, that will be helpful from their unique vantage points, that can aid from a reflective perspective, and for improving current and future efforts? The following comments are helpful for learning about ways of engaging others.

I had heard that the directors of all the federal agencies in the past met once a month to coordinate their prevention activities called the Drug Prevention Roundtable. I suggested that we should start doing that, so we reinstituted the roundtable. I think that also helped to contribute to the success by coordinating efforts across federal agencies.

Karol Kumpfer

Let's join hands, the suicide community and the alcohol community joining hands because we have clearly realized that there is a tie in between suicide, alcohol use, and lots of other factors.

Bill Modzeleski

"If you aren't part of the solution, you are part of the problem," I think it is that simple. I have a hard time getting faculty on board. Our business school has no classes on Fridays and so not surprisingly our business students drink more than any other academic department.

Kim Dude

It still surprises me that people haven't had that "aha moment" themselves and realize that they could help be part of the solution.

Kim Dude

My sense of the word accomplishment is the ability to influence behavior on the part of anyone in that constituency.

Jeffrey Levy

I really don't have any regrets because this was just something that I was a volunteer in the sense that I did as much as I could do and I really didn't have a lot of opportunity to do more, I did everything I could do kind of thing.

Jeffrey Levy

We understood the importance of working together across states and so the prevention network kind of evolved from that discussion. And we had lots of help from our federal counterparts from NIDA and NIAAA, and we developed regions which each federal agency had a completely different set up for regions geographically so we really had to come to some conclusion of what were the common boundaries of regions so that we could say yes we have a lot in common there.

Darlind Davis

We were always working on getting that empty seat filled with the right perspective, whether it was law enforcement – some communities flat-out didn't want to work with law enforcement or some communities where their whole prevention effort was law enforcement and they didn't feel like they needed anybody else.

Darlind Davis

I think people just fall short of being able to put themselves on the line about it. When it comes to it they may, and then maybe everybody does to that extent.

Darlind Davis

People support what they create. If they are not part of it they will not do it and they will not like it.

Darlind Davis

I think we've made a bit of progress. And I'm just thinking again about some of the response that we hear from others. I think back in the day we probably didn't even ask youth what they thought about the issues so much and so I think today we are engaging them so I think we are making progress. Again if you look at the metadata I know it's a bit disconcerting but I think there are some success stories out there that just haven't spread, or the efforts, or their strategic approach has not necessarily spread so that it's impacted that broader data set. So I think we are making progress and I think we are heading in the right direction on our thinking about engaging youth, and thinking about those environmental factors where we haven't made progress obviously and resourcing the efforts.

Mary Wilfert

The power of peer influence is so important: we need to empower students with understanding about the forces that might contribute to their behaviors to not intervene and when they might want to. And once you empower them, for lack of a better word, once you provide them the understanding and the tools, they can just run with it. And we as professionals obviously do a lot of work in a top-down way; we do a lot of coordination, we do a lot of connecting, you know, gathering data of that work, that foundation of work that needs to be done. But when it comes to real-time alcohol and other drug problem behavior, what is happening in front of you is usually not happening in front of us as professionals; it is happening in front of their peers or their family members. So the more we can help youth, the college students or whatever that target is, to understand what they can do to facilitate an intervention, and it may be something very indirect, it may be going and getting help, and it may not be putting themselves in the middle of something. But the more we can help them understand that they do have a role, and a very powerful role, to play in spotting for their teammates and stepping up and intervening when appropriate, the better off everyone is.

Mary Wilfert

The most important things that can be done ... everybody has a role to play and the community, the larger community, again in establishing a social norm, in this case a more responsible norm has to be involved. And I really think that to some degree it's there, the question is whether this different from community to community, and I think there's got to be a commitment on all sides, to sort of figure out the best way forward.

Ralph Blackman

And getting state government officials to realize that colleges and communities want you to work with them, not tell them what to do, but to work with them.

Steve Schmidt

I think the state official mindset often is, unless you come to me with a problem, I'm not going to be real quick to reach out. And what we were really doing I think was forcing our partners at the state level to come together, and the state associations as well. It wasn't just government – it was key state associations, the league of cities, or enforcement groups or even some of the statewide groups and getting them to come to the table and to ask "what is it that we can do for you?"

Steve Schmidt

The importance of developing relationships would be one of the surprising things. It's a constant string of building relationships.

Deb Thorstenson

Summary

Having a sound planning process is essential to being more likely to achieve the desired outcomes. This chapter specified the overall construct of "planned change," stressing that having a clearly defined process will aid with organizing the strategies and achieving results. Through use of a strategic planning framework, decision-makers and leaders can engage others to achieve shared visions and shared processes. This investment by other organizations, constituencies, groups, and individuals will be helpful not only for shared ownership, but also for optimizing desired outcomes.

Notes

1 Lewin, K. (1951). *Force Field Analysis*. Cambridge, MA: MIT Institute for Social Research.
2 www.samhsa.gov/capt/applying-strategic-prevention-framework.

8 Resourceful Approaches

Chapter 7 (Helpful Processes) emphasized the variety of processes important for orchestrating comprehensive strategies. The focus was upon having a plan, and grounding that plan in a quality process that engages a range of individuals, groups and constituencies. This chapter builds on that plan, and focuses on various strategies that might be considered to constitute the efforts. This is the "what" and the "to do" initiatives; it is the efforts, the initiatives, the things, and the tangible approaches. Chapter 9 (Personal and Professional Strategies) incorporates the range of communications efforts, helpful for bringing to life, and making consistent and clear, the efforts included in this chapter.

Resourceful approaches are determined based on the goals and objectives identified in the previous chapter. The goals represent the high-level aims, and the objectives are more tangible and measured in nature and scope. The objectives are the shorter-term outcomes; these are what the planners want to see different as a result of what they do. The objectives do not just happen; they are achieved by implementing something, whether this is a campaign, a policy, an educational effort, some training, a media effort, or a blend of these and other initiatives. Each objective is achieved by implementing something; and it is this "something" (or "some things") that is the focus of this chapter.

This chapter is organized around four overall constructs. First, attention is provided to evidence-based foundations; whatever is identified for implementation must be grounded in theory, science, and/or prior documentation. Second, some guiding principles from an organizational perspective are offered; these complement the guidelines and standard-setting offered in the chapter on Prevention and Education. Third, a menu of potential strategies is included; this provides an overview of approaches and initiatives that can be considered. Finally, and building upon the strategic planning approach from Chapter 7, a way of pulling together the various strategies and the engagement of partners is highlighted.

Evidence-Based Foundations

In preparation of specific strategies or approaches identified to address needs, a critical element is the incorporation of sound approaches. Through the planning processes identified in the previous chapter, or through other strategic planning processes, it is vital that the approaches selected represent current and grounded thinking.

Within the context of having strategies that are locally appropriate as well as based on identified needs, the identification of strategies should also be based in science. One approach for having science-based approaches is to review best practices that have met, successfully, the rigor of prior, successful implementation. Through published articles and repositories of best practices, communities, schools, worksites, and other settings can benefit from these compilations. It is helpful when evidence already exists that specific strategies have been proven to work – at least under certain circumstances with identified settings and audiences and for specific purposes. A good example of that is with alcohol and the higher education community, specifically. CollegeAIM represents a distillation and review of published articles on a wide range of strategies, and provides summaries of these within the broad classification of individual and environmental strategies.[1] It highlights the evidence (or lack thereof) of multiple strategies, as well as the source of evidence (e.g., from settings other than higher education).

A caution is that, just because an approach has been proven to be effective under certain circumstances does not mean it will necessarily be helpful under the local setting; the prior evidence is just a helpful starting point.

Similarly, just because an approach has not been documented to be effective does not make it ineffective or counterproductive. Should the documentation of ineffectiveness be present, that should be respected. However, lack of evidence is simply that. When evidence is nonexistent, what can be helpful, however, is to have sound theoretical grounding for attempting the identified approach. Organizers may wish to adapt an approach used in another setting for the current setting; or they may wish to apply one or more theoretical principles to the current need.

Further, it is helpful to understand that different professional disciplines have varying standards regarding alcohol and drug issues, as well as other issues. For example, professional standards vary among health, counseling, law enforcement, education, and other professionals. To be effective and appropriate, within the context of a local setting, the engagement of key constituencies around the same issue is critical. This will be further illustrated in the last segment of this chapter, and reflected in the "planning grid" regarding "who can do what."

The important thing with this consideration is that there be substantive grounding with whatever is planned. This approach is important as it helps ground and focus the planning efforts.

A helpful starting place for further understanding evidence-based foundations is with the observations from a couple of long-term advocates, as well as with the summary insights found in Professional Perspective 8.1.

Professional Perspective 8.1

The Dichotomy of Data: Slow Is Smooth and Smooth Is Fast

Dave Closson, M.S.

Planning and organizing efforts to address the range of drug and alcohol problems is a tall order. Fortunately, many programmatic leaders and stakeholders gather data to help identify specific needs and guide their efforts. All too often, these leaders stop short with their assessment and only collect data such as past 30-day consumption rates, quantity and frequency of substance use, and perceptions of others' use. This is when I share a line from my military days, "slow is smooth and smooth is fast." It is okay to slow down when that means digging deeper and doing a more in-depth assessment. With that context, I have four key points regarding "data."

The first key point is not digging deep enough with the data. The opioid epidemic is fast moving and ever changing. It is the current drug/alcohol-related crisis in the U.S. as of the writing of this book. There have been many before it and there will be more to come. I have seen firsthand many clients who feel the pressure of the overdose rates and begin selecting strategies based on that rate. I then ask them who is experiencing the highest rate of overdoses, where are they occurring, what substance is most misused, and what are the risk and protective factors for their community. The answers to these questions lie in their data and will help direct where and to whom to distribute naloxone, what messaging to use, specify the needed treatment and support services, and identify audiences for education such as prescribers, pharmacists, or families.

Second, leaders often find that the problem is not what they originally thought. As a result of looking more in depth at their data, some may see the problem is much different from, or more nuanced than, their original conclusions. They may have felt overwhelmed, that the crisis is too much, and that their efforts (however well-intended) were going to be futile. Once they slowed down and thoroughly looked at their current data, they realized these factors were, in fact, changeable and they could make an impact! For example, in most cases, people obtain prescription opioids from friends or relatives. Having this knowledge, efforts can be focused on education for community members, healthcare professionals, and patients. Additionally, prescription drug take-backs and drop box programs, prescribing and dispensing regulations, and prescription drug monitoring programs can be implemented to address the access to prescription opioids.

To produce real and long-lasting change you will want to target the risk and protective factors influencing the behavioral health problems; this is the third key point. Identifying what factors put individuals at risk, and make them more vulnerable, as well as what helps protect them from harm, can reveal new opportunities to influence both current and future substance use patterns and behaviors. To be most effective, prevention strategies must address the underlying factors driving these patterns and behaviors. It doesn't matter how carefully a program or intervention is implemented. If it's not a good match for the risk and protective factors for the particular audience, it's not going to be very effective.

The final key point is to focus on identifying and prioritizing needs. Remember that the factors driving an issue in one community may differ from the factors driving it in another community. Because every community is unique, it is important to determine which factors are contributing to substance use and related problems in your community and address those. To help you identify and prioritize your community's needs, consider the following steps:

1. Start by looking for data already being collected by others which can include surveys, hospitals, law enforcement agencies, state agencies, and community organizations.
2. Examine the gathered data and determine whether you are missing any pertinent information that relates to the problem, behavior, or population groups.
3. If you are missing data or information, determine who may currently have that information, or the best method of collecting that information. This could include surveys, focus groups, or key informant interviews.

The dichotomy of data, slow is smooth and smooth is fast. Take time to gather current and quality data. Get focused and dig deep to the root causes and let that data drive your decision-making. The process of using quality and current data can be powerful in making sound decisions for your efforts.

Dave Closson, M.S., is a national expert on substance misuse prevention and law enforcement. He is the author of *Motivational Interviewing for Campus Police* and brings a unique experience to substance misuse prevention, having served as a campus police officer at Eastern Illinois University.

The main thing was bringing research-based interventions to the federal government and to state governments. I didn't want taxpayers' money being spent anymore on programs that didn't necessarily work or we didn't know if they worked. So rigorous evaluations were necessary to test the hypothesis that the intervention was effective in reducing later drug use in kids.

Karol Kumpfer

We looked at what the research and the science said worked and then began to bring people together based on what we knew was the best policy, the best science to solve the problem, and the classic cases in the area of college alcohol use.

Steve Schmidt

Guiding Principles from an Organizational Perspective

When planning initiatives at the local level, some overarching principles or guidelines are helpful. These are helpful whether the efforts are designed at the local community level, from a statewide perspective, within an educational setting, or at a broader level. Further, it is helpful for the planning constituency to develop its own guiding principles; these can be helpful with aiding the group to be relevant and appropriate with its local needs, as well as to stay on track with whatever is identified as key elements for the setting.

First, it is important to remember the *societal context*. Whatever the scope and nature of the specified needs, the context is that drug and alcohol issues are, and have been, part of a larger societal and cultural context for centuries. Localized issues may vary from the recent past, or from the larger setting; however, concerns surrounding drugs and alcohol are broad and extensive. As such, addressing drug and alcohol abuse is a large job and requires extensive resources.

Second, *needs-based approaches* are essential. Efforts should address identified and documented needs, and not be done just to "check off a box." To be effective, the approach should consider the continuum from prevention to intervention to recovery. Strategies vary from institution to institution and from community to community because of different missions, contexts, cultures, and needs.

Third, be both *evidence-based and creative* with planning efforts. It is important to respect and rely upon scientific foundations. Be grounded and use respected resources and protocols. At the same time, incorporate innovation, build upon stakeholders' hypotheses, and create new science.

Within this context of being both evidence-based and creative in planning activities and strategies, some specific ideas about ways of encompassing creativity are found with Professional Perspective 8.2. Further, some comments and insights from long-term advocates are helpful for stressing the importance of the planning process being open. With these processes, especially those of a creative nature, it is important to maintain the scientific grounding of these so the initiatives identified are not simply of a "feel-good" nature; rather, the use of creativity can further expand the reach and ideally, the impact of planned efforts.

Professional Perspective 8.2

Let's Dream! Employing Creativity and Innovation in Working with Alcohol, Other Drugs and Related Issues

John Watson, M.S.

Professionals working with alcohol, other drug, and related issues are quite well versed in their areas of competence and expertise, whether that is clinical work, prevention efforts, policy development, advocacy, orchestrating community coalitions, or more. Best practices and scientific grounding abound; however, many issues still remain. In fact, no "silver bullet" or "magic answer" exists. Therefore, it is incumbent to continue to explore new ideas, creative approaches, and inventive programs and interventions. Incorporating creative and innovative approaches can be both daunting and freeing at the same time. That said, from my work with clients, families, communities, administrators, policymakers, advocacy groups, and state and national leaders I have identified five considerations for incorporating creativity in our work.

First, be confident. We all know the work with alcohol and other drugs is challenging, and can feel overwhelming. But it's helpful to remember, regardless of our role, we do know a lot about the issues. I first got involved in this work as a clinician. Through my work as a clinician I first began to infuse creativity into my work. I remember working with an individual who'd lost a father to an overdose after years of substance abuse. In processing his grief, we hit a wall. Luckily he had a background in acting so we pulled from that and together decided on him writing a short screenplay, in which he could explore all he needed to say and all he needed to hear. This process allowed him to move forward and find a sense of closure.

Second, be curious. Explore best practice, evidence-based, and evidence-informed approaches as well as approaches grounded in science; what a great foundation. But don't stop there, investigate and learn about approaches used in other fields, such as from education and business, to the arts as well. This does not negate the science that has gone into developing evidence and science-based practices, but it takes us back to the beginning, as all approaches start with a new and innovative idea. Often, we need to push the boundaries and find a new and creative approach in working with alcohol, other drug, and related issues and pull from a variety of sources including work with other special populations. All evidence and science-based approaches started with recognizing the need for a new and innovative approach. In looking for a model to connect students in recovery with each other and with supportive peers, I borrowed from the early gay–straight alliances that emerged in the early 2000s, which provided a good framework for connecting students in recovery with a variety of safe social supports.

Third, be collaborative. Work with others on your team, your coalition, your advisory group, or your staff, if you have one. The group can be most helpful to brainstorm ideas, share thoughts, ask and answer questions, get feedback, help flesh out an idea and develop a plan to implement and assess a new approach. When developing coalitions and/or a task force to address specific drug/alcohol issues, I found myself looking to churches and faith-based organizations as a model for bringing diverse groups of people together around a common cause. A church I worked with was excellent at finding common ground among a broad range of constituents to bring multiple parties together with passion, energy, and mutual respect to explore how this specific church could meet the needs of those in the community and provide an environment that is inclusive of all. The motto "to be of service to each other" was a great tool and one that is great to keep in mind when collaborating with others.

Fourth, be bold. Take a leap of faith and try something new, or modify, borrow, reinvent, or combine existing approaches to meet the needs of your population, the goals of your organization, or your work with individuals. Consider incorporating or infusing your current work with approaches used in other fields; being bold means doing something that isn't (yet) popular, institutionalized, or perhaps even on someone's radar screen. So far, the examples I've shared, while creative, admittedly are not radical or particularly bold, so let me share an approach that was truly bold. In the late 1990s and early 2000s club drugs were big with multiple populations including late adolescents and young adults.

These drugs were often used at dance parties known as "raves." So, in my effort to find a different, creative approach that might get students' attention, I borrowed from the rave culture itself and held a mock-rave (dance party) on campus. We built on an experiential learning model that would also address multiple learning styles. Student volunteers were engaged in the development and implementation of this approach where participants were exposed to the effects of various club drugs, how to recognize and respond to a problematic situation, and ways to think on their feet. It got students' attention and for a time was a good part of a more comprehensive prevention approach.

Fifth, do not be afraid to fail! It is never our intent to fail, but so often when we try something new, it doesn't land exactly where we thought it would or it goes in a somewhat different direction than expected. That's fine, we can learn from those experiences, as much as from the successes. No matter the outcome, we will never know the potential of new and innovative approaches unless we try.

Without creativity and innovation, we are left with the existing tools and approaches in our field. While these may be plentiful and helpful, we always encounter new issues, problems, and populations that may benefit from work that is outside the box! Keep on dreaming!

John Watson, M.S., NCC, L.P.C., is Director of Counseling Services at Holy Family University, having previously served as Director of Alcohol, Other Drug, and Health Education, Assistant Director of Counseling, and Adjunct Assistant Professor at Drexel University. John has served as Chair of the Network Addressing Collegiate Alcohol and Other Drug Issues and a member of the board of directors for the Council for the Advancement of Standards in Higher Education.

I met people open to think outside the box, who gave me license to do that.
BJ McConnell

It appears that we sort of have a downhill but we can always move forward. I always thought that sometimes you can become creative when you have problems. That's when you become creative. And even though we've lost some of our major programs, that help people in the field to become qualified, to receive training, we don't quit. We try to figure out ways that we can get around this so we can go forward.
Mary Hill

I was probably most surprised when the money pretty much dried up. Shocked is probably a better word because it just seemed like, you know, again until recently we were in the business of collecting data to show our effectiveness, and it would've been nice to have been given that opportunity because I think there are an awful lot of good things out there, a lot more good things to come from it if we had a little more funding. On the other hand I've also been very surprised at what we can do with no money at all.
Carla Lapelle

So transparency is defined as really trying to open up the process to different ideas.
Ralph Blackman

Fourth, it is important to design any initiatives as part of a *comprehensive effort*. Single strategies may be helpful, yet are typically not sufficient for addressing the needs. Being successful means including both environmental and individualized approaches. Comprehensive approaches include multiple different strategies with many individuals and groups involved. Approaches should consider strategies within the paradigm of universal, selected, and indicated initiatives.

Fifth, *use a variety of efforts*, as the range of approaches helps with each one complementing or reinforcing other approaches. This variety also helps to acknowledge different learning styles (e.g., experiential, reading, reflecting, discussion).

Sixth, be *organized and strategic* with a clear plan and timelines. Orchestrate efforts for small successes and timely results. Ultimately seek environmental change. Address the ultimate audience (e.g., youth, elders, residents) as well as intermediaries (e.g., healthcare providers, educators, parents).

Finally, emphasize *shared responsibilities and accountability*. This involves extensive collaboration, acknowledging that many partners can have a role to play, large and small, short-term and longer-term. Document outcomes and processes, gather data, assess short-term and longer-term outcomes, be accountable, and share results.

With attention to these guiding principles, local and community leaders can help efforts be more planful and, ultimately, successful. Complementing these with locally appropriate guiding principles will aid with effective planning efforts, overall sustainability, and likelihood for successful impact.

Two long-term advocates offer some of their reflections and recommendations for planning appropriate initiatives.

So my deliverable at the end of the game will be to get those numbers back on course in any way that we can, most especially in a collaborative way.
Kurt Erickson

If we were allowed to research for effectiveness I think there are fantastic ideas out there, a lot of sort of growth from a little piece of knowledge, you know what you could do with it, you could do this and that, but there's not the money to try.
Carla Lapelle

A Menu of Strategies

The strategies identified for implementation to achieve the desired outcomes will vary. Ideally, the various strategies will complement one another. The critical point is that these strategies are designed to be balanced and, ultimately, effective. It is like a meal: having a balance of salad, vegetable, starch, meat, and (perhaps) dessert. Various individual needs, constraints, and preferences may enhance or restrict specific elements of the meal; further, within any category, there are choices. For implementation of drug and alcohol initiatives, the menu of strategies parallels those of a meal: based on needs, constraints, and choices. This also includes priorities based on factors such as local needs and interests, costs, implementation or sustainability considerations, and resources.

For example, implementing policy approaches only will not be sufficient, although certain policies may be more effective for specific results; further, implementing a wide variety of policies may indeed be appropriate, yet preferably orchestrated over a period of time. Necessary to complement the policies will be enforcement with followthrough and consequences; also necessary will be awareness by the audience about the existence of the policies and their consequences, as well as training of those charged with implementing and reviewing the policies.

The ideal way of approaching the various approaches to be considered is within the construct of the goals and objectives. As noted in the previous chapter, having an objective means having a specified outcome that has clearly defined endpoints or measures, so that their attainment can be monitored and reviewed. The objective is not, therefore, the strategies that will be implemented; the strategies are chosen to help achieve the objective. For example, training law enforcement personnel is a strategy to achieve a level of knowledge or skill about a specific topic or issue; and that outcome combines with other outcomes to support the achievement of an overall goal (such as safety). It is the training itself that is the strategy chosen. Similarly, if the aim is one of having greater public awareness about the dangers associated with the use of a particular illicit drug, strategies may include public awareness campaigns, media approaches, training of educators, enforcement of violations, and education about enforcement efforts and consequences.

A variety of strategies is helpful for consideration with a comprehensive effort, whether at the group, institutional, community, state, regional, or national level. These strategies can be organized within 14 overall approaches, summarized briefly here.

Policies and Laws: Policy statements cover numerous issues and can be prepared in many different formats. These represent standards that are important to the constituency. They can be national, state-based, or community-centered; they are also found in organizations, worksites, schools, volunteer settings, and more. Policies can be laws or regulations, ordinances or procedures. Policies can reflect overlapping jurisdiction, also; while federal laws may exist, states or localities may have additional laws, as well as the policies established by a locality, institution, group, or organization (e.g., a drug-free workplace). Topics are widespread, and may include access, pricing, taxation, marketing, qualifications of vendors/servers, hours of operation, quality standards, zoning and land use, age requirements, use of equipment, responsibilities when transporting others, driving, and industry sponsorship.

The importance of laws and policies is paramount with substance abuse prevention efforts. Some of the insights and recommendations from long-term advocates are helpful in putting this into context.

> *We can do all kinds of things like our policy development and pretty much enforcement; if we start at the beginning, it doesn't have to cost any more than we are already spending but I think that the research on the trial and error does take some money and I would like to see us have it.*
>
> Carla Lapelle

There was very little discussion about alcohol and drugs. More about alcohol than drugs but I think the knee-jerk insert every time you saw an alcohol problem was a referral to AA, so everybody got referred to Alcoholics Anonymous whether they needed it or not. For younger kids there really wasn't any answer, as I think back in the late 1960s it was hoping that they do well, there was some counseling but not a whole lot of counseling based on science or anything. It was more like a "do well and if you don't do well we're going to punish you," so there were not many carrots but there were a lot of sticks back then.

Bill Modzeleski

I understand it's not easy but I think you've got to stay focused on getting policymakers to understand that good prevention is about policy, it's not the easy stuff and to me that's going to be generational. I think we have to stay focused on that and not allow ourselves to slip back into doing, to use another phrase, simple educational message programs; it just doesn't make sense in all alcohol and other drugs.

Steve Schmidt

Enforcement: Policies and laws alone are not sufficient; they must be supplemented with enforcement and followthrough, to ensure compliance with them. Based on the setting and scope of the standard (e.g., law, ordinance policy, or procedure), different personnel have responsibility to do the enforcement. Laws and ordinances are handled by law enforcement personnel, who are trained to observe and intervene as appropriate; this may also include investigative activities and complementary deterrence efforts. Procedures at all levels are important to maintain consistency and offer review of the efficacy of these approaches. Strategies may include, among others, sobriety checkpoints, pre-employment and current employee drug screening, ignition interlock devices, and compliance spot checks of vendors. Other enforcement efforts may include behavioral consequences (e.g., tough love), monitoring of procedural compliance, assessment of knowledge acquisition or understanding, attitudinal monitoring, environmental scans, and evaluative reporting. Whether for a law or a generalized policy for a setting, it is important that the nature and spirit of the standard is followed by actual implementation.

Information Dissemination: Communication is essential about so many issues surrounding drugs and alcohol. This must be accurate, current, believable, and done in ways that are understood by the audiences targeted. Topics are widespread, including facts about the range of substances that exist, as well as new ones and combinations of substances; how the human body processes and reacts to their presence; short- and long-term effects; how individuals handle substances differently; and consequences of use. It also includes how to evaluate new or confusing information, facts about others' use, resources and trustworthy sources, tips for decision-making, strategies for promoting quality choices, and ways of promoting healthy decisions among others. An important aspect of this element links with the first two items: communication about the policy as well as about its enforcement. Numerous tips and channels (e.g., print materials, television, public service announcements, media, billboards, social media, and more) are highlighted in Chapter 9.

While the blend of a variety of approaches and an orchestrated effort are deemed essential for success, the importance of good information dissemination and messaging is also viewed as vitally important, as cited by several long-term advocates.

> *I hope we become seamless. I think one of the things that's really going to help is when we are all giving implicitly or explicitly the same message to people about alcohol and other drugs. So I'm very hopeful when I see that coalitions and national agencies and others are working together I'm really hopeful.*
>
> Carla Lapelle

> *We never viewed this issue as a marketing issue, and I always go back to marketing and so I as an adult who is 50 or 60 years old I'm going to tell you what's right or wrong, rather than saying "okay, get a group of kids and say that I want to sell you something, what's the best way to sell it to you?" And so you get that input. There was this reluctance for the longest period of time to use those people who we were targeting as resources for steering us in the right direction. And we relied solely on "we know what's best for you."*
>
> Bill Modzeleski

> *In a lot of ways we are victims of our own success, because there were some great programs, some good progress, obviously some of the self-reported surveys showed that, but unfortunately the media doesn't spend a lot of time on the issue today and as a result we have just lost a lot of momentum, I believe, whether it's funding or whether it's just getting people to understand these are important issues.*
>
> Steve Schmidt

Affective Approaches: Complementing the information is attention to the importance of personalized choices and values. These efforts address clarification of individual standards and guidelines, as well as shared standards for a group or organization. Attention is provided to approaches using personalized feedback as well as ways of discussing issues of importance to individuals and groups.

Campaigns: Having a focused, multi-pronged approach on a specific issue or topic serves as the foundation of a campaign. This will typically include a range of strategies, such as a proclamation, kick-off event, articles, large-scale events, discussions, fact sheets, interviews, social media initiatives, resources, information pages, public service announcements, and media coverage. A campaign may be linked to a time of the year (month, week, day, season) or be tied into a policy change or current identified need or issue.

Curriculum: These efforts are included in traditional education settings, and also with in-service training activities as well as self-directed learning. Content should be current and grounded in good science, illustrate where areas of confusion or controversy exist, and be presented in ways that allow for retention and application of the content. Quality efforts include the overall context, science, applications, resources, and references. Grounded with rubrics for organizing and monitoring goal attainment, these efforts can be found in traditional classroom settings, workshops, online training; they include approaches such as lectures, guided discussion, experiential learning, self-learning, practice sessions, mentoring and coaching, reflection and writing.

Skill-Building: Often incorporated within curricular efforts is skills training, generally of a hands-on, applied nature. Individuals gain competence with implementing strategies for themselves or with others. Skills include goal-setting, strategy development, self-monitoring, and evaluation of impact. They also include stress management, time management, assertiveness, effective communication, interpersonal relationships, organization, financial wellness, and other life skills.

Peer Approaches and Mentoring: Whether in the workplace, school, community, or other setting, the engagement of peers and mentors is helpful and effective, and is often viewed as essential. Within the self-help/mutual aid community, for example, the importance of efforts being run by volunteers, and the role of sponsors, exemplify the importance of these efforts. School-based groups such as SADD (Students Against Destructive Decisions) and college efforts such as BACCHUS Peer Education further demonstrate how these efforts can help. Based on the "helper therapy principle,"[2] peer approaches can demonstrate results to the intended recipient as well as the individual offering assistance. These efforts can include information sharing, advice, consultation, support, referral, challenge, and safety.

Programming: Having a range of activities and services is helpful for promoting the desired outcomes, whether at a school, worksite, community, or other setting. It is not sufficient to simply be organized or to have policies in place. Within the context of what a group or organization (or society) aspires to be, programming is one of the vehicles for achieving that outcome. These may include educational, cultural, recreational, and social events; audiences may be targeted (e.g., teens, tots, tweens, elders) or varied. Some efforts may be designated as substance free, and others may include responsible use of beverage alcohol. Programming may be part of the campaigns, and it may incorporate skill-building or training, all cited in this section.

One of the long-term advocates highlights some of the contextual aspects associated with implementing programs:

> *And by the way I am not just talking about politicians but I'm also talking about professionals in the field, that they still focus on programs that just are not science- and evidence-based. We still do a lot of programs that are feel-good programs, we still do a lot of programs that don't show impact, but it's a way of crossing that checkmark off on a book or saying to people, or saying to the politicians "Yep I'm out there doing all of this educational stuff." And politicians certainly don't understand what the science says and I don't think that the professionals in the field have held their feet to the fire as best they can.*
>
> Steve Schmidt

Training: These efforts help prepare individuals implement their responsibilities in a more skillful and informed manner. Whether focusing on new information, a change in policy or law, expedited procedures, or a more consumer-oriented style, the training prepares participants with the specified outcomes and processes. Audiences may include vendors and service providers, law enforcement personnel, or educators; they may involve students, parents, or community leaders or volunteers. Topics range widely and include bystander intervention, refusal skills, public presentation and persuasion, referral, and media advocacy.

Community Engagement: Getting community members involved is central to effective and long-lasting initiatives, as highlighted in the planning model described in Chapter 7. This involves leadership training, recruitment, retaining quality personnel, ongoing commitment, organization, planning, meeting management, and ongoing monitoring. These same processes can be applied in varied settings, other than the community at large. Further, the efforts are relevant for those in paid or volunteer roles, and include those in appointed or elected positions, as well as those with a role of interested participant.

Long-term advocates have some observations regarding community involvement and engaging others:

> *I'm also personally curious to the point of being a pain in the butt. I have an insatiable curiosity, I think people are wonderful and it's so cool to ask them their ideas. I also believe that people like to figure stuff out. "Don't lecture me, make it interesting give me the parts, give me the challenge and I'll figure it out to do"; they are great at it.*
> BJ McConnell

> *We get a fair chunk of public funding, but we don't for our SoberRide program where we are reliant on industries which may not be normally associated with this effort but have a responsibility – or want to have a responsibility – in this public safety and public health issue, especially with any absence of more traditional public funding.*
> Kurt Erickson

Media Involvement: Helping to get the word out, about whatever is undertaken, is the media. This includes the traditional media (newspaper, magazine, television, and radio) as well as the newer or emerging media (including the web and social media). The central focus is that efforts are enhanced significantly by the engagement and, ideally, the support of the media. This includes media relations, with the cultivation of good relationships with those who manage access to these various media channels. In also involves media advocacy, so that efforts involving media approaches engage them to be in support of the initiative. Media leaders may take a stand on a proposed ordinance change, a substance abuse issue or need, a promising initiative, or a dedicated leader.

Support Services: With substance abuse, needs for immediate or longer-term medical, health or support services exist. A critical element of a comprehensive set of initiatives is having the necessary support services; this is true for organizations and agencies as well as communities or society at large. Services include brief and more intensive screening protocols, individual and group counseling, mutual aid/self-help groups, treatment services, medication, and trained personnel. Cost factors are essential for addressing the needs of individuals, whether through use of sliding fee scales or universally provided services. The complexities associated with quality support, and within the context of a caring culture, evolving clinical definitions, and improved understanding of effective services, requires ongoing attention to this factor.

Needs Assessment and Evaluation: Through all programs and services, whether policy, curriculum, training, or support services, it is important to have helpful and efficient standards and procedures to document and assess the processes and outcomes associated with the efforts. Initially, it starts with an appropriate assessment of the needs, and then the design of strategies to address those needs. The initial question involves whether the efforts accomplished what was specified. The follow-on question is what contributed to and what hindered the outcomes. This involves the use of quantitative and qualitative assessments, process and outcome measures, and careful planning and monitoring. Most important, it requires a commitment to attend to this element.

The importance of quality evaluation as part of the overall strategic planning efforts has been emphasized throughout this book. The long-term advocates also highlight the vital nature of quality with evaluation, metrics, data, and outcome-focused information. Blended with this is also the importance of understanding processes that helped or hindered the outcomes received, all done with an eye toward improvement and quality results.

> *One of the most important things that can be done is collecting good outcomes. If I had the data in front of me when my client presented that supported her treatment based on the success or failure of those who came before her I could develop a more accurate care plan. When we combine science with compassion I believe we achieve the best outcomes.*
>
> Robert Lynn

> *One of the things that contributed to their success was having data demonstrating outcomes. Success builds success.*
>
> Jeff Linkenbach

> *We need to have good data as we move forward, we need to have strong policy and clearly communicated to folks; obviously we need to work together so that we're all sort of on the same page if you will. But for all of those I think we can't forget that if or not engaging at a true, true dialog with students and recognizing that they have the power to make those decisions, that we can't make it happen. We can help things to happen but we can't make their choices for them. So if we are not engaging with them in true dialog, then those behavior changes won't happen on their end and we will be still struggling with these issues the same way we have for many years.*
>
> Mary Wilfert

> *Contributing to the success has been, is a focus on the bottom line, not just doing programs that presumably make the world a better place, but actually measuring them,*

and trying to be as evidence-based as we can. We actually incorporated the measurement device recently, albeit self-reporting, about how we move the needle. For example, between the beginning of the presentation and at the end of the presentation or sometimes even a week later, we can see whether there is an attitudinal change or an educational change of what kids think about alcohol, or the effects, or the laws or the consequences of such.

Kurt Erickson

Is it working and why it's working? The mind frame of higher education is an advantage because we are always looking at what is working and what needs to be studied further.

Deb Thorstenson

I am proud of being able to collaborate with researchers all over the country using their various longitudinal studies and having been invited to work with them and get the experience of working with different groups because everybody does their research differently.

Helene White

I think I've been a part of, an exciting part of, an absolutely infant field that was in complete and total infancy and I got to participate in that. I wish that everything we had done had had research hand in glove, but we could never afford it. That's the other thing I wish that the purists and the research world somehow understood – that kids aren't a petri dish and you can't have control and treatment and tests in one day.

BJ McConnell

Each of these 14 strategies can be considered for adoption by concerned individuals from a variety of roles. To be addressed further in the next section, enforcement efforts, while important for those in law enforcement roles, are not the total responsibility of law enforcement personnel; similarly, support services does not "belong only" to counselors, and "programming" is not just for youth. In addition, the strategies identified in Chapter 9 (Personal and Professional Strategies) stress the range of communications efforts; these can be helpful as they overlap these 14 strategies. Throughout any comprehensive effort, it is important to have a blend of strategies, by a range of individuals and groups, and using various communications approaches.

Pulling It Together: A Planning Grid

With the variety of potential strategies that constitute a comprehensive effort, multiple individuals or groups must be involved for the overall effort to be as effective as possible. Three distinct elements are central to this. First, *individual efforts*, while helpful, will have limited reach and effectiveness. Second, using approaches that *complement* one another are helpful as they address the same issue from different perspectives. Third, the various individuals and groups should, ideally, work in conjunction with one another, offering *consistent messages*. This compilation is an overall systems approach.

With the first consideration, individual initiatives are important. Sometimes, a single voice can make a tremendous difference. What may happen is that an individual is concerned and strives to make a difference. This individual may encourage an existing group to undertake some effort, join another group, or do things alone. An individual voice may be helpful in getting things started or energized; however, success is more likely when others get engaged.

Second, having various perspectives is important for having a broad understanding and a wide reach. For example, the participation of law enforcement, health professionals, educators, and policymakers promotes different perspectives and insights. Each of these viewpoints, as well as those from other groups and constituencies, are helpful. In addition, within the context of a comprehensive effort, some individuals will be responsive to messages from a health professional, while others will benefit from messages from a law enforcement point of view. Further, messages can build upon one another; someone may hear a message from one source, but its impact may not be felt until it is heard from another, perhaps different, source.

Finally, with the ideal of collaborative initiatives, groups of various areas of interest and expertise benefit from working together. It is important that the voice to the larger constituency (e.g., a school, community, worksite, state) is consistent. While the language and context of the message may vary due to the source or the framework (e.g., health vs. legal vs. interpersonal), the ultimate message should be the same.

This represents a systems approach, consistent with the planning framework outlined in Chapter 7. Such a systems approach is based on being organized and planful, and working in a collaborative way. For issues as complex as substance abuse prevention, intervention, treatment, and recovery, it is vital that strategies be seen within the context of a comprehensive effort. To have an impact, a broad-based, overall program, working together, is important.

The long-term advocates offered some final perspectives about ways of orchestrating quality efforts from a systems perspective:

What has changed, however, is we have better funding resources. We still have stigma but hopefully less. We do have people now who are conducting more research; we have more universities and professors involved, and looking at this I think that's important. We need to bridge the gap between science and treatment, not just bench to trench but trench to bench as well. I believe we've made a lot of progress in those areas and there's more opportunities for psychologists, researchers, sociologists to add value to the field.
Robert Lynn

Use your resources in areas where you get the most bang for your buck.
Deb Thorstenson

A classic example illustrating the importance of this systems approach is with impaired driving. If the governing body establishes a law to help reduce the incidence of fatalities or injuries due to impaired driving, that alone is not sufficient. The systems approach requires the buy-in of the enforcement element as well as the adjudication approach; further, education about the routine and potential

228   Confidence

consequences is essential. If the law is too rigorous, law enforcement personnel may choose to not enforce it; similarly, if the law is too strict, those in adjudication roles, such as judges, may provide a weak sanction. If the judge is lenient, this may communicate back to the law enforcement personnel that the effort of enforcement is not valued. Ideally, whatever law is implemented has the buy-in of enforcement personnel as well as judicial personnel, so each views the law as meaningful and appropriate. Complementing all of this is effective information with these constituencies as well as the audiences to be reached; this can be accomplished through education, training, campaigns, and curricular efforts.

One way of visualizing the comprehensive nature of efforts to address substance abuse issues is with the following planning framework. Orchestrated here for a college campus, the same concept can be used for a worksite, school, local community, state, nation, or other setting. This framework includes the "What" and the "Who"; the "What" is represented by the eight components identified, and the "Who" includes various individuals or offices. The components are the clusters of strategies that are done; it is within these broad categories that the initiatives, efforts, and approaches are found. These ten groups illustrate the variety of potential partners within this setting; these may represent areas of interest and expertise.

Important within each of the 80 cells in this example is that each identified group has roles to play within each of the eight components. For example, within the component "enforcement," it might be assumed that this is the primary, and sole, responsibility of the Police and Security group. While police and security have an important role to play with enforcement, each of the other groups also have opportunities and responsibilities to be involved with this. Another way of seeing this is to take a specific group and determine ways in which its members can be helpful and involved in each of the eight components. As another example, the Student Government group can be involved with Policies and Implementation, with Awareness and Information, with Training, and with the other components. Noteworthy with this specific product is that documented best practices and potential strategies were compiled to illustrate, specifically, ways in which each of the ten types of groups and organizations could be involved with each of the eight types of strategies or components.[3] When this was done, a total of 311 distinct strategies were identified.

Viewing the efforts to address substance abuse from a systems approach can help with orchestrating successful outcomes. This systems approach helps remove or reduce the impact of a "silo" perspective where different groups and individuals do separate things; it also helps these factions from competing with one another. This organized framework helps with pulling together a consistent message for the specified audience, with, ideally, the range of approaches complementing one another.

The theme with the planning grid is that various individuals and groups each have a role to play with the process of planning and implementing quality efforts. In short, this is a "shared responsibility," where categories of initiatives are not relegated to a particular group or organization. As noted, each of the groups has a role to play with each of the components associated with a comprehensive program. To provide one illustration, from the perspective of one of the groups, is Professional Perspective 8.3; this segment offers specific insight from the viewpoint of law

GROUPS

COMPONENTS

	Policies and Implementation	Curriculum	Awareness and Information	Support and Intervention	Enforcement	Assessment and Evaluation	Training	Staffing and Resources
Campus Leadership								
Drug/Alcohol Coordinator								
Health and Counseling								
Student Life								
Police and Security								
Faculty								
Residence Life								
Student Government								
Student Groups								
Community								

Figure 8.1 Comprehensive Approaches

enforcement personnel. Undoubtedly, views are also held by those in other areas of specialization – whether as a counselor, a medical professional, an organization leader, an instructor, a parent, a bar owner, a youth leader, and many more. These perspectives are helpful within the context of collaboration, as highlighted with this final perspective from a long-term advocate.

> *Unfortunately, there is no one silver bullet to defeat drunk driving otherwise we would've used such. Rather, it's going to take both collaboration as well as a multi-faceted approach.*
>
> Kurt Erickson

Professional Perspective 8.3

Successful Leadership Requires Collaboration in Law Enforcement

Ryan Snow, M.Ed.

Working in law enforcement is a difficult job. Increased opposition from the public due to snapshots of incidents seen on the news causes many officers to feel like the public they are serving does not support their efforts. This is making recruitment and retention a difficult thing to accomplish for police departments around the nation. Leadership and collaboration with other community organizations have a big impact on the way officers feel about their jobs. The work officers do should be recognized by not only the leadership in the police department, but other groups that are working toward the same goal. Often, the work police officers are tasked with is far from capturing an armed robber or chasing down a wanted felon. Officers often are faced with issues like solving an emerging drug issue or ensuring the younger generation understands the dangers of drinking and driving. These issues have been tackled in many ways over the past several years, but the problem persists.

Communities often see drugs and alcohol issues as someone else's problem. It is important to remember that there is no age, gender, race, or sexual orientation associated with drugs and alcohol. The issues are non-discriminatory, and no community is immune from issues that stem from drugs and alcohol. Many property crimes, thefts, domestic violence, and sexual assault cases start with either drugs or alcohol. The public needs to understand the root of the issue rather than just the result. It is easy to see the impact alcohol has when it comes to impaired driving but recognizing that the individual just arrested for shoplifting was stealing a bottle of vodka to feed an addiction requires a little more investigation. Officers are faced with these realities every day and have seen firsthand the destructive nature of these substances. Without sounding rude or callous, it is often difficult to explain to the average citizen the results of addiction or other problems resulting from problematic drug/alcohol use. Developing educational opportunities for diverse groups in communities is important. Recognizing differences in educational backgrounds or financial support before developing communications will help as many people as possible connect to the message.

Law enforcement agencies find it difficult to connect to the public and share this information for a variety of reasons; one is decreasing staffing numbers, available officer priorities, time commitments, and overall resource allocations. This is where collaboration with other community organizations is so important. Many great agencies and foundations have been set up with the purpose of supporting individuals that may have fallen victim to addiction or other substance problems. Leaders from police departments should reach out to these groups and ask how they, as law enforcement, can collaborate with them. Officers often feel like they are imposing or pushing their way into these organizations if they don't have an invitation. It isn't enough for social workers, addiction counselors, or other prevention-based groups to say officers are always welcome to come by or participate in their efforts to educate others on addiction or effects of drugs and alcohol. These invitations need to be provided to the officers with details about when, where, and how they are expected to participate in an event. Officers often feel like they are the outcast or afterthought, and this probably stems from the fact that when they walk into the room, people stop what they are doing and stare at the officer like, "What are you doing here?" Providing ways to make officers feel welcome is important to the success of the collaboration.

Police officers often feel as though their efforts are going unnoticed by members of the community. Often, members of law enforcement feel as though they are facing an uphill battle when dealing with larger societal issues, such as social injustice and discrimination based on factors such as race, ethnicity, language, sexual orientation, and socioeconomic status. It is important to highlight the good work that is being done by officers all over the profession of law enforcement and public safety. Something as simple as providing social media posts that recognize the work being done and showing the police officers interacting with the public are key to reinforcing the feeling of belonging and success within the job. Leaders from other organizations can include officers in their newsletters, awards banquets, social media, or online presence to provide the public with feedback of the work being done. This not only helps the public see officers doing something else other than giving citations; it helps reach a wider audience due to sharing on social media and other news outlets.

Based on these varied perspectives about law enforcement, the following are five action steps. First, ensure that your police, sheriff, or other law enforcement personnel are proactive as well as reactive with addressing drug and alcohol problems. They would rather spend their time trying to reduce problems from happening in the first place. Second, help youth and others see law enforcement personnel as doing more than enforcing the laws. The broad approach by these personnel, as community members, will help the partnership. Third, remember that these law enforcement personnel are all about public safety; this is the larger "mission" to which they are committing their lives. Fourth, find ways to recognize them for their good works, and their important contribution to the community. This also means communicating publicly about their public safety and public service roles. Finally, continue to identify ways to collaborate better, and to plan and implement this collaboration on a more systematic basis. Through these action steps, among others, our communities will be better off for all served.

Ryan Snow, M.Ed., has served as a police officer for eight years, with specialties in impaired driving and drug investigations. He also serves as a trainer on emerging drug trends and a conference speaker emphasizing the impact of drugs and alcohol on communities.

Summary

Important for resourceful approaches with addressing substance abuse, regardless of whether it is pure prevention or recovery issues, is having a comprehensive effort. This is true for a school, a community, a college, a faith-based setting, a worksite, and more. The essential point is that single, targeted efforts will likely not be effective in addressing the issue of importance and interest. It is vital to think and plan more broadly; and within that larger context, the individualized efforts can be implemented.

Starting with the foundation of evidence-based approaches and a theoretical construct, some guiding principles for the organized approaches are helpful. Individual groups can determine their own such principles to aid with the focus of their efforts. The foundation of having a systems perspective for the comprehensive undertaking, and incorporating various strategies from a broad-reaching menu of approaches, is helpful for the effort. Using the tools from planning (Chapter 7) and communication (Chapter 9) further help with quality efforts.

Notes

1 National Institute of Alcohol Abuse and Alcoholism. CollegeAIM. Retrieved www.collegedrinkingprevention.gov/CollegeAIM/Default.aspx.
2 Riessman, F. (1965). The "helper" therapy principle. *Social Work*, 10(2), 27–32.
3 Anderson, D. and Milgram, G. (1998). *Task Force Planner and Task Force Planner Guide. Promising Practices: Campus Alcohol Strategies*. Fairfax, VA: George Mason University.

9 Personal and Professional Strategies

Vitally important is the ability to make the case for appropriate strategies to address substance abuse issues, regardless of whether this is primary, secondary, or tertiary prevention. While science-based approaches and sound evidentiary documentation may point clearly in a specific direction, getting others to buy in may be challenging. Central to persuading others to support desired initiatives is effective communication.

Much of communication is an art, using various styles and incorporating a range of strategic approaches. The quality of communication can be improved upon over time and with practice. Learning specific approaches that can be included, as appropriate, will enhance the likelihood of achieving support from various audiences.

Many in the counseling setting often rely upon self-discovery, mutual aid experiences often rely upon support, enforcement often relies upon deterrence to avoid consequences, and education often relies upon critical thinking and recall. With communication for advocacy work, attention is placed on confidence and expertise; the persuasive abilities are enhanced by being grounded and organized, and by incorporating different techniques throughout the process.

This chapter begins with some communication basics; while generally accepted, these tips are helpful to reinforce effective practices. Second, attention to some specific tools and strategies is highlighted. The third segment builds upon general communication and specific strategies, with a focus on persuasive components. Finally, tips for advocacy are addressed.

The combination of these elements, when coupled with practice, will likely result in greater achievement of results. This is true regardless of the specific message, and regardless of whether the setting is prevention and education, intervention, treatment, or recovery services.

Communication Foundations

The basic, essential foundation of communication is on having a message that delivers, clearly and accurately, what is intended; also, that the planned and desired message is, in fact, what is received and understood. Without this symbiotic relationship, misinterpretations and conflicting views are likely. To help achieve this desired outcome, the communicator (whether a counselor, educator, peer supporter, policymaker, healthcare provider, law enforcement person, or other) must know clearly what is wanted as a result; specifically, what is it that the communicator wants the recipient(s) to know, feel, or do? For example, what knowledge is desired, whether new knowledge, replacement of old or faulty knowledge, or understanding? Separately, or in conjunction with knowledge, the communicator must know what is desired with the recipient(s) regarding feelings, attitudes, beliefs, and values; this may be new, revised, or alternative perspectives, and it may be a changed appreciation or feeling about a situation or issue. Further, the communicator should know what it is that may be wanted for the recipient(s) to do; what action is desired, what behavior (new, revised, or reinforced) is wanted, and what skills may be reviewed for application.

As highlighted in several places in this book, attention to sound theoretical grounding is important. This is true with communication, as a grounded understanding about how the desired outcome(s) might be achieved can be better articulated through incorporating the approaches such as the Health Belief Model and the Stages of Change Model.

With this clarity of the desired outcome, the communicator benefits from knowing the audience, and their current and prior beliefs and experiences. Knowing what is important to the audience, as potential recipients of the messages being communicated, will help the communicator organize and plan the approaches to best meet the audience "where it is." In this context, the communicator can also clarify what knowledge, attitude, and/or behavior is being reinforced, what is being introduced, what is being modified, and what is being challenged. This type of framework helps narrow the nature and focus of the message.

When communicating, it is helpful to share both a personal and a professional perspective. While it is appropriate to speak with authority, it is also vital to acknowledge the limits of one's knowledge and experience. The expertise held by professionals is important and helpful; also vital is an acknowledgment of the changing nature of knowledge with advances in scientific activities. Beyond the professional aspect, it is vital to speak from the heart; sharing personal stories and insights, "aha" moments, and challenges can help the communicator better connect with the audience. The blend of grounded knowledge with personal applications is essential.

With substance abuse issues in particular, the challenges are many with regard to communication. In part, this is due to the widespread personal exposure by virtually every person to some aspect of substance abuse; this may be through personal and direct experience, involvement with a family member or loved one, challenges facing a friend or co-worker, reading about situations in the news, and general public awareness. These experiences are valid and real; they are also the same and different, at the same time. Individual differences in how substances are handled exist, and the application to current and future situations requires the utilization of broadly defined constructs with individualized application. Further, within substance abuse issues, so much is known, yet so much remains unknown; so much has existed for centuries, and so much is new and is changing. Thus, the application of core principles and strategies, with adaptation for current issues and audiences, is important for achieving the desired outcomes.

Finally, with any communications effort, through public presentations or testimonials, with counseling or teaching, and with group sharing or public service announcements, repetition is helpful. A common mantra regarding effective speech-giving, for example, is "tell them what you're going to tell them; then tell them; then tell them what you told them." The idea is one of bookends. In a classroom, for example, outline what is to be covered, and then go through the curricular design, and end with a brief review. This helps ground and organize the communication, and most importantly provides clear focus with what is intended for the audience to know, feel, and/or do.

An important aspect of communication is being translational. That means taking some scientific grounding and providing adaptations for localities and other settings. Professional Perspective 9.1 provides an overview of an internationally based approach with various adaptations. Long-term advocates also provide some rich insight about the importance of translational work.

Professional Perspective 9.1

Translating Research into Practice on a Global Scale: The Health Information National Trends Survey Global Research Program

Gary L. Kreps, Ph.D.

The Health Information National Trends Survey (HINTS), conducted regularly every one or two years since 2002 by the National Cancer Institute, is a large-scale example of the nexus of research and practice. The HINTS research program helps identify opportunities for improving health education efforts to people who desperately need relevant health information to make informed decisions about their health. These nationally representative, repeated measure surveys examine a broad range of health issues and provide relevant audience analysis data about the groups of people who are seriously underinformed or misinformed about important health issues, involving food and drug safety, substance use, nutrition, exercise, prevention of health risks, screening, access to care, symptom management, social support, and best strategies for health care and health promotion (Finney Rutten et al., 2011).

HINTS data suggest the best ways to communicate relevant health information to at-risk audiences include identifying the information sources members of these groups trust to provide them with health information, the communication channels and media they prefer to use to access health information, as well as the kinds of messages that they are likely to understand, relate to, and respond well to. For example, the HINTS-USA results have shown that most consumers want to receive relevant health information from their primary physicians, but more often use the internet to get health information due to ease of access. However, the internet can often be an imprecise and misleading communication channel for consumers to access health information that is directly related to their specific health needs. These HINTS data suggested the need to develop online communication channels, such as patient portals from healthcare delivery clinics, where patients could easily seek and receive relevant health information online from their healthcare providers. Similarly, the HINTS-China research showed that Chinese healthcare consumers, especially older consumers, typically sought health information from television shows. However, the health information provided on television shows in China was not always accurate, nor was the information always directly relevant to consumers' health concerns. Therefore, the HINTS-China data suggested the need to improve the quality and currency of health information provided on televisions, as well as to include mechanisms (call-in telephone numbers and digital response systems) for consumers to ask follow-up questions and receive answers about specific health issues of concern. The HINTS data enabled development of evidence-based health education and information dissemination strategies for addressing important health issues (Kreps et al., 2017).

Several strategies have been developed to translate HINTS research data into practice, including designing survey questions that examine health information gaps and generating data that guide the design of targeted health communication efforts for key groups of healthcare consumers. For example, the HINTS-USA data indicated that many consumers were confused about cancer screening guidelines for diseases such as breast cancer, prostate cancer, and colorectal cancers, especially members of immigrant and minority populations. These findings suggested development of targeted educational programs for members of these populations to increase their understanding about where and when to seek cancer screening tests. The educational programs were designed to match consumers' levels of understanding, health literacy, and language preferences, with examples and recommendations these consumers could relate to. The HINTS-USA data also found that women, especially mothers, were the family members who were most likely to seek health information, not only for themselves, but for other family members too. These findings were translated into health education programs concerning healthy behaviors, such as nutrition, drug and alcohol use, and exercise designed specifically for mothers to help their family members make important health decisions.

Special survey modules have been added to the HINTS surveys, to address emergent health issues that arise in the different settings (Finney Rutten et al., 2012). For example, for the HINTS-China survey a special module was added to ask questions concerning food and drug safety, which has become a serious health problem in that country. The data gathered were used to identify public concerns about food and drug use to address with health education efforts. In the U.S., special modules have been added to different HINTS administrations to address salient health concerns such as consumer knowledge about health issues such as tobacco product risks, drug and alcohol use, side effects from cancer treatments, and nutritional guidelines. Results from these special modules have guided development of targeted federal health campaigns addressing areas of misunderstanding about healthy behaviors.

Results from the HINTS surveys have been disseminated widely in many publications, health briefings, websites, and presentations, with specific recommendations made for implementing findings for guiding health promotion efforts. Relevant partnerships have been established with important health promotion and regulatory agencies and organizations. There has been direct outreach to many local public health departments, and clinics to encourage their adoption of HINTS data for guiding health promotion programs. The results of the HINTS research program have been used to identify specific health information gaps among the populations these local health organizations serve that can be addressed with evidence-based health campaigns, educational materials, and health promotion programs offered.

The take-away message from the HINTS research program is that health promotion efforts are most effective when they are based on accurate assessments of consumer health information needs and concerns. By identifying serious information gaps and needs among specific audiences, efforts can be taken at local, regional, national, and even international levels to communicate relevant health information to guide informed health decision-making. The HINTS research program provides up-to-date and revealing data about what different groups of consumers understand about important health issues and what they are confused about. The HINTS research results also provide important guidance about the best ways to communicate needed health information to different groups of consumers to help them address relevant health issues. Information about the HINTS research program is available from the National Cancer Institute, including recommendations for applying HINTS data for promoting public health.

For more information about the HINTS research program visit the website: hints.cancer.gov/.

References

Finney Rutten, L.J., Davis, T., Beckjord, E.B., Blake, K., Moser, R.P., & Hesse, B.W. (2012). Picking up the pace: Changes in method and frame for the health information national trends survey (2011–2014). *Journal of Health Communication*, 17(8), 979–989.

Finney Rutten, L, Hesse, B., Moser, R., & Kreps, G.L. (eds) (2011). Building the Evidence Base in Cancer Communication. Cresskill, NJ: Hampton Press.

Kreps, G.L., Yu, G., Zhao, X., Chou, S.W.Y., & Hesse, B. (2017). Expanding the NCI Health Information National Trends Survey from the United States to China and beyond: Examining the influences of consumer health information needs and practices on local and global health. *Journalism & Mass Communication Quarterly*, 94(2), 515–525.

Resources

Finney Rutten, L.J., Blake, K., Moser, R.P., & Hesse, B.W. (2010). Partners in progress: Informing the science and practice of health communication through national surveillance. *Journal of Health Communication, 15*(suppl. 3), 3–4.

Kreps, G.L. (2012). Translating health communication research into practice: The importance of implementing and sustaining evidence-based health communication interventions. *Atlantic Communication Journal, 20*, 5–15.

Kreps, G.L., Oh, K.M., Zhou, P., & Kim, W. (2014). Applying the HINTS research model to studying Korean American immigrants' access to and use of health information. In *A Decade of HINTS: Quantifying the Health Information Revolution through Data Innovation and Collaboration* (p. 31). Bethesda, MD: National Cancer Institute.

Nelson, D.E., Kreps, G.L., Hesse, B.W., Croyle, R.T., Willis, G., Arora, N.K., Rimer, B.K., Viswanath, K., Weinstein, N., & Alden, S. (2004). The Health Information National Trends Survey (HINTS): Development, design, and dissemination. *Journal of Health Communication, 9*(5), 1–18.

Ramírez, A.S., Willis, G., & Rutten, L.F. (2017). Understanding Spanish-language response in a National Health Communication Survey: Implications for Health communication research. *Journal of Health Communication, 22*(5), 442–450.

Gary L. Kreps, Ph.D., is University Distinguished Professor of Communication at George Mason University where he directs the Center for Health and Risk Communication; his prior role was Founding Chief of the Health Communication and Informatics Research Branch at the National Cancer Institute. His research, reported in more than 450 frequently cited publications, examines health information needs and targeted applications (programs, policies, technologies, and practices) to guide informed health decision-making, support, and improved health outcomes.

I would say that there are a couple of things for professionals – they need to understand how to ask every patient, every visit about tobacco, alcohol, and drug use. And they have to understand that these are medical diseases that can be treated and that there are experts available who have taken specialty training who can help them if they don't know what to do. Those are the three things they need. What surprised me is the number of residency slots and even training slots in medicine for people going into internal medicine or surgery or psychiatry is almost at the point of time during the Johnson administration when the Medicare law was initiated.

Mark Gold

I think education is necessary, probably more than anything, to inform others in your field. Policymaking, policymakers, and others.

Steve Schmidt

Wouldn't it be wonderful if we could take Al-Anon principles of how you can negatively hurt people by enabling, and translate that into more of an understood public view.

Thomasina Borkman

Technology is changing but the family has changed, kids have changed, and technology has changed the family. I'm not sure that the field, rooted so far down in the weeds of the substance, has really done a great job and we are challenged ourselves. I'm not being critical of others without recognizing our own challenges, but we all have to look at how we communicate differently because at the end of the day the best information that isn't communicated in a quick, attractive, accessible manner is good information that will never get used. And then we have failed.

Ralph Blackman

We don't do as many flashy, visible activities as we used to.

Deb Thorstenson

Tools and Resources

As highlighted throughout this book, the challenges with communicating clearly and in a convincing manner are many. As highlighted by authors of the Professional Perspective segments and interviews with long-term advocates cited throughout this book, different perspectives and experiences are prevalent; individual frameworks and biases are many.

To help address these issues, and to obtain, ideally, the outcomes sought by program planners and advocates, some tools and strategies are identified. These can be mixed in with any of a variety of strategies, whether public speaking or news interviews, with public service announcements or posters, and with campaign materials or with social media. These various approaches should be viewed like a tool box: become acquainted with them, incorporate specific ones for various purposes, blend various items, and review and update as needed.

Data and Documentation: In its simplest form, this involves facts, numbers, and results. This is perhaps the most commonly used "tool" with communicating a need or priority. All types of data can be helpful, and may include incidence and prevalence elements. Data may include mortality as well as injuries or other negative consequences, such as those noted in Chapters 1 and 2, and also repeated or adapted for local application. Changes over time can be helpful, whether it is increased problems or concerns, decreases in those factors, or lack of change. Perceptions and attitudes can be incorporated within data, as well as areas of awareness, knowledge, and access (or lack of these factors). Data may include observational findings, and data may incorporate the presence as well as the implementation of policies and procedures. Further, data may be examined based on demographic factors, such as age, gender, socioeconomic status, setting, and region of the country.

Examples: These serve to illustrate what might be expected as a result of doing, or not doing, an initiative. They help provide specific illustrations of how an approach might be implemented. With a policy of reducing access to substances, examples might include hours of operation, training of sales personnel, and identification card enhancements. With an aim of increasing knowledge, examples might include instructional approaches, self-training opportunities, public service announcements, and campaigns. Similarly, with a goal of quality treatment services, examples may include ways of attending to cultural appropriateness, incorporating a variety of psycho-educational strategies, updating staff with current techniques, and conducting a systematic review of the attainment of goals identified in clients' management plans.

Testimonials: These are real life examples of the issue being addressed; typically these are quotes from those affected by the issue or situation in question. These may demonstrate the consequences from an action or an inaction. The various considerations in this book's first three chapters could each be illustrated with a testimonial, such as how substances affected a person's life, what helped make an intervention successful, what type of mentoring, policy, program, or service made a difference with not using substances, or the nature of supports that aided with successful recovery. Testimonials help provide depth, passion, and connections to discussions for or against various programs and services.

Expert Statements: These are observations or quotes from those with detailed and specialized knowledge on the issue. It might include observations from a counselor or health professional, and it may also include insights from someone with law enforcement experience. When reviewing programmatic, legislative, or funding options, experts may be engaged to describe research and evaluation findings.

Scenarios: Often viewed as "what if" situations, the approach can describe, generally and specifically, what can be expected to occur as a result of action or inaction. This approach can "paint a picture" and incorporate data as well as sample testimonials that can be expected. When seeking a change, the results expected, ideally, as a result of implementing the vision can be articulated. The impression sought could outline potential consequences of inaction or delayed responses.

Creative Epidemiology: Also known as "social math," this approach takes data and numbers and restates them using brief, visual, and ultimately persuasive approaches. A classic example is that used with the number of tobacco-related deaths annually in the U.S.; with numbers nearing 600,000 deaths, this is restated by saying that is the same as having two jumbo jet airplanes (each filled to capacity) crashing every day with no survivors. This "creative epi" approach typically provides the real number and then says "this is as if …" or "that is equivalent to having…." When restating the data with images, these may be done in a variety of ways. One is visual (e.g., filling a stadium with people, the population of a region, or the volume of liquid in a swimming pool). Another approach is with a time equivalent (e.g., time spent, comparison of outcomes with a time investment). A third approach is with a cost equivalent (e.g., comparing the cost of a drug's negative consequences with the budget of a public resource or the cost of a prevention strategy). The messages are dramatic and visual, and brief and true. It is important to not exaggerate with these, and to find examples that resonate with the audience.

Social Marketing: The classic four Ps of marketing are Product, Place, Price, and Promotion. Within the public health arena, attention to Product can address tangible products (such as alcohol-free beverages, recreational activities), services (such as wellness checkups, counseling, treatment options), practice (such as motivational interviewing, self-monitoring), and intangible items (such as self-esteem, quality of life, enjoyment). For Place, it may address where services or resources are advertised, how this information is communicated or distributed, and locations. With Price, attention is provided to the financial cost (e.g., admission charges, cost for treatment services, medication costs); it can also include psychological costs, access considerations, and time factors. The fourth P – Promotion – includes ways of promoting the service or "product," maintaining the demand or interest in it, and the use of marketing and advertising strategies.

Social Norms Marketing: This approach is designed to correct the many misperceptions about others' behaviors and attitudes. Typically, individuals underestimate others' health-promoting behaviors, and overestimate problematic or abusive behaviors. For example, a perception is that "everyone is doing drugs" (or at least a lot of people are); with that mindset, one may be tempted to "join the majority" and use drugs. The reality, however, is typically that the perception is overstated. Social Norms Marketing attempts to correct those misperceptions, by providing factual information, based on current data, of what others are actually doing, and what their attitudes actually are. Within this, it is important to identify what the majority are, in fact, doing and to also point toward the desired behavior.

Linking and Pairing: This approach helps to provide associations with something that already exists, so that the message does not have to stand alone or be represented in isolation from a larger context. If there are plans to have an initiative or kick-off event, such as for a campaign, consider linking that to a national day, week, or month. Similarly, with such an undertaking, tie it into something historical (e.g., "on this day 20 years ago ..."). This tool can show how the strategy represents something new, or is in contrast with another approach. It can be celebratory, and it could include an endorsement (thus linking to a celebrity). It can include images or be associated with a season or holiday. There can be something unique with the approach, or a twist, or a blending of various approaches. It can include comparisons, perhaps based on some demographics. It can be fun. And most important, it should be relevant to the audience so it resonates for them.

Positioning: This dovetails with the previous tool, as it seeks to identify ways that the strategy can stand out from the many others. An initiative can be first, best, most cost-effective, longest existing, most relevant, culturally appropriate, highest rated, most valued, locally prepared, multi-generational, or other designation that distinguishes itself from others. The aim is to identify a relevant factor (or more) that helps this initiative be valued at a higher level than another, in the minds of the audience. The specifics will be based on what is appropriate for the initiative and what might be salient to the audience.

Bookends: This tool is a classic with speeches: "Tell them what you're going to tell them, then tell them, then tell them what you told them." It is a way of framing what is being said, whether this is with a 30-minute talk, a day-long workshop, or a short three-minute request of a governing board. It might include a story (a beginning, and the end later on), some facts, several key points, or a memorable acronym. The point is one of repetition, and helping anchor the key message in ways that are convincing and memorable for the recipient.

Blending: While data and documentation are essential parts of any planning or retrospective effort, they are not sufficient; they should be complemented with other elements. It is vital that discussions about current or planned strategies have multiple appeals – to both the mind and the heart. Data without a personal touch or emotional pull will appeal to some, but likely will not be sufficient to make a difference; similarly, personal stories may be compelling, but will likely not result in impact without some clear documentation.

This variety of tools is designed to provide some traditional and non-traditional approaches that can be useful in any of a variety of settings. Whether working with an individual client or a group of clients, or working in an educational setting and training teachers, parents, youth, or others, these strategies can be incorporated when appropriate to help engage the audience toward the desired endpoints. These can be useful with presentations to traditional naysayers, or they can be used to empower those who are already committed to working with the issues being addressed. Since individuals learn in different ways, it is vital that communication approaches be tailored to reach this variety and disparity of audience styles and needs. What may not be heard, believed, or accepted through use of one approach may find success with another approach; plus, the blending of various approaches can complement, in positive ways, one another toward the achievement of the desired outcomes.

As part of the communication strategy and the use of various tools, understanding the importance of language is critically important. Professional Perspective 9.2 provides a foundation for this; additional insights are provided from the interviews with long-term advocates.

Professional Perspective 9.2

Coming to Grips with a Common Language

Barbara E. Ryan

Alcohol and other drug research, treatment, prevention, and policy has found itself in the midst of language conflicts and controversy for decades. That's because words have a potent effect on what people think and feel about problems related to alcohol and drug use and thus influence consideration (or non-consideration) of potential solutions and policies that can be applied to reduce such problems.

Over the past 30 years a number of efforts have been undertaken to come up with a "common language" to assist those working in a range of capacities in the alcohol and other drugs field. In 1989 the National Institute on Alcohol Abuse and Alcoholism (NIAAA) entered into an ambitious joint project with the U.S. Center for Substance Abuse Prevention (CSAP) in order to "provide a conceptual map of the multidisciplinary field of AOD research and practice, as well as a standard terminology." Primarily developed as a tool for librarians, among other objectives the resulting thesaurus aimed to improve communications through standardized taxonomy and terminology. This technical document is not readily available, but a synopsis is posted on the internet.[1]

In 1994 the World Health Organization developed a lexicon of alcohol and drug terms providing a set of definitions of terms concerning alcohol, tobacco, and other drugs designed to be useful to clinicians, administrators, researchers, and other interested parties in this field.[2] Main diagnostic categories in the field are defined, as are key concepts in scientific and popular use. Social as well as health aspects of drug use and problems related to use are covered.

In January 1995, the U.S. Center for Substance Abuse Prevention and the now defunct International Council on Alcohol Policy (ICAP) – a non-profit organization that was sponsored by major beverage alcohol producers – established a Joint Working Group on Terminology to:

- review current terminology used by public health advocates and others in relation to alcohol abuse;
- identify key concepts so as to achieve a better understanding of different definitions; and
- explore opportunities for promoting greater consensus on terminology, taking into account international and cross-cultural dimensions.

The group promulgated a set of working papers and the publication *What Do Others Hear When We Speak about Alcohol? A Guide to Some of the Words, Phrases, and Slogans Most Likely to Engender Controversy, Offense, and Misunderstanding*, which was motivated by the idea that the "beverage alcohol industry and the public health/public policy communities need to find a common language." Despite those lofty intentions, according to "ICAP and the perils of partnership,"

> In the opinion of some of the limited number of reviewers who responded to the draft of the Working Papers "major sectors of thinking and concern in the alcohol issue arena" were left out and the effort was seen as addressing the "concerns of the industry not the concerns of the scientific or prevention community."
>
> (McCreanor et al., 2000)

Nevertheless, these efforts underscore the impulse in the alcohol and other drug problem prevention and treatment fields to get agreement on terminology and language to meet a number of objectives, not the least of which is to improve communication among researchers, administrators, policymakers, practitioners, and the public. However noble that objective, the ongoing debate over various terms illustrates the difficulty in coming to agreement on a common terminology for developing prevention communication messages.

The reason that many debates about alcohol terminology become heated is because the political stakes are enormous. The economically powerful alcohol industry is often pitted against public health interests. And within both camps disagreements about language and its influence on public policy are legion. Despite decades of communication research, there is little hard information about what people think the words mean.

In "What's In a Name? Let Me Count the Ways," William DeJong noted that Mothers Against Drunk Driving fought to banish the word "accident," thinking that the term perpetuated the mistaken idea that drunk driving crashes cannot be prevented (DeJong, 2004). But a 1999 survey found that 83% of U.S. adults associated the concept of "preventability" with the word accident, while only 26% thought that accidents are controlled by fate (Girasek, 2001).

The language used to communicate prevention messages and policies needs to be tested rigorously so that those charged with implementing prevention policies and practices can have some confidence that people hear and comprehend what is intended. In other words, more research is needed.

Notes

1 www.webharvest.gov/peth04/20041014225849/http://etoh.niaaa.nih.gov/AODVol1/Aodthome.htm.
2 www.who.int/substance_abuse/terminology/who_ladt/en/.

References

DeJong, W. (2004). *Prevention File: Alcohol, Tobacco and Other Drugs*, 19(2), Spring.
Girasek, D.C. (2001) Public beliefs about the preventability of unintentional injury deaths. *Uniformed Services University of the Health Sciences*, 8.
McCreanor, T., Casswell, C., & Hill, L. (2000). ICAP and the perils of partnership. Addiction, 95(2), 179–185.

Barbara E. Ryan has over 40 years of experience in the alcohol, tobacco, and other drug prevention field as a writer and editor. Among numerous publications, she edited the quarterly magazine *Prevention File: Alcohol, Tobacco and Other Drugs* (1990–2009). She currently works as an editorial consultant at the University of California-San Diego.

Not only are the key concepts of what we were trying to get across rooted in data, but so too is their delivery, from people who are both researchers as well as practitioners.
Ralph Blackman

We need to turn what we're dealing with in prevention into practical language that educators know and understand because if we can't do that, it's not going to be taken.
Bill Modzeleski

Story trumps data. And what I mean by that is that a lot of us as professionals have now gone to a point where we really value the data. I mean we are researchers, we are practitioners that are consuming the science and the data, and we think therefore that we can somehow convince different publics with this information that the data will be transformative, when in fact it is not. It's that the story carries the power and the story is imbued with emotion and values and perceptions and assumptions.

Jeff Linkenbach

People feel threatened when addressing alcohol prevention particularly when seeing it as a moral issue, i.e., if you drink, you are a hypocrite. Having conversations with students in the context of health and safety, it makes the issue much more palatable. People, then, don't see you as Carrie Nation reincarnated, i.e., we're not going to take your right away to drink (which, by the way, isn't in the Bill of Rights). Having respectful conversations helps people to see the issue differently.

Deb Thorstenson

And if we continue to allow ourselves to frame this debate around consumers, then you already started with a couple of feet in the grave for good policy because the argument is with more access there will be more jobs or more revenue; there's very little discussion about public health and social impact.

Steve Schmidt

I think when you can guide people through the process and give the people the opportunity, they will do the right thing.

Deb Thorstenson

What I believed earlier, that I no longer believe ... is the scare tactic I think, but partially scare tactics that hasn't been proven.

Bill Modzeleski

Persuasive Components

The appropriate starting point with applying the various tools and resources is to have a careful consideration of what it is about the audience that the appeal is going to be made to. Aristotle offered three elements with his means of persuasion; these include *logos*, *pathos*, and *ethos*. This means that planning a persuasive appeal benefits from deliberation about each of these three elements. With an emphasis on *logos*, which emphasizes logical and rational thinking, appropriate strategies would include the use of data, examples, evidence, social norms marketing, and similar factors. *Pathos*, which addresses the passion, might incorporate testimonials as well as elements of creative epidemiology, as these approaches can help "bring home" and make personally relevant the issue. With *ethos*, the message is about one of doing the right thing, and being ethical. This might involve positioning, personal examples, data, or other strategies that stress disparities, faulty paradigms, or unjust approaches.

Additional considerations are most helpful with the development of persuasive approaches. These factors are most helpful and appropriate for large-scale and group initiatives, whether a workshop, public speech, testimony, public awareness campaign, media initiative, or group discussion. They are also helpful with individual, one-on-one approaches.

- Credibility – It is vital that the source and the information provided are credible. Include the sources of information, and ensure that these sources are grounded and of high quality. Spokespersons and experts can help with this.
- Up to Date – Any data used should be the most current. Language used to communicate the message should reflect common and current words and phrases.
- Points to the Next Step – The content should clearly specify what is desired as an outcome, and what the audience should do. This may include consciousness-raising, information gathering, change of attitude, targeted behavior, or other result.
- Attention-Getting – Particularly true with public awareness activities, the approach should be inviting and visually appealing. By being visually engaging, the approach helps the message stand out from others.
- Clear – Any language used should be appropriate for the audience; it should be neither too simple nor too complex. The desired message should be obvious.
- Actionable – The message should specify an outcome that is within reach, and something that can be done and achieved within a reasonable period of time. While longer-range goals and visions are important, these should be contextual and encompass more manageable tasks.
- Personally Relevant – The strategy should clearly connect to the audience, whether through appropriate examples and illustrations, language, or timeliness.
- Blend Approaches – Include both facts and emotion, addressing the "head and heart" of the audience.
- Consistent – The words and illustrations should match; stylistic approaches should be parallel. Documentation and examples should complement one another. The action steps should link clearly with the background.
- Error-Free – Ensure that spelling, grammar, dates, and information are accurate. Avoid any exaggeration or dramatization. Be precise and clear.

Each of these standards or guidelines can be helpful with being persuasive. As with any communication, it is important to engage the recipient or audience in ways that are relevant to them, and appropriate for maximizing their understanding and engagement with the topic or issue. Just as with viewing substance use disorder on a continuum, and with intervention being a series of events and processes, persuasive strategies can be viewed in the same manner. Ensuring that these components of persuasion are present, the presenter or persuader can continue in an ongoing manner to affect the audience or recipient in the desired direction. While no quick fix or magic answer exists to ensure that the audience will "get it" or act in the desired manner, these suggestions can help toward the ultimate greater success with desired outcomes.

Complementing effective communication is a view of marketing. While the "product" is not one in the traditional sense, marketing principles are most helpful. Professional Perspective 9.3 is offered to suggest some ways of thinking about substance abuse prevention efforts with a marketing mindset. In addition, the views of long-term advocates regarding messages and communication are helpful.

Professional Perspective 9.3

Don't Fear Change – Initiate It

Thomas Hall, Ph.D.

Behavior change is, ultimately, the goal of drug and alcohol abuse prevention policies. Change starts with challenging beliefs – and this includes understanding how raising doubt challenges specific beliefs, or well-established habits (Miller & Rollnick, 2013). Health-risk messages are used by public health professionals to raise awareness about health and safety concerns – marketing strategies designed to increase ambivalence and to suggest actions to remediate or reduce the risk of harm (Strong et al., 1993).

Successful campaigns identify a target audience and include messages that boost the likelihood of behavior change. The Institute of Medicine (IOM) identifies three audiences for prevention messaging – universal, selected, and indicated (Springer & Phillips, 2007). Universal prevention includes a non-specific population, such as everyone in a community. Selected prevention includes at-risk sub-populations, such as people who drink and drive or people who mix alcohol and prescription drugs. Indicated prevention also includes at-risk sub-populations, however, the unit of measurement is an individual or small group such as patients who abuse prescription opioids or who regularly black out due to drinking alcohol.

Marketing establishes a narrative that highlights risk and encourages the use of protective behaviors. Creating an accurate and engaging campaign involves answering the following questions:

- Who am I trying to engage?
- Will the content be viewed as an observation about health or a judgment or negative appraisal about a behavior?
- How do I get the attention of my audience – will stirring-up emotions work?
- Does my message create ambivalence or doubt about a belief or behavior?
- Does my message include clear action steps that support self-efficacy?
- Is there something useful to do with the information provided in a health marketing campaign?

Two components influence effective messaging. First, a health threat is defined; next, a strategy to address the risk is introduced. It's not enough to point out risk alone; effective marketing gets the attention of the audience, and then provides a range of options tailored for the audience. Supporting self-efficacy changes a narrative from teaching skills to recognizing autonomy and self-determination (Maddux, 1995).

Messages focused on threat alone typically appeal to a group that needs no persuasion; the message "preaches to the crowd." Information *only* does not change behavior or attitudes; however, supporting self-efficacy does. This simple idea – balancing a health threat with identifiable and attainable action – increases the odds of sustainable change. Healthcare professionals often have a long list of things people should do or avoid, and a longer list of negative outcomes if the advice is ignored. Fear-based appeals are often rejected because the threat is too high; balancing threat appeal with a self-efficacy message enables the target audience to thoughtfully consider both options – change or resisting change.

An example of a fear-based appeal is the 1987 "Just Say No" anti-drug campaign "this is your brain, this is your brain on drugs." The campaign featured an egg frying in a pan. It implied drug users "fry" their brains. The implicit message was don't use drugs. However, it was not clear what drugs should be avoided or what to do next if you tried to stop using drugs unsuccessfully. An example of a successful public service message is the 2004 "Click It or Ticket" campaign. Click It or Ticket balanced threat appeal – a citation and fine for not wearing a seatbelt with self-efficacy, "Click it" served as an auditory confirmation a seat belt was in use.

Balancing threat appeal with supporting self-efficacy is also relevant in micro-level communication. Think about a relational conflict you recently experienced. In your effort to educate a co-worker, friend, partner, son, or daughter, did your advice lead to change or resistance? What did you emphasize in your appeal to change a behavior? Was it danger or intrapersonal competence? What could you do differently to lower the threshold of threat appeal and raise support for your target's self-efficacy?

You can assess the effect of persuasion by listening for change talk. Using focus groups or surveys administered to random members of a target audience provides useful information before launching a marketing campaign, and during a campaign. I created a mnemonic – I WANT TO change to measure the impact of health messaging. Keep in mind that any change toward adopting healthy behavior is a win.

- First, does my target audience IDENTIFY good reason to change?
- Do they WISH to change?
- Are they AWARE of their options?
- Do they have the NECESSARY skills needed to create and maintain change?
- Are they TAKING steps toward change and TAKING action to change?
- Lastly, do they have a plan for ONGOING reflection of what has changed and how they feel about the behavioral modifications they have made?

Health communication is a two-way interaction. Changing behavior, especially habitual behavior, is a process. Sustainable change starts with ambivalence, results in action, and promotes ongoing self-reflection (Prochaska et al., 1994). Persuasion, not threat appeal, accounts for the movement between identifying something that needs to change, becoming aware of alternatives, discovering the skills needed to change, taking concrete action steps, and doing ongoing reflection of the benefits of change. While it is easy to sensationalize, tantalize, stigmatize, and strike fear in an audience, supporting self-efficacy accounts for lasting change. Resisting the impulse to rely solely on threat appeals requires persistence, skill, and practice, but in my experience the effort pays dividends.

References

Maddux, J.E. (1995) Self-efficacy theory. In Maddux, J.E. (ed.), *Self-Efficacy, Adaptation, and Adjustment*. The Plenum Series in Social/Clinical Psychology (p. 3). Boston, MA: Springer.

Miller, W.R. and Rollnick, S. (2013). *Motivational Interviewing: Helping People Change* (3rd ed.). New York: Guilford Press.

Prochaska, J.O., Norcross, J.C., & DiClemente, C.C. (1994) *Changing for Good: A Revolutionary Six-Stage Program for Overcoming Bad Habits and Moving Your Live Positively Forward*. New York: Avon.

Springer, J.F. & Phillips, J. (2007). *The Institute of Medicine Framework and Its Implication for the Advancement of Prevention Policy, Programs and Practice*. Department of Health and Human Services. http://casdfscorg/docs/resources/SDFSC_IOM_Policy pdf. Accessed: October 23, 2013.

Strong, J.T., Anderson, R.E., & Dubas, K.M. (1993). Marketing threat appeals: A conceptual framework and implications for practitioners. *Journal of Managerial Issues*, 5(4), 532–546.

Thomas Hall, Ph.D., serves as Associate Director of substance use disorders, prevention, treatment, and recovery services, Student Health Services at the University of Central Florida, and has over 25 years of experience providing substance abuse and mental health treatment. He frequently partners with university faculty and government agencies to develop, implement, and evaluate evidence-informed prevention and intervention strategies.

Without question, more public attention is needed on the issue. Having the public understand that drunk driving is completely preventable is important especially noting that, currently and locally, we're losing the fight against drunk driving.

Kurt Erickson

One regret is probably not embracing technology early on, especially social media. I think that we all missed a golden opportunity with young people early on, as they were beginning to embrace and understand and engage with social media and technology. I think there would have been opportunities to use that, whether it was using it for brief intervention screening or for other evidence-based efforts to engage young people; probably that would've been valuable.

Steve Schmidt

I think sometimes we are open to receive things and sometimes we are too busy or cluttered, but there are some that have the teachable moment, the "aha," and how are you going to have an "aha" unless you keep repeating the message, and it can't be a hackneyed message, we need imaginative messages.

William Kane

What surprised me was the incredibly powerful role that spirit is playing, meaning the emotions and the common views and that by opening up spirit in a conversation it completely shifts the conversation, and then science and action can serve that spirit. What surprised me was like this hidden influence of spirit on these issues that no one is even discussing.

Jeff Linkenbach

Do we really challenge ourselves to deliver messaging in a different way so we don't give up one of those very, very influential channels? The challenge and the observation is not just about going from the web to email to social media which is still typing in words, but even in terms of the challenges that visual communication gives us in terms of how we deliver our message.

Ralph Blackman

Preaching is not going to work; you have to set some examples as a role model. Not that you don't have to talk about the issues; you can't preach about the issues. So I would convince 21-year-olds and 18-year-olds to listen to adults; in the end they're going to have to make up their own minds. I have also come to the realization that they're not going to totally do what I say, but I do think as parents and adults, we can set the guideposts and we can set the pathways that we think they should take. We should provide all the help and support that we can, but in the end they're going to have to make those decisions.

Bill Modzeleski

If I ever said I think we ought to do this and people said oh, yes, let's do that, I think I would faint. I usually have to spend a great deal of time trying to persuade them.

Kim Dude

When I was growing up, the scare tactics about heroin worked. And they were scare tactics and they don't have scare tactics now, heroin doesn't have that. So it was something that we had then, whether it was true or not, it worked. You've gotta be truthful; you can't fabricate things.

William Kane

Advocacy

Advocacy goes hand in hand with persuasion. To be able to advocate successfully for an initiative, service, policy, approach, or other strategy requires persuasion skills. It is vital for the advocate or presenter to harness various elements identified in this chapter, and then craft the approach in ways that will maximize the attainment of the desired outcome.

For context, advocacy starts with a cause or initiative. This may be the presence of treatment services in a community, or a policy change in a school setting. It may include expanded training for supervisors in a work setting, or it may be for a local ordinance to address specific areas of concern to residents. It may involve dedicated funding, a shift of priorities, or attention to a particular point of view. Advocacy may be general in nature (such as heightened compassion for those in recovery or a general shift toward life skills building as part of prevention) or more targeted (such as the availability of free meeting space for mutual aid groups or funding for after-school mentoring activities). Advocacy can occur by individuals, and it can also be conducted by intact or new groups or organizations.

Several steps for advocacy efforts will aid with a positive outcome. These build upon and incorporate many of the communication strategies specified in this chapter.

First, *identify clearly the situation* where attention is needed or change would be appropriate or helpful. As part of this, it is vital to have good information and data regarding the situation, and to be sure this documentation is current. This could be through existing data or examples, or with the development of a needs assessment in the region or area. It may also involve an understanding of similar circumstances elsewhere. This clear understanding of the situation, and the likely or possible outcomes of action or inaction, will help ground the initiative.

Second, *specify the desired outcomes*. This may include long-range, intermediate, and short-term goals. In this process, the aims should be both broad and narrow: general and specific. Both are needed, as the shorter-term results are necessarily encompassed within the longer-range goals. To the extent possible, the shorter-term and intermediate goals should be as specific as possible, so they are amenable to being measured or documented. These shorter-term and intermediate goals should be realistic, reasonable, and attainable.

Third, *understand and assess the decision points*. This requires knowing what approval processes are needed for whatever approvals are needed. Whether it is funding, resources, prioritization, policy, or other endorsement, it is vital to know where the decisions will be made. As part of this, it is helpful to know what the priorities are, and have been, for these individuals or groups. Know what is important to them, and what their own areas of attention or neglect have been. Know also their understanding of the issues being proposed, as well as their mindset regarding alternate perspectives.

Fourth, *identify resources and assets* that can be helpful in promoting the initiative. This may include groups or organizations, as well as influential individuals. From understanding the decision-makers' priorities and perspectives, and individuals, groups, or points of view to which they will listen, reasonable approaches can be developed. The approach can be framed within the organizational, institutional, and/or societal context (such as its mission statement or strategic priorities).

Fifth, *build a strategy* to promote the initiative. This includes the key communicators, both individual and group. It considers a gradual nurturing of the audience to prepare for the advocacy work, so that surprises are minimized. The strategy would address issues such as timing so as to maximize success. It will likely include media-related initiatives, through quality media relations and media advocacy. It may include large-scale events (such as a rally or letter-writing or campaign) in addition to smaller-scale approaches. The initiative can link or dovetail with other related efforts, as each can support the other.

Sixth, *conduct periodic reviews and monitoring*. This assesses the strategy process identified, and includes the identification and assessment of milestones relevant to the pursuit of the larger goals. Similarly, identify obstacles and challenges. With these reviews, the results can be helpful for identifying any necessary changes in tactics or strategies; they can also help with encouraging participants to reflect upon their success.

Finally, *nourish and support those engaged* in the initiative. The context of advocating for substance abuse issues is often an uphill battle, due to a variety of factors (including misinformation or outdated facts, faulty perceptions, biases, assumptions, personal fears, avoidance, or other priorities). It is important to become educated, continue to learn, remain confident, and stay engaged. Further, it is critical to have the courage to get involved, to speak up, and to stay involved.

Becoming an advocate, as an individual or as a group or organization, is an essential aspect of promoting necessary change within any setting. While communication skills in general are important and helpful, the advocacy mindset is one that can help further the specified cause.

A final view from a long-term advocate offers some insight about the challenges with advocacy efforts.

> What I do know is that using the measure of drug use alone has not been able to influence people. We have not been able to engage decision-makers, so is there a better measure that we can use to engage, that strikes the heart of decision-makers so they say, "Oh, we better do something about this."
>
> Bill Modzeleski

Summary

Personal and professional strategies are important elements of the Confidence focus for addressing drug and alcohol abuse issues. While professionals as well as volunteers working on substance abuse issues typically have great knowledge, the challenge is one of getting others to understand and accept that knowledge and those perspectives. Educators face this all too often; they can see the knowledge and attitudinal gaps with students and others to be served, and aspire to effective strategies to affect change with their audiences. Similarly, although in a more complex way, counselors face similar situations, as they help clients have a realistic view of themselves, and seek to prepare the client to improve. The various communication tools – those of a generic style, those involving more persuasion, and more advocacy-oriented approaches – all combine to achieve positive and healthy outcomes with the specified audiences. Having greater familiarity, through awareness and practice, helps further the confidence of those working to achieve reduced substance abuse.

Part III
Commitment

Commitment, as the third component in the *Pyramid of Success*, emphasizes the perseverance required to make a difference with substance abuse issues. While commitment is similar to confidence, it is separated to emphasize much of what is unique with drugs and alcohol. Based on the resistance and obstacles, the widespread presence of individualized impact of substance abuse problems, the lack of current knowledge among the majority of people, and limited resource attention, commitment is essential for achieving results.

This aspect is central, because simply being skillful and having sound self-belief, while essential, are not sufficient for sustaining quality efforts with substance abuse issues. Leaders have a vision, thus propelling themselves and others into the future. With challenges, limited success, and the many complexities associated with substance abuse issues, leaders must maintain self-belief and continue to get others inspired and motivated. The dedication to the cause of substance abuse prevention is central to this component of the *Pyramid of Success*, as issues with drugs and alcohol require a long-term perspective, comprehensive strategies, planned efforts, nourishment, and revisions to achieve and sustain the healthy outcomes.

10 Leadership and Advocacy within an Evolving Societal Context

For professionals working with drug and alcohol issues, thinking about having a role of leadership may seem out of place or inappropriate. After all, many professionals are working in clinical settings, and many other professionals are educators or community health specialists. What, then, does leadership have to do with these roles? And where does advocacy fit? What does it mean to advocate regarding substance abuse issues, and to whom?

This chapter acknowledges the important role that knowledgeable and committed professionals can play regarding drug and alcohol issues, beyond the "standard" or traditional roles. Specifically, substance abuse professionals typically work in a regular setting, such as counseling, treatment services, education, community outreach, and related roles. These professionals hold a tremendous amount of information and insight that can help inform decisions at the local, regional, state, or national level on these same issues. The presumption is that these professionals have much to share, and that policy, programmatic and services discussions and decisions would be better informed, and the audiences affected by these efforts would be better served, if those discussions and decisions were grounded in sound experience and current research.

In this chapter, readers gain insight into the important contributions that can be made in settings and through roles that may be outside of their regular roles and responsibilities. Within the context of the *Pyramid of Success*, this chapter emphasizes leadership and advocacy. This is done with the knowledge that societal norms can and will change, with some of these changing quickly and others changing more slowly. Laws may change to catch up with what people are doing, and people may change to catch up with what the laws have established. The important element, and central to this chapter, is the various and important roles of professionals with substance abuse expertise in this process.

This chapter encompasses five broad sections, and draws upon many of the concepts and skills covered elsewhere in this book. First, attention is provided to leadership in general. Second, the issue of ethics is highlighted. The third section attends to the context of a continually changing society. Movements is the focus of the fourth section, and is followed by a synthesis of leadership and advocacy.

Leadership

Leadership is a quality about which volumes has been written, and about which numerous views and perspectives are found. Leadership encompasses visioning and planning, organizing and managing, reviewing and funding, and communicating and assessing. Leadership involves courage and power, intuition and organization, negotiation and flexibility, and standards and confidence. Leadership attends to outcomes and processes. Leadership can be natural and it can be developed; it can be improved and refined; it can be revised and reversed. It can be situational as well as sustained; it can be crisis oriented and it can be transformational. Leaders may be elected and they may be selected; leaders may be vocal and leaders may be working behind the scenes. Leaders may have defined and historical roles, and leaders may find temporary or emergent responsibilities or opportunities.

In this book, the focus on leadership is intentionally broad and encompassing. The message throughout this book is that everyone working with substance abuse issues is and can be a leader. Some individuals will have an identified position, whether paid or volunteer. Others are specialists with focused expertise, and can be leaders in a variety of ways. The importance of addressing leadership with substance abuse issues is because of the need. As documented in the first two chapters, substance abuse permeates the environment and affects so many individuals directly or indirectly. One of the main challenges is that, because virtually everyone has some level of experience with drug and alcohol issues, different (and valid) experiences shape the world view. Different values and priorities exist, lack of current and broad-based understanding of substance abuse issues exist, and a clear direction forward is not present. Thus, leadership is vital at all levels of society – local, state, and national.

What leadership looks like can and will vary. What is important is to have leadership, and to enhance individuals' knowledge and abilities with their leadership responsibilities and opportunities. Just as with substance abuse not having a single or magic answer, thus necessitating a comprehensive approach, so also is leadership conceptualized. Leadership is essential, and varied styles and strategies are helpful.

The professionals interviewed among the long-term advocates offer a range of insights regarding leadership in general. These views can be helpful in shaping current and future discussions regarding how leadership is orchestrated.

> *I was at the Office of National Drug Control Policy, and I give the leadership credit for listening to us; when we would say something, the opinion was that we were the experts.*
>
> Darlind Davis

> *I think that quite frankly the field and the government, instead of applying pressure to stay out, could have applied more pressure certainly on our funders to do more.*
>
> Ralph Blackman

Alcohol is produced legally under legal auspices, as opposed to drugs which flow illegally and we don't really have a handle on it. I think the government has a whole lot more potential to impact the flow of alcohol than it does the flow of drugs.

Jeffrey Levy

What I would recommend to National Leaders: The political motivations for the War on Drugs are no different than the historical motivations behind alcohol prohibition. The War on Drugs is an archaic approach that reinforces institutional racism. This approach does not reduce substance use; it just creates more incarcerated for those who have the least resources, who are the most impoverished, and among those who come from diverse racial and ethnic populations. Prison does not rehabilitate, treatment does!

Claudia Blackburn

The hard part of it is it became very politicized. In my opinion members of Congress were going to "save your children from drug abuse, so reelect me." And so members of Congress run every two years, but who's going to solve that in two years, and thus it became a political pawn. To sustain change it doesn't happen in a two-year election cycle so every two years there are some new ideas that we were going to do and it was going to rescue the children of the world. But there was no way to change that because it became a political pawn and every member, every Secretary of Education, every HHS Secretary, every new Attorney General, everyone had an idea.

BJ McConnell

The students are smarter than we were. And many of them are tremendously accomplished and so we have improved. I grew up in the civil rights era and marched and protested for civil rights and we have great diversity where we didn't have any. And so the combination of public education, improved access to universities, and diversity itself will help us move forward. We have some of the best young people and their commitment and accomplishment are often drowned out by students that are more self-centered and less productive.

Mark Gold

I think that the younger people are pretty sophisticated, they see a lot of stuff and I am more hopeful that the young people are going to stay clean and want to have a clean society. I really do think the younger kids are smarter and they know what's out there; they are not coddled. Maybe the other generations were a little bit in the dark but not these kids. I think there's optimism. And they came up with models that are very different from what we had found in the past, so I'm sitting here waiting for the new models to come.

Darlind Davis

Six overall constructs will help with specifying leadership vis-à-vis drug and alcohol abuse prevention issues: (1) The Course; (2) The Boundaries; (3) The Focus; (4) The Collaborators; (5) The Style; and (6) Evolution.

260   Commitment

The Course: Overall, a leader will help guide the efforts with the group, organization, setting, or entity. This includes the initial *setting of the course*: what direction is wanted, what the vision is, what processes are to be used, what resources are needed, and related factors. This may be from a start-up phase (e.g., the community needs to have a policy to address a concern; an organization needs training and skills for effective intervention; a state needs accessible and cost-effective treatment services). This may also be improvements in what already exists; setting the course can include reviewing existing efforts and determining that enhanced attention, skills, or resources are needed. As part of meaningful and appropriate leadership, having a vision of a cause or issue that is larger than oneself can be most helpful as a foundation or anchor. After setting the course, the leader must *maintain the course*. This is a critical effort to assess how well the established course is being met. Are things on track for obtaining the desired results? If not, what needs to be done to achieve the results? If things are on track, what support and encouragement is appropriate to help continue those results? Finally, the leader will *modify the course*, as needed. If the efforts are on track, and the outcomes are not what was desired, what changes are needed? That is, if all the well-planned strategies and resources are in place, but the results are not what was expected, what can change? For example, if the planners and program designers believed having online support resources for those in recovery would help reduce relapse, but that this was not the result for some or all of the audience, then an examination and potential retooling of approaches would be warranted.

A couple of perspectives from the long-term advocates help illustrate the nature of the direction, often inspired by the leader.

> *So we often use the analogy if you put a stop light out there at an intersection, a whole new stoplight system is going to cost $100,000, that's just what it costs the highway department now to put up the poles and all of that stuff to have the lights. And yet a community can't afford $100,000 for its drug prevention efforts. It's criminal, it's so sad that our priorities just can't seem to make room for the allocation of enough resources to enable us to be able to move throughout the year in a planful way.*
>
> Darlind Davis

> *What occurred to me is that knowledge has more to do with inquiry than it does with having all the answers. So for me it is the path of growth, it's the path of being able to ask questions and question myself, it's about those things; it's not about being the most clever. It's about being smart enough to know when I don't know.*
>
> Robert Lynn

> *A major reason that the professionals ignore AA is because it is experientially knowledge based rather than professionally knowledge based.*
>
> Thomasina Borkman

The Boundaries: Related to setting and modifying the course is a leadership thrust of managing the boundaries. An effective leader is one who manages the boundaries. This can include establishing a vision, beyond what is currently done; the effect would be one of moving the boundaries outward. It could be changing direction so that the boundaries are defined in a different way; for example, a group may determine that enforcement of policies needs to be increased, thus changing priorities. Managing the boundaries can include areas of responsibility, for one's own group or for others. For example, what are the appropriate boundaries for action in a school when discussing drugs and alcohol, and what are the appropriate messages, and for what age group? What are the respective roles of parents and families, and what is within the purview of the school? Managing the boundaries is also one of attending to the process; who has responsibility for what, what timelines will be appropriate, and what processes will be used to make decisions? Finally, managing the boundaries has a focus on the group or organization, as well as on the individual; to help avoid floundering or burnout, it is appropriate for the leader to help the focus and limit overextension.

The Focus: A critical aspect of leadership is helping define the scope of the effort. Dovetailing with managing the boundaries, this addresses the nature and overall emphasis of the effort. Is the vision one of "solving" or "curing" the problem? In the context of the "War on Drugs," is it one of "winning"? While it is appropriate to have aims such as these, it is also appropriate to acknowledge that full attainment, or perfection, with such grandiose aims is not reasonable. What is vital for leaders is to establish realistic outcomes, based on the needs, priorities, and resources of the setting. As highlighted in Chapter 7 addressing goals and objectives, the focus should be upon what is reasonable and attainable; SMART goals[1] are appropriate for identifying the focus. This helps direct the focus to what is attainable, and can help leaders identify small steps that become achievable. Related to this is a redefinition of the focus – rather than "solve" a particular issue (such as underage drinking, opiate addiction, limited support for recovery, inattention to parental conversations about substances), consideration should be given to "better managing" these issues.

Long-term advocates have various perspectives about the focus of their efforts, with an eye on future initiatives.

> *The most important things that can be done ... is to make the misuse and abuse of alcohol and other drugs issue a "front burner issue." I think in a lot of places it is not even on the stove. Unfortunately, it takes a disaster to get it on the stove and to get it front burner. And I think we should all be proactive enough to do everything we can to prevent it from being a disaster.*
>
> Kim Dude

> *We're not going to eliminate drug and alcohol use. I think that as a society we need to have some clear understanding of where we are going to put our resources.*
>
> Bill Modzeleski

> *It's not a priority now.*
>
> BJ McConnell

> *What surprised me most was with all of this policy stuff, and I have been shocked at how effective it has been. Policy is really important. If you've got maybe a few rules*

> here and there, then you can institute some guidelines that can be very effective in changing attitudes, because that is changing and behavior and then maybe later the attitude changes.
>
> Darlind Davis

> In the big picture it is considerable progress. But again not when you have 31% of traffic crashes still caused by drunk drivers, so it's considerably less than what it was.
>
> Kurt Erickson

The Collaborators: As highlighted in Chapter 7's Planning Framework about organizing initiatives to address drug and alcohol issues, a central factor for strategic planning is engaging with others. Partnerships are vital, and the leader plays a critical role with promoting these. This can be done by supporting and nurturing current collaborators as well as identifying those not currently included as collaborators. It may also involve gaining the cooperation of those individuals or organizations identified as challenges or obstacles to the implementation of desired efforts. The focus with collaboration is one of avoiding doing something alone, and finding ways that "win–win" scenarios can be obtained. An additional essential part of collaboration is that different types of leadership skills and approaches are needed for different times and situations; thus, complementary styles and approaches can be most beneficial.

The important theme of working with others, through engagement, collaboration, and shared perspectives is provided by the long-term advocates:

> I think leadership has to recognize that it needs to walk hand-in-hand with the peer movement, with empowering young people. Obviously policy is important, information and data collection are important for all of these leaders to do, and to pay attention to.
>
> Mary Wilfert

> Recommendations for a policymaker: The experts are not only the professionals who have the academics, awards, and publications. Go local and find your AA leaders and sit down with them.
>
> Thomasina Borkman

> My recommendation: treatment. Treatment has to be available, it really does.
>
> William Kane

> We began working on standards for prevention programs and we looked at the various aspects of quality programming because I was working in the state office at that time and it was critical that we provide guidance to the county plans so that they would have a good prevention program.
>
> Darlind Davis

The Style: So much of what is written about leadership focuses on the individual in the leadership role. Attention is provided to "what makes a good leader" and different qualities emerge. As noted at the introduction to this chapter, leadership takes a variety of different forms, and is found in a wide range of settings. Leadership qualities include the individual being adaptable, understanding, compassionate, communicative, consistent, engaging, planful, organized, courageous, and bold. These styles will likely vary based on the type of situation (e.g., long-term planning versus crisis management). These will also vary based on the setting: an elected official in a public office, a volunteer on a board of directors, a paid administrator for a facility, a professional offering his/her expertise or advice, or a concerned individual with no specific role. Using one's personal style so as to build upon individual strengths, and incorporating the variety of tactics and strategies noted in the previous chapter, can be helpful for having a quality leader.

Evolution: Central to effective leadership is modification over time. With changes in the setting (whether a group, community, or society), new knowledge, turnover of key individuals, as well as personal experience, updates and modifications in leadership are essential. This evolution attends to each of the previous five elements: The Course, The Boundaries, The Focus, The Collaborators, and The Style; with each of these, changes occur over time, and leadership approaches and areas of emphasis must also change. With attention to individuals, attention to this evolution and incorporation of the requisite attitudes and skills can help good leaders become great leaders.

Just as leaders know, long-term advocates also report the importance of changing with the times. This may mean new perspectives, new strategies, new sources of information, new resources, and more.

> *I think that the rigidity came, it started because of money and then because politics has become black and white, it seems like you can't discuss it; if you say young people consume alcohol with their parents and they are learning, it becomes, you are allowing or you are supporting.*
>
> Gail Milgram

> *Treatment personnel and people involved in planning programs should learn some of this basic stuff from Al-Anon; that you can't change anybody or force things down their throat. You can enable and make it worse. A lot of people don't understand that they excuse a lot of drinking and drugging. You know, "I'm rich, my son has had three drug trips; why should I deny him a place to live, he'll grow out of it."*
>
> Thomasina Borkman

> *We weren't taking something that might work very well in this part of the country and trying to apply it in rural areas. We were beginning to realize that there was no one-shot deal and we wanted to move away from that kind of thing. Prevention at that time was basically getting up and doing school assemblies. So we kind of moved from that direction.*
>
> Darlind Davis

> *One of the potential concerns is that you may not have professionals that have the training on the issue but you certainly have dedicated professionals who are concerned about it. I'm talking about human resources and funded positions, but also providing funding for strategic development, for whatever it might take to support those*

264   Commitment

professionals for going to meetings and those types of things, such as establishing those centers where there's a focus on some of this effort.

Mary Wilfert

I think you've got to move with the times, you have to listen to what they tell you, and then you have to design your program to meet their needs.

Mary Hill

We are treading water. We are going backwards, we are going backwards in education, we are going backwards in our social policies trying to support the nuclear family. I think we are increasingly polarizing the views on those issues, I won't say for no reason at all but I think there is a lot more common ground than people would like to believe. But again because we are being driven in our thought by what has become a commercial newsmaking media.

Steve Schmidt

We know that opiates are more likely to cause overdose death and we know that alcohol is more likely to cause withdrawal-related death and for cannabis we are likely to see problems like we see in alcohol dependence. Plus problems like we see in countries with high levels of cannabis use.

Mark Gold

Attending to these six elements is appropriate for quality and effective leadership. Just as with any effort with substance abuse, no magic or single answer exists; a blend of qualities and skills help comprise effective leadership. As a summary mantra regarding leadership, the title of a publication written for college and university presidents is worth repeating: "Be Vocal. Be Visible. Be Visionary."[2]

What does leadership look like, more specifically, in a variety of settings? One unique environment is found with higher education; colleges and universities often operate as distinct, independent entities. With ongoing research and evaluation occurring, and compilations of resources and strategies existing for the setting encompassing colleges and universities, attention to this higher education setting is helpful. In a sense, colleges and universities can be viewed as a microcosm of the workings in other settings, whether a workplace, a community, a high school, a faith community, or even a state or the national government. Offered with Professional Perspective 10.1 is a view of this higher education setting.

Professional Perspective 10.1

Strategies to Minimize College Drinking and Related Problems

Gail Gleason Milgram, Ed.D.

College students are a unique population. Many students at four-year institutions leave home and parental supervision and are on their own often for the first time. For many students and various situations, young people are doing things never done before, which is a challenge for them. Not only is no one there to do things for them; no one monitors their behavior. They sleep (or not) when they want; going or not going to class, and studying, are individual decisions. Most students have reached the age of majority of 18, so institutions of higher education no longer assume the role of "in loco parentis." Community college students have different issues, as they often attend the two-year institution while living at home. These colleges also need to look at how alcohol impacts their community.

College and university leaders need to understand the reality that many young people arrive on campus having consumed alcohol in high school. Though the major focus of this essay is on alcohol, a legal commodity in the USA, marijuana and other drugs are also on campus.

Every institution of higher education has the opportunity, and the obligation, to examine their role in the prevention of alcohol-related problems on campus. The first decision is to decide if alcohol is allowed at all on campus and, if so, by whom and in what circumstances. When making this decision, it is critical to consider if the focus is on students only, or upon the entire campus community. When alcohol is misused, it can have a negative effect on an individual's life and on the campus. Policies need to be written, published, and widely disseminated, including in various handbooks for various campus populations.

A Task Force, established at the highest levels (e.g., the president or chancellor) should be established and maintained. The members should represent all segments of the institution (i.e., administration, faculty, staff, and students) and also represent all levels of the institution. The significance of the Task Force's findings and recommendations will be based on the membership representativeness, diversity, and scope of influence. One of the Task Force's first jobs is to determine the pattern of alcohol use on campus. If a campus survey has recently been conducted, the findings as to use and related problems will be available. If not, a survey should be designed to assess this information.

Although there are many social outlets on campus, fraternities and sororities are often singled out as they are a unique part of campus life in many institutions. With the dozens of fraternity-related deaths, and other deaths (e.g., car accidents, falls) not counted as fraternity-related, it is particularly incumbent upon this group to address alcohol issues aggressively. Efforts such as that by the North American Interfraternity Conference (NIC), a coalition of 66 national fraternities on more than 800 campuses, are important; they recently announced that its members would continue to work to reduce hazing and will ban hard liquor from fraternity facilities and events by September 2019. Since the same amount of alcohol is in 12 oz. of beer, 5 oz. of wine, and 1.5 oz. of distilled spirits, one could wonder why only hard liquor has been banned. This makes sense because grain alcohol, which is cheaper, often contains a higher percentage of alcohol by volume and is mixed with sweet drinks to make a punch, which makes it difficult for a drinker to determine how many drinks have been consumed. The NIC also adopted a Medical Good Samaritan policy which ensures that a student who calls 911 to get help for someone with a medical emergency won't be prosecuted. Related to fraternities and their role with reducing alcohol problems, colleges and universities must decide when a student can join the organization. Policies are needed regarding how alcohol can be served in these settings, who will monitor this use, consequences of policy violation, and dedicated roles for those with oversight responsibilities.

Related to the overriding policy regarding alcohol use on campus, answers to the following questions need to be considered by the Task Force:

- Can students access available and safe transportation at night?
- Are classes scheduled on Fridays? If not, the realization that Thursday is "party night" needs to be considered.
- Are alcohol-free activities (e.g., cafés, movies, pool hours) available to compete with alcohol-focused parties?
- Are protocols in place to prevent and address underage and heavy drinking at events such as tailgates?
- Are educational programs on alcohol and problems related to use available for administrators, faculty, staff, and students, including those who are peer educators?
- Is curriculum infusion of alcohol information in academic courses supported?
- Are peer-based approaches implemented widely?
- Are Student Assistance and Employee Assistance programs available for individuals who are experiencing problems related to their alcohol use?
- Has outreach occurred to local sources of alcohol (liquor stores, bars), local police, hospitals, community residents, and others to get a sense of their perspective on what's taking place?
- Is a substance-free living environment available for those students who would like to live in alcohol-free housing?
- Is support available for individuals (i.e., spouse or family member, girlfriend or boyfriend, roommate) who are experiencing second-hand effects related to someone else's drinking?
- Is space available for self-help groups (i.e., Alcoholics Anonymous, Al-Anon)?
- Are surveys, program evaluations, and monitoring of effectiveness occurring on a regular basis?
- Is attention provided to the campus environment and campus culture, to identify ways support can be provided to healthy decisions and reductions made regarding factors contributing to high-risk drinking?

Answers to the above questions will provide the ground work for the Task Force's discussions, as well as those of other campus leaders. Ultimately, each

> institution must supplement these core questions with questions pertinent to their campus, to make the discussion relevant to their campus.
>
> Gail Gleason Milgram, Ed.D., is Professor Emerita, Rutgers, the State University of New Jersey. She served as Director of the Education and Training Division, Center of Alcohol Studies for over three decades, and has authored books, articles, and pamphlets.

Long-term advocates provide insight about some ways that leadership can be involved for moving toward positive outcomes.

I don't see that there are easy answers for what to do about these things.
Thomasina Borkman

So leadership, I think that classic someone willing to use their position for a bully pulpit to get leaders involved, it was very helpful.
Steve Schmidt

Because when they are confronted with a public policy issue that has to do with actually preventing it or precluding it, they aren't sure that that's going to do anything about it.
Darlind Davis

Ethics

Important for inclusion in leadership are ethical considerations. This includes a myriad of factors, from individual to organizational to global. This section attends to some of these, acknowledging that much deeper and encompassing discussions are necessary and warranted among advocates for any of a variety of issues surrounding drugs, alcohol, dependence, recovery, intervention, overdose deaths, overprescription, and more.

How are ethics relevant, specifically? Consider the following:

- What is the appropriate consequence for the first offense with an impaired driver? How about the second, or third, or fourth offense? How might this be different based on the substance – alcohol, prescription drugs, or illicit drugs? What differences result when incorporating the age of the driver?
- What level of information about substances is appropriate in the school setting? Should distinctions about what and how it is addressed be made based on the substance and its legality or illegality? How would this be different if the setting was in a faith community, or a youth-serving organization? How would this be different if the audience was adults being trained to work with youth?
- What type of education, intervention, treatment, and/or recovery services are appropriate for those incarcerated? Is jail time designed as punishment, rehabilitation, reduction of the potential for recidivism, direct services, or something else?

- In what ways should hiring decisions for a job be based on prior substance use? To what extent does the extent of use, consequences associated with use, substance dependence, legal aspects, age of use, and specific substance(s) involved affect the consideration?
- What is the responsibility of accrediting organizations and certification agencies for ensuring adequate training and competence of professionals on drug and alcohol issues, in preparation for and delivery of professional services? What responsibilities exist for the organization doing the hiring?

These situations are just a sampling of the many ethical dilemmas embedded with substance abuse issues. Attention, albeit brief, to ethics is deemed important for inclusion in this chapter, just as Chapter 3 (Why Be Concerned?) is included in the book. Its incorporation is valuable for highlighting and inclusion at all levels of leadership.

First, it is helpful to distinguish between ethics, morals, and the law. Overlap exists among each of these, particularly between ethics and morals. Ethics can be seen as the overarching guiding principles, as well as the standards for behavior. These may be embodied in codes of conduct for an organization or profession. Morals reflect the principles on which individual (or group) judgment of right or wrong are based. Often cited is the importance of having a "moral compass" which can help maintain the valued course of action. Laws are formalized codes of conduct for a jurisdiction, such as a city, county, state, or nation. Laws can reflect the overall priorities of the jurisdiction regarding standards of behavior, with typically wide overlap with ethics.

Second, the consideration of ethics has been woven throughout this book, although without this specific designation. The book's title – blending "Leadership" with "Drug and Alcohol Abuse Prevention" – boldly pronounces the need for leadership within this field. The noted specification of "Why Be Concerned?" addresses some of the many issues warranting attention and, ideally, resolution (and practically, better management). The inclusion of specifying guiding principles for organizations (Chapter 8) and setting personal guidelines (Chapter 6) both reflect the importance of attending to these issues. With the strategic planning efforts, practical suggestions about how to infuse ethical foundations into organizing this work on drug/alcohol abuse prevention is found with the proposed incorporation of a clear planning framework (Chapter 7). Even the communication approaches (Chapter 9), with distinguishing attention to *logos*, *pathos*, and *ethos*, provides a specific example of the ethical elements.

Third, ethics can be embodied in various written documents, whether existing or to be created. Many groups, organizations, educational institutions, and other entities have a mission statement. The words in these documents are typically broad and help illustrate the overall direction and emphasis desired. In essence, these mission statements are reflective of core values. Groups may consider reviewing these, and potentially revising them, to reflect more accurately the current sentiments and needs.

Fourth, when looking at professional organizations, standards or codes often exist. In a general sense, the Hippocratic Oath includes the phrase "First do no harm"; this is often ascribed to those in the medical profession, yet can easily be adapted to others. More specifically, the American Medical Association has a Code of Medical Ethics; its Preamble states "As a member of this profession, a physician must recognize responsibility to patients first and foremost, as well as to society, to other health professionals, and to self."[3] The Code of Ethics of the Coalition of National Health Education Organizations (CNHEO) states "The responsibility of each health educator is to aspire to the highest possible standards of conduct and to encourage the ethical behavior of all those with whom they work."[4] This CNHEO Code promotes responsibility to the public, to the profession, and to employers; it also stresses members' responsibility in the delivery of health education, in research and evaluation, and in professional preparation.

Similarly, and outside of the health-specific focus and in the public service arena, the American Society for Public Administration (ASPA) has a Code of Ethics; its introduction states: "The Society affirms its responsibility to develop the spirit of responsible professionalism within its membership and to increase awareness and commitment to ethical principles and standards among all those who work in public service in all sectors."[5] ASPA's code includes, among others, principles about advancing the public interest, upholding the constitution and the law, strengthening social equity, demonstrating personal integrity, and advancing professional excellence.

Fifth, attention to the specific role of leaders within the context of ethics is highlighted within two broad areas. One area is the function or role of the leader in helping guide the group or organization. With the various functions of the leader cited earlier in this chapter, an important one is to help the organization be ethical. That is not suggesting a focus on due diligence with budgetary management; it is the large picture of visioning, agenda setting, prioritizing, managing, and orchestrating the efforts in a positive direction. It is helping the group maintain its course, and to adjust and refocus as necessary (such as with the changes in marijuana laws or increases in opioid overdoses). It is the important role of guiding and steering. The other area is with the individual him/herself, and being an ethical leader. This includes appropriate role modeling, and actually living ethical standards; this can be done through how decisions are made, open communication, transparency, attention to an inclusive process, and incorporation of scientific and research foundations for decision-making. It is also about prioritizing, through vocalization and attention, a sound ethical focus for the group or organization, thus helping to achieve the desired aim of preventing the specific identified concerns regarding substance abuse.

As noted near the beginning of this segment, distinctions are made between ethics, morals, and the law. The legal construct is an important one to maintain, as so much of society is based on the rule of law. That is not to suggest that all decisions and directions are determined by the law; in fact, the law itself continues to evolve, and different interpretations of the same law are often found. What is important is to have a sound respect for and some understanding of the law. To this end, and acknowledging the overwhelming nature of legal considerations, another microcosm of society – in the focused higher education setting – serves as the basis for a scholarly, grounded, and resourceful review of current issues in this environment (Professional Perspective 10.2).

Professional Perspective 10.2

The Changing Legal Landscape for Prevention in Higher Education

Peter Lake

Editor's Note: This segment addresses the college and university setting, and illustrates the importance of blending legal considerations with broader-based prevention needs. While the details and implications are applicable to higher education only, similar attention to the juxtaposition of legal with health and safety issues should be conducted in other settings (such as business, faith communities, communities, and beyond).

For decades, college alcohol and other drug prevention efforts have faced legal rules that have not incentivized proactive, science-based harm/risk reduction efforts. Indeed, some legal rules have functioned to *dis*-incentivize such efforts – pitting legal compliance against prevention, wellness, and safety. The good news for prevention leaders and advocates is that the legal landscape is changing to become more supportive of science-based alcohol and other drug prevention efforts.

To understand how the climate for prevention work is changing, it helps to consider the following key points:

The Fall of Prohibition in the 1930s Correlated with the Rise of the "Proximate Cause" Rule

In the twentieth century, alcohol was largely the "drug of choice," and legal rules regarding safety focused on alcohol-related hazards. As lawful drinking increased after the fall of Prohibition, the law began to rely more heavily on the notion that a voluntary drinker (of any age) is the sole "proximate cause" of harm related to alcohol risk – including accidents or victimization (even sexual assault) caused by others while intoxicated. In the early times there were strong moralistic overtones of blaming the drinker for moral irresponsibility; in modern times the tone has shifted to a focus on "personal responsibility." The practical result on campus? Colleges can often deflect responsibility to a student who voluntarily consumes alcohol.

The law has been resistant to accept public health perspectives on the use of alcohol and has also been slow to develop a focus on safety issues related to *other* drugs, although user-blaming rules are evident in that dimension, as well. The "War on Drugs" has taken a different path from the fall of prohibition, and only recently have some states (and not the federal government) begun to relax rules prohibiting the possession, use and distribution of marijuana.

"Dram Shop" Laws Have Limited Applicability for Colleges: Social Hosts Are Generally Not Liable

Dram shop law arose in the 1970s primarily to combat drunk driving arising from over-service at bars. These laws are limited, strictly construed, state statutory law exceptions to the "proximate cause" rule. Dram shop laws usually only prohibit the sale of alcohol by *vendors* for *on premises consumption* (bar/restaurant) to visibly/noticeably intoxicated adults or minors. Critically, other forms of furnishing or enabling alcohol use usually have been considered "social host" situations. Some states, like Massachusetts and Florida, have begun to impose responsibility on social hosts in some settings, but many other states have not. (For example, Florida's Open House Parties statute 856.015 makes it a criminal offense to knowingly allow minors to use or possess drugs or alcohol in a residence.) Even in states that have ended categorical social host protections, the law might not protect the *voluntary drinker* who is injured – only third parties injured by a voluntary drinker are protected.

Alcohol and Other Drug Prevention Efforts on Campus Lack a Legal "Driver"

State law has largely focused legal responsibility on efforts to reduce vehicular alcohol-related injuries – and not on college-related risks *per se*. The rise of services like Uber may be reducing vehicular risks to college populations, with the somewhat ironic effect of reducing pressure on public policymakers to address alcohol and drug issues on campus. The ongoing opioid issues are often viewed as background issues for the general population, not specifically college issues. Alcohol and other drug prevention efforts have also been overshadowed by other public policy safety/wellness issues related to college, such as active shooter violence and sexual violence. Indeed, alcohol and other drug prevention efforts generally lack consistent governmental funding; counterintuitively, even insurance programs generally do not significantly underwrite prevention efforts showing a distinct preference for claims management over prevention. This may instead reflect a long history of "winning" most college alcohol-related injury cases through victim-blaming arguments in court.

Federal Law Has Had Minimal Impact: State Law Varies Significantly

The Safe and Drug-Free Schools and Communities Act (SDFSCA) and Education Department General Administrative Regulations (EDGAR) Part 86 rules dealing with alcohol and drug abuse prevention have not been enforced aggressively by the federal government. Alcohol responsibility law is therefore primarily rooted in state law, which varies particularly with respect to social host rules. Individuals without significant legal training are at risk of being confused by subtle, yet critical, state law variances. This makes education about legal standards a priority for campuses, as populations may have significant misunderstandings about legal mandates. One area that is particularly problematic for colleges is that federal law is not permissive of marijuana usage despite the fact that some states have relaxed their laws. Students may perceive that marijuana use and possession are lawful, or subject to only minor punishments, but colleges receiving federal funding must enforce restrictive federal policies or risk a variety of major legal consequences.

College Students Generally Are Considered Legal Adults in "Social" Settings – Even If Not 21 Years Old: Deflection and Victim-Blaming – Once Common – Are Eroding Particularly Because of Title IX and Hazing Issues

Beginning with a series of court decisions in the 1970s, college students have been considered legal adults for purposes of safety law. One implication of these cases – referred to as "bystander" cases in higher education law and policy scholarship (*see* Lake, 2013) and various court opinions – was that colleges had "no duty" (and therefore no legal responsibility) to "rescue" students from dangers associated with the voluntary consumption of alcohol. Another implication of "bystander" case law was that institutions might be better off legally by *not* engaging in proactive, science-based alcohol and other drug prevention programing. Knowledge implies foreseeability; prevention efforts might be seen as "assuming a duty" that does not otherwise exist. Contrary to good prevention work, the law incentivized colleges to (1) deflect responsibility, (2) gather data hesitantly, and (3) blame victims (under the proximate cause rule and defenses such as assumption of risk) rather than engage the learning environment proactively.

This has been *changing*. In more recent times, some courts have held that the college–student relationship is sufficiently "special" to create legal duties, thus ending "bystander" approaches. In fact in 2018, two state supreme courts – Massachusetts in *Nguyen v Mass. Inst. of Tech.* and California in *Regents of University of California v. Superior Court* – recognized the special nature of the university–student relationship in a student suicide case (*Nguyen*) and a case involving a violent attack with a weapon in a classroom (*Regents*).

Moreover, most states eliminate victim-blaming rules in hazing matters. Critically, there has been a discernable eroding of proximate cause rules related to alcohol when a Title IX issue is at stake. Rape is a criminal act; rapists cause rape, not the voluntary consumption of alcohol by a victim. Therefore, the voluntary drinker is *not a proximate cause* of sexual violence perpetrated upon victims whether or not the victim is a voluntary drinker. Also, a number of states are changing social host rules: consider again, for example, the state of Florida, which has a "house party" statute prohibiting the hosting of parties for underage drinkers.

Courts have also made it clearer that knowledge alone does not create a legal duty – encouraging the collection of data – and that having policies regulating alcohol or other drug use does not itself create legal duties. Courts have thus made it more attractive for campuses to collect and collate data and proactively intervene in the educational environment. Perhaps most notably, some courts are moving away from moralistic, pre-scientific attitudes about alcohol from the mid-twentieth century – and even shifting rhetoric away from assigning blame to creating rule systems that incentivize safer behaviors and student wellness.

The law is slowly trending toward congruence with science-based, public health models for prevention. Campus leaders can accelerate trends in the law favoring good prevention work by understanding the core legal concepts that have impeded congruence in the past and by emphasizing a critical and emerging legal counter-narrative – the law functions best on college campuses when encouraging prevention and wellness, not working within a conceptual framework of assigning blame. In other words, and to some extent, the pace of legal reform on campuses lies in the hands of campuses themselves.

The path of the law is slowly, perhaps inexorably, moving to align with, and facilitate, science-based alcohol and other drug prevention efforts. But the law changes methodically, and requires dedicated leadership from campuses to move down this pathway more expeditiously.

Reference

Lake, P. (2013). *The Rights and Responsibilities of the Modern University*: The Rise of the Facilitator University (2nd ed.). Durham, NC: Carolina Academic Press.

Peter Lake is Professor of Law, Charles A. Dana Chair, and Director of the Center for Excellence in Higher Education Law and Policy at Stetson University College of Law.

Continually Changing Society

Whether by intent, neglect, circumstance, or other reason, society changes over time. Substance abuse issues are no different; witness the evolution of how alcohol, alone, has been viewed: from a moral failing of the individual, to the problem with the substance, to a more environmental approach.[6] Marijuana's reference as "green death" and the 1936 movie *Reefer Madness* are contrasted with recent changes, with the majority of states allowing marijuana use for medical reasons, and an increasing number of states allowing recreational use of marijuana. Opium's role has evolved, from opium dens to the opium wars, from prescriptions for opioids to use of heroin and fentanyl and the opioid crisis.

The interaction between society and substances is complex and multi-dimensional. Societal changes, and the rapidity of changes, can be seen as causes of drug and alcohol abuse. Similarly, drug and alcohol issues can be seen as the causes of changes in society.

For the former, consider the continued introduction of new technology, whether with manufacturing or communication. As documented in *Future Shock*,[7] the rapid changes in society contribute to upheavals in security and feelings of connectedness. Faster pace, whether with automobiles or airplanes, increases stress. With technology, the more recent changes with communications via cell phones, smart phones, and texting, can arguably have contributed to lessened interpersonal, face-to-face interaction. Technology can result in quick responses and instant gratification. With these and other factors in society, individuals, particularly youth, may feel isolated or lonely; the paradox is that they are, in fact, more connected, yet often feel less connected. The expectations of technology curing all problems are high; thus, when needs are not gratified (or not gratified immediately or completely), insecurity, isolation, anger, and frustration may set in. With this societal context, the response with drugs and/or alcohol can be to attempt to address problems: drink or drug to reduce the stress; drug (or drink) to help sleep; take a pill or more to alleviate physical pain or get high; and obtain a prescription to address emotional pain. Further, societal intolerance of pain, as seen with "pain clinics," pain scales for patients, and the goal to "feel no pain" helps promote the use of substances. With medications, a "fix me," and a "fix me now" approach can be found; and patients who, when seeing a doctor, may not be satisfied if they don't receive a prescription to "fix" the ailment.

How can drugs and alcohol be causes of changes in society? One example is having sanctions, ever more stringent, to catch and punish those driving while under the influence of alcohol or drugs; further, these efforts, particularly if publicized, can have a deterrence effect among these same individuals and others throughout society. Another example is with drugs being sold to youth, resulting in drug-free school zones. Consider also requiring those serving or selling alcoholic beverages (and more recently, those selling cannabis) to have the requisite training to maintain the laws and policies around responsible sales and service. With the recent infusion of electronic smoking devices, regulations become promulgated for the setting of their use as well as the contents consumed. With the witnessing of problems associated with the use of drugs or alcohol, public awareness campaigns may be developed that suggest how to address the issue most effectively.

The point with this is that the relationship between the substances themselves and society overall (as well as segments or subsections of society) is not a simple cause and effect relationship; it is dynamic and interactive, and constantly changing.

Those in specified leadership positions, as well as those in unspecified leadership roles, can continue to see opportunities for action. John Rohr helps merge the previous section on ethics, and put this in perspective: "When Machiavelli told us to look at the way things are and not as they ought to be, he made us modern men; but in so doing he bequeathed us a sorry legacy of trained incapacity for sound moral debate."[8]

With the changes in science and greater understanding of "what works" and "what doesn't work," and for whom, changes in approaches for prevention, treatment, and recovery are relevant. At the same time, changes occur regarding awareness of the issue, whether with parents or youth, with clinicians or educators, or with policymakers or leaders at the local, state, or national level. These changes can result in how the issue is itself viewed – as a problem to be addressed, or an opportunity; as a reflection on inadequacies of an individual (e.g., dependent person), or a confluence of circumstances; as issues to be solved, or as issues to be managed better; as areas of concern that people just live with and accept, or as areas for substantive improvement.

Essential to this are seven salient points:

1. Change is occurring. Changes in society happen quickly in some arenas, and more slowly in others. New substances, designer drugs, derivatives, and other products appear; these include legal and illegal substances. The important message for appropriate leadership is to be prepared.

2. Change isn't necessarily bad; change can be occurring for the good. With increased scientific understanding, greater awareness of professionals at all levels can be forthcoming. Positive change occurs with evidence-based practices; with research grounding that supports effective practices, these then can be shared for replication and adaptation in other settings.
3. Be prepared for change, and engage in planned change. Consider the saying "Are you doing it or is it doing you?" The fact that change is occurring means that it would be wise and appropriate to try to understand what is occurring, and to attempt to make steps to manage it. This means reducing the impact of what is viewed as negative, and striving to enhance the effects of the more desirable aspects of change. This reinforces the efforts of "Planned Change" highlighted in Chapter 7.
4. Be grounded in science. The implication of this is that those seeking to manage drug and alcohol issues better must remain vigilant and up to date with the latest substance abuse issues, as well as approaches for addressing them. The latest science may be on neurobiology or adolescent development; it may address the physical or psychological aspects; and it may focus on effective prevention education or treatment and recovery with minimal relapse. Consider the awareness in recent decades about neurotransmitters and the neurobiology of cocaine addiction, or the understanding of the development of the adolescent brain and its increased susceptibility to substance dependence until one's mid-twenties.
5. Keep an eye on progress and improvement. Just as current science is needed for grounding efforts, the ongoing monitoring of local efforts and needs is essential. With proximate outcomes identified, progress can be assessed and processes reviewed. When opportunities present themselves to do so, it is vital to applaud good work; when reviews and modifications are needed, adjustments should be made.
6. Keep a critical perspective. The changes in science and the changes in society will necessitate changes at local, state, or national levels. Major successes and progress, while certainly desired, will be a challenge to obtain. The aims will vary based on the changes, as well as the priorities of those in leadership positions (particularly those with influence and power). With substantiated good progress, the aim can reasonably shift to more ambitious and ultimately more positive goals.
7. Manage what you can. The perspective is that you can't control everything around drug and alcohol issues. These are issues that are long-standing and far-reaching; it is important to not establish unreasonable goals (such as "eliminate" or "solve" or "win"); rather, establish outcomes within the framework of better managing or increasing awareness or enhancing attention to the specified target area and target audience.

These perspectives can be helpful with the leaders at the local, state, or national level as they seek to have desired and positive effects with drugs and alcohol. Change is constant, and the important orientation is to maintain the vision, manage the process, engage the resources, and persevere toward small steps and modest results. The aim is to bring solid commitment and quality skills to good use within this overall context. The need for personal relevance and engagement seem higher than before.

Acknowledging that change surrounds the work with drugs and alcohol, and how important it is to stay up to date, Professional Perspective 10.3 offers some strategies about how to accomplish this. In addition, interviews with long-term advocates are helpful in providing direction on this issue.

Professional Perspective 10.3

Knowing What's New: How to Stay Current and Effective in an Ever-Evolving Landscape of Prevention, Intervention, and Initiatives

Shannon K. Bailie, M.S.W., and Jason R. Kilmer, Ph.D.

As professionals committed to maximizing our effectiveness addressing alcohol and other drug concerns, we are often bombarded with the latest online program, the hottest topic, or the most recent research that turns what we thought we knew about health and well-being (particularly among young adults) on its head, leaving us scratching our own heads and trying to figure out, "what is truly effective?" What is considered a trusted source for research, and how do we stay current? Here, we will discuss strategies for sifting through the noise and how to create partnerships that can help us stay up to date and informed.

We are living in an exciting time for understanding and exploring health of people of all ages and backgrounds. Along with these advances comes the challenge of knowing what works and what has evidence behind it. Organizations like the National Institute on Alcohol Abuse and Alcoholism (NIAAA) have taken the guess work out of sorting through the decades of research and reviewed and collected the most effective, evidence-based strategies for addressing alcohol prevention and intervention. For the college audience, in particular, their College Alcohol Intervention Matrix (CollegeAIM) helps college and university leaders identify approaches to prevention and intervention by categorizing strategies into relative effectiveness and relative cost to a campus. This tool alone can help colleges and universities assess and prioritize existing programs and identify gaps. With scheduled updates in the future, CollegeAIM can be a very useful tool in helping us stay up to date and informed with regard to the latest advances and research, and can guide strategic planning on campus. They note that a mix of strategies is best, and this tool provides a way to consider the balance and mix that will best meet individual campus needs.

For other prevention settings, consider the Substance Abuse and Mental Health Services Administration's (SAMHSA's) searchable database of programs, campaigns, initiatives, technical assistance centers, or resource centers. Noteworthy, however, is the approach used to prepare the CollegeAIM: evidence-based strategies reviewed and codified in a useful format. Unfortunately, a similar review based on relative cost and relative effectiveness has not been implemented for other settings such as worksites, elementary and secondary schools, and the community at large. Hopefully, similarly rigorous and helpful codifications for other settings will be forthcoming.

Another useful strategy for staying current is often found in our own back yard. Some of the most beneficial partnerships can be made by building bridges between research and practice, and this can be particularly true with those studying alcohol and other drugs given the rapidly changing landscape. Getting to know those who do research and evaluation better, finding out what is piquing their interest, learning what new areas of research they are exploring, and hearing about the latest studies can help us stay apprised of what new advances are coming down the pike. Collaborating with researchers allows us to bridge the theoretical with the practical, offering opportunities to work together to test theories and propose solutions that can benefit both researchers and practitioners. Researchers benefit from knowing and understanding the "on the ground" realities of the work currently being done with people of all ages (whether with elementary or high school youth, young adults, or older adults) as well as in various settings, such as worksites, faith communities, community-based organizations, or treatment services. Through this, researchers can often learn about emerging issues before they have surfaced in the published literature; community leaders, managers, administrators, and service providers benefit greatly knowing what practices and services have evidence behind them and are worth our limited resources of time and money.

Finally, it's critical we understand not all research is created equal. When we look at alcohol and other drug education, for example, it is important to have a clear understanding of the motivations behind the research or the way in which the findings are being reported or portrayed. We encourage people to think critically about data and findings, and we should be continuing to do so as well. It is important to apply a critical thinking lens to research, particularly if it is being summarized by a group with commercial interest. In order to assess potential effectiveness it can be helpful to ask:

- Did the published article acknowledge limitations that are not being recognized or considered by the source citing their work?
- Are conclusions about the findings by a secondary source going well beyond what the original article is reporting?
- Can you find independent, peer reviewed research that validates a claim or findings identified in the conclusions (including if findings have been replicated)?

Studies and research conducted by, or funded by, organizations promoting a particular product or service may have inherent conflicts of interest and need to be carefully evaluated. If you are not a researcher but want to know whether or not the research methods being touted are scientifically sound, don't hesitate to ask colleagues, professionals in the field, or those with research expertise; you might even contact the person who conducted the research. That is where the relationships you build with researchers and other professionals can be beneficial and can provide a potential sounding board for your questions or concerns.

Staying up to date and feeling confident in current best practices can be challenging, but it's important to remember you are not alone. Building bridges with research partners, tapping into nationally recognized programs that do the heavy lifting of reviewing and assessing best practices, and using a critical eye to assess the motivations and methods utilized in research can help us narrow down the programs, services, and research that promise to enhance our prevention, intervention, and treatment services.

Resources

NIAAA's College Alcohol Intervention Matrix (CollegeAIM): www.collegedrinkingprevention.gov/collegeaim/.

SAMHSA's Programs and Campaigns database: www.samhsa.gov/programs-campaigns.

Shannon Bailie, M.S.W., is Director of Health and Wellness at the University of Washington, a holistic program that addresses the overlap of multiple issues on college campuses through education, prevention, intervention, and strategic outreach. Prior to this position, Shannon worked as a sexual assault and relationship violence information specialist, providing both response and support to survivors of assault, as well as being actively involved in prevention efforts in the college setting.

Jason R. Kilmer, Ph.D., works at the University of Washington in both a student affairs and a research capacity. As Associate Professor in Psychiatry and Behavioral Sciences, he serves as an investigator on several studies evaluating prevention and intervention efforts for alcohol, marijuana, and other drug use by college students; as Assistant Director of Health and Wellness for Alcohol and Other Drug Education in the Division of Student Life, he works with different areas across campus to increase student access to evidence-based approaches.

By the time we figure out one channel, technology has changed and that's a fabulous thing because again technology is changing communication to make it more accessible and lower the bar. The question is how do we keep up with that in order to make our communications as accessible as somebody else's.

Ralph Blackman

Back when I started in the field, I felt I was at the right place at the right time. The field was burgeoning, particularly with family. Today, I continue to think how best I can contribute to the field, while keeping up with the many advances. It's exciting, but we have so much more work to do.

Claudia Blackburn

One thing I am concerned about is the legalization of marijuana.

Thomasina Borkman

I am also worried about the decriminalization of marijuana; I predict in probably ten years it will be legal everywhere. And that scares me, for it is going to add to our list of health issues we've got to deal with.

Kim Dude

There are going to be changes, of course our generation changes, and you must change with your generation. We now have two major groups, we have the millennials and our veterans, who are too different from what we've normally had and so you have to train with meeting their needs.

Mary Hill

If you look at the SUD field, there are many examples where you could easily say we did this 40 years ago and that things have not moved. But then, there are other examples where the field has moved so quickly that it took a decade to catch up, e.g., the introduction of managed-care dating back to the 1990s. Health care and how it was delivered and reimbursed changed in a heartbeat. We are facing this today as it relates to patterns of use. It's a national crisis regarding opioid misuse, and the field and communities are struggling to keep up with the needs and the losses.

Claudia Blackburn

Our efforts have been limited pretty much to alcohol and illegal drugs, like heroin was a 1% problem and alcohol was a 15 times problem. And so with the increased access and de facto decriminalization the assumption is that cannabis problems will be at least equal to alcohol problems, and we have no treatment capacity set up for that and no roadside drugged driving testing.

Mark Gold

Other countries have different definitions, and their terminology was different than ours. I think we need almost a global initiative that says 'let's have some common understanding, let's try to define things' so that we are all talking about the same thing.

Gail Milgram

Movements and Campaigns

Within the field of alcohol and other drug abuse prevention, numerous movements have occurred. In brief, a "movement" is when individuals or groups work together to promote a cause or an initiative, with an aim of societal or policy change. Generally, a movement is organized to some degree, and is strategic with its aims and tactics. A movement is designed to bring about a change of thinking and ways of dealing with an issue.

Within the realm of drugs and alcohol, consider Prohibition, the outgrowth of the Women's Christian Temperance Union movement.[9] This was followed shortly by the movement to repeal prohibition, with the Twenty-first Amendment to the U.S. Constitution. There's the movement with drunk driving, spearheaded in large part by the formation of Mothers Against Drunk Driving. Youth became involved with this area also, with the formation of SADD (Students Against Drunk Driving, and renamed Students Against Destructive Decisions). Movements were found to address illicit drugs, brought on with the surge of cocaine-related deaths in the 1980s. There have been movements such as "Just Say No," focusing on youth. And movements exist to change the legal landscape surrounding marijuana, from legislation regarding the use of marijuana for medical reasons to legislation allowing for its recreational use. Movements also exist to advocate for attention to the needs of those in recovery, as well as for necessary and appropriate treatment services.

While outside the direct scope of this book, movements have appeared in other areas. Consider the many initiatives regarding tobacco, from restricting where tobacco products may be used as well as with it advertising, sales, and labeling. More recently, movements about e-cigarettes and vaping are found. Counter-culture movements of the 1960s, while more focused on freedom of expression and lifestyles, also included the use of drugs. Movements are found with women's rights, civil rights, and LGBTQ rights. Movements exist for appropriate services and resources for veterans, as well as for those affected by the 9/11 attacks on the U.S.

The importance of reviewing movements is based on several factors. First, examples from movements demonstrate that change is possible. Working together, toward a common cause, can result in the desired outcome. Second, some insights from what helped make a movement successful, what hindered its success, and what lessons can be learned from them can aid in future efforts. Third, the concept of a movement is worthy of consideration; while all change does not require a movement per se, the lessons of movements can aid with efforts at the local, regional, or national level.

While the vision of a movement may be one of a larger societal shift, leaders may consider a less tangible (yet nonetheless valuable) outcome. For example, a focus may be upon changing the view of a person with a substance use disorder or substance-related concerns as "a problem" to more of a result of the confluence of personal, environmental, or other factors. It may be a focus on increased respect for the challenges faced by individuals in recovery, and the value of their perspectives and insights. It may be a shift in the conversation, to include increased acceptability of talking with others about concerns surrounding drugs and alcohol. There may be increased attention to dependence and addiction as a disease, with concomitant care and respect. A movement may also be focused on a particular audience – like having attention to the specific substance-related needs and issues associated with older adults, with adolescents, with persons of color, with veterans, with LGBTQ individuals, with women, or others. There may also be a movement toward greater health literacy and critical thinking, to help people be more knowledgeable about drugs and alcohol, as well as to have outlooks grounded in current science. This is not to diminish a movement regarding a policy change (e.g., advertising, drink specials, hours of operation, training standards), but to expand the focus of what might be encompassed within a realm of possibilities.

Professional Perspective 10.4 is helpful in providing specific details about ways of becoming involved with a movement, participating with one, or even starting one. This is followed by some movement-related comments and insights from long-term advocates.

Professional Perspective 10.4

Movements: Key to Making Change!

John Watson, M.S., and Brad Luna

Movements come in many forms, big and small, local and national, social and political; most of which are designed to help orchestrate and facilitate change on an issue of importance to the few and the many. From a reflection on various movements from civil rights to the War on Drugs and many others, common essential elements emerge. Some of the key essential elements include the focus on *change*, the importance of clear *goals*, the need to be *inclusive* of many, the call for *leaders* and *volunteers*, and the use of activism, advocacy, and other strategic action at the *grassroots* level. This piece highlights and provides examples to illustrate each element.

Movements often start in response to a societal need, crisis, or simply a personal experience. We think of movements as large-scale multi-dimensional efforts with marches, media campaigns, and legal and policy initiatives; we typically think of these as having structure, a mission, and clear goals. Movements may get to that point, but they often start at the individual and local level. Most movements begin when an issue hits close to home and affects one personally, thus prompting some form of action. One may see the need for *change* and begin to take action by sharing concerns with friends and colleagues. This is evidenced when people first took notice of the opioid crisis or the consequences of drinking and driving, working one-on-one to facilitate change for someone you know in a professional or personal capacity. This is further seen with helping someone who is struggling to overcome addiction, or with responding to the call of others and joining a local action group or finding other ways to support a call for action.

As movements begin to take shape it is critical to clearly define a shared *goal*, or set of *goals*, in a way that is broad enough to be inclusive yet focused enough to be achievable. The War on Drugs had a goal of reducing drug use and related problems, initially specifically addressing the crack epidemic in the 1980s. Over the lifetime of a movement, goals may change based on the successes, challenges, and failures of the movement as well as the ever-changing sociopolitical climate. Thus, it is helpful to think long term and short term. As the War on Drugs evolved, goals moved from awareness, to policy initiatives, to care for those on the street who might not survive, to education in our schools through the Drug Abuse Resistance Education (DARE) program. And DARE itself evolved over time based on lessons learned.

As movements bring people together for a common purpose, it is important that all who are, or might be, interested in being a part are *included*. To achieve this, a critical philosophy is "nothing about us, without us," meaning we include all, and no one who truly wants to be a part is left out. In the movement to address drunk driving, both those who had been directly affected by the consequences of drunk driving as well as those who genuinely cared about this issue were included in moving things forward, raising awareness, and creating change. This became clear with the formation and growth of Mothers Against Drunk Driving (MADD), Students Against Drunk Driving (SADD), and other like organizations. We also see this in various civil rights movements such as the push for marriage equality and hate crimes legislation for the LGBTQ community. LGBTQ people came together with friends and allies to push forward a movement that brought about significant change; this could not have been accomplished without the support and action of many.

For movements to develop and take shape, the most essential resource is people; people with passion and commitment who will take on different roles. This is seen from the efforts of the War on Drugs, the movements to address drunk driving, efforts to address tobacco issues and LGBTQ rights. Movements need *leaders* with a variety of skills. Some assume leadership roles by choice and others by circumstance. Fortunately, many individuals are looked to as examples of leadership – from Martin Luther King Jr., to Harvey Milk, to the local community organizer, and more. Movements also need *volunteers*; movements go nowhere without people volunteering in myriad ways from getting the word out, to knocking on doors, making phone calls, passing out literature, or using social media, all to help make their voices and their messages heard. A movement thrives when those who take part approach the effort with energy, persistence, and tenacity. These participants must also remember to stop, take stock, and remember to recharge; self-care is not a given, however, it is a must.

As most movements do grow out of local-level activities, it is essential to acknowledge that grassroots efforts and initiatives are a key feature of a movement. *Grassroots* efforts take the form of activism, advocacy, or other strategic action. These may include letters to the editor, campaign pieces, op-ed articles, public forums, boycotts, sponsorships, speakers, fundraising, the involvement of local charities, and civic or political action groups. These may also include coming together for marches, rallies, and other social or political campaigns that grow out of the local grassroots efforts to form and fuel large-scale initiatives or movements.

No matter the goal, cause, or size, if the action can be a part of improving the quality of life around some issue or audience, the key message is that movements are about making change. All professionals and volunteers addressing drug and alcohol issues must remember four points. First, change is possible. Second, change takes action. Third, change takes time. Fourth, change comes in all forms and sizes. Therefore, the action of one or the actions of many make a difference in the lives of others and in our world. So, the change you imagine, dream of, or think is impossible is, in fact, possible and just may happen. Take the action steps that resonate with you; you never know where that may lead!

John Watson, M.S., NCC, L.P.C., is Director of Counseling Services at Holy Family University, having previously served as Director of Alcohol, Other Drug, and Health Education, Assistant Director of Counseling, and Adjunct Assistant Professor at Drexel University. He has served as Chair of the Network Addressing Collegiate Alcohol and Other Drug Issues and as a member of the board of directors for the Council for the Advancement of Standards in Higher Education.

Brad Luna, B.A., is the founding partner of LUNA+EISENLA media, having previously served as Communications Director for the Human Rights Campaign, where he oversaw communications strategy on the passage of the Matthew Shepard and James Byrd, Jr. Hate Crimes Prevention Act. He has also worked on Capitol Hill as Press Secretary to Brad Carson, former U.S. Congressman and later Undersecretary of Defense.

Just as we see if we could take apart the magic of the smoking and tobacco thing I think recovery and alcohol has gotten better as well. There is something there, there was some yearning, craving for recovery and health that these guys had, and then to put some system into it that's a major miracle, it really is.

William Kane

The most important things that can be done ... We need to balance public health and safety with economic development, with what government agencies need to do. I'm not a prohibitionist by any stretch, I do think that it's important to try and craft policy that's balanced and I think in order to do that, and I think that just goes for a variety of areas that have to do with our social fabric, we just need to stay balanced. I think that as far as quality of life I don't think we put enough resources into public education. We just have to have policies that are focused on supporting the nuclear family, whether it's better childcare, better work rules or whatever it is we don't do enough to support parents raising kids.

Steve Schmidt

This whole movement towards legalization of marijuana just really concerns me because the average person just says "what's the big deal" and they just don't understand addiction and how insidious it is. It just gets in there and by the time it's caught on, you don't realize how it's affecting your life and that kind of thing. So obviously we don't want, for the younger population, a lot of access to more substances.

Darlind Davis

I was pleasantly surprised that lawyer recovery got its own legs. Because I wasn't totally, how should I say, confident, you know I thought we'd have this little cubbyhole of people getting better, and the more the better. But we treated 4000 people in 20 years, and in the past five years we treated more people than we did in the prior 15. And lawyers are a tough breed, they have fear, pride, the fact that they are helpers and so on, and then they intellectualize, and they want to fix things, but when they want to get better they can read the directions on the box and I think that they are better clients because of that. They know what consequences are and they can read the directions on the box.

William Kane

I used to believe in the War on Drugs. At this point, I have no idea about how society can stop the scourge of drugs. On one level, it may be partly spiritual and having meaningful work.

Thomasina Borkman

It does take prioritizing and resources for there to be some effective movement on this issue and I think we've sort of seen little blips where there have been infusion of funds and resources. We've seen some changes and then, like it's just human nature that other problems then creep up and so we put resources and effort into other issues so that this takes an ongoing effort.

Mary Wilfert

I think it's like a cycle, I think it's going to have to get worse before it gets better.

BJ McConnell

At that time they were not allowed to have psychiatry residents because addiction wasn't considered a part of mainstream psychiatry.

Mark Gold

I view myself as a transformational leader. And what I mean by that, is to see and act beyond surface-level changes – which is working in a system or framework – toward transformational leadership which works on the system or framework itself. So what I find is as I move into a role or path where I am engaged in change, but then is just a matter of time before I find that I'm engaged in transformation meaning working on the system itself.

Jeff Linkenbach

There was no alcohol and drug section in ASA, and a group of us put it together.

Helene White

Related to a movement is a campaign. These can go hand in hand as a campaign can feed into a movement; further, the presence of a movement can help inspire or invigorate a campaign. In short:

A campaign is an orchestrated initiative around a specific health or safety topic, designed to reach a specific audience through a range of approaches. A campaign is typically targeted within a given time period, so the focus on an issue is concentrated with its message. What a campaign does is to have dedication to a specific issue that incorporates a range of venues or approaches.[10]

This means that a campaign may have much of the same vision or aim as a movement; what a campaign offers is a specific period of time (such as a week or a month), and a variety of strategies (including approaches such as public service announcements, educational components, print materials, training activities, seminars, billboards, and media support).

A campaign can work nicely within a movement. Whether the aim is a policy change, an educational reform, a service-based initiative, or a shift in the mindset of people, a campaign can have a specific focus and attempt to achieve the desired results. Similarly, a campaign may draw inspiration from a movement, or it may link to a movement's activities or efforts. When campaign planners are organizing their efforts, they often have testimonials and expert personnel providing their insights and expertise; these can be used in interviews on television, radio, cable, or print publications. Consider campaign examples and resources available with several national organizations addressing drug and alcohol issues: the Substance Abuse and Mental Health Services Administration, the National Highway Traffic Safety Administration, the Ad Council, Community Anti-Drug Coalitions of America, and the Partnership for Drug-Free Kids.

The important implication of this overview of movements and campaigns is to have leaders understand the important role that these approaches can have with promoting the outcomes sought. Further, it is vital to be prepared with approaches and messages, talking points, current research, local and relevant information and scenarios. The role of professionals or committed volunteers being involved in a movement or campaign is central to the success of these initiatives. These prepared individuals provide the expertise and insight helpful to promote a clear and credible message to the audience. This is not to suggest that the leaders must necessarily be the ones to lead a campaign or movement; while this may be the case, the participation of these individuals is vital to the success of the initiative.

Synthesis of Leadership and Advocacy

This chapter has provided highlights about leadership opportunities faced by many individuals. Whether in a specified position of leadership (as an executive director, member of a board, or other clearly identified leader) or in an unspecified role (using professional expertise to be engaged and vocal as appropriate), various insights and perspectives have been emphasized. The overall aim is one of being a positive and constructive leader in whatever setting one finds oneself, with the outcome of achieving desired results for both reducing unwanted issues or problems, and promoting positive outcomes. Beyond leadership traits and approaches, attention is provided to ethical foundations, the context of a changing society, and the role of movements and campaigns.

The previous chapter (Chapter 9, Personal and Professional Strategies) addressed communication, related tools and resources, and tips on persuasive communication. In addition, seven steps for advocacy efforts were presented: (1) identify clearly the situation; (2) specify the desired outcomes; (3) understand and assess the decision points; (4) identify resources and assets; (5) build a strategy; (6) conduct periodic reviews and monitoring; and (7) nourish and support those engaged.

These advocacy steps represent the culmination of leadership, all within the larger societal context of change. Ultimately, leaders must act on what they know, and help orchestrate or seek to achieve change within their spheres of influence. Leaders help manage the boundaries. This may mean restricting influences from outside, including societal changes or even movements that are counter to the aspirations of the leader's vision or those of his/her group or organization. This also may mean expanding the boundaries, by taking on new initiatives, new approaches, new philosophies, and new partners.

Blending leadership and advocacy means remembering what drove the leader (as well as the group or organization) to be doing this work. It means recalling what inspired them to be part of this. It means remembering, both cognitively and viscerally, why there is concern about whatever issues – large or small, broad or focused, long-term or immediate, chronic or acute – were instrumental in getting involved.

To blend leadership and advocacy, consider three overarching themes. First, emphasize clear communication. To advocate effectively, it is essential that communication be very clear, and that the desired outcomes are very clear. Focus on what is wanted with the audience – what the audience should "know, feel, or do." This means sharing data and stories, blending quantitative and qualitative approaches, incorporating facts and examples, and addressing the "head" and the "heart" of the audience. Further, part of clear communication is sharing passion: what got the leader involved, and what might similarly get the audience involved.

Second, identify various opportunities for engagement. For appropriate advocacy, it is vital to have a presence at appropriate settings, both long-term and immediate. Identify ways to "have a seat at the table." With decisions being made about drug and alcohol issues, or related issues, find ways to be connected to and engaged with those settings. With decisions being made about allocation or resources generally, about priorities, about policies, and about initiatives, find ways to have the advocacy voice heard. While these decisions may have nothing to do, specifically, with substance-related issues, leaders can have a presence and demonstrate how attention to substance-oriented issues warrants consideration. Leaders advocating for drug and alcohol issues should always have project proposals conceptualized and ready for inclusion when funding opportunities arise. Similarly, leaders should always be ready to speak up and speak out when the unfortunate and tragic situation arises, whether locally or more broadly; this may include having campaign resources, testimonials, expert opinions, proclamations, public statements, and letters to the editor. Leaders can continually look for acts of commission or situations of omission and make observations and recommendations.

Third, attend to the role of policymaker. While the public health professional, educator, treatment provider, counselor, mentor, law enforcement person, healthcare provider, and others are prepared and best suited for their specific roles and responsibilities, they can also have a role as policymaker. They, as specialists, can consider themselves as more expert in their fields of study than the elected or appointed policymaker; similarly, the policymaker is viewed as more expert in that role of developing and refining policy. What is important is to work collaboratively and on an ongoing basis with those in policymaking roles. Having informed leaders, at all levels, is the foundation for effective action. Thus, the leaders in substance abuse prevention activities can help those in policymaking roles, by aiding them to be informed leaders. The policymakers, as informed leaders, can be guided toward addressing various behavioral health issues, and moving the setting of interest toward a healthier and safer standing.

The long-term advocates have some summary perspectives regarding leadership and the important roles that professionals can play.

> *We became aware that we were not doing what we needed to do. And still today, I suppose, trying to keep up with what's new, where are the trends, as of right now your personnel are all concerned because of the tragedies that have happened in the last year or so.*
>
> Mary Hill

> *I believe that many well intentioned people have brought us to this point in time. My optimism is based on my belief that most folks really care about the struggling addict, and that by treatment professionals and science beginning to come together we can all move forward to achieve better outcomes.*
>
> Robert Lynn

> *Evidence-based practices have been important additions to the field of SUDs. And it is imperative that we all become scientist-practitioners so that you providing the best-known treatment for the client's presenting problems. You surely won't want to go to a cardiac specialist who hasn't read a journal article in the last five years. However, evidence-based practices don't replace the importance of the relationship between the client and the counselor. Nor should we assume that an evidence-based practice fits all populations in SUDs; they don't. Yet we can easily mandate an approach without knowing the science and population that it supports.*
>
> Claudia Blackburn

Summary

Leadership is essential to being effective with the specified cause. Starting with the basis for getting involved with drug and alcohol issues (and reflecting upon the first three chapters of this book), it is helpful to remember and recall that foundation and passion. That serves as the continual inspiration and motivation for action as well as for renewal. Specific skills and perspectives about leadership are important, acknowledging that leadership is not restricted to those in appointed or elected roles; leadership permeates all settings and provides various opportunities. With ethical grounding and retaining the vision and focus, leaders can maintain the desired course through the changing society. Incorporation of the skills of advocacy can help leaders articulate the vision and maintain the initial vision.

Notes

1. Doran, G.T. (1981). There's a S.M.A.R.T. way to write management's goals and objectives. *Management Review* (AMA FORUM), 70(11), 35–36.
2. Higher Education Center for Alcohol and Other Drug Abuse and Violence Prevention. (1997). *Be Vocal, Be Visible, Be Visionary*. Newton, MA.
3. www.ama-assn.org/sites/default/files/media-browser/principles-of-medical-ethics.pdf.
4. www.cnheo.org/ethics.html.
5. www.aspanet.org/ASPA/Code-of-Ethics/ASPA/Code-of-Ethics/Code-of-Ethics.aspx?hkey=5b8f046b-dcbd-416d-87cd-0b8fcfacb5e7.
6. Rorabaugh, W.J. (1979). *The Alcoholic Republic: An American Tradition*. New York, NY: Oxford University Press.
7. Toffler, A. (1970). *Future Shock*. New York, NY: Random House.
8. Rohr, J. (1978). *Ethics for Bureaucrats*. New York, NY: Marcel Dekker, p. 3.
9. Rorabaugh, 1979.
10. Anderson, D.S. & Miller, R.E. (2017). *Health and Safety Communication: A Practical Guide Forward*. London: Routledge, p. 113.

11 Believing in and Taking Care of Yourself

Working with drug and alcohol issues is a challenge. This is undoubtedly the case regardless of whether working full-time with treatment services for substance use disorders or doing prevention education; whether volunteering or working as a paid staff member; whether doing training or research; or whether in a focused community or work setting, or in a state or national role. The challenge is, to the largest extent, because of the topic: drugs and alcohol.

What is particular to drugs and alcohol that makes working with it a challenge? One dimension revolves around the range of problems associated with drugs and alcohol; as documented in the first three chapters of this book, problems can and do arise from the misuse and abuse of these substances. Again, this is not to negate the fact that healthful and positive outcomes from the appropriate use of drugs or alcohol are often found, and for most people. A related dimension is the personal exposure of virtually all, if not all, people to drug and/or alcohol problems; this may be with themselves, family members, neighbors, co-workers, or strangers. Related to this is the lack of accurate or current knowledge about so many substances, as well as having the attitudes or skills to do something to promote healthy and safe decisions. Beyond this is the reality that one of the factors of the public health model – the agent – continues to change with the creation and dissemination of new substances and/or methods of use of those substances. Finally, many obstacles surrounding drugs and alcohol exist, some of which were highlighted in Chapter 3.

Within that context, those working to promote these healthy and safe decisions from an individual and environmental perspective are thrust into the re-imagined "hard sciences." While "hard sciences" typically refers to those conducted in laboratory settings, with the use of protocols, procedures, and experiments, and with topics such as chemistry, physics, biology, and geology, it is appropriate to consider work with drugs and alcohol as, actually, "hard sciences." This substance abuse prevention work is conducted within the context of dynamic and changing individuals and environments. While new knowledge, evaluation and identification of best practices, and enhanced dissemination efforts abound, challenges remain because of the factors identified, as well as others. For drug and alcohol issues, the world is the laboratory.

Knowing the challenges, difficulties, obstacles, and uncertainties in this world laboratory, how then, can concerned and dedicated individuals persevere? What helps individuals believe in the work, within this type of environment? What will help maintain a positive attitude, as well as taking care of oneself, with these issues? This chapter, within the Commitment construct, addresses this issue. The focus is on perspectives, strategies, and tips that help put this challenging, yet rewarding, work into context; the aim is to provide nurturance to individuals, and to identify ways to help them sustain their focus and energy. To this end, eight elements are provided: (1) Mission; (2) Growth; (3) Support; (4) Balance; (5) Management; (6) Perseverance; (7) Refreshment; and (8) Legacy. Within each of these, several tips are provided, with the acknowledgment that each individual's path for these issues will be developed personally, and will be done based on local circumstances and needs.

Mission

Just as organizations and agencies have mission statements, so also can individuals have a mission or identified purpose for their lives. This may be for their life overall, or for a phase of their life. While an individual may have a unifying theme or purpose that encompasses all aspects of their life, it may also be compartmentalized among work, family, community, and other aspects of life.

A key question for those involved with drug and alcohol issues is why they are involved. As illustrated by some quotes from the long-term advocates, many just "happened into" the field. The clarification of mission is an important anchor – "remember why you are here" can serve as a grounding mantra. The societal needs are widespread including, yet certainly not limited to, drunk driving, opiate overdoses, underage drinking, substance use disorders, dysfunctional families, and harm to self or others. The societal needs can also be framed within a more positive context, such as correcting injustices, opportunities for enhancing human potential, the promotion of healthy life skills, collaboration to address a shared mission, and the lessons learned from changed lives.

Tips

- Prepare a mantra or slogan to remind yourself of your mission or calling.
- Share publicly why you are involved, to help hold yourself accountable.
- Continue to remind yourself of the needs that exist.
- Display a photo or memento that reminds you of the overarching mission.
- Keep a journal to reflect upon the mission and your overall accomplishments and challenges.

The long-term advocates continue to provide their perspectives about their mission. Regardless of how they started with their work with drug and alcohol issues and substance use disorders, the sense of purpose and overall "calling" is evident for each of these individuals.

> It can be a stark reality to find out, after gaining education and training in the SUD field, that it is not a field that provides good salaries for most. Even though you are often working with clients who have greater needs and higher risks for co-occurring

disorders, you are also dealing with agencies that have minimal resources, including those surrounding professional development. This fact alone creates staff turnover, and attrition in working within the field.

Claudia Blackburn

They did this because they believed in that and maybe they had issues and their families are the personal lives that made them realize how critical this drug and alcohol issue is in a community, to people whose potential is damaged. I mean I certainly lost good friends and loved ones from alcoholism and substance abuse; and you feel like there's nothing you can do about the past, but maybe you can help someone face this in the future. So it was basically commitment.

Darlind Davis

I didn't seek out to do anything; that's basically been my entire career where I've sort of fallen into things or where things have fallen into me rather than me going out and seeking them.

Helene White

When studying psychology at the University of Vienna for my junior abroad, my main instructor was a graduate student of Dr. Victor Frankl, who wrote Man's Search for Meaning. Hence I learned about life in concentration camps. Also that having purpose in life, meaning, and dreams and goals were very important for survival. These are the most important qualities for getting through and being resilient. They can help kids in overcoming the pressures of living in a family with parents who are substance abusers and were sometimes violent, with major mood swings.

Karol Kumpfer

What I believed earlier, that I no longer believe … Is that I could make a huge difference. And I think more realistically I can make a difference, and anyone can make a difference. And that is going to eventually add up to a huge difference.

Carla Lapelle

I contributed to the growth of those along with a lot of other really great people. I think that along the way I touched a number of children. I still hear from some of them.

BJ McConnell

I'm hopeful that maybe we can prevent it from happening again, but overall on a personal level it's hard to be optimistic when you see this kind of stuff going on.

Jeffrey Levy

Growth

Continued nurturance and growth is critical for ongoing commitment. Many professionals are required to have continuing education activities to maintain their credentials, typically for the purpose of keeping them up to date with the latest science and best practices. This is vital so they are providing the best possible services for their patients, clients, guests, staff, co-workers, and others. Complementing this rationale is the importance of the professional staying refreshed and relevant both personally and professionally.

By identifying opportunities for growth, individuals will find that they stay timely and relevant for those with whom they interact, whether colleagues or those being served or affected by their engagement. Growth-oriented activities help provide challenges for learning; they encourage individuals to stretch their boundaries and perhaps engage in new ways of thinking or strategies for their work. Individuals may experiment with alternative approaches, and practice different strategies. Helpful for growth-oriented efforts is the identification of ways that approaches, paradigms, or ways of thinking in other fields of study might be applied or adapted for the drug and alcohol field. When learning of strategies in construction, cooking, travel, or engineering, for example, inspiration and creative adaptations may be relevant or appropriate; even if the conclusion is that nothing can be used, the process of attempting to do so can be engaging and growthful.

Tips

- Stay up to date by reading and attending workshops and conferences.
- Identify those who can serve as mentors, and engage them.
- Identify people for whom you can be a mentor.
- Engage individuals new to the field, and learn their perspectives and knowledge, as well as sources of these new learnings.
- Experiment with new strategies; practice, review, and welcome critiques.
- Identify ways of ensuring you remain relevant and contributing in meaningful ways.

Continuing to grow personally and professionally is an important theme for all individuals working with drug and alcohol issues. Staying challenged, finding mentors, doing some mentoring, and specifying other strategies are identified with the long-term advocates interviewed. Further, ways of accomplishing this growth are identified in Professional Perspective 11.1.

Professional Perspective 11.1

Keepin' It Green: Staying Professionally Challenged

Robert J. Chapman, Ph.D.

Wherever one happens to be on the continuum of professional development as a healthcare professional, there are challenges that threaten to sabotage effectiveness or, worse, short-circuit one's empathy. For those new to the field of addressing substance use disorders – as clinician, prevention specialist, administrator, or educator – the challenges of working with individuals with such disorders appear daunting ... and little prevents this perception from generalizing to self-doubt regarding one's ability to make a difference. For the experienced veteran, the challenge is to avoid reaching a point where preoccupation with the diagnosis precludes empathy for the individual who has it; either scenario is equally devastating for the substance-dependent individual.

My grandfather used to say: you know what you've learned and learned what you were taught ... but you will never know all there is to be known. As an early adolescent I was likely unsure what that meant, but these words have guided me through my entire professional career. In 45+ years of practice, I never once managed to be as good a healthcare professional on a given day as I was going to become in the future. That meant, at times, I was going to work with individuals whose needs were greater than my abilities at the time I was introduced to them. The resulting doubt found me, more than once, teetering on the edge of burn out.

But as I reflected on my grandfather's wisdom, it dawned on me that I had neglected the most important part of his advice. I may not have been as good a counselor "that day" as I could become in the future ... but I was also a better counselor "that day" than I was the day before. You see, although there is a limit to one's knowledge and experience at any point in a career, to paraphrase Theodore Roosevelt, you do what you can, with what you have, where you are. Wisdom is the gift received when recognizing the limits of one's knowledge, and when aware of the limits of one's knowledge and experience, it is this wisdom that suggests asking for help.

Americans specifically – and others from Western-oriented cultures in general – have great difficulty asking for help. Unfortunately, such requests are often perceived as a sign of weakness, an admission that, "I don't know what to do." Ironically, it is the humility inherent in such requests that ensures the gaining of the knowledge and experience necessary to become that "better health care professional tomorrow." Fortunately, "help" and the acquisition of knowledge come in many forms: "going back to school," identifying a mentor, learning from a gifted supervisor, or simply talking and interacting with peers. As I look back over my career, I realize that I took advantage of each of these opportunities and then some, attending and eventually presenting at conferences and workshops, monitoring and eventually posting on listserv discussion groups, maintaining a blog, publishing monographs, book chapters, and journal articles, and teaching. But among the best ways to learn is to observe or, as Albert Bandura postulated 40-years ago, engage in observational learning. Observing skilled and experienced practitioners results in both learning as well as the opportunity to identify potential mentors.

There are many ways one can learn from others and emulate their behavior: from reading biographies and autobiographies, to watching documentary films and "bio-pics," to simply watching those who have mastered a skill you wish to add to your repertoire, or listening to them as they share their stories. This "observational" learning starts when I realize that what I wish to do, can be done. Once acknowledged, the next step is an act of humility that allows me to recognize that these others *have done* what I have been unable to do, meaning, "this skill is doable." This humbling admission is only possible when I let go of the belief that my previous shortcomings were evidence of being a disappointment as a practitioner and repurposing them as indications of a need for more work on a skill yet to be mastered. Remember, *thoughts are not facts; if you want to grow professionally, change the way you think about yourself as a professional.*

Once I viewed my shortcomings as indications of missing steps rather than personal deficiencies, I was ready to learn. At this point the adage *I hear and I forget; I see and I remember; I do and I understand* took on great significance for me. It is in the doing – repeatedly – that I develop the skills that become the confidence and professional challenge I seek – in short, you do best what you do most. As I become comfortable with learning from others and then practicing what I have learned, I not only develop confidence in myself as a healthcare provider, I also discover that I have grown as a professional. This, in turn, may result in my one day becoming the accomplished practitioner that someone else seeks to emulate on his or her quest to remain, if not become, professionally challenged. To illustrate this point, an allegory shared by a supervisor years ago:

> The circus's arrival in town each spring was heralded by its parade down Main Street, the elephants traveling single file, "trunks on tails, trunks on tails." This one year there was a baby elephant just recently born and therefore the last elephant in the parade as it left the train yard and proceeded down Main Street to the circus grounds, firmly holding its mother's tail. Well, as the years passed and the circus continued to visit the town, new baby elephants joined the circus and the little elephant no longer found itself the last in the procession. As is the circle of life, the pachyderm's mother eventually passed away, leaving our protagonist without a tail to grasp with its trunk and therefore no one to follow. In bewilderment, as she turned to glance behind her in hopes of finding a new leader to follow, she saw a long line of elephants following her … trunks on tails, trunks on tails; you see, she had become the lead elephant.

The secret to staying challenged professionally is, for me anyway, found in the last phrase of my grandfather's counsel almost 60 years ago: but you will never know all there is to be known.

Note

1 For an overview of Bandura's theory of observational learning, see Fryling, M.J., Johnston, C., & Hayes, L.J. (2011). Understanding observational learning: An interbehavioral approach. *Analysis of Verbal Behavior*, 31(2), 153–161. www.ncbi.nlm.nih.gov/pmc/articles/PMC3139552/.

Robert Chapman, Ph.D., is an experienced counselor educator with 45 years of experience addressing substance use disorders, the last 30 of which were focused on working with colleges and universities to develop effective, evidence-informed strategies to prevent high-risk collegiate drinking and intercede with at-risk users.

I think most of my things that I ever accomplished in life was because I had a problem and had to find a solution for it.

Mary Hill

It has always been about mentors. Mentors coming in at the right time for me.

Robert Lynn

As people become more mature in this field, I think they need to reach out to people who are just coming into the field. I think we need to mentor, I think we need to pass the experiences of the last 20, 30, 40 years on, I think we have to go out of our way to bring them into meetings and decision processes that will get them hopefully even further ahead than we were at that age. So I just think that we owe that to our colleagues and to the field, to go out of our way to find young people who are interested in this work.

Steve Schmidt

Selden Bacon stepped in, and he believed that young faculty should meet with senior faculty on a regular basis and he did that with graduate students also.

Gail Milgram

I have evolved as a professional by implementing what I have learned from professional conferences, research in the field, and evaluating what works. I have gone from trying to teach students how to make good choices to implementing comprehensive prevention efforts that include significant social norming campaigns, environmental management strategies, health protection and harm reduction approaches, and bystander intervention.

Kim Dude

Somebody helped me design an experiment, support an experiment, run an experiment, do the data analysis, and then write the paper up. So I think that's an example of the great mentoring. I think it's really good mentoring.

Mark Gold

I would probably obtain some more specialized credentials. At one point I was working towards the certified prevention specialist and I let that drop. And it's a factor where you are in your job, is it a requirement of your job and if it's not then other things take your time and your effort so you kind of let that slide. So that would be one regret is that I didn't get some more specialized certification that would provide me just a little bit more confidence and maybe help me in presenting myself with more credibility to others.

Mary Wilfert

Support

With the challenging work of addressing drug and alcohol issues, support is vital. Challenges of all types permeate this field, in particular. These may include those who do not believe problems are urgent or should be prioritized (societally or individually), as well as those who have a mindset of having a specific approach (e.g., enforcement, harsh sanctions, education). It may be with those who do not believe in collaboration, or with an individual who does not comply with the professional's guidance. It is within this context that ongoing support is essential. While recalling the personal or organizational mission can be helpful, times will occur when that is just not sufficient.

Support can come from those with similar challenges or experiences. Just as those in recovery find support from mutual aid groups, those working professionally to address drug and alcohol issues can find necessary support from co-workers, colleagues, and others. This can be accomplished from intentional discussions about obstacles and challenges, and ways of addressing them. Consider the Force Field Analysis approach outlined in Chapter 7 (Helpful Processes), with identification of driving and restraining forces; with the restraining forces, for example, attention to what would help reduce its strength or impact can be helpful.

Support can be grounded in individual relationships as well as with intact groups. Individuals may seek out those who are like-minded in their approaches or orientation; these may be ad hoc in nature, or more structured with regular discussions and problem-solving efforts. There may also be groups, such as a work group in a workplace or community, that can regularly provide support and direction.

Gaining different points of view for analyzing a situation or issue can be helpful. Fresh perspectives from those not involved directly can enhance the decision-making process. These may be people who know nothing about professional efforts to address drug or alcohol issues; it may also be from those who are in different settings but who share knowledge or expertise from the substance abuse prevention field.

Also helpful is a larger, higher-level perspective about what is reasonable to expect as an outcome. From an individual or client-oriented perspective, the progression of an individual on the continuum of a substance use disorder is typically a long-term process; thus, addressing that disorder successfully is also a long-term process, and recovery becomes a lifelong journey. From a community or societal perspective, the issues associated with drugs and alcohol are long-term in nature, with contributions such as different cultural standards, inattention or non-communication, misinformation and not addressing underlying issues. Progress with addressing these issues will necessarily not be quick and easy. Support to help reflect upon these contextual considerations, and provide reminders about the paths of progress, are vital for maintaining a sense of hope and engagement.

Finally, while most of the narrative on support is designed as a proactive way of addressing the challenges inherent in this work, also important is to be reactive as needed. Individuals may find it helpful to obtain support from a mentor, as well as from individual or group counseling, to help gain greater understanding of the situations and to bolster personal attitudes and perspectives regarding this work.

Tips

- Identify various ways of having support at the individual and organizational level.
- Find specific anchors that help offset the challenges and lack of immediate success.
- Ask for help or guidance as needed.
- Start a support group with others in similar circumstances.
- Be proactive with acknowledging the need for support and ways of nurturing this.
- Identify situations where you can offer support to others.

The long-term advocates felt strongly that support of others was vital to their success, their achievements, and their long-term commitment. Helpful are the various perspectives and insights offered by these interviewees:

> *I would just like others to know that this field came from nothing and it's there at the table that substance abuse prevention became a legitimate discipline. It is made up of people with a variety of professional backgrounds and that has strengthened it. No one field owns it; it is driven by collaboration and it recognizes the importance of planning and evaluation and it is full of a lot of very, very good people.*
>
> Darlind Davis

> *What surprised me was my own personal growth as a part of being in this field. It has held a mirror up to me, it has made me walk the talk, it has helped me become a better person, not only in my professional but personal life. I think I'm a better friend, I think I'm a better family member. It has really raised the quality of my life. A profession became a life; it was really hard to make this just a career, it was more than a career, it defined who I was and defined the relationships in my life.*
>
> Robert Lynn

> *We were always up against a lot of resistance so we had to support each other and we had to create the systems to provide support to one another. If we only had to touch base once a year we could do it.*
>
> Darlind Davis

> *We had to create these systems to provide support to each other. Now it is much easier to collaborate – capital "C" for Collaboration. Not to get credit for it individually, just to move it forward.*
>
> Darlind Davis

Balance

Vital to sustaining efforts is maintaining good balance. Just as a person walking requires staying balanced, so also does a person working with drug and alcohol issues need to keep in balance. It is so easy to get out of balance with these issues, in part because of the all-too-common heart-felt nature of the grounding of those working in the field. The personal nature of the work, the "calling" often described by experts, specialists, and volunteers, and the uphill nature of the effort are all factors that cause the dedicated person to overextend himself/herself. Individuals seek success, and it is not uncommon to have limited success or limited positive rewards, beyond the intrinsic rewards of "doing good work."

To help with balance, a key strategy is to be as proactive and prevention oriented as possible. This means setting boundaries and limits, and striving to maintain good quality without overextension or burnout. Just as the recommendation was made in Chapter 10 (Leadership and Advocacy) to manage the boundaries, it is also important for individuals to do the same. In a collaborative work setting, this may be done well by establishing appropriate boundaries for oneself and for the work group; it may also involve identifying situations where others would benefit from assistance in managing boundaries.

Helpful for maintaining balance is ensuring that all aspects of wellness and well-being are attended to. This means taking stock periodically of where gaps or deficiencies exist, as well as setting personal goals for addressing these and for improvement. Whether the area is financial or self-care, relationships or spiritual, or vocational or physical, the important point is to assess, monitor, and refine on a regular basis.

It is vital for each individual to find ways to achieve balance with these responsibilities, and for maintaining the overall quality of life. For many, this is a healthy exercise regimen; for others, it is careful time management. Some individuals need significant cultural or educational rejuvenation; others benefit from a sound nutritional component. Certainly, there are times when overextension in one area may occur (such as a large campaign or media blitz, or an overly intensive client load); however, the norm should be one of striving to minimize those and to find positive outlets that will help with recharging.

Tips

- Monitor yourself to ensure a balanced life; consider keeping a log of time spent on various wellness components.
- Schedule appointments with yourself for exercise, yoga, or other self-maintenance activities.
- Find colleagues who will help you stay balanced, check in on you, and call you out if they sense you are getting out of balance; and you would do the same for them.
- Deal with exhaustion before getting exhausted.
- Manage time by beginning and ending on time; having a carpool, public transportation or other timely obligations may help with leaving work on time.

Balance and organization are so vitally important for continuing activities of taking care of oneself. As found with Professional Perspective 11.2, as well as the insights of long-term advocates, this challenge has some basis in specific strategies and mindsets.

Professional Perspective 11.2

Staying Refreshed

Darlind Davis, M.Ed.

As I reflect on my decades of work in the substance abuse prevention field, I know that so many of us worked tirelessly – because of our heart-felt belief in the importance of our work. We gained strength and energy not just from the good that we saw accomplished, but from our colleagues and friends who shared our work and our purpose. In fact, every state created support networks of prevention workers to charge up our batteries, share successful experiences, and revitalize our commitment to move forward.

As we continue to move into continuous changes in our society, some unimaginable just a decade ago, the prevention practitioner is challenged with the legalization of medical marijuana, a national opioid pandemic, and other issues. De-regulation has eliminated many of the safety nets that helped protect communities from risk in the past (i.e., lax norms regarding public intoxication; availability of prescription drugs).

Advertising and social media seem to have no boundaries as messaging pressures young people at a time when they are formulating their attitudes about whether to try substances.

The practitioner will continue to be confronted with constant changes in laws and norms. Leaders will need to be able to relate the experience of the past, cite the current findings, and forge ahead with practices and policies that will curtail the risks of substance abuse. The problem is not going away, and the ability to problem solve in an intelligent manner still holds true.

People support what they create; given a process that examines data is the most informed method of preventing problems among our youth and families. Keeping ourselves on task and up to the challenge is the goal.

Each of us discovered methods to: clarify our purpose; acknowledge the efforts of others; and re-create/update the message. The following concepts have helped me stay on course:

- Refresh by keeping skills honed/sharpened. Seek new knowledge from both research and practice; find colleagues with similar populations or challenges; renew past connections. Do not isolate.
- Reevaluate your assumptions; hold hearings and focus groups; listen.
- Acknowledge others. Put out a great aura of hope. There are many small miracles that occur, and when appreciated, give energy to the next steps in the work.
- List close associates whom you can call at any time. They are your team. We cannot expect immediate goodwill from obvious partners in this endeavor. Since change is often difficult, to achieve the fastest results – go slowly. You will save a lot of time in the long run and you will find this builds the support needed to get through the rough spots.

- Hungry; Angry; Lonely; and Tired (HALT acronym commonly used in aftercare) reminds us to keep ourselves on course. Stay well in spirit, mind, and body. Eat right, get your rest, harness your energies, and reach out. Work to understand others and then to be understood in return.
- Renew your spirit by developing healthy outlets. Meditation, yoga, biofeedback, massage, and regular physical exercise are examples of methods of holistic cleansing.

We are often asked if we have succeeded. The brief answer is "Not always; Maybe sometimes." One thing is certain, we can never give up. With a shared sense of purpose comes the realization that there is just too much at stake. Society needs everyone to reach his or her potential in life. Preventing substance abuse is a life and death issue. Our nation's health, safety, and emotional stability is dependent on each person's role. The important thing is to exemplify bravery and keep moving ahead; it is our collective future that depends on us.

Darlind Davis, M.Ed., is a former coalition director, prevention branch chief for the White House Office of National Drug Control Policy, and 30-year veteran of the substance abuse prevention field.

I wish I had maybe balanced my time better. I wish I had exercised more, had better pacing because I am a zealous worker.

BJ McConnell

It's hard to have an overall sense of optimism and hope, having had the experiences that I've had. Obviously I would hope that others could avoid, you know. If I had to do it all over again I would pick all of the same fights.

Jeffrey Levy

Management

Consistent with the prior issue of balance is the one of management. One part of this is maintaining a healthy and appropriate perspective. It is remembering the context of all the work on drugs and alcohol that is being done, and what needs to be done. It emphasizes keeping in perspective all of the challenges, heartaches, non-success, and criticism that occurs. It means celebrating small successes as they occur, and reflecting back on them over time. It means not expecting overnight accomplishments or a complete resolution of the issues being addressed.

Just like the goals and objectives prepared for a project or agency, it is important to keep these achievable. Make sure there is "low hanging fruit" in addition to the larger, more grandiose, and longer-term aims that are important. In addition to being achievable is being reasonable. It is important to not set oneself up for failure; while the dream may be to solve something (or someone else's issue), determine what is reasonable and appropriate. Having a schedule of reasonable activities and specified measures of accomplishment are helpful to manage oneself effectively.

With the management issue, consider the dichotomy of what is important versus what is urgent. Often called the Eisenhower Matrix or Eisenhower Box, this puts things into one of four categories, based on how important it is, and how urgent it is. Items identified as both urgent and important are classified as "Do" items; those not urgent and important are labeled "Decide": for the not important items, those that are urgent are marked as "Delegate," and those not urgent are identified as "Delete." Consider using these two factors of importance and urgency to decide how to manage a situation, and who might be involved with it.

Tips

- Make sure your personal and organizational goals and objectives are reasonable and appropriate.
- Identify strategies that work for managing time well. These may include personal deadlines, time allocations for various tasks, calendaring reminders, and limiting email correspondence to specific times of the day.
- Collaborate with others to share specific personal management strategies.

The long-term advocates interviewed offered some perspectives about managing their time, as well as how they looked at the issues surrounding various aspects of drug and alcohol abuse prevention. Whether it was a frame of reference, or a mindset, or other views, their observations are instructive.

> *I bought into some rather rigid models and I think I was banging a lot of square pegs into round holes. I think back on it and it feels uncomfortable, disrespectful and I just try not to dwell on it. My excuse has always been I did the best I can with what I had. I believe I should have been more open, and I think that was a challenge of mine at the time.*
>
> Robert Lynn

> *In retrospect, I would say I wish I was smarter. I mean, I would like to be able to figure things out but I'm not always able to in the timeframe that I have, but I keep the project active in my mind and struggle with it. So I would say the hardest things for me are working on problems all the time and not able to figure out solutions. I wish more of my scientific papers solved problems.*
>
> Mark Gold

> *What has contributed to our success is never giving up. If you try one thing and it doesn't work you just backup, recalibrate, and then try another way.*
>
> Kim Dude

> *When I think about drug and alcohol problems, we will certainly never end them. We're never going to stop the abuse of chemicals.*
>
> BJ McConnell

> So I tell you I've been interested in this since the early 80s and failed data for 30 years and recently picked up steam as I figured out what was wrong with my approach.
>
> Mark Gold

> Be willing to change your mind; be willing to look at other evidence that guides decision-making. What works at one point in time may not work at another point in time, what works in one community or with one culture may not work in other communities or other cultures. So be flexible and be willing to look at evidence and persuaded by it.
>
> Tom Griffin

> The other thing is that I think there does seem to be a bit of impracticability in the sense that people do want to change their mind, they do want to change how they feel. We need to look at whether there are ways that we can help people do that with safe and low-risk efforts.
>
> Tom Griffin

> I am never satisfied and I am always looking for the next challenge. All of the data that we have gathered over the years has certainly helped. Nobody is going to listen to me but if I have data that illustrates where our problematic areas are, people listen.
>
> Kim Dude

Perseverance

Within the context of the work with which drug and alcohol personnel are involved, it is not uncommon to experience burnout or frustration. It is not surprising to hear these dedicated people describe how others "just don't get it" when dealing with various aspects of this work, whether when seeking legislative or community leader support, or parents who say "not my child," or organization or education leaders who report "we're no worse than everyone else." For those in counseling or therapeutic roles, frustration and disappointment may arise when clients state that they don't have a problem, or clients who don't follow through on what was agreed upon. These are just among the many issues that cause frustration among those dedicated to making a difference in others' lives.

So how can this be addressed, and what can help these dedicated individuals persevere? Perseverance is the stick-with-it mentality, and maintaining dedication to the larger cause. It is having reminders about the positive impact that has been made and constructive results that have been achieved. Usually these are small, so attending to these various focused and limited items will be helpful in maintaining engagement with this work.

Helpful in this process is attention to the first item cited here: mission. It is reminding oneself of the motivation for getting involved in this kind of work. It is also about perspective; while the challenges and limited outcomes do exist, it is helpful to recall the successes when they occur. The perspective can also remind individuals of what life would be like – for individuals, groups, a community, or society – if their involvement was muted or not present at all. Further, it is about attitude; the old adage about the cup being half empty or half full is a helpful reminder.

Most important, perseverance blends these various factors, and is grounded in one's personal inspiration. Hopefully, this is based in the intrinsic positive and affirming feelings about doing good work for an individual, a group of individuals, or a larger community or society. Hopefully it is built upon the small successes that are helpful in moving things forward. Hopefully it is from the inside out, and the positive feelings that come from one's heart. The reward comes from the knowledge and the attitude that this work is, indeed, important and valuable.

Tips

- Reflect regularly upon why you are involved with this work.
- Focus on the positive things that have been done, and accomplishments made, that likely would not have been done without your involvement.
- Have inspirational quotes in various venues: posters, bookmarks, mugs, screensavers, and more.
- Avoid settings or social media that are grounded on complaints and negative perspectives.
- Listen to music that provides self-nourishment and positive inspiration.
- Seek others for mutual support and affirmation, in all directions.

To persevere is an important quality, particularly within the realm of addressing substance abuse issues. One way of addressing this is to be a sound and quality role model; this type of consistency with what one espouses for others is vital for professionals, as highlighted with Professional Perspective 11.3. Further, insights from the long-term advocates offer additional views that can be helpful.

Professional Perspective 11.3

Accepting the Role of Role Model: A Work in Progress

Ann Quinn-Zobeck, Ph.D.

As professionals in the alcohol and drug prevention and treatment field, much of our work is teaching the tools and strategies for people to change behaviors so they may live happier, healthier lives. As we are assisting others to make life changes, they see us as role models. This is true regardless of whether they are clients, students, employees, or others reached by us.

The thought of being a role model for another person can be frightening. While I strive to be healthy, I occasionally struggle to consistently use the tools and strategies to maintain a healthy lifestyle. Because I am willing to acknowledge these struggles and continue to address them, I can be a role model for others. We can model our imperfection, our learning from our struggles, and our continued progress toward wellness. Among the many behaviors we model for others, among the most important are self-exploration, respect and compassion, being authentic, and self-care.

Self-Exploration

By exploring our own health behaviors, and challenges to maintain them, we can mentor others in their journey to live healthfully. Self-exploration is taking the time to reflect on our own behaviors and their impact on our lives. As we work with others about new skills, we can take the opportunity to examine ourselves. If we assist others find positive outlets for relaxation or stress reduction, we can reflect on what we have done for ourselves, how effective our approaches are, and whether we need to explore new techniques.

Take time to reflect on how you are doing as a role model. Reflection questions include:

- What skills or values do I feel others can learn from me? How do I role model these?
- How well have I been listening to others' feelings and needs without interpreting them through my own experiences?
- Am I letting my frustration with someone's lack of progress interfere with understanding where they are in the change process?
- Do I recognize the signs of burnout and how that interferes with my ability to provide quality service to others? What actions am I taking to prevent burnout?
- Do I actively engage in self-exploration, by attending conferences, reading current studies, and trying new things? Sharing your efforts to be a life-long learner and develop new skills encourages others to recognize that learning is ongoing. One can continue to seek opportunities for improvement throughout one's life.

Respect and Compassion

We would not be very effective as caring helpers if we did not have respect and compassion for others. Compassion can be difficult, particularly when we work with someone who continues to repeat destructive behaviors. At times, if I develop a plan with someone and they do not follow it, I remind myself that this is their journey and not mine. We talk about what has been learned from slips or struggles and what could be done differently. It's important to be non-judgmental regarding someone's ability to "get it"; not only are we modeling respect and compassion for others, we are teaching others to have respect and compassion for themselves. The goal is not perfection but progress.

Change can be scary. When beginning the change process, especially with addictive substances, it is not unusual for others to be resistive and to lash out at the helper. We can role model non-defensiveness by recognizing reasons for resistance (fear); utilizing the "Roll with Resistance" techniques of *Motivational Interviewing* (Miller & Rollnick, 2002), we can help others explore fears about change.

Being Authentic

To be healthy and resist the temptation to escape through abuse of substances, individuals must learn to be authentic and true to oneself. We role model this by being genuine, kind, and honest. We identify what we value and develop our moral compass based on our values. We can express our feelings and disagree with others respectfully and without malice.

People with addictions may find it difficult to be authentic because of their upbringing or past experiences; many will be dealing with a lack of self-esteem and shame. Some may have rigid ways of thinking and may find it difficult to accept the opinions or lifestyles of others. We can role model authenticity by treating others as equals. Others can evolve and change through being open minded and learning new things about other people and other cultures.

Self-Care

While it makes logical sense that I will have more to give to others if I am happy, well rested, and relaxed, it is very easy to put off self-care activities. Many individuals' lives are out of balance and they may use substances to fight the stress, exhaustion, and shame that comes with feeling out of control. What greater gift could we give than to model how to set healthy boundaries and how to ask for help.

Setting healthy boundaries means setting a healthy schedule. To avoid burnout, you need time for friends, family, sleep, relaxation, and renewal. Have a set work schedule when you are available for others. Work with colleagues to share on-call duties to avoid constantly handling unexpected emergencies. Keep consistent office hours as much as possible, and block out time during your day for phone calls, emails, and report writing. Take your vacation days to enjoy time with friends and family, and to relax.

As someone trained in the helping field, many professionals may believe they should be able to help themselves. We all have times when we need to reach out to someone else for assistance, and there is no shame in seeking ways to improve our situation. Whether it is meeting with a professional counselor, asking a friend to listen, or requesting more help at home from a significant other, we are role modeling for others the importance of reaching out.

Being a role model is a large responsibility. Once we enter the helping profession, we must recognize that our lives will be under some scrutiny, both public and private. Modeling healthy behaviors is inherent in the professional role. By taking the time to think about ourselves as role models, we will not only assist others to improve their lives, but will improve our own in the process.

Reference

Miller, W.R. & Rollnick, S. (2002). Motivational Interviewing: Preparing People for Change (2nd ed.). New York, NY: Guilford Press.

> Ann Quinn-Zobeck, Ph.D., has 30 years experience working in health promotion and higher education. She most recently served as Senior Director of BACCHUS Initiatives and Trainings for NASPA – Student Affairs Administrators in Higher Education.

I think we've pushed an enormous rock up a huge mountain, but not all of it was smart or right, and a lot of it was downright stupid.

BJ McConnell

I am a hopeful person, I'm an optimistic person and you just can't stop me, that's all there is to it. I would find a rainbow in your mud puddle. And I think recovery does that.

William Kane

I think we need to be happier with our baby steps of progress; it is a giant heavy, heavy thing that we are trying to move and we should be satisfied when we move it at all. We shouldn't stop there, it should just motivate us to keep working towards that. That's all.

Carla Lapelle

To actually write and conceptualize the School Aid bill, and that was in 1980, that really started drug education and student assistance programming in Minnesota schools. I think a lot of schools started addressing substance use a little more formally as a result of the establishing student assistance efforts.

Tom Griffin

I think that if we realize the importance of that individual who makes up our nation and their quality of life, it will carry on. And where it's all of the different political things that we're hearing if you watch the news, then we have to realize that as we work with young people and we instill in them some skills to maybe cognitively want to go forward we will see things happen. And so, we can't quit.

Mary Hill

It is important for people working in this field to never give up, never give up. That's the case for individuals AND programs.

William Kane

All of us really felt as if we were in the Peace Corps – we were on a mission. And we all supported each other at the state level and at the local level and helped each other whenever possible. There were so many times as a prevention person you felt like you are the only one who cared about these things because you're just kind of outnumbered, either systems wise or you're dealing with resistance.

Darlind Davis

I let some of the pressures of the current or next funding get in the way of doing diligence to publishing some of what we are learning. And I just feel there are so many nuggets and breadcrumbs and trails that I have left and I really regret not getting more of that out there to others, for young or entering professionals to learn from. So I am trying to really take time to in this next phase of my career to make sure that I am addressing that. So more time to publish and share lessons learned.

Jeff Linkenbach

It was kind of a blend, of getting engaged with state agencies, by being "nervy" if I may, to say "you need someone like me."

Mary Hill

I would have probably been more assertive. I think there were times when I kind of folded my cards too soon. I tell young people that all the time "if you believe in something you go for it, you go for it."

Darlind Davis

Being an advocate for change can be very challenging. Sometimes you get a little beaten up at open hearings because people can get very upset about change. Patience is not my strong suit; some of our efforts have taken three or four years to get passed.

Kim Dude

Assessing initiatives is critical so that you are spending time and resources doing what works.

Deb Thorstenson

Refreshment

Staying refreshed is vital for everyone. However it is one of those life skills that is often relegated to a lower priority, neglected, or not honored. To draw a parallel, sleep is vital for all human beings to sustain life, just as is food and water. Sleep is a time for the body and the mind to rest, renew, and get recharged. All too often, individuals neglect sleep or have difficulty sleeping, resulting in a variety of negative consequences. Similarly, the body – in its entirety – needs to be refreshed regularly.

With this work with drug and alcohol issues, the nature of the work (with its many challenges) compounds the importance of being refreshed from any type of work. Both short-range and longer-range refreshment are vital for continued quality work with clients, patients, audiences, colleagues, and oneself.

The larger-scale refreshment is typically found with vacations. These can be extended over many weeks. Ideally, this is a time to disconnect and become removed from the daily responsibilities and routines with the work. It is also a good time to disconnect from other activities and settings: experience different cultures, enjoy the outdoors, and become engaged in totally different experiences. When one is disconnected from the regular news of the day, the experience can be quite freeing. It is a great time to not be involved with social media as well as the larger media.

More regularly, short vacations, long weekends, quick trips, weekends, and non-work times are very helpful. Staying refreshed means planning these activities and opportunities ahead of time so that, ideally, burnout does not occur (or occurs less often or less intensively). While these shorter and more regular times away from the regular activities of the professional life may be less intense (i.e., not as fully disconnected), the specific strategies need to be identified as appropriate for each individual. Some people will turn off telephones at home, and only respond to voicemail messages; others will limit the time when email is checked.

With staying refreshed, the important factor is attending to oneself. Each person must listen to personal needs and wants, and respond appropriately. For some, this involves long weekend naps, or quick naps daily; for others, the importance of quiet, alone time is central; and for others, meditation or inspirational readings are vital. The choices made are individualized and help with staying refreshed; these all help one be more attentive and productive with the responsibilities and opportunities of the professional work.

Tips

- Identify ways of staying refreshed on a regular basis; specify boundaries for professional work and personal time.
- Prioritize yourself by permitting, or demanding, alone time.
- Periodically do extensive disconnecting time, such as an extended vacation.
- Experiment with other ways of staying refreshed.
- Engage with others to learn what strategies they use to stay refreshed.

The long-term advocates illustrate ways of staying refreshed. These views are highlighted with some of their personal views, as well as strategies used.

> And I think we need to take care of ourselves, it is pretty easy to get overwhelmed in this work and to think you are the only one who can do it so you've got to take care of yourself.
>
> Steve Schmidt

> So that broad acceptance I think for everything that we do is how we think we succeed.
>
> Ralph Blackman

> I think I was very idealistic. My idealism, I shed it with a lot of fighting and mourning but I shed it, I have shed it.
>
> BJ McConnell

> I found that during my college experience I learned a lot more outside the classroom than I did inside. I wanted to provide similar learning opportunities outside the classroom for my students.
>
> Kim Dude

Legacy

Legacy is defined as "something transmitted by or received from an ancestor or predecessor or from the past."[1] It also means how someone is remembered, and what contributions were made while they were alive. For the purpose of this section, the approach of legacy is connected with mission. In part, this is about beginning with the end in mind, one of Steven Covey's seven habits.[2] Focusing on legacy is also helpful for the establishment of priorities.

Each person, throughout their lives, has encountered a wide variety of people, and recalls personal experiences with teachers, relatives, parents, neighbors, friends, leaders in the community, and others. In addition, there are also impressions held of others, whether through media or other public events. Some of these encounters are more meaningful than others; and some are more positive or more negative than others. The initial question is whether the memories or impressions of these individuals – whether positive or less than positive – are what the other person intended.

The second, and more relevant question for this section, is with the focus on oneself. Specifically, it is helpful for individuals to be reflective and determine what legacy is wanted. Legacy can also be achieved in various different dimensions: some may be professional, some may be with family, some may be with community activities, and some may be totally individualized. Legacy is about how one wants to be remembered. With that in mind, individuals can make effort to achieve that outcome.

In specifying one's legacy, greater focus is obtained about the desired endpoint; thus, personal and professional efforts can be channeled toward that aim. Having a legacy focus helps individuals direct energies in a somewhat organized and planned way so that they are remembered, ideally, in desired ways. Having a focus on a legacy does not mean, necessarily, that this legacy will, in fact, be achieved. However, one is more likely to achieve a legacy when being intentional about it.

Having a focus on legacy (or legacies) is something that helps drug and alcohol professionals and others committed to this work. It can serve as an anchor, and can dovetail nicely with the mission perspective offered here. Observing others' activities and approaches, and what legacies they are establishing, can be further helpful for the determination and refinement of one's own legacy. Legacies are lasting, and can also serve to be inspirational on a day-to-day basis.

Tips

- Write one paragraph (or less) of what you want your legacy to be; do this in a journal or other special place, or prepare a vocal recording of it.
- Share the desired legacy with others, and seek feedback for how realistic or achievable it is.
- Stay observant of others – friends, colleagues, and those in the news – and learn from their legacies, both desired and unintentional.
- Review the legacy and revise it periodically.
- Assess periodically the extent to which you are on track with your own legacy.
- Ask others about what legacy they want, and what they are doing to achieve that.

Legacies among the long-term advocates take a variety of forms and hold a range of messages and themes.

> *What I want them to say is that he was terribly committed, that he made some mistakes, there were things he could've done better, that we are proud of some of the things that he pushed and that he did. But in the end I hope that people say that it's a good example of the fact that government can do some good things. And you know I think we're in this whole battle, this philosophical debate about the size of government and the role of government and I hope we can look back and say he is a good example of government actually working.*
>
> Bill Modzeleski

> *I would like my legacy to be that I was a fighter; I didn't quit. If you were to ask 20 people who knew me what adjectives would describe me, "passion" would probably be the number one. It is because I really do love what I do and I believe in what I do and it is hard for me to ever turn it off. Even when I am home I'm thinking about work. Passion is probably going to be my legacy, that these things were worth fighting for, the young adults are worth fighting for, and the changes I am trying to have are worth fighting for.*
>
> Kim Dude

> *I would like my legacy to be associated with downward trends whether it be in tobacco or alcohol use by teens, or drunk driving trends in general.*
>
> Kurt Erickson

> *I hope my legacy will be these young people that are out now who went through our program earlier.*
>
> Mary Hill

> *My goal has been to change one kid's behavior and if I can change a lot of "one kid's" behavior it would be great and I've made the effort to do that. I'm satisfied that it was time well worth spending and if maybe I contributed to the one person or some other family not having to suffer the way my family suffered, then the legacy is established.*
>
> Jeffrey Levy

> *I would like my legacy to be that I was of service to others, the Center for Young Adult Addiction and Recovery, and my six children.*
>
> Teresa Johnston

> *For a legacy, I just hope that the lawyers assistance momentum will continue.*
>
> William Kane

> *I hope my legacy has something more to do with my family and grandson than it does with my career. But careerwise I would like my legacy I think to be a model of persistence.*
>
> Carla Lapelle

I would like my legacy to be this work of the science of the positive and how to make transformation achievable.

Jeff Linkenbach

I think that my legacy is helping other parents; helping them be better parents, however they define that, with whatever and however they meet those challenges and that their kids ultimately grow up to be productive adults. This is defined as not abusing, misusing, over consuming, whatever the politically correct terminology might be, alcohol, and if I had some role to play with that then I guess that's a pretty good legacy.

Ralph Blackman

I would like my legacy to be understanding beverage control agencies could be leaders, that they can be the big tent. They have the ability to interact with the beverage alcohol industry, public health, law enforcement, local communities. They are in a unique position. The beverage control agencies have a very unique place and they really don't have a lot of support at the federal level.

Steve Schmidt

I think my legacy is going to be the conversations because I have staff now who have seen the value of just sitting down and having conversations with people, and the importance of bringing people to the table who you probably never would have in the past.

Deb Thorstenson

I would like my legacy to be changes in some way, shape, or form, I know that some of the work that we did in Minnesota has already had, has already lived on and will continue to live on in terms of policy for schools. I think some of my publications will have had impact and will continue to have impact.

Tom Griffin

I would like my legacy to be having pushed for promoting empowerment of students and student athletes. I'm hoping that part of that is my legacy, that I was looking at things like bystander intervention, and at the importance of empowering peers to take charge of their own health and choices. With the population of student-athletes, unfortunately, sometimes their choices are taken away from them at an early age; they are told what to do, when to do it, and how to do it from the time they start showing ability until the time they leave college, and I think sometimes it's difficult for them to feel that they can and they should make their own choices.

Mary Wilfert

I want others to say that he really believed in what he was doing ... he was honest and I knew he really cared. Paying it forward as a mentor is the most important legacy for me.

Robert Lynn

Summary

This chapter emphasizes the importance of taking care of oneself. While this is valuable for any individual, the field of drug and alcohol abuse prevention is particularly fraught with challenges and obstacles. Many uphill battles exist with the work involving drugs and alcohol, whether in the prevention or treatment aspects, whether in policy or enforcement, or whether in research or societal change. To aid with the dedication and ongoing commitment of those involved, eight elements are highlighted. While many of these overlap with one another, they provide various perspectives that are helpful for individuals charting their own direction for themselves. With collaboration and honesty, the considerations of mission and growth, support and balance, management and perseverance, and refreshment and legacy can all blend for healthy and sustained futures.

Notes

1 Merriam-Webster Dictionary. www.merriam-webster.com.
2 Covey, S. (1989). *The 7 Habits of Higher Effective People*. New York, NY: Simon & Schuster.

12 Vision for the Future

Stephen Covey said it best: "Begin with the end in mind."[1] With drug and alcohol issues, this is most appropriate for all who are committed to making a difference. The work – whether in prevention or treatment, recovery or interdiction, policy or education, or research or parenting – is much more than routine activities or pro forma efforts. The work with drugs and alcohol is all part of a larger mission, as it is about human lives, families, workplaces, educational settings, communities, and society. The work addresses problems, both mild and serious; the work also encompasses unmet potential and helps release the accomplishment of dreams.

Having a vision for the future is vital for the work with individuals, groups, organizations, and larger societal entities. Just as many businesses and organizations have mission statements, a similar construct is appropriate for work with drugs and alcohol. Vision is essential for setting the course, for monitoring progress, for making adjustments, and for helping individuals and groups sustain their effort.

The vision is generally long-term in nature. It represents that toward which individuals and groups aspire. It is the dream, the ultimate, and the ideal. It can be broad or narrow in scope. Ultimately, it is that upon which committed people place their faith and heart-felt effort.

This chapter addresses vision from four different perspectives: What, Why, Contents, and How. First, what is meant by having a vision? Second, why is vision important, and what is the consequence of not having clear and sustainable visions? The third consideration is what constitutes the vision, and includes specific elements. The "how" aspect addresses the sources of vision, and encompasses strategies for building a vision.

What Having a Vision Means

In essence, a vision is an overall dream or concept. The vision is a generalized conceptualization of what the planners want to see. The vision may be outcome-focused and quite broad, such as a "drug-free society" or people living with minimal pain. By contrast, the outcome-focused vision may be much more narrow and specific, such as having low- or no-cost treatment services, having those in recovery feeling valued and not stigmatized, or ensuring that parents feel confident with having open and honest discussions with their children about drugs and alcohol. Similarly, the vision may be more process oriented, such as wanting those in any kind of leadership position respecting the expertise and insights of professionals who are experienced and knowledgeable about topics such as substance use disorders, prevention, and environmental strategies. This process focus may also seek to have those who may be affected by policies and strategies involved in the planning and implementation phases.

A vision can be fuzzy in nature. It is designed to prepare a broad framework about what the group, organization, or societal structure (e.g., a state government) wants to achieve. A vision provides a general sense of what is desired for the setting. What is it that the leaders or planners would like to have, ideally? The answer to the global question is something that can be described in very general terms, including what planners desire for how things are designed to "feel" or "seem" for the specified setting. Typically, the vision is constructed in reference to an overall initiative, project, or set of projects.

It is within this broad and general vision that greater specifics are developed. From the vision comes a mission as well as goals and objectives. As highlighted in Chapter 7 (Helpful Processes), it is the objectives that are clear, specific, and measurable. The mission typically refers to the organization, and its overall "charge" or areas of focus; the mission statement may provide a sense of the organization's values and some general direction of its goals. While the vision is often more project or initiative focused, the vision could be for the organization as a whole and help serve as the framework for the mission. Goals are broad-based, sweeping, and not particularly time-limited in nature. Objectives help support the goal, and focus on the end result that can be specified at the beginning and measured during or at the end of the initiative.

Consider a vision that is sweeping and fuzzy, such as wanting a community to be drug free. The mission for organizations that are part of a community-wide effort would help guide toward a specification of their particular roles. The mission may be focused on educational efforts involving parents, adults, and older siblings; goals within that overall mission then may focus on parenting skills, communication expertise, knowledge of drugs and alcohol, and confidence building. Objectives, then, would highlight specific outcomes, such as inter-generational dialog, knowledge of substance abuse disorders, skill-building around interventions, and self-esteem; based on the various organizations' areas of expertise, influence, and interest, the outcome-focused efforts would be specified for different organizations.

The vision can be helpful in setting the overall direction. Having a vision articulated can help with the specification of the mission, as well as of specific goals. The vision can be a basic foundation that aids with planning efforts, and is something to which planners can refer to help ensure that initiatives are consistent with the initially conceptualized aims.

Overall, a vision is designed to be proactive, and to stress an ideal state of affairs. It helps "paint a picture" about the lives of people and their families, about their communities, about schools and workplaces, about safety and health, and about dreams and futures. A vision helps orient a group or organization, and it can be as idealistic as its designers want it to be.

A helpful starting place for conceptualizing a vision is having a historical perspective. What did a vision entail 30 and 40 years ago? How did that process unfold, to bring things forward to where they are today? Some retrospective observations are helpful, as found in Professional Perspective 12.1.

Professional Perspective 12.1

Substance Abuse Prevention: A Retrospective

Darlind Davis, M.Ed.

One of the challenges of working within the area of drug and alcohol abuse prevention has been facing the external pressures occurring from politics, social trends, and shifting community norms. Every culture, whether it be ethnic or socioeconomic, demonstrates standards of alcohol and drug behaviors. In the United States, various local, state, and national laws, ordinances, rituals, campus norms (as a few examples) all contribute to the attitudes of young people. Those pioneers in the field of substance abuse prevention, myself included, had to embrace the reality of so many powerful variables, often working against our heart-felt and grounded efforts.

The 1970s brought a burgeoning of youth substance abuse that ignited the concern of a nation. Resources were assigned to address the widespread experimentation with alcohol, drugs, and tobacco. Staff were pulled from every aspect of the issue – medical personnel, educators, social workers, pharmacists, psychologists, and higher education leaders. For example, some states re-assigned programs to form a special gubernatorial agency on drug and alcohol abuse using personnel from health, education, labor, criminal justice, and social services.

Federal agencies were re-organized in a similar fashion. Offices were created with the mandate to include multiple disciplines to analyze findings and implement strategies to address this complex phenomenon. A thousand seeds were sown, sharpening the direction needed to power the effort. Research from various disciplines was gleaned to create a common language that made it easier to share evidence-based principles. Many fields could utilize this knowledge to reach many populations. This was an exciting time and energy was generated to provide focus to this new field.

Margaret Mead once related (during a convention speech to an audience of child development people) her retrospective that when the emerging disciplines of sociology, child development, psychology, anthropology, etc. were forming in the 1920s, these specialized scientists were supposed to study the findings from their own discipline and then return to the table to collaborate. Instead, she rued, they each saw their own field as the "true" answer, thus thwarting the real collaborative goal. Substance abuse prevention had to bring everyone back together because a multiple disciplinary approach was essential for progress to occur.

Through assessment techniques, prevention researchers and practitioners were still faced with the challenge of creating new concepts while producing results. It was a dark and uncertain path and we lacked the support of the many existing disciplines (some of which remained parochial in their philosophies or limited by lack of knowledge that led to stereotyping and bias).

Some fields were unwelcoming of a new government entity. They saw this as an infringement on their valuable, limited resources. However, we remained relentless as a field. We saw ourselves as the agents of change and were open to new approaches. Relying largely upon our instincts and experiences, we borrowed the best from every nook and cranny, to find relevant wisdom. The field of community psychology gained attention at this time and provided much needed process data on various risk factors and methods to address gaps and needs. The dynamics of community/grassroots action fueled these efforts.

It was both exciting and frustrating at the same time. Adequate research and evaluation monies accompanied early successes and the field grew in its mission and public support. While our sibling fields (such as mental health) were aligned with long-standing associations and research institutes, we initially had no support systems for prevention efforts.

The prevention practitioner was a lonely and sometimes stressed-out player in the human services field. We were competing for available resources, frequently unwelcomed at the table. Careful not to be seen as siphoning off funding for treatment, we sought support from related disciplines (i.e., child development, social science, public health/epidemiology) who seemed intrigued by our interest in the precursors to drug use, abuse, and addiction. We were borrowing from everybody, meshing it together, and due to a paucity of standards in those times, were free to try everything. We enjoyed the freedom of our distance from bureaucratic systems but lacked protection enjoyed by the status quo human services.

Public health provided a model that became our mantra, utilizing the trinity of agent, host, and environment, promulgated in the Institute of Medicine (IOM) Prevention of Mental Disorders Study (1994). Everyone carried around this tome, and it provided the organizing principles needed at the time.

Once, at a national meeting at which the topic of "availability" was discussed (i.e., underage tobacco use), a presenter advocated policy initiatives as opposed to providing services to individuals. To reduce tobacco use we should work to limit availability by (1) increased prices which deter young people from starting to smoke; (2) monitored product locations in stores; and (3) checks at point of sale. One colleague stood up and said, "That is an interesting means to a similar end, but I don't think we are equipped to stop youth tobacco use by instituting policies." That is almost laughable now because we have come a long way since then.

The implication for this example is that our assumptions are always being challenged and even when something may seem to be impossible, it is important to voice those ideas and share them to improve results.

One of the most important milestones in the advancement of substance abuse prevention, was the creation of a national grassroots movement. Now there was a collective voice that mobilized neighbors, politicians, and other stakeholders. The thousand seeds were growing. Groups learned how to monitor local indicators that reflected conditions that contributed to or reduced alcohol and other drug use among youth in the community. A partnership formed between university academics and grassroots leaders and they bolstered success.

We were blessed with the understanding that good solid planning and evaluation was just as important to our success as delivering services. We had to look ahead both short and long term. Plus, we had a broader support system to keep up the momentum. When colleges, schools, police, treatment providers, parents, elected officials, all work on the same local plan, the effort is more easily sustainable.

Darlind Davis, M.Ed., is a former coalition director, prevention branch chief for the White House Office of National Drug Control Policy, and 30-year veteran of the substance abuse prevention field.

Why Have a Vision

The importance of a vision is grounded in the belief that people want improvement, and that they want life to be better. Typically, a vision is about dreams of the ideal, and is grounded in the belief that many qualities of life and living can be better. A vision is a belief that the world (or a part of it) can be a better place.

A vision does point in a general direction. It is not just about problem reduction or elimination of areas of concern. It is a direction going forward. Without a vision, there may just be problem resolution, or even floundering in aimless ways.

Reflecting on the first two chapters of this book, the focus is upon what issues surround drugs and alcohol. Attention was provided to these issues, problems or concerns, from an individual perspective as well as from an environmental perspective. Related to these, a vision may be to have these concerns or problems addressed. However, a vision is much more than that, as it can focus on what life would actually be like if these problems were addressed. What is it that a group, or society as a whole, is actually seeking? If the problems were reduced or removed, what would life be like? That is what can be encompassed within a vision.

Another rationale for having a vision is incorporated in an optimism orientation, grounded with having a sense of hope. While many problems associated with drugs and alcohol do exist, it is vital to maintain a positive orientation that these problems can be addressed, or at least minimized. While solutions at a level of 100% may not be realistic for many of these issues, having some basic grounding in hope serves as the foundation upon which realistic and reasonable strategies can be built. The vision, then, provides some overall direction, and is rooted in the belief that change is possible.

Some additional considerations serve as a rationale for having a vision.

1. A vision can provide a general orientation and direction for an organization, community or entity.

2. A vision can help focus these efforts, and help direct strategies most important for inclusion or exclusion in the initiatives.
3. The process of building a vision can be inclusive and grounded with an overall orientation of creating a "shared vision."
4. The vision development process helps tap the creative and futuristic energies of leaders and participants.
5. Through the process of preparing a vision, energy and empowerment of participants are likely.
6. Having a vision helps with the identification of goals and specific objectives.
7. Vision processes and outcomes set the stage for ongoing monitoring and evaluation efforts.

While having a vision is not essential for all initiatives, it can be helpful regardless of whether the focus is large-scale or more focused. Whether outcome- or process-based, a vision can be an important factor for making progress with drug and alcohol problems and issues.

Contents of a Vision

When preparing a vision, the old adage "the sky is the limit" is appropriate. The vision can be short-term or long-term; it can be narrow or broad; it can be practical or grandiose. Once a vision is developed, the other mechanics fall into place, with goals and objectives, and then strategies and metrics.

Consider some of the following as potential areas of focus or emphasis with a vision statement. These can be clustered into large and long-term, focused and immediate, and moderate.

Large-scale visions might include:

- A drug-free culture
- Elimination of drunk or impaired driving
- No drug overdoses
- No availability of substances made in clandestine laboratories
- Attention to substance abuse as an issue to be better managed without being an uphill battle
- Substance use disorders being viewed and treated as a disease
- General societal understanding of a substance use disorder
- No stigma or shame associated with dependence or recovery
- Comfort discussing a range of issues associated with drugs and alcohol
- High level of respect for the human body, thus not allowing for harm caused by drugs or alcohol
- A societal desire to maximize human potential
- Attention to the root causes underlying drug and/or alcohol problems
- Substance use problems seen as a societal issue and not just a youth problem
- Grounding with science-based approaches for prevention, treatment, and recovery

The interviews with the long-term advocates asked directly about their vision for the future. Some of their words are insightful and reflect some grandiose, large-scale, and vitally important considerations that will be helpful for making a substantive difference with drug and alcohol concerns. The following represent some of these views.

> *We do need to integrate behavioral health and medical health. What fascinates me at this point in my life is to see how mental health and physical/medical health took two divergent roads. Given the fact that the brain is part of the body we continue to operate as if anything above the head isn't a part of medicine. For national and state leaders I would say that behavioral health and substance use integration is critical. I think developing communities of care and concern is needed. We need to focus and support parents by providing education to them as well. I think it's really critical for us to raise our children with values and purpose in such a way that they know when they are making their decisions that are absent values.*
>
> Teresa Johnston

> *It's a multi-faceted approach, not one or the other. It's not just about harm reduction or addressing environmental issues, it's not just about social norming. It's all of those things.*
>
> Kurt Erickson

> *We need to keep working to get the laws changed – state, national and local – and to become involved with the political scene of it.*
>
> Mary Hill

> *There's no follow on and it amazes me that national leaders are well aware that this kind of stuff is going on but they don't do anything about it.*
>
> Jeffrey Levy

> *This issue is still at the crux of an enormous amount of problems in various sectors. Whether you like it or not you need to know as much as you can about the dynamics of this problem in your sector. In order to be a good manager, in order to do your job, you have to understand the dynamics of this issue, of addiction and the dynamics of use and abuse in your various community efforts or whatever in these sectors. You need to support those who are in positions to be able to do something about it and you've got to support your staff because they are not going to have an easy job dealing with this issue. And if at the top, if you're not giving them the support they need you are doing a disservice to your area.*
>
> Darlind Davis

> *Essential is more science that's defensible and replicable to inform care and add value to the field.*
>
> Robert Lynn

> *Focus on and do the physical work of talking about what it is we are for. I have a vision that we want to grow and there need to be conversations that are broader than alcohol and drugs, but then they put the role of alcohol and drugs in perspective. So what I'm talking about is creating communities and cultures that are inclusive of and protective of all. We're talking about social justice issues and we are talking about dignity and worth and understanding that there are going to be differences in values and lifestyles within this and yet that is what weaves together and makes the fabric of a community or culture so beautiful.*
>
> Jeff Linkenbach

> *Have this treated as a health and safety issue; getting people to think about it on that level, and I don't know if people shy away from it because they thought "well I drank and so I would be a hypocrite if I started addressing that."*
>
> Deb Thorstenson

Moderate visions, which are still broad yet more manageable in a relatively limited period of time, may include:

- Quality education of medical and healthcare professionals regarding the prevention of and intervention with alcohol and drug problems
- Adequate and affordable treatment services for those with a substance use disorder
- Healthy family discussions about drugs and alcohol, and responsible decisions about their use and non-use
- Understanding of brain health, with particular attention to the adolescent and young adult population
- Availability of, interest in, and engagement with quality activities and substance-free options
- Responsible use of prescription drugs
- Laws and policies that are equitable and do not target specific groups or cultures
- Humane treatment of and respect for those in recovery
- High levels of knowledge about facts and current science regarding substances
- Respect for innovative approaches within a framework of theoretical and scientific grounding

The long-term advocates offered various vision statements that can be classified within this moderate classification, as these are still broad yet can be accomplished within a reasonable period of time.

> *To the legislators I would go to the price issue. We need to increase the price of alcohol and tobacco at least through an increase in taxes. It would make a huge difference, it would solve a lot of our healthcare problems by giving us more revenue. Plus fewer people would smoke and drink.*
>
> Kim Dude

We certainly have the data to show that we need to keep working with education. And the programs that are working, that we know through our model programs.

Mary Hill

I want people to receive treatment based on science, compassion and individual needs, not pseudo-science and politics. I would like to see more time and energy spent in developing professional programs based on science and outcomes. We should be developing curricula regarding addiction that reflects best practices based on research for psychologists, counselors, and the medical profession. Corporate and political leaders need to address stigma so that we can combat this barrier through things like parity and funding. When I speak about stigma I don't just mean drugs and alcohol I also mean mental health as well.

Robert Lynn

I would say stay with us, recognize that we have had success with tobacco control, we can have success with alcohol control as well. I would say the same thing about prescription drugs and probably a list of drugs, that norms can change; they are open to change based on strong and consistent messages. I would encourage people to continue funding interventions that are at the population level. I would encourage them to retain some sense of hopefulness; that even though these problems have been with us for a long time and they continue to create concerns in communities and in families, change can happen and does happen.

Tom Griffin

Smaller-scale visions, which are more immediately achievable but not any less important, might include:

- Quality parental skills and comfort with discussions surrounding drugs and alcohol
- Preparation of school, business, collegiate, and community leaders to identify and address drug and alcohol problems in their settings
- Documentation of efficacy of policies and programs
- Resources for local application
- Adoption of individual and organizational guidelines
- Quality education at individual, group, and societal levels

Some very practical perspectives are offered by the long-term advocates. These are within the larger context of the long-term, large-scale visions offered; however, these are more directly applicable at the current level of effort by any individual, group, or organization.

The most important things that can be done ... generally we need to establish norms and policies that support informed decisions about use that don't allow and encourage intoxicated behavior. I think there are things that just would fit into this in terms of the shift of direction of prevention more toward an environmental approach, social norms approach, that we really do encourage people to pay attention to the risks of alcohol-impaired driving, alcohol-impaired working, alcohol-impaired parenting.

Tom Griffin

I would like to see us targeting the highest risk youth with more funding and evidence-based selective prevention rather than just doing universal school programs like we are now. It is possible to do an inexpensive saliva test to find the youth who have risk genes and vulnerability to drug addiction, like Dr. Brody found the youth who had the Strengthening Families Program ten years earlier were much less likely to use drugs, have a criminal record, have HIV, or be pregnant. This means that we also should find ways to reduce stress that turns on the risky genes, because the real leading cause in these kids to use alcohol and drugs is stress. It's the high levels of cortisol and stress that turn on these risky genes. We need more supportive families, schools, and communities to bring down people's stress to not turn on these risky genes.

Karol Kumpfer

I think it is important to fund promising practices and evaluate them and report what was learned.

Kim Dude

I'm afraid that community leaders would just like the thing to go away because they don't perceive the threat as being as real as it really is. And I recommend to community leaders that they look a little bit deeper to see what the real consequences are on what the real threat is. And for the college or university presidents, my advice is that they need to stand up and be counted.

Jeffrey Levy

The broad-based recommendation is don't forget these issues when you're making your decisions, such as leadership and decisions about hiring. When it comes to academic issues, if you close your eyes to that issue, then you are really closing your eyes to the success of the overall educational institution; it has to be woven into a number of the decisions that are made.

Bill Modzeleski

These young men and women coming back from the army are trained to do one thing. There's something we can do with them to help them transition back into the community, train them to be something positive whether it's helping out in schools and doing a little bit of intervention.

BJ McConnell

I think that this has always been a field where everybody's final goal has always been the same. And the problems that arise along the way are that everybody has got a different way of achieving that goal. Certainly everybody wants kids who are underage to be safe, to not put their lives in danger. The way they do that, whether that is a legal *drinking age, whether that is education, whether that is abstinence, whether or however you see your role there, I think everybody's goal is the same. I think that at this stage of the game there is no educational void out there. I think at the end of the day the issues are really cultural and quite frankly, the issues are about empowering, if we are talking about underage, the issues are about empowering young people to change their own culture.*

Ralph Blackman

Don't base your decisions and your initiatives and your plans on your gut or on conjecture or anecdote or what you think a politician wants to hear. I think being a leader means that you go out and get the best information possible.

Steve Schmidt

The language issue is a big one. It's getting some kind of consensus as to the term binge drinking, and I know there are some journals that won't even accept any articles that talk about binge drinking of four or more drinks for women in one setting or five or more drinks in one setting for men.

Deb Thorstenson

I think we have to be mindful of the message we're sending about alcohol and drugs. I don't think alcohol and drugs in particular are the enemy. But I think we need to be realistic and have conversations that include the fact that people are at risk for addiction and are in fact developing addictions in college. There is still a great deal of stigma associated with addiction and we need to talk about it openly. We need to provide addiction prevention education and talk about how students who learn through experience are at risk.

Teresa Johnston

Your voice matters, and so does your silence. You need to speak up. You carry a disproportionate weight in shaping perception and public conversation and it is critical that you speak up. But you need some guidance in how to do that. It is critical that your voice is out there, especially in areas like this where there is ambiguity. And you need to speak up for what it is you are for, not just what it is you are against.

Jeff Linkenbach

The various visions identified here are intended as a starting point for individuals and groups as they embark on or update their journey of addressing drug and alcohol issues. The distinction between large-scale, moderate, and smaller-scale is a basic one, and is offered to illustrate how the vision can move from the larger, grandiose approach toward something more manageable. As will be discussed in the next section of this chapter, the ultimate focus is to take the vision and translate it into something that is reasonable and appropriate. For example, the large-scale vision of "a drug-free culture" is appropriate for a vision, but will not actually be fully achievable. The challenge then is to translate that vision into something that will be helpful in guiding and shaping efforts toward that end. If the aim is one of "elimination," such as with drunk or impaired driving, that would then be translated into strategies that would reduce, and even drastically reduce, that type of outcome. The vision can thus be recalibrated into goals that reflect what is reasonable; rather than "eliminate," a goal may emphasize "better manage" or "more effectively address" the area of concern.

Thinking about these many visions – large and small, long-term and shorter-range – can be somewhat daunting. These are included to illustrate how important having a vision is to a sound and quality initiative with addressing drug and alcohol issues. Providing some additional insight, from a local need and idea to a large-scale, relevant, and influential initiative is the narrative and inspiration for all with Professional Perspective 12.2.

Professional Perspective 12.2

The Power of an Idea

Gerardo M. González, Ph.D.

Sometimes the simplest ideas can have the greatest and most enduring impact.[1] I'm a Cuban refugee who arrived in the United States shortly after Fidel Castro came to power. My parents were not educated people – my father was an auto mechanic and my mother a homemaker – but they used every possible means to impress upon my younger sister and me the importance of education and hard work.

Despite the challenges of immigration, I did attain a college education and eventually became an academic. Along the way, in the fall of 1974, I was offered a graduate assistantship at the University of Florida working for Dr. Thomas Goodale, dean of students. Dr. Goodale was all too familiar with the devastation alcohol abuse wreaks on college campuses and asked me to take the lead in developing an alcohol education program at the university.

This was an exciting challenge. My first task was to dig into the research on campus alcohol abuse and learn as much as I could. I was surprised that, despite the widespread use of alcohol and its serious effects on college students, research was scarce. Intrigued, I turned to the literature on alcohol and other drug use among young people in general. I found that the most promising education and prevention programs used positive peer pressure to get their message across. I thought, why not organize students to be a voice for moderation and responsibility?

Late in the fall of 1975 I called a meeting of students to discuss ways of accomplishing that goal. We brainstormed. Finally, we decided to become an official student organization called Bacchus – the Roman mythological god of wine and revelry, famous for his debauchery. With a name like Bacchus, no one would mistake us for a temperance group. But we needed an acronym. I suggested calling ourselves "Boost Alcohol Consciousness Concerning the Health of University Students (BACCHUS)." It was a hit.

We had built the foundation for what eventually became America's largest collegiate organization for preventing alcohol abuse. With the help of a board of trustees and national advisory council, I led BACCHUS as president and CEO for ten years. When I retired from the organization in 1986 to pursue my professorial career, I was honored and humbled by the many congratulatory notes I received. One came from the esteemed Otis R. Bowen, MD, former BACCHUS advisory council chair and U.S. Secretary of Health and Human Services. He wrote,

> For the usual retirement celebration – we would call this a final tribute. But, for you Gerardo, your work will be seen for generations … All the efforts that you and others have made for BACCHUS will be part of the American way of life.

He added,

> Knowing how modest you are, I thought that if you heard it from someone else, you would really believe that you have made an extraordinary impact on the lives of young people of this nation. I have enclosed a special message from the White House.

The message said:

> I understand that for the last 10 years you have dedicated yourself to developing a successful alcohol education program for college students. It is comforting to know of your efforts … Nancy and I are proud of the work you have done to help make a safe and healthy tomorrow for our nation's young people. That's a fine contribution to your adopted homeland.
> Signed: President Ronald Reagan.

I sat in my office and read and reread President Reagan's words: "your adopted homeland." The president of the United States. I was overwhelmed. The president – the man in the White House – wrote those words. He acknowledged I was an immigrant, a refugee in an adopted homeland. He praised my contribution. I'd overcome my difficult beginnings, and done something meaningful.

Years later, famed author Dr. Stephen Covey co-authored a book in which he profiles people from all walks of life who have brought creative solutions, peace, and healing to some of the world's most perplexing problems. Writing about BACCHUS, he said:

> Gerardo and his friends set in motion an entirely new approach to helping young people avoid risky behaviors, what is now called the "peer education" or "peer support" movement … and it works, perhaps better than any other approach out there.

(Covey, 2011, p. 188).

Recently, I published a memoir (González, 2018) where I wrote about my experiences and examined my own trajectory from Cuban refugee to leading American educator. Several key influences contributed to my success: a loving and supportive family, a community that provided me a sense of belonging, and caring mentors who guided me along the way. I believed in taking advantage of what life brings rather than being bound by fixed goals, being willing to take a leap of faith when unsure where to turn, finding and pursuing a passion with vigor, listening to others who care, remembering my roots, and giving back.

These attitudes sustained me and led to opportunities that empowered me to turn a simple idea – that young people could be mobilized to have positive impact on one of America's most intractable health problems – into a national movement. Not every good idea can grow to have that kind of impact; however, every good idea can make a difference. Whether working as a parent, volunteer, health professional, educator, or whatever at the international, national, community, family, or individual level with college students, children in poverty, the infirm, immigrants, disabled people, or any other population in need, the key is to never give up. When I first started BACCHUS, initially I was being asked to speak to small groups of local students and then to various audiences from one end of the country to another. Some events were highly attended and some not, but I never refused an invitation to promote our work. I believed in the idea, planted the seed, it grew and made a difference. So can your work if you persevere.

Note

1 This brief topical segment is based on excerpts from the author's memoir. Reprinted with permission.

References

Covey, S.R. (2011). *The 3rd Alternative: Solving Life's Most Difficult Problems.* New York, NY: Free Press.

González, G.M. (2018). *A Cuban Refugee's Journey to the American Dream: The Power of Education.* Bloomington, IN: Indiana University Press.

Gerardo M. González, Ph.D., has long been a noted and fearless education activist. He is Dean Emeritus of the Indiana University School of Education and Professor of Educational Leadership and Policy Studies.

How to Prepare a Vision

Preparing a vision is both energizing and frustrating. It is energizing because it draws upon the creative nature of leaders and participants in the process. It is energizing also because it helps address areas of concern, and provides a sense of focus and priority to how to ameliorate these issues. It is frustrating because in developing a vision it is often difficult to conceptualize what is wanted, particularly if it is more than "address the problem." It is frustrating because many people are not used to engaging in a visioning process.

Consider, for example, the perspective offered in Chapter 6 on prevention and education; this distinguished between "prevention" and "promotion" approaches. With "prevention," the emphasis is typically upon what is not wanted: examples include prevent harm, prevent automobile crashes, prevent overdoses, prevent underage drinking, prevent dependence, and more. With "promotion," the focus is upon what is wanted, and what one wants others to actually do; this may include healthy decisions, appropriate interactions, engagement in quality activities, balanced lifestyle, excitement about life, embracing culture, and related issues. For many, it is a challenge to think about what *is* desired; similarly, it is hard to envision what one wants the culture, a community, an educational setting, a family, or a person's life to really look like and to feel like.

As a first step for preparing a vision, it is important to have key individuals identified for engaging in the process. They should understand what the purpose is, and how it is important in preparation for the follow-on discussions and strategic planning efforts. It is important to have them buy into the process, and to know how it can be valuable to their personal, group, organizational, and potentially societal efforts.

A second step is to have participants specify what they want the setting under consideration (the group, school, community, worksite, or other setting) to look like or feel like. Have participants write or share their impressions of this, whether in words, phrases, attributes, images, or other approach. This is done in a general, broad way, and is very open-ended in nature and content. One strategy is to provide a blank magazine cover and ask participants to compose an article for their best dream for drug and alcohol issues for a future year, such as 2030 or 2050. These can be shared among participants, and can help identify similarities and differences among their visions; common goals for the future can be created, thus resulting in group cohesion and energy.

Third, they can then be more specific and identify aims regarding various audiences. Think about whomever is within their reach (based on the setting), and think about the ultimate audience as well as intermediary audiences. For example, in a school setting the ultimate audience may be the students; the intermediary audiences may be teachers, guidance counselors, principals, parents, and even older youth. Audiences may not be within a confined setting, but may be more general, such as individuals in recovery; it may include those convicted of a first offense of driving while intoxicated. It could even be a setting-specific audience, such as those at a party when alcohol poisoning or a drug overdose is apparent and an intervention may be needed.

Fourth, with these audiences, the planners can think about what they want various audiences to know, feel, or do. This is all part of the visioning process, but the clarity about the vision is important within the framework of what the audience should, ideally, know, feel, or do. It may be "better preparation to address overdose whenever it occurs," similar to how many people are prepared with CPR for potential heart attack situations or with the use of the Heimlich maneuver for choking situations.

Once this foundation is done, the leaders can help develop some guiding principles. These would be any factors they believe should be foundational for the group's efforts. These may include areas such as (but not limited to) philosophical foundation, individual behavioral results desired with self or others, underlying emphasis of the programmatic effort, focus of the group's efforts, audience(s) served, context, and process of implementation. This process helps identify beliefs, values, and philosophies of life that serve as the foundations for their visions.

Next, the planners can assess current realities. These planners can examine positive and negative trends as well as identify challenges, obstacles, and distractions associated with their desired vision. What will emerge is a gap between vision and current reality; this tension can result in creative energy, which then can further propel the group toward positive action.

Finally, the effort with vision can end up with the establishment of strategic priorities. This is the place where much of the planning identified in Chapter 7 with the establishment of goals and objectives comes into play. The visioning is general and broad, whether long-term or shorter-term in scope. The specific strategic planning is where the resource allocation, timelines, personnel involvement, needs assessment, and program and policy preparation all come into play.

Some final thoughts and perspectives are helpful from the long-term advocates regarding the development of a vision. Further, Professional Perspective 12.3 is helpful in providing some specific guidance about how to proceed with preparing vision-based initiatives and processes.

This is about process, not programs. We so quickly jump to programs whether they be evidence-based or not, red ones or blue ones; it doesn't matter but we jump to programs when it's really this process that is critical. The process comes through getting people together in conversations, discussions around policy, whatever they be, but it's the process that matters.

Jeff Linkenbach

Just get involved. Just get involved and get on different committees.

Mary Hill

I would like to see more people on the same page. I would like to see more work in prevention, that people take that seriously. I think as we move out of silos agencywide and as we begin to work together we still aren't looking at the entire impact of alcohol and other drug use. I don't think when we talk about what we do that we do it in a language that is real clear for our legislators or our city council. They are very smart people but we're using a jargon that they don't understand. So probably changing that a little bit will help. If we can demonstrate our effectiveness we will be way ahead of the game but that's just hard to do.

Carla Lapelle

For state, community, federal leaders, don't forget this issue. We are going to need people to continue to stand up and fight for this. I would also say that there has to be a willingness on the part of the people who are fighting for recognition and more funding to join hands and partner with other people. I think smart leaders are going to say, "Who can we partner with? Should we partner with those people who are involved in suicide? Should we partner with those people who are involved in violence prevention?" They should ask who should be partners because it may be that as individuals we are not going to be successful in getting added funding for other efforts, but as part of the growing coalition I think that that's where the answers are.

Bill Modzeleski

Professional Perspective 12.3

Helping Others Create Shared Visions: Generating More Light Than Heat

Robert J. Chapman, Ph.D.

As we prepare to enter the second quintile of the twenty-first century, it would appear our approach to addressing problems appears more focused on circling wagons than exploring new ideas.[1] Unfortunately, the adage, if you always do what you've always done, you always get what you've always gotten, tends to trump the merits of collaborative problem solving.

Although research has proffered new insights regarding the etiology of SUDs, which in turn has encouraged the development of new approaches to their prevention and treatment, these have remained unfortunately localized to academics and those working in the hard sciences. Funding this research and more specifically the application of its findings in preventing and treating these disorders has remained principally the responsibility of those who make and implement public policy. Therein lies the challenge healthcare professionals face when considering how best to effectively address SUDs … navigating the cleft between evidence-informed practice and the public opinion that shapes public policy.

The chasm that separates public policy from research is wide and deters if not prevents healthcare professionals from implementing evidence-informed approaches to prevention and treatment. Consequently, yesterday's theories, strategies, and programs remain stubbornly a mainstay in many a healthcare professional's toolbox, thereby ensuring that we always get what we have always gotten.

Helping create shared visions is an underserved objective of many contemporary healthcare professionals. Accomplishing this objective is no small task, however, and necessitates nothing short of a change in the culture that surrounds substance use and substance use disorders. That said, there are steps contemporary healthcare professionals can take to initiate this culture change and maintain its momentum once started. These steps start with civility and an effort to generate more light than heat as we debate options.

- We need to remember the adage of countless thousands of recovering alcoholics in AA, "In order to keep it, you have to give it away"; It's all about our work with SUDs and those affected by them. If we are people first, counselors, prevention specialists, and administrators second, then we need to be vigilant that the Sirens of hubris do not call us to our spiritual demise. Sharing ideas, information, and strategies across ideological boundaries will further the advancement of SUD treatment and prevention.
- Prevention is a process. It is not an event. Just as any counselor who ever mounted a successful intervention with an addicted client did so by standing on the shoulders of numerous others who had previously intervened, people who change their behavior do so as the result of an epiphany that results from the concerted efforts of myriad others ... scientists, physicians, nurses, researchers, academics, administrators, and health educators to mention but a few. We all make a difference, everyone. It is when we play fair and realize that rare is the occasion when we are the be all and end all of change in a person with a SUD's life. Again, borrowing from AA, we can do together what we could not do alone.
- Again, I borrow from AA, "Continued to take personal inventory and when we were wrong promptly admitted it" (10th step of AA). Some call it a reality check ... others, "Keepin' it green." Whatever we call it, it is important to always remember that we are people first and our role/profession second. Remember: Even with an advanced degree or position of responsibility and "power," I am still my parents' child when I step across the threshold of their house.
- After the mistake has been made, after someone sees us acting contrary to our professional message, after we have missed the deadline, failed to file the report, "whatever," do what needs to be done to assuage the guilt/make amends and then, "let ... it ... go."
- Acknowledgments, kudos, and heart-felt thanks, be they from supervisors, administrators, or colleagues are good; accept them, smile, and say thank you. More to the point, and as a mentor of mine once told me, "Find someone to thank for something each day and then thank him or her."
- Attend a workshop, present at a conference, take a colleague to lunch and refuse to talk shop, play hooky from an afternoon at the professional conference and ride a horse. Adopt the M.A.S.H. philosophy of human service: Never give less than your best and all of it you've got, but when the work is done, don't be afraid to laugh ... with each other and at yourself.
- Every one of us is a better healthcare professional today than we were yesterday ... and none of us is as good as we will become tomorrow. We

know what we have learned and learned what we have been taught ... but never forget that that is not all there is to know. Growth is the realization that more is available if we are willing to ask for it and listen as those who have what we need instruct us.
- No healthcare professional ever changed any person with a SUD ... not one. Those practitioners we recognize as effective in their fields are actually able to motivate others to change themselves.
- On our best day we can help those we serve; we cannot save them. Suicides will occur. Alcohol poisoning will happen. Sexual assault will take place. The truth be told, we cannot prevent these – at least not all of them – but we nonetheless make a difference. My job is to help ... saving is in much larger hands than mine.

Note

1 The inspiration for this essay was Robert Fulghum's marvelous tome, *All I Really Need to Know I Learned in Kindergarten*. New York, NY: Ivy Books, 1986.

Robert Chapman, Ph.D., is an experienced counselor educator with 45 years of experience addressing substance use disorders, the last 30 of which were focused on working with colleges and universities to develop effective, evidence-informed strategies to prevent high-risk collegiate drinking and intercede with at-risk users.

Summary

This visioning process is an important foundation for addressing, successfully, drug and alcohol issues. It is positive and proactive in orientation, and can be done in a variety of ways. The key elements of visioning, from contents to rationale to how-to approaches are highlighted briefly in this chapter. Further, many of the dreams and visions of those professionals interviewed help provide perspective as well as inspiration for future initiatives. While the visioning activities and approaches discussed are important for groups and organizations, the same process and rationale applies to individuals as they find their place and roles with grounding, group work, leadership, and shared visioning for all whom they serve – currently and in the future.

Note

1 Covey, S. (1989). *The 7 Habits of Higher Effective People*. New York, NY: Simon & Schuster.

Index

Notes: Page numbers in *italics* refer to figures. The term "workers" refers to "individuals working with drugs and alcohol." (LTA) = long-term advocate.

abstinence 13, 101, 104, 105
abuse of drugs and alcohol 13, 104, 106; *see also* use of drugs and alcohol
ACoA (Adult Children of Alcoholics) 135
"addict" label, public perceptions 44, 45
addiction *see* substance use disorder (SUD)
adults: older adults 20; overview 13; young adults *see* young adults
advocacy 251–252, 282, 307; and leadership 286–287; *see also* persuasive communication
Al-Anon 41, 135, 263
Ala-Teen 135
alcohol and alcohol use disorder: alcohol-related mortality 25, 27, 29, 37, 61, 101; appropriate language 174–175, 242–244, 245, 323; assessment and screening 119, 125, 129; BACCHUS peer education 223, 324–326; binge drinking *see* binge drinking; as chronic disease 73, 92, 107; guidelines 170–171; ICAP 243; medical perspective 74–75; NIAAA *see* National Institute on Alcohol Abuse and Alcoholism (NIAAA); policies, in higher education 111, 265–267, 272–273; risk factors 16; as separate from "other drugs" 12, 48, 64–65, 72, 175; societal attitudes 72, 85, 169, 230; societal cost 28, 37, 38; support for family members 135; underage *see* underage drinking; usage patterns, adults 13, 169; usage patterns, college students 21, 23, 72, 174–175; usage patterns, sexual minorities 22–23; usage patterns, young adults 21; *see also* drugs and alcohol; substance use disorder (SUD); use of drugs and alcohol
alcohol industry, attitudes towards 79, 206

Alcohol Use Disorders Identification Test (AUDIT) 129
Alcoholics Anonymous (AA): effectiveness 140, 146; as long-term 107, 127; misconceptions 86, 93; professional awareness and attitudes towards 113, 260; social acceptability 45; spirituality 139–140, 142; as "unusual" 141; *see also* self-help groups
allies, vs. champions 199
American Medical Association 269
amphetamine 97
Aristotle, on persuasion 245
assessment and screening: AUDIT 129; BASICS 125; CUDIT 129; Cultural Formulation Interview 103, 119; DAST-10 129; motivational interviewing 129–131; RAPI 119; social history 131–132
associations, as communication "tool" 241
athletes and athletic groups 35, 77, 170, 311
authenticity 305
awareness step (in four-part intervention process model) 118–119

BACCHUS peer education 223, 324–326
Bailie, Shannon K. 124–126, 275–278
balance, for workers 297–300
barriers to change 75–80; environment 47, 48, 49–50, 148
behavior change, factors influencing 109–110; models and frameworks *see* change models and frameworks
binge drinking: defined 13, 174; adults 13, 20; college students 21, 174–175; cost 37; sexual minorities 22; terminology

174–175, 323; young adults 21; youths 16, 50
binge/intoxication phase 67
biopsychosocial disease model 80, 93, 95–96, 98; *see also* brain disease model
Blackburn, Claudia (LTA) 36, 46, 52, 85, 127–128, 136, 137, 138, 145, 188, 259, 278–279, 287, 290–291
Blackman, Ralph (LTA) 37, 39, 65, 79, 92, 113, 160, 172, 176, 177–178, 191, 210–211, 219, 239, 244, 250, 258, 278, 308, 311, 322–323
blended approach: achieving balance 219–210; in communication 242, 248; frameworks/models 95; and learning styles 219; to prevention 169; to treatment 108, 129; *see also* comprehensive/holistic approach
Borkman, Thomasina (LTA) 14, 24, 29, 39, 73, 86, 92, 93, 107, 113, 127, 138, 139–141, 141, 142, 149–150, 172, 177, 239, 260, 262, 263, 267, 279, 284
boundary management: of strategies/programs 260–261; of workers 298
brain, and reward processing 67
brain disease model 96–99; *see also* biopsychosocial disease model
brain health 95–99, 100, 136, 320; *see also* biopsychosocial disease model
Brief Alcohol Screening and Intervention for College Students (BASICS) 125
brief interventions 124–126, 171
buprenorphine 143–144
burnout 41, 261, 298, 302, 304, 305, 308
"bystander" cases 272

campaigns 26–27, 36, 220, 222, 236, 284–285; defined 284–285; impaired driving 26–27, 29, 202, 204–206, 244; links and tie-ins 241; *see also* education and training; movements
cannabis *see* marijuana
Cannabis Use Disorders Identification Test (CUDIT) 129
causes for involvement with drugs and alcohol: addressing root causes 80–82, 159–160; biopsychosocial disease model 80, 93, 95–96, 98; environmental/societal 43–44, 81; individual 24, 25, 81, 83, 93
Center for Substance Abuse Prevention (CSAP) 154, 175, 243; *see also* Substance Abuse and Mental Health Services Administration (SAMHSA)
Center for Substance Abuse Treatment (CSAT) 136, 149; TIPS 69, 136–137;

see also Substance Abuse and Mental Health Services Administration (SAMHSA)
Centers for Disease Control and Prevention 14
change, planning for *see* planning
change models and frameworks: guiding principles 55–56; Health Belief Model 51, 94, 109, 166; Lewin's Force Field Analysis 52; Self-Determination Theory 181, 182; Social Cognitive Theory 109; Social Ecological Model 56–58, 109, 111, 165; Stages of Change (Transtheoretical) Model 51–52, 57, 94, 166, 167; Theory of Planned Behavior 109; *see also* paradigms/frameworks/theories
Chapman, Robert J. 292–295, 329–331
chemical health 161–162, *162*
Closson, Dave 192–194, 213–215
Coalition of National Health Education Organizations (CNHEO) 269
coalitions and partnerships: CADCA 53; coalitions 53–55; college students 210, 218, 266; community leaders/members 111, 138, 219, 224, 230–232; faith-based communities/organizations 53, 71, 164, 217; leadership in 262; media 224; in planning 204, 208–211, 217, 227, 327–328; removing "silo" perspective 228; in research 226, 227, 277, 317; youths 205–206, 210
cocaine: driving impairment 27; neurobiology 67, 275; stigma 45; usage patterns, adults 14
Cocaine Anonymous 140
CODA (Co-Dependents Anonymous) 135
codes of ethics 268–269
cognitive behavioral programs 17
cognitive impacts 26, 29, 38, 98, 119
Cohen, Allan 90–92
collaboration *see* coalitions and partnerships
college students: athletes 35, 311; BACCHUS peer education 223, 324–326; BASICS 125; "bystander" cases 272; College Alcohol Survey 63; consequences of alcohol use 29; environmental influences 35; fraternities 265–266; Harvard School of Public Health College Alcohol Study (CAS) 174; as higher risk group 20–21, 63; intervention 125; mock-rave program 218; prevention 176–179, 227–230, 245, 265–267, 270–273,

324–326; as program partners 210, 218, 266; usage patterns 21, 23, 72, 174–175; *see also* higher education; young adults
CollegeAIM initiative 68, 69, 114, 213, 276–277
commitment, in Pyramid of Success framework 4, 255
communication: advocacy *see* advocacy; channels 278; effective 233–235, 239, 244–245; persuasive 245–249, 286; preferences, health information 235–236; tools and strategies 239–242; visual 250; *see also* messages and language choice
community: blocking change/recovery 47, 49–50, 76, 79; capacity building 181–183; education and training 36, 69, 93, 182, 214, 321; facilitating prevention 53–54, 71, 77–78; facilitating recovery 151; influencing effect of 35–36, 43, 51, 164; leaders/members, as program partners 111, 138, 219, 224, 230–232; perceptions of environment 57; psychology 316; risk/protective factors 164, 214; and school programs 64, 205; *see also* environment and society; workplaces
Community Anti-Drug Coalitions of America (CADCA) 53
COMPASS: A Roadmap to Healthy Living 81, 82, 159
compassion 304
compassion fatigue 40–41
competence, in Pyramid of Success framework 4, 9
comprehensive/holistic approach 81–83, 93, 109–114, 115, 219, 220, 226–230, 229; to prevention 109–113, 154–155, 158, 161–162, 162, 169, 315; to recovery 149; strategy approaches (overview) 220–226; *see also* blended approach
concern: in intervention process model 120–121; in prevention planning framework 166
confidence, in Pyramid of Success framework 4, 185
consequences of drug and alcohol use *see* harm and consequences
contact(s) step (in four-part intervention process model) 121–123
context: local, and program selection/effectiveness 213, 216; political 56, 137, 166; societal 216
continuum of care 107–109, 117, 124; *see also* intervention ("response process"); prevention; recovery; treatment programs/services

continuum of use 101, 104–107, 117, 142
cost (societal) of drug and alcohol use 28, 37–38, 274
cost of treatment 129, 140; *see also* funding for programs/research
counseling 75, 77, 108, 128, 133, 145; with Medication-Assisted Treatment (MAT) 144; vs. therapy 142
Covey, Stephen 309, 313
craving 67, 96
creativity 216–218, 324; creative epidemiology 240
Cultural Formulation Interview 103, 119
cultural sensitivity 36–37, 103, 128
cycle of addiction 67–68, 80; *see also* substance use disorder (SUD)

data, as communication "tool" 239, 240
data/research gaps 61, 69, 91, 150, 213, 215, 244
data/research sources 32, 63, 68–69, 198–199, 213, 235, 276–277; challenges 31; needs assessment *see* needs assessment and data collection/documentation; usage patterns 14, 15, 22–23; *see also* evidence-based practice
Davis, Darlind (LTA) 64, 73, 78–79, 113, 158, 172, 176, 178, 191, 200, 209–210, 258, 259, 260, 261–262, 263, 267, 283, 291, 297, 299–300, 306, 307, 315–317, 319
decriminalization 42; of marijuana *see under* marijuana
DeJong, William 109–113, 244
"denial" 125–126
dependence *see* substance use disorder (SUD)
detoxification 132
Diagnostic and Statistical Manual (DSM): continuum in diagnostic categories 101, 104–107, 117, 142; Cultural Formulation Interview 103, 119; DSM-5 30, 48–49, 80, 102–104, 105–107, 119, 129–130; pre-DSM-5 30, 48, 102
dimensional approach 103
distance from the plant, and drug potency 100
dopamine 67, 97; Dopamine Deletion Hypothesis 99
dosage: defined 13; binge drinking *see* binge drinking; and drug effects 100; overdose 25, 26, 71, 214; and tolerance 97
Double Trouble in Recovery 150
driving, impaired: campaigns and movements 26–27, 29, 202, 204–206, 244; collisions and fatalities 16–17,

25, 262; as "completely preventable" 85, 249; comprehensive approach 227–230, 229; detecting impairment 26, 27–28; drug-impaired 27–28; ethics 267; public recognition as problematic 57, 249
Drug Abuse Resistance Education (DARE) program 17, 76, 282
Drug Abuse Screening Test (DAST-10) 129
drug effects 99–101
Drug Enforcement Administration 37
drug properties, and effects 99–100
drugs and alcohol: definitions/scope (for the book) 12–13; harm see harm and consequences; use of drugs and alcohol; see also alcohol and alcohol use disorder
Dual Recovery 150
Dude, Kim (LTA) 14, 19, 64, 79, 167, 189, 200, 202, 203, 209, 250, 261, 279, 295, 301, 302, 307, 308, 310, 320, 322
Dunn, Michael E. 16–19, 129–131

Earley, Maureen 53–55
e-cigarettes 274
economic deprivation 37
ecstasy 69
education and training: accreditation 268; community leaders 69; community/public 36, 93, 182, 214, 321; doctors/healthcare professionals 49, 61, 62, 180, 214, 238; families 134; limitations 158; parents 48, 155, 172, 311, 319; police 26, 28, 220; in prevention 179–183, 266; principles 222–223; professionals/paraprofessionals (non-healthcare) 49, 61, 69, 180; schools 77, 111, 155, 158, 161–162, 162, 306; skill-building 223; workers 291–295, 299, 304; see also campaigns; information dissemination
Education Department General Administrative Regulations (EDGAR) 271
effects of drugs, principles defining 99–101
Eisenhower Matrix 301
emotional impacts 26, 29, 34, 38, 40, 119
environment and society: defined 34, 35; blocking change/recovery 47, 48, 49–50, 148; causes of involvement with drugs and alcohol 43–44, 81; changes due to drugs and alcohol 274–276; and effects of drug on individual 100; influencing effect of 35–36, 51–58, 147, 148, 158, 315; societal risk factors 164; supply and demand framework 42–44; see also community; families; peers
environmental strategies 42–44

Erickson, Kurt (LTA) 58, 79, 85, 155, 179, 183, 191, 202, 219, 224, 225–226, 230, 249, 262, 310, 319
Espinoza, Joseph 181–183
ethical considerations 267–269, 277
ethnic groups, higher risk 20, 63
evaluation: accountability 219; design 203, 207; "easy" programs 73; importance 200, 207–208, 215, 225–226, 307; in Strategic Prevention Framework (SAMHSA) 193
events 218, 223
evidence-based practice: critical appraisal 277–278, 287; data/research gaps 61, 69, 91, 150, 213, 215, 244; data/research sources see data/research sources; importance 188, 198–199, 202, 212, 275; knowledge dissemination 68–69, 91–92, 136–137, 201, 210, 237, 307; needs assessment and data collection/documentation 197–198, 213–215, 216, 225, 251; policy translation 329; in prevention 155, 158, 161–163; privilege of laboratory trials 91, 92
examples, as communication "tool" 239–240
experimentation, defined 104, 105
expert statements, as communication "tool" 240, 285

faith-based communities/organizations: influencing effect of 36; as program partners 53, 71, 164, 217
families: compassion fatigue 40–41; coping tips 40–41; education and counseling 134; enabling/perpetuating the problem 39, 41, 134, 164; impact on 38, 39–41, 82, 85, 134–135; involvement in intervention/treatment 110, 134–135, 136; risk/protective factors 164, 165; self-care 40; support for 41, 135, 263; "survival roles" 39–40; see also parents
family therapy 38
fear-based appeals 248, 250
"feel-good" programs 69, 85, 202, 216, 223
five-step contact process 121–122
Flori, Jessica N. 16–19, 129–131
follow-up care 134
follow-ups (in four-part intervention process model) 123–124
Force Field Analysis 52, 75, 188–191, 296
four-part intervention process model 118–124
frameworks see paradigms/frameworks/theories
functional family therapy 38

336 Index

funding for programs/research: by alcohol industry 79, 92; development funding 263–264; government/public agencies 198, 206, 224; partnerships 329; prevention 73, 171, 316; shortfall 218, 219, 260, 271, 284, 291; treatment 80, 138; *see also* cost of treatment

genetics, as risk factor 21, 30, 80, 93, 95–96, 99, 177; targeting high-risk individuals 322
goals and objectives 201–202, 212, 220, 261, 275; personal 300–301; vs. vision 314; *see also* outcomes of strategies/programs
Gold, Mark S. (LTA) 14, 42, 64, 66–68, 73, 78, 99, 136, 179, 238, 259, 264, 279, 284, 295, 301, 302
González, Gerardo M. 324–326
Griffin, Thomas M. (Tom) (LTA) 37, 82, 154–155, 161–163, 169–171, 171, 178, 188, 201, 302, 306, 311, 321, 321–322
Griffin-Wiesner, Jennifer 161–163, 169–171
group interventions: prevention 167; therapy 108, 133; *see also* self-help groups
group support, for workers 296–297
growth, for workers 291–295, 299, 304; personal growth 297; *see also* education and training
guidelines 106, 170–171
guiding principles 55–56, 77–78, 215–216, 268, 328

Hall, Thomas 44–46, 247–249
"hard sciences," drug and alcohol work as 289
harm and consequences 25, 26, 29–30, 37–39, 60–61; cognitive impacts 26, 29, 38, 98, 119; cost 28, 37–38, 274; defined 13; emotional impacts 26, 29, 34, 38, 40, 119; extending beyond individuals concerned 29; impact on families 38, 39–41, 82, 85, 134–135; mortality *see* mortality; not fully understood 74; physical impacts 16, 26, 29, 119; social impacts 26, 119; of underage drinking 16–17, 19; violent behavior 38, 39, 65
harm reduction approach 81, 84, 85, 94, 107–108, 153–154, 156–158
Hart, Carl L. 96–99
hashish 15
Haveson, Randy 105–107, 134–136
Health Belief Model 51, 94, 109, 166

Health Information National Trends Survey (HINTS) 235–237
health promotion: COMPASS: *A Roadmap to Healthy Living* 81, 82, 159; and health information needs/preferences 237; in prevention 154, 161–162, *162*, 327; *see also* public health perspective
Heard, Robert 204–206
helpline 41
heroin 14, 76, 100, 143; black tar 71; driving impairment 27; fear-based appeals 250; shame and stigma 45; *see also* opioids
higher education: alcohol policies 111, 265–267, 272–273; CollegeAIM initiative 68, 69, 114, 213, 276–277; leadership 63, 64, 265–267, 273, 322; legal duties 272; *see also* college students
higher risk individuals/groups 20–21; college students *see* college students; economically disadvantaged 37; ethnic groups 20, 63; genetic factors *see* genetics, as risk factor; homeless people 21; LGBTQ/sexual minority people 21, 22–23, 63; minority stress 22; offenders 21, 267; veterans 21, 322; women 63; youths 15, 17, 68, 99, 113, 275
high(er)-risk use of drugs and alcohol 13, 104, 106; *see also* binge drinking; problematic use of drugs and alcohol; substance use disorder (SUD)
Hill, Mary (LTA) 83, 160, 167–168, 179, 218, 264, 279, 287, 295, 306, 307, 310, 319, 321, 328
holistic approach *see* comprehensive/holistic approach
homeless people 21
humility, importance of 293–294

important vs. urgent items 301
indicated approaches, defined 114
individual characteristics: and drug effects 100; risk/protective factors 164
individualization of strategies/programs 222; recovery 145; treatment 128–129
information dissemination 221–222; campaigns *see* campaigns; media *see* media; messages and language choice *see* messages and language choice; research 68–69, 91–92, 136–137, 201, 210, 237, 307
inhalants 154; usage patterns, youth 19
Institute of Medicine (IOM): audiences for prevention messaging 247; framework

Index 337

for strategies 114; Prevention of Mental Disorders Study 316
institutional programs 110, 111
International Classification of Disease-10 (ICD 10) 102
International Council on Alcohol Policy (ICAP) 243
intervention ("response process") 116–126; defined 116–117; acute 117; brief 124–126, 171; decision to intervene 120–121; early 117; follow-ups 123–124; Johnson model 121, 124; making contact 121–122, 124–126; as a process (four-part model) 117–124; "Small i" and "Big I" 118, 123

Jellinek, E.M. 30, 90
Johnston, Teresa (LTA) 47, 48, 62, 78, 113, 119, 132, 138, 165, 172, 177, 310, 319, 323
"Just Say No" 160, 167, 248

Kane, William (LTA) 52, 62–63, 65, 101, 121, 132, 142, 151, 176, 189, 250, 262, 283, 284, 306, 310
Kilmer, Jason R. 124–126, 275–278
Kreps, Gary L. 235–238
Kumpfer, Karol (LTA) 38, 50, 99, 138, 160, 165, 176–177, 209, 215, 291, 322

labeling, avoiding 125–126
Lake, Peter 270–273
Lange, Jim 56–58, 195–197
language choice see messages and language choice
Lapelle, Carla (LTA) 14, 65, 79, 80, 83, 151, 177, 207, 218, 219, 220, 222, 291, 306, 310, 328
laws, policies and regulations: "bystander" cases 272; "dram shop" laws 270–271; EDGAR 271; enforcement, as strategies 221, 228, 230–232; vs. ethics 269; and evidence-based practice 329; federal laws 271; influencing effect of 36, 42, 76–77; police see police; policymaking leadership 286–287; post Prohibition 270; SDFSCA 271; state law 270–271; as strategies 220–221, 261–262, 265–266, 316, 319, 320
leaders and leadership 2–3, 257–267; adaptable 263–264; and advocacy 286–287; allies and champions 199; boundary management 260–261; in collaborations 262; community, as program partners 111, 138, 219, 224, 230–232; considerations 7–8; constructs for 259–264; course-setting/maintaining/modification 260; and ethics 269; focus identification 261–262; higher education 63, 64, 265–267, 273, 322; lacking commitment 63, 64, 79, 322; lacking knowledge/understanding 74; maintaining status quo 49–50, 319; in policymaking 286–287; scope 257–258; style 262–263; transformational 284; values 86–87
legacy, for workers 309–311
Levy, Jeffrey (LTA) 19, 29, 48, 51, 64, 65, 74, 79, 86, 93, 138, 177, 178, 206, 209, 259, 291, 300, 310, 322
Lewin's Force Field Analysis 52
LGBTQ/sexual minority people: as higher risk group 21, 22–23, 63; language and terminology 21–22; minority stress 22; sensitivity of services 23; usage patterns 22–23
Life Ring 149–150
Life Skills Training 17
Linkenbach, Jeff (LTA) 35, 37, 72, 78, 83, 179, 206, 225, 245, 250, 284, 307, 311, 320, 323, 328
low-risk use of drugs and alcohol: defined 104, 105–106; 0-1-2-3 guidelines 106; choices 170; see also use of drugs and alcohol
Lucey, Richard 198–200
Luna, Brad 281–283
Lynn, Robert (LTA) 35, 65, 74, 80, 83, 107, 132, 137–138, 151, 178, 206, 225, 227, 260, 287, 295, 297, 301, 311, 319, 321

management, for workers 300–302
marijuana: CUDIT 129; driving impairment 27; federal vs. state laws 271; lack of media interest 50; legalization (as negative/neutral) 47, 48, 73, 92, 273, 279, 283; legalization (as positive) 39; usage patterns, adults 14; usage patterns, college students 23; usage patterns, sexual minorities 22; usage patterns, youth 15, 50, 77
marketing mindset, in prevention communication 247–249
marketing of prescription medication 70, 71
McCabe, Philip T. 21–24
McConnell, BJ (LTA) 52, 64, 93, 114, 160–161, 165, 178, 218, 224, 226, 259, 261, 284, 291, 300, 301, 306, 308, 322

media: engagement 224; health information in 236; influencing effect of 264; lack of coverage/interest 50, 222; see also campaigns; social media
Medication-Assisted Treatment (MAT) 71, 143–145
Medina-Kirchner, Christopher 96–99
mentoring, for workers 295, 296, 311
messages and language choice: alcohol 174–175, 242–244, 245, 323; consistency 222, 246; currency 246; fear-based 248, 250; importance 242–245; jargon 328; LGBTQ/sexual minority people 21–22; limitations of words 176; message evaluation 173; message planning 173; in prevention 167, 173–179, 247–249; in recovery 148; taxonomies and terminologies 242–243, 279; in "War on Drugs" 156; see also communication
methadone 143–144
methamphetamines: driving impairment 27; neurotoxicity (lack of evidence) 97–98; usage patterns, adults 14
Milgram, Gail (LTA) 14, 24, 62, 93, 113, 127, 137, 141, 165, 263, 264–267, 279, 295
Minnesota Model 140
minority stress 22
mission, for workers 290–291, 302, 306, 309
mission statements: outcomes and steps 63; values 86, 87, 268, 314; vs. vision 314
misuse of drugs and alcohol 13; see also binge drinking; use of drugs and alcohol
Moderation Management 150
Modzeleski, Bill (LTA) 14, 58, 74, 78, 155, 158, 165, 184, 188, 189, 191, 200, 202, 208, 209, 221, 222, 244, 245, 250, 252, 261, 310, 322, 329
Monitoring the Future Study 15
morals, vs. ethics 268
morphine see opioids
mortality: alcohol-related 25, 27, 29, 37, 61, 101; drug-related 20, 25, 27, 61, 71, 101; tobacco-related 31, 65, 101
Mothers Against Drunk Driving (MADD) 26, 204–206, 244
motivational interviewing and interventions 91, 124–125, 138, 304; for assessment 129–131; as under-explored 91; for underage drinking 17, 124–125
movements 279–283; defined 279; "Just Say No" 160, 167, 248; MADD 26, 204–206, 244; SADD 223; "War on Drugs" 69, 156, 203, 259, 281–282;

Women's Christian Temperance Union 280; see also campaigns
mutual aid groups (MAG) see self-help groups

naloxone 76, 214; see also opioids
naltrexone 143–144
Nar-Anon 41; see also self-help groups
Narcan 76, 77; see also opioids
Narcotics Anonymous 35, 46, 140, 146; see also self-help groups
National Cancer Institute 235–237
National Institute on Alcohol Abuse and Alcoholism (NIAAA) 14, 37, 68, 198, 209, 242–243, 276; "Rethinking Drinking" website 125
National Institute on Drug Abuse (NIDA) 14, 37–38, 127, 198, 209; principles of effective treatment 128
National Survey on Drug Use and Health (NSDUH) 22, 32
natural world 82, 159
needs assessment and data collection/documentation 197–198, 213–215, 216, 225, 251
neurobiopsychosocial disease model 80, 93, 95–96, 98; see also brain disease model
neurotoxicity (lack of evidence) 97–98
neurotransmitters 96
nicotine see tobacco

observational learning 293–294
offenders 21, 267
older adults 20
O'Malley, Kate Y. 96–99
opioids 69–72; driving impairment 27; history of 69–71; mortality 25, 27; needs assessment and program planning 214–215; programs 71, 76, 136, 143–144, 214–215; societal cost 28; stigma 45; usage patterns, adults 14; see also heroin; oxycodone
outcomes of strategies/programs: and addressing root causes 81; defining 78, 84–85, 190, 201–202, 251, 261; expectation management 118, 122–123; harm reduction 81, 84, 85, 94, 107–108, 153–154, 156–158; positive 62, 63, 81, 84–85, 153–154, 157–158; in prevention 156–158, 167; specificity 157–158, 201; and values 84–85; see also goals and objectives; vision
overdose 25, 26, 71, 214; see also mortality
Oxford Houses 150
oxycodone 70, 71, 76, 143; see also opioids

Index 339

painkillers *see* opioids; prescription medication
paradigms/frameworks/theories 90–95; biopsychosocial disease model 80, 93, 95–96, 98; blended 95; brain disease model 96–99; of change *see* change models and frameworks; continuum of care 107–109, 117, 124; continuum of use 101, 104–107, 117, 142; five-step contact process 121–122; Force Field Analysis 189–191, 296; four-part intervention process model 118–124; harm reduction approach 81, 84, 85, 94, 107–108, 153–154, 156–158; Institute of Medicine framework for strategies 114; outdated 75, 90–91; Planning Framework 191, 194–211, *194*; Principles Defining the Effects of a Drug 99–101; professional group differences 75; Public Health Model 94, 289; Pyramid of Success 4–5, *4*; Strategic Prevention Framework (SAMHSA) 169, 191, 192–194; supply and demand framework 42–44, 93–94; zero tolerance approach 94
parents: educating 48, 155, 172, 311, 319; influencing effect of 77, 111; lack of knowledge 51; *see also* families
Parisa, Jenna 146–148
partnerships *see* coalitions and partnerships
peers: influence, risk/protective factors 17, 110, 111, 164, 165, 210; peer providers 127–128; and recovery 147, 149; *see also* self-help groups
perseverance 302–307, 311
personalization of strategies/programs 222; recovery 145; treatment 128–129
persuasive communication 245–249, 286;*see also* advocacy; communication
physical impacts 16, 26, 29, 119; *see also* effects of drugs, principles defining
planned change 51, 187–189
planning 187–211; building the plan 202–203, 226–230, *229*; for campaigns 248; creativity in 216–218; Force Field Analysis 189–191, 296; goals and objectives *see* goals and objectives; implementation design 203–204; importance 187–189; message planning 173; needs assessment and data collection/documentation 197–198, 213–215, 216, 225, 251; organizational principles 215–216, 219; partnerships 204, 208–211, 217, 227, 327–328; pilot testing 207; Planning Framework 191, 194–211, *194*; planning grid 226–230, *229*; in prevention 166, 248, 262; seven Ps 187; Strategic Prevention Framework (SAMHSA) 169, 191, 192–194; Theory of Planned Behavior 109; WRAP 179; *see also* vision
police: collaboration 230–232; DARE program 17, 76, 282; education and training 26, 28, 220; enforcement 27, 76, 205, 228, 230–232; perspectives 57, 230–232; *see also* laws, policies and regulations
policies *see* laws, policies and regulations
politics: as context 56, 137, 166; privileging 14, 201, 202, 223, 259; "rising above" 198–200
prescription medication: adverse reactions 28, 38; marketing 70, 71; misuse, prevalence 22, 64; misuse, societal cost 28; misuse, stigma (lesser) 45; overprescribing 76; programs 71; *see also* opioids
prevention 107–108, 153–184; definition/scope 153–156; college students/young adults 176–179, 227–230, 245, 265–267, 270–273, 324–326; COMPASS: A Roadmap to Healthy Living 81, 82, 159; comprehensive approach 109–113, 154–155, 158, 161–162, *162*, 169, 315; ecological approach 56–58; education and training 179–183, 266; evidence-based 155, 158, 161–163; evolution of strategies 154–155, 160; funding 73, 171, 316; and genetics 322; vs. intervention 172; "Just Say No" 160, 167, 248; laws/policies and 220–221; medical model 154; messages 167, 173–179, 247–249; methodologies 166, 168–169; outcomes 156–158, 167; planning 166, 248, 262; as process 330; and promotion 161–162, 327; public health perspective 155, 272–273, 316; retrospective 315–317; Strategic Prevention Framework (SAMHSA) 169, 191, 192–194; "War on Drugs" 69, 156, 203, 259, 281–282; youths 160–165, 172, 176, 221
privilege, as sociological construct 44; sober privilege 44–45, 46
proactive and reactive approaches 94
problematic use of drugs and alcohol 104, 106; *see also* abuse of drugs and alcohol; harm and consequences; use of drugs and alcohol
process (vs. outcome) perspective 84, 224, 225, 296, 313, 328; intervention as process 117–118
programs *see* strategies/programs

protective factors *see* risk/protective factors
psychiatric disorder, and substance use disorder 150
Public Health Model 94, 289
public health perspective: prevention 155, 272–273, 316; as under-represented 245, 270; *see also* health promotion
public perceptions of substance (ab)use 44–46, 66, 90
Pyramid of Success framework 4–5, *4*

Quinn-Zobeck, Ann 303–306

reasons for use of drugs and alcohol *see* causes for involvement with drugs and alcohol
reasons for working with drugs and alcohol *see* mission, for workers
recovery 145–151; defined 145, 149; appropriate language 148; counseling *see* counseling; four dimensions (SAMHSA) 145; individualized 145; people in, as peer providers 127–128; public perceptions 44–45, 146–148, 151; Recovery Oriented Systems of Care (ROSC) 149–150; residences 150; self-help groups *see* self-help groups; supportive environment for 147
refreshment, for workers 299–300, 307–308
regulations *see* laws, policies and regulations
relapses 146; as discouraged term 148; relapse prevention training 133
relationship health 82, 159
repetition, as communication "tool" 235, 241–242, 250
research: blended into practice 195–197, 235; collaborations 226, 227, 277, 317; funding *see* funding for programs/research; gaps 61, 69, 91, 150, 213, 215, 244; mentoring in 295; *see also* evidence-based practice
"response process" *see* intervention ("response process")
reward processing 66–67
Ripley, Dana 69–72, 143–144
risk, higher risk individuals/groups *see* higher risk individuals/groups
risk/protective factors 164, 214; community 164, 214; families 164, 165; individual 164; peers 17, 110, 111, 164, 165, 210; schools 164
Rohr, John 274

role modeling 303–305
Rullo, Diane 101–104
Rutgers Alcohol Problem Index (RAPI) 119
Ryan, Barbara E. 174–175, 242–244

Safe and Drug-Free Schools and Communities Act (SDFSCA) 271
scare tactics *see* fear-based appeals
scenarios, as communication "tool" 240
Schlabach, Kelly 181–183
Schmidt, Steve (LTA) 48, 72, 73, 172, 176, 178, 189, 201, 211, 215, 221, 222, 223, 238, 245, 249–250, 264, 267, 283, 295, 308, 311, 323
schools: chemical health model 161–162, *162*; community engagement in programs 64, 205; guidelines 170–171; program engagement 78, 79; risk/protective factors 164; SADD 223; student education programs 77, 111, 155, 158, 161–162, *162*, 306; suspension policies 77; *see also* youths
screening *see* assessment and screening
Secular Organizations for Sobriety (SOS) 149–150
selected approaches, defined 114
self-care: in COMPASS 82, 159; family members 40; when intervening 126; for workers 290–312, 330; *see also* emotional impacts
Self-Determination Theory 181, 182
self-exploration 304
self-help groups 73, 138–142, 146, 149–150; AA *see* Alcoholics Anonymous (AA); Al-Anon 41, 135, 263; BACCHUS peer education 223, 324–326; Cocaine Anonymous 140; Double Trouble in Recovery 150; Dual Recovery 150; effectiveness 140, 150; lawyers 63, 151, 284; Life Ring 149–150; Moderation Management 150; Nar-Anon 41; Narcotics Anonymous 35, 46, 140, 146; professional cooperation with 140; SADD 223; SMART 149, 150; SOS 149–150; sponsors 223; Women for Sobriety 149
Self-Management and Recovery Training (SMART) 149, 150
setting, and drug effects 100
sexual minorities *see* LGBTQ/sexual minority people
shame and stigma 45–47, 151, 321, 323; hierarchies of 45–46
Snow, Ryan 26–28, 230–232
sober privilege 44–45, 46

Social Cognitive Theory 109
Social Ecological Model 56–58, 109, 111, 165
social history 131–132; *see also* assessment and screening
social impacts 26, 119; *see also* driving, impaired; families
social marketing 241
"social math" (creative epidemiology) 240
social media 249–250
social norms approach 241, 321–322
social use of drugs and alcohol *see* low-risk use of drugs and alcohol
societal cost 273
societal level programs 110, 111–112, 164; *see also* comprehensive/holistic approach
Stages of Change (Transtheoretical) Model 51–52, 57, 94, 166, 167
stigma and shame 45–47, 151, 321, 323; hierarchies of 45–46
strategic planning *see* planning; Strategic Prevention Framework (SAMHSA)
Strategic Prevention Framework (SAMHSA) 169, 191, 192–194
strategies/programs: approaches (overview) 220–226; comprehensive/holistic approach *see* comprehensive/holistic approach; continuum of care 107–109, 117, 124; counseling *see* counseling; education and training *see* education and training; events 218, 223; "feel-good" 69, 85, 202, 216, 223; funding *see* funding for programs/research; individualized *see* individualization of strategies/programs; institutional 110, 111; intervention *see* intervention ("response process"); Medication-Assisted Treatment (MAT) 71, 143–145; outcome focus *see* outcomes of strategies/programs; prevention *see* prevention; prioritization 64, 65, 75, 155, 214–215; proactive and reactive 94; selected (defined) 114; self-help groups *see* self-help groups; societal level 110, 111–112, 164; therapy 114; treatment *see* treatment programs/services; universal (defined) 114
students *see* college students
Students Against Destructive Decisions (SADD) 223
Substance Abuse and Mental Health Services Administration (SAMHSA) 20, 31, 276; CSAP 154, 175, 243; CSAT *see* Center for Substance Abuse Treatment (CSAT); MAT-PDOA program 71; National Helpline 41; Recovery Support Strategic Initiative 145; Strategic Prevention Framework 169, 191, 192–194; TIPS 69, 136–137
substance use disorder (SUD): alcohol *see* alcohol and alcohol use disorder; assessment and screening *see* assessment and screening; as chronic disease 73, 92, 107, 127, 148; in continuum of use 105, 107; cycle of addiction 67–68, 80; DSM classification and diagnosis 30, 48–49, 65, 102–104, 106–107, 119, 129–130; medical perspective/disease models 65–68, 74–75, 80, 90, 91, 93, 95–99; prevalence 31; and psychiatric disorder 150; public perceptions 44–46, 66, 90
supply and demand framework 42–44, 93–94
support, for workers 296–297, 299, 303
support services 224–225; counseling *see* counseling; self-help groups *see* self-help groups; treatment *see* treatment programs/services
Surgeon General's report 199
"survival roles" in families 39–40

teenagers *see* youths
testimonials, as communication "tool" 240, 285
Theory of Planned Behavior 109
therapy, vs. counseling 142
Thorstenson, Deb (LTA) 14, 35, 47, 52, 74, 93, 158, 179, 211, 226, 227, 239, 245, 307, 311, 320, 323
time management 301
tobacco 31, 92, 189, 316, 320
training *see* education and training
Transtheoretical Stages of Change Model 51–52, 57, 94, 166, 167
Treatment Improvement Protocols (TIPS) 69, 136–137
treatment programs/services 108, 127–145; defined 127; blended 108, 129; components 133–134; cost 129, 140; counseling *see* counseling; evidence-based *see* evidence-based practice; foundations 128–129; funding 80, 138; individualized 128–129; medication-assisted 71, 143–145; peer providers 127–128; purpose 142; self-help groups *see* self-help groups; settings 132–133; stagnation in 137–138; 13 principles 128; 28 Day Program 127; withdrawal (detoxification) 132; youth 132–133

twelve-step programs 133, 139–140, 142, 146, 149; professional cooperation with 140; *see also specific programs*
28 Day Program 127

underage drinking: community perceptions of 57, 165; defined 16, 204; lack of media interest 50; prevalence 15–20, 50; strategies for reducing 17–18, 57, 111–112, 124–125
universal approaches, defined 114
universities *see* higher education
urgent vs. important items 301
use of drugs and alcohol: defined 13; causes *see* causes for involvement with drugs and alcohol; data sources 14, 15, 22–23; societal cost 28, 37–38, 274; usage patterns, adults 13–14, 169; usage patterns, college students 21, 23, 72, 174–175; usage patterns, sexual minorities 22–23; usage patterns, young adults 21; usage patterns, youth 15–20, 23, 50, 77, 91; *see also* abuse of drugs and alcohol; high(er)-risk use of drugs and alcohol; misuse of drugs and alcohol; problematic use of drugs and alcohol

vacations, importance 305, 307–308
values 81, 82, 83–87, 159, 328
veterans 21, 322
violent behavior 38, 39, 65
vision 313–331; conceptualization 313–317; content 318–326; creation 326–331; vs. mission, goals and objectives 314; in Planning Framework 195; rationale 317–318; *see also* outcomes of strategies/programs
visual communication 250

Wagstaff, Jenny 39–41, 69–72, 143–144
"War on Drugs" 69, 156, 203, 259, 281–282
Watson, John 216–218, 281–283
Wenzinger, Michael L. 66–68
White, Helene (LTA) 29, 37, 39, 48, 65, 72, 73, 93, 99, 119, 121, 132, 171, 179, 226, 284, 291
Wilfert, Mary (LTA) 155, 158, 167, 172, 176, 177, 203, 210, 225, 262, 263–264, 284, 295, 311
withdrawal (detoxification) 132
withdrawal phase of reward cycle 67
women: as higher risk group 63; recovery groups 149, 151
Women for Sobriety 149
Women's Christian Temperance Union 280
workplaces: guidelines 170–171; supporting recovery 147
World Health Organization (WHO) 37; ICD-10 102; lexicon of alcohol and drug terms 243

young adults: advice for 176–179; COMPASS: *A Roadmap to Healthy Living* 81, 82, 159; programs 81, 82; usage patterns 21; *see also* college students
Youth Risk Behavior Survey 15, 23
youths: advice for 176–177; brain development 99, 176, 275; as higher risk group 15, 17, 68, 99, 113, 275; lack of media interest in increasing substance use 50; prevention 160–165, 172, 176, 221; as program partners 204–206, 210; SADD 223; treatment programs 132–133; underage drinking *see* underage drinking; usage patterns 15–20, 23, 50, 77, 91; *see also* parents; schools

zero tolerance approach 94

Made in United States
North Haven, CT
19 December 2022